ISLAM AND THE HEROIC IMAGE

STUDIES IN COMPARATIVE RELIGION

Frederick M. Denny, *Editor*

ISLAM
AND THE
HEROIC IMAGE

Themes in Literature and the Visual Arts

by **JOHN RENARD**

UNIVERSITY OF
SOUTH CAROLINA PRESS

Library of Congress Cataloging-in-Publication Data

Renard, John, 1944–
  Islam and the heroic image : themes in literature and the visual
  arts / by John Renard.
  p. cm.—(Studies in comparative religion)
  Includes bibliographical references and index.
  ISBN 0–87249–832–8
  1. Islamic countries—Civilization. 2. Heroes in literature.
  3. Heroes in art. 4. Islamic literature—History and criticism.
  5. Islamic art. I. Title. II. Series: Studies in comparative
  religion (Columbia, S.C.)
DS35.62.R46 1993
909 .097671—dc20   92–18558

To my Heroine
Mary Pat

CONTENTS

Contents

Contents

FIGURES

Figures

Figures

TABLES

SERIES EDITOR'S PREFACE

The academic study of Islam and Muslim peoples has proceeded along several courses in the past century, when it became an independent field of critical-historical inquiry. The early phase was dominated by textual and philological approaches, sometimes heavily influenced by Christian and Jewish viewpoints. As the field developed, social scientific approaches augmented the more literary and historical emphases, bringing Islamic studies to focus more on local contexts and current realities. More recently, textual and contextual concerns have increasingly been brought together, providing more balanced and thickly textured understandings of Islam and, especially, of Muslims.

For most of its history Islamic studies has had a strong Middle Eastern bias, whether the focus has been on the Arab world, Iran, or the Turkish tradition. The very term *Middle East* betrays another bias, that of the hegemonic Western powers that drew the maps and named the regions under their authority. There are compelling historical reasons for scholarship's long preoccupation with the old Islamic lands of the "Nile-to-Oxus" regions. Marshall Hodgson's non-political label for the great expanse that was the stage for the development of the classical Islamic civilization still provides the ideal for Muslims everywhere. But Hodgson made a breakthrough in thinking about Islam as a global reality, not reducible to a regional and therefore intrinsically limited and often exotic phenomenon, especially when viewed from the West. The title of Hodgson's masterpiece says much about his global and empathetic approach to his subject: *The Venture of Islam: Conscience and History in a World Civilization.*

John Renard is clearly in the tradition of Marshall Hodgson with this book on Islam and the heroic image, especially insofar as it takes the whole Islamic world—and by implication the rest of humankind—as its subject. The hero is a universal phenomenon but has specific and idiosyncratic characteristics within the many varying social, cultural, and literary traditions where the figure is found. Relatively little has been written on the hero in Islamic contexts. Renard's comparative survey and comprehensive classification of the phenomenon across a wide range of Islamic regions, periods, and traditions is a pioneering work.

Scholars, including adherents of Islam, sometimes get confused about what is truly "Islamic" about the tradition and what is merely cultural or derivative or relative. Most often people in this quandary resort to the Qur'an and Muhammad's Sunna and settle on stipulative grounds what Islam should or should not be. The problem with that approach is that it fails to take into account the rich complexity of real human communities of faith and experience. Thus much of what Islam has been and can be in embodied forms is lost, or at least seriously undervalued. Renard has sought to avoid the hazards of scripturalism and doctrinal stipulation in discerning authentic and unique aspects of Islam through those Muslims have held up as their heroes. The heroic image is also a good reference point for discerning ways in which Islamic doctrine becomes translated into everyday life as authentic piety. It is here that Renard, like Hodgson, shows the power and pervasiveness of religious conviction throughout all levels of Muslim society. Formal theological and legal discourses may not indicate what ordinary people experience as Islam; popular stories and widespread visual data provide much greater documentation about what Clifford Geertz felicitously called the "long lasting moods and motivations" of religion.

Renard has chosen four main avenues of approach to his subject, which he integrates throughout his survey: psychology, art history, literature and folklore, and history of religions. Although the author includes scriptural and other authoritative doctrinal sources in his study, he does not apply them like some "Grand Inquisitor" to the varied visual and literary as well as folkloric data on heroes. These latter sources span a vast realm of historical, spiritual, and cultural experience and include both elite and common traditions. The heroic image Renard shows to be everywhere, both conveying and sustaining Islamic convictions and acting as agent of Islamization, moral-code patterning, and legitimization of local phenomena—as in the Malay world—within the Islamic worldview. It is not often that a comparative study of this magnitude is attempted these days; within Islamic studies it is almost unheard of. But a comparative approach is essential for the author's subject, because it helps us understand what is "Islamic" across a bewilderingly varied and sometimes even contradictory global religious culture.

Islam and the Heroic Image is modestly put forth by its author as a survey. But the book is far more than this: it is a pioneering and convincing effort at establishing a new subfield within Islamic studies as well as a major contribution to the humanities.

Frederick Mathewson Denny

Preface

Islam in relation to its heroes, and heroes within the context of that vast religio-cultural phenomenon called Islam, are the twofold subject of this investigation. Both key terms, hero and Islam, are broad and need clarification, which the introduction and first two chapters provide. Though the project's scope is ambitious, its purpose is less grandiose. It brings together and organizes several complexes of themes through which one might approach its topic. As a self-confessed survey, its primary purpose is to afford teachers and students a basis for further and more detailed investigation of this rich humanities theme as it has developed in relation to the Islamic religious tradition and to the various cultures within which that tradition has flourished.

Numerous problems arise in such an attempt as this, for it suggests from the outset a host of major methodological and hermeneutical issues. One must ask, for example, in what sense one can apply the term "Islam" and its adjectival form "Islamic" to cultures so diverse as those of Morocco and Malaysia. And what of the term "hero"? Does it mean to an Albanian Muslim what it means to a Sudanese? Even if one can demonstrate important connections among the stories of major characters from more than one cultural milieu, can one assume that the stories and characters have performed similar functions within their respective surroundings? What about critical differences among the literary sources? Is it not essential to distinguish clearly between a heroic story of folk origin and one that arises out an elite or courtly life setting? Is it not presuming too much to draw upon both popular and high artistic traditions for visual interpretations of heroic themes?

Another set of problems has to do with the choice and the availability of literary and visual materials. Though the book is designed to encompass themes popular across a wide swath of Islamicate cultures from Morocco to Malaysia, its treatment remains rather uneven, for several reasons. One is that my own first-hand acquaintance with the principal literary works and their illustrated versions is limited largely to the Arabic and Persian materials. Another is that although the number of editions and translations in all areas is growing, much primary source material remains available only to highly specialized scholars. One such area to which this survey has paid far too little attention, therefore, is that of the Indian subcontinent, with its several important Islamicate languages. That the bulk of this book deals with works from the central Middle East is due in part to the dominance of Arabic, Persian, and Turkish works relevant to our topic. I wish to emphasize, however, that this survey, broad as it is, has managed to include only a small fraction of what remains to be brought to light and appreciated.

It is my hope that this compendium of themes will serve as an invitation to a part of our world at once variegated in its cultural manifestations and unified in its association with a global religious tradition. If *Islam and the Heroic Image* gives to one scholar the reason to write the book(s) this one might have been, to one teacher the encouragement to offer that impossibly broad course, to one student a moment of puzzlement as to how all this richness could have escaped his school's curriculum for so long, then it will have served its purpose.

A word about transliteration is necessary. Serious difficulties in maintaining an uncluttered consistency arise when one deals with material from so many literary traditions. For the sake of simplicity, I have tried to retain names and terms in their most common Anglicized or Arabized forms, rather than in transliterations that might more readily approximate their pronunciations in the languages in which they are more frequently found. For example, Rustam instead of Rostam; *Shahnama* rather than *Shahnameh*. Where no common Anglicized or Arabized form is available some other widely used transliteration appears; as, for example, Köroghlu. All quotations retain their authors' transliterations.

The bibliography of over five hundred entries is by no means exhaustive. It does offer a representative sample, especially of secondary material published by scholars across the spectrum of specialities that touch on our subject. References to some material still unavailable to the author at publication time have been retained as a help to students and scholars who might wish to do further work in the topic.

The black-and-white pictures are intended as generic illustrations of a number of the major characters. Various practical considerations have limited them to but a small sample of what is available. Notes include references to over five hundred color plates illustrating the material discussed. These are for the most part in sources readily available in or through college and university libraries. References are to plate number, if available, or to page number in the work cited. The quality of the reproductions listed varies considerably, but is generally adequate for instructional purposes. Scenes or characters found in multiple examples, produced in a variety of cultural contexts, offer an excellent opportunity for further comparative study of the range of visual interpretations of some heroic themes. The book refers often to material from Firdawsi's *Shahnama*. I have not given specific page citations in many instances. Interested readers can find the stories easily by using the extensive index in the Warner translation. (Each volume contains its own table of contents and index, and volume nine contains both a general table of contents and a general index.)

Finally I wish to express my thanks to those who have assisted in many ways in my completing this book. Thanks to the College of Arts and Sciences of St. Louis University for making available Mellon faculty development grants that funded research and writing over several summers. To the faculty and staff of Washington University's Center for the Study of Islamic Societies and Civilizations, I am grateful for the Rockefeller Fellowship that allowed me to complete the project during the fall of 1990. For their helpful suggestions on various drafts, I thank Peter Heath, Bridget Connelly, Julie Meisami, Fred Denny, and Ken Scott. For advice on, or assistance in obtaining illustrative materials, I thank Annemarie Schimmel, Oleg Grabar, Shreve Simpson, Esin Atil, William Hanaway, Lee Vinzant, and Carolyn Kane. And thanks to Jan Harbaugh for her help in producing camera-ready tables and charts, and to the University of California Press for permission to use material published in Mounah Khouri and Hamid Algar's *Anthology of Modern Arabic Poetry*, copyright 1974 © The Regents of the University of California.

Introduction

For over 1,400 years, Islam has contributed to the worldview and value systems of peoples across the globe. Every serious observer of Islam's impact on our world has finally to ask, "What is authentically Islamic about the myriad religious, literary, political phenomena that come to be associated with Islam?" Muslims and non-Muslims alike have characterized numerous social movements, political entities, and artistic works as Islamic, evidently convinced that one can discern in remarkably diverse phenomena the signature of Islam. On the other hand, apt as the term "Islamic" may be in characterizing Andalusia's architecture, or the government of the Republic of Iran, or the Moro National Liberation movement in the Philippines, it is hardly an exhaustive description of any, let alone all, of these.

One question behind the present survey is this: how can one discern and appreciate the interplay between ordinary human beings in their varied cultural settings and the emergence within those settings of value systems that have come to be known as Islamic? In order to understand both the Islamic unity and the enormous diversity of the Islamic world from Morocco to Malaysia, one needs to find some common theme that has flourished wherever Islam has taken root. Across that world the theme of the hero provides such a cultural constant. In popular and elite epics, folk and princely arts alike, Muslims have told and retold tales of exemplary figures. Literary and visual images of such folk heroes as Antar, royal scions of Persia, and spiritual descendents of Muhammad have inspired, entertained, and epitomized the aspirations and values of tribes and peoples for centuries.

This book therefore proposes the theme of the hero in art and literature as one key to understanding both what is Islamic about the Islamic world and what is unique to any one local setting—a key that will make it possible to speak meaningfully about an Islamic Culture without denying that Albania remains half a world away from Afghanistan. A study of heroic themes across the Islamicate world offers the prospect of an entrée into fundamental human questions, to an understanding of relationships between religion and culture, to questions about each other that Muslims and non-Muslims need to ask. The hero provides an invitation to explore the breadth and depth of Islam's role in shaping the aspirations and values of many hundreds of millions of people.

Joseph Campbell's *The Hero With a Thousand Faces* discusses the importance of the hero as a global theme and underscores the need of some kind of survey of how peoples within the orbit of Islam have celebrated the hero. Campbell seeks to make a contribution to "the perhaps not-quite-desperate cause of those forces that are working in the present world for unification . . . in the sense of human mutual understanding."[1] As a result, he emphasizes the homogeneous character of the hero as a global phenomenon and does not attend so keenly to important cultural differences. Moreover, even at his homogenizing best, he gives only the merest hint as to the breadth and richness of Islamicate tradition. Persia's national epic, *The Book of Kings,* and its most famous hero, Rustam, for example, barely rate a mention in Campbell's book. And the Islamicate heroes he does treat are quite marginal, given the enormous breadth of material now available.

Scholars have produced studies of heroic themes in the Islamic world from a wide range of approaches. Most are literary studies. Of those, the majority focus on either a single work or genre. Others may trace a single hero, such as Iskandar (Alexander the Great), through a series of literary metamorphoses. Some art historical investigations have looked into narrative and iconographic themes in illustrations of the literary works. More often than not, such studies tend toward formal and stylistic analysis, showing little interest in why the subject matter evidently held such fascination for the patrons of the arts. A few art historical essays have moved toward a more integrated visual/verbal interpretation, but they have on the whole confined themselves to one or a few illustrated manuscripts or other objects.

As for the media used to communicate heroic themes, this study will concern itself only tangentially with either formal or functional issues. Such matters belong more properly to the domain of philology, literary criticism, and art history. My study will, nevertheless, take account of the data made available through such

2

media and genre studies as, for example, Albert Lord's *Singer of Tales,* M. Shreve Simpson's *The Illustration of an Epic,* and Allesandro Bausani's work on the *Structure of the Classical Malay Hikayat.* In short, my investigation will focus on the hero as theme, rather than on attempts to define what qualifies as truly epic literature and so forth.

A survey of so broad a subject virtually requires an eclectic method, one that borrows elements from several disciplines in attempting to define the hero. First, we shall make use of some insights from a psychological interpretation of myth. Campbell, for example, describes the hero largely from the psychological perspective, as an individual who has battled past "personal and local historical limitations" to the outer boundaries of human potential, through submission to the suprahuman, whose vision is fed from the "primary springs of human thought and life," and who returns transfigured with a message of renewal.[2]

Second, literary and folkloristic studies see heroic stories as the common possession of all humanity, often with specific details and names seemingly interchangeable within the context of episodic frameworks.[3] In the Islamicate case we find material converging from the West (especially the Alexander tales) and from Central Asia (stories of Rustam) and expanding as far westward as Spain and eastward to South Asia.

Third, art history uncovers some distinctively Islamicate features in the pertinent works, as well as local variations and chronological developments in style. Just as multiple literary and oral traditions contribute to the verbal image of the Islamicate hero, so the visual influences are as diverse as Byzantium, pre-Islamic Sassanian Persia, China, and Central Asia. Finally, the history of religion discerns the importance of such figures as the thaumaturge, shaman, holy person (or saintly figure), prophet, and perfect person. Such religious types share a number of critical attributes with some heroes who are not so clearly religious.

To sum up, one can describe the book's overall purpose this way: to study data from two major manifestations (visual art and literature) of a global culture (the Islamicate), to trace therein the threads of a universal human theme (the heroic), and to discover some of the ways in which a major religious tradition (Islam) has shaped and inspired those visual and literary manifestations of culture in Islamdom.

3

The five major sections of the book encompass twelve chapters and a lengthy appendix. Each section and each chapter within it is meant to be able to stand alone as well as to interlock with other individual parts. Part one locates the study of heroic themes within the context of the humanities. Chapter one opens with some suggestions as to how heroic themes can serve as an invitation to the study of the Islamic world and its various cultures. Those themes can form a unifying thread, not only among the cultures of Islamdom, but across the broader world of religious and cultural traditions as well. Heroic themes have performed various religious, social, and psychological functions within the world of Islam over the centuries, and continue to do so. The twin dynamics of Islamization and indigenization provide key insights into how heroic themes suggest both unity and diversity within the world of Islam. Chapter two examines some questions the survey raises for the broad discipline known as Islamic studies. Studies of the themes as expressed in literary and visual media evidence a variety of interpretations.

These first chapters deal therefore with a number of theoretical issues and include a fair amount of "scholarly apparatus" and may not provide the most congenial entrée for the non-specialist. Readers who wish to postpone the theoretical and methodological questions pending greater familiarity with the heroes and their stories may profitably move immediately to part two. The appendix can likewise be used several ways. It can serve as a general reference guide in its present location at the end of the book. Teachers, however, may find it useful either to treat that material as a unitary survey at the beginning of a course, or to insert sections of it wherever an excursus on sources would help to deepen students' general background knowledge.

HEROIC THEMES
AND THE
WORLD OF ISLAM

PART ONE

Chapter One

Heroic Themes as Invitation to the World of Islam

Yesterday the Republic of Indonesia's first warship and a Malaysian frigate, both named *Hang Tuah,* sailed within sight of each other through the Straits of Malaka. This evening an Egyptian raconteur entertained a packed coffeehouse with tales of Abu Zayd and Antar, and a bard in eastern Turkey charmed his listeners with the story of Köroghlu. Tomorrow a Central Asian couple will name their newborn child Rustam, or perhaps Manizha. Heroic themes live on as an integral part of Islamicate cultures from North Africa to Southeast Asia. The present survey will provide a sample of some of those themes as an entrée into the world of Islam. This chapter will look at some issues that will clarify how and why those themes have endured in Islamicate societies and will suggest several ways of understanding how the heroic image can serve to highlight both religious unity and cultural diversity within that world. These are highly complex matters, and any treatment so brief as this can only skim across the surface of some major questions.

Three sets of global issues arise from a study of heroic themes. The first concerns the prevalence of such themes across the world and the place of Islamic heroic themes within that larger context. The other two concern how those themes are manifested within contexts explicitly modified by the Islamic religious tradition. One has to do with the various ways heroic narratives and images function within Islamicate societies. The other has to do with the twin phenomena of Islamization and indigenization. We shall approach each of these sets of issues in turn.

Before we discuss those matters, however, several crucial terms need to be clarified. In *The Venture of Islam,* Marshall Hodgson addresses the need for a more precise terminology that would allow for a distinction between the religious tradition called "Islam" (with its corresponding adjective, "Islamic"), and the societies and cultures that have come under the strong influence of Islam but cannot be understood simply in terms of that religious association. So, for example, one can legitimately speak of "Islamic Law" or "Islamic Mystical Literature." But because much of the literature and art produced even in regions where Islam is the belief system of the majority is not uniformly "religious" in the same way law and mystical literature are, Hodgson devised terms intended to reflect that complex relationship: "There has been . . . a *culture*, centered on a lettered tradition, which has been historically distinctive of Islamdom the *society*, and which has been naturally shared in by both Muslims and non-Muslims who participate at all fully in the society of Islamdom. For this, I have used the adjective 'Islamicate.' I thus restrict the term 'Islam' to the *religion* of the Muslims, not using that term for the far more general phenomena, the society of Islamdom and its Islamicate cultural traditions."[1] We have on the whole adapted Hodgson's distinctions to our purposes, but will use the term "religious tradition" where he uses "religion."

Treating a subject as far-ranging and intricate as this involves unraveling and disentangling numerous long threads. Since the beginnings and endings of those threads almost never come readily to hand, it becomes necessary simply to grasp them somewhere—true to the epic spirit—*in medias res* and follow where they lead. Throughout this chapter and the next, the reader will encounter names of many as yet unfamiliar heroic figures. A better acquaintance with those characters has been deferred to part two and subsequent chapters, in the interest of first laying a methodological foundation.

Islam's Heroes in Global Perspective

Asked what Odysseus, Mother Teresa, John Henry the Steel Drivin' Man, Aeneas, Joan of Arc, Batman, Judith, and Nelson Mandela have in common, many would no doubt respond that they are all heroic figures. Yet the reasons for which people have conferred on them the mantle of heroism vary enormously. One general characteristic that links them, perhaps, is such exemplary virtues as resourcefulness, strength, fidelity, thirst for justice. But is exemplary virtue sufficiently precise to define a class of persons across a wide range of cultural, ethnic, and religious lines? Does one not need more specific attributes to delineate a category called "heroic figures?" Part two proposes more precise working descriptions of the three major heroic types—folk, royal, and religious.

For the moment, however, we will keep our definition of the heroic rather general, employing only the following distinction between form and function. From a formal point of view, the hero or heroine is the protagonist: any character who plays a starring or strong supporting role in either major literary works or the visual arts, or both. The heroic figure must in addition function as a model, an ideal of exemplary behavior as worked out in the context of adversity.

Every people and culture has its national treasures, or their equivalents; and what a people prizes most dearly is invariably an important clue to what that people regards as constitutive of the human ideal. If it were possible to gather into one image or person all of a people's national treasures, one might fully appreciate what that culture sees as the truly and essentially human. An old Arabic proverb says, "Wisdom has alighted on three things: the brain of the Frank, the hand of the Chinese, and the tongue of the Arab." It suggests that the gift of wisdom has been granted to many peoples, that it is manifested in a characteristic form among each of them, and that eloquence and wit are a uniquely Arab treasure. One could say something similar of the image of the hero as human ideal: it is a virtually universal phenomenon and, at the same time, bears the unmistakable signature of every people and culture in which it is found. Another proverb might have said, "The hero has a thousand faces: Rama, Buddha, the Confucian Scholar, Jesus, Moses, Muhammad. . . ."

Study of Islamicate heroic themes highlights the striking extent to which major religious traditions and cultures have always interpenetrated. A broad spectrum of Muslim attitudes toward non-Muslims is evidenced in the literature. Alexander's celebrity among Persians and Turks is a measure of the esteem Hellenistic culture has enjoyed. A look at the array of visual materials reveals the stylistic and iconographic heritages of Byzantium, Central Asia, India, China. As for literary sources, A. Bausani has made a preliminary analysis that indicates material from: tribal Arabic stories, either pre-Islamic or contemporary with Islam (such as Antar); parts of Islamic tales (such as that of Hamza); Hellenistic and middle eastern (Alexander); Iranian legend (Bahram, Nushirwan); Hindu legend and myth (Indra and his heavenly attendants); Buddhist legends (Jataka stories); and local tales (Baluchi, Sindhi, Kurdish, etc.).[2] In short, the hero is capable of leading one on a

9

journey with stopovers in every place human beings have called home. Let us look now at the ways heroic themes have functioned within the world of Islam, and at several ways those themes can assist in our analyzing relationships between Islam and the cultural settings in which we find it.

Functions of Heroic Tales in Islamicate Societies

A study of the ways heroic themes function in Muslim cultures across the world provides an important key to appreciating the unity and diversity of Islamicate societies. Opinions vary among Muslims as to the continuing relevance of the classic heroic figures as models for twentieth-century societies. Just two examples from recent Arabic poetry offer an instructive hint as to the spectrum of views. The Egyptian Salah Abd as-Sabur's "Dreams of an Ancient Knight" suggests that heroic imagery has by no means lost its appeal, even if it represents a rather distant and idealistic—perhaps even unrecoverable—mode. His is an ideal of romantic heroism, about which we shall see more in part two. The poet talks of how the lover has, at least for now, left the hero behind. To his beloved he laments, "I was once in bygone days / O my enchantress a steadfast warrior, a heroic knight [fata, fáris] / Before my heart was trodden underfoot." As hero he felt deeply, laughed like a brook, grieved, had compassion for the suffering, and would willingly have been set ablaze to offer them light. "What befell the heroic knight?" he asks. "His heart was plucked out and he took to flight dropping the reins." To the beloved he offers "the experience and skill bestowed on me by the world / In return for a single day of innocence / No it is only you who can make me again the ancient knight / Without any payment / Without any reckoning of profit and loss."[3]

At the other end of the spectrum, Syrian-born Nizar Qabbani makes it clear that he believes the classic heroes have nothing more to say to him or his contemporaries. "Bread, Hashish and Moonlight" decries the uncritical clinging of ordinary folks to the past and its legends. "In my land, / In the land of the simple, / Where we slowly chew on our unending songs— / a form of consumption destroying the east— / Our east is chewing on its history, / Its lethargic dreams, / Its empty legends, / Our east that sees the sum of all heroism [butula] / In . . . Abu Zayd al-Hilali" (a major folk hero who will appear in chapter three). In his "What Value Has the

People Whose Tongue is Tied?" Qabbani complains how people of his time remain blind to the crucial problems. They "Make heroes [*abtal*] out of dwarves, / Make the noble among us, vile, / Improvise heroism [*butula*], / Sit lazy and listless in the mosques, / Composing verses and compiling proverbs, / And begging for victory over the foe / From His Almighty presence."[4]

In the course of this chapter we shall encounter several other Muslim opinions as to the relative importance of the more traditional themes. For the moment, we look at some of the classic works' religious, social, and psychological functions within Islamicate societies.

Two obvious religious functions are the renewal of devotion and religious education. Sacred figures from the greatest prophets to the local holy personage inspire and encourage when times are hard. One way to connect present with past is to associate a contemporary figure with a classical religious hero. This method is clearly evident in Iranian revolutionary posters that depict Khumayni as a new Moses who confronts a Pharaonic Shah. Husayn's tragic journey to martyrdom and Muhammad's triumphant odyssey into the unseen world and back still move Muslim audiences across the world. Such heroic accounts supply a great deal of what many Muslims know about their faith tradition.[5]

A link between the specifically religious functions and the more general social functions mentioned below is the following example of heroic themes as exhortation to bravery. In addition to giving listeners a sense of connectedness to historical antecedents, heroic narratives, at least in Malaysia, also seem to have carried the power to bestir warriors on the eve of battle. Brakel cites a fascinating text from the *Sejara Melayu (Malay Chronicles)* well worth quoting here. The setting is Malaka in 1511, the night before an expected Portuguese attack on the city. The two principal heroes mentioned are Hamza, an uncle of Muhammad, who will reappear in chapter three; and Muhammad al-Hanafiya, another but more distant relation of the Prophet, whom we shall discuss again in chapter five.

> It was night and all the captains and young men were on guard in the palace. And the young men said, "Of what use is it for us to sit here in silence? It would be better for us to read some story of battle so that we might benefit from it."

11

"You are right," said Tun Muhammad the Camel. "Tun Indra Sagara had better go and ask for the story of Muhammad Hanafiah, saying that perhaps we may derive advantage from it, as the Franks attack tomorrow." Then Tun Indra Sagara went into the presence of Sultan Ahmad and submitted their remarks to his highness. And Sultan Ahmad gave him the romance of Amir Hamza, saying, "Tell them, I'd give them the story of Muhammad Hanafiah but I fear they'll not be as brave as he: if they are like Amir Hamza it will do, so I give them the story of Hamza." Tun Indra Sagara came out carrying the story of Hamza and told them all Sultan Ahmad had said, and they were silent not answering a word. Then Tun Isak said to Tun Indra Sagara, "Tell his highness that he is mistaken. His highness must be like Muhammad Hanafiah and we like the captains of Baniar." Tun Indra Sagara submitted Tun Isak's remark to Sultan Ahmad, who smiled and answered, "He is right." And he gave him the story of Muhammad Hanafiah too.[6]

Heroic themes provide a number of broader social functions, not the least of which is simple entertainment. Heroic stories bring people together. One result of that interaction is the strengthening of national pride.[7] A major social function is the capacity to inculcate a sense of honor and shame. In classical Arab tradition, for example, a sense of private honor was based on an awareness of one's natural goodness, independent of social consideration. That in turn was linked to *futuwwa* ("bravery in battle") and *muruwwa*, a value associated with protecting refugees and with vengeance, courage and generosity. The leader required most of all *ʿird* ("dignity," "good repute") and *hilm* ("intelligent forebearance"). The former consisted in ancestral nobility and illustriousness combined with natural praiseworthiness (*ash-sharaf, al-hasab* and *al-khaliqat al-mahmuda*). All of these the heroic narrative extols and reinforces. Heroes and heroines model a range of social virtues that preserve family honor as well. Blood vengeance restores balance, closes the circle of shame, and restores honor. Single combat with its decisive duel in turn links the individual to the group. Honor and its opposite, shame (*ʿar/aʿyar*), were thus key concepts governing relations between individual and society. Heroines often modeled values of virginity, "love of the eyes," and readiness to aid a prisoner. Shame for women typically involved false accusal of adultery, adultery, and various forms of treachery.[8]

A related issue is the sense of tribal or racial identity. In the Antar story, for example, much is made of contact between blacks and whites. Important Arabian themes are intermarriage of human and jinn to explain the marvelous and single combat between an Arab and an Ethiopian, or between black and white serpents. Key themes in both the Sayf and Antar stories include an assertion of the unity of warring Ethiopians and Arabians, as shown through a rediscovery of common ancestry. According to H. T. Norris, combat between black and white symbolizes either political conflict (in which case the Black may be identified with Abraha, the sixth-century Abyssinian invader of Arabia), or ethnic and religious accord (when the Black is identified with the Christian Abyssinian king, the Negus, who helped Muhammad in 615 by giving asylum to his community).[9]

S. Hurreiz comments more specifically on this aspect of the psychological function of stories of Bani Hilal among the Muslim Ja‘iliyyin people of the Sudan. "Among the other narratives that perform psychological functions are the local variants of the romance of 'Abu Zeid the Hilalite.' Dealing with the earlier Afro-Arab or North-South relations, these narratives have great psychological significance for the Ja‘iliyyin who belong to both ethnic groups. The audience identifies with the hero who is an Afro-Arab, or an Arab noted for his blackness. They implicitly realize the tensions underlying their identity and emerge from the tale triumphant and reassured of their social and moral worth. After all, Abu Zeid is the leader and rescuer of his tribe."[10]

Finally, heroic narratives are said to provide a number of personal psychological benefits. Listening to a hero's tale can soothe and quiet anxiety. Firdawsi asks his wife on the darkest of nights to help him find rest; she responds by telling him the story of Bizhan and Manizha.[11] Iskandar asks Aristotle to tell him stories from the *Shahnama* when he is discouraged, and the accounts move the king to tears.[12] One of king Hurmuz's last three wishes of his son Khusraw Parwiz is that Khusraw send the king a warrior of long memory to regale him with the exploits of kings and campaigns past.[13] Zal tells his young son Rustam that he should delay setting off to confront the rampaging Turanian King Afrasiyab and take some time to be inspired by the lays of heroes.[14]

13

Islamization and Indigenization

A major religio-cultural issue for students of Islamdom concerns the persistence of pre-Islamic ways and ideals after the coming of Islam, or the co-existence of Islamic and non-Islamic value systems. Here we shall frame the question this way: how can the theme of the hero facilitate a balanced approach to the study both of the Islamicate world as a whole and of the unique cultural traditions that make up that world? Two large complementary dynamics come into focus: Islamization and indigenization. In the general sense, Islamization is the process by which the religious tradition of Islam becomes a major factor within a culture or ethnic group or region. Some understanding of that process can help clarify to what extent one can speak of Islamdom as a unity. Indigenization is the process by which a culture, ethnic group, or region puts its own stamp on Islam, and it accounts at least in part for the diversity within Islamdom.

Scholars have long debated the question of the continuity or discontinuity one finds in the expression of cultural and religious values in the process of Islamization. Seventh-century Arabia is the prime example. I. Goldziher sees a major disjunction between Jahiliyya and Islamic values.[15] T. Izutsu describes a somewhat less dramatic transformation of pre-Islamic virtues into the Qur'anic ingredients of a faith-informed value system.[16] M. Bravmann describes the transition still more explicitly as a continuum rather than a definitive break. Quoting the Arabic saying, "There is no religion [din] without 'manly virtue' [muruwwah]," Bravmann says, "the virile ethics of the heathen period were appreciated even in the Islamic period, [but] in the course of time other qualities, of purely religious character, were added to them."[17] In his study of fatalism in Persian epic literature, Helmer Ringgren makes a similar point in connection with a theme to be brought up again in chapter seven—that of "Destiny." He concludes that "the attitude towards Destiny does not develop into indifference and complete resignation. . . . Even the fact that man complains of his fate shows that the fatalism of the epics is modified and mitigated by the belief in a God who acts righteously. But the latter belief, in its turn, has not been without traces of fatalistic ideas. There is a tension between fatalism in the real sense of the word and belief in a personal

God as the Master of man's destiny, and this tension is never entirely removed."[18]

Islamization has also come to occupy the attention of scholars who study regions now solidly Islamized but originally far from the birthplace of Islam. Soewito Santoso, writing on early Indonesian and Malay literature, defines Islamization as "the process of reforming any cultural product from another culture into something acceptable to Muslims and in accordance with the basic principles and notions of Islam."[19] He also makes a useful distinction between "Islamic" and "Muslim," somewhat analogous to Hodgson's coining of "Islamicate" as distinct from "Islamic." Santoso uses "Islamic" to denote something "in accordance with the basic principles and notions of Islam." "Islamic" thus explains the existence of a common element from Morocco to Malaysia, but it does not explain how those cultures differ. The term "Muslim culture," on the other hand, can help explain how Indian Islamic culture differs from Spanish Islamic culture: "As culture is the product of the minds of people, and as the adherents of Islam who bring forth this kind of culture are called 'Muslims,' I feel that consequently it should be called 'Muslim culture.' And as the Muslims of India differ from the Muslims of Spain, the products of their minds are also different; they are either Indian or Spanish. So in fact the two cultural products are Indian and Spanish adjusted to basic Islamic principles or in other words *the cultures in both countries are in the course of time Islamized by the Muslim culture-bearers of those countries.*"[20] In relation specifically to heroic themes, Islamization is the process by which an originally non-Islamic heroic figure (such as Hang Tuah, Köroghlu, Iskandar in Persia, Rustam or even Antar) gradually takes on a more or less distinctly Islamic religious cast. An Islamized hero thus participates in the legitimation of a religious tradition by conferring on it the kind of credibility it needs to take hold in new cultural circumstances.

Referring specifically to Malay and Indonesian heroic themes, Santoso notes two types of Islamization. One occurs through the insertion of Islamized stories, or of stories transplanted in their entirety from another Muslim literature, into indigenous works of non-Islamic origin. The *Sejara Melayu* exemplifies this type. Stories of Iskandar, a king who has already been Islamized before arriving in southeast Asia, serve to Islamize in turn other stories of pre-

Islamic origin in the *Sejara*. The second process involves the insertion either of phrases that extol the God of Islam as superior to other deities, or of meetings of the hero with famous Islamic figures who confer on the hero religious legitimacy.[21] The latter occurs in *Hikayat Hang Tuah* where, for example, the hero meets the mysterious and ubiquitous Khadir (Khizr). The prophet gives Hang Tuah a bottle of wondrous water that, when poured on his ears and lips, enables him to speak and understand foreign languages (Hang Tuah knows Siamese, Tamil, Turkish, Nigrama, among other tongues).[22]

The corollary to the process of Islamization is that of indigenization, whereby the receiving culture makes acceptable to itself stories from other cultures. By the term "indigenization" I mean the process whereby an originally Islamic hero (such as Ali in Persia, Muhammad in East Africa), or a hero previously Islamized en route to a farther destination (such as Hamza or Iskandar in India or Malaysia), begins to take on the features of a local character. An indigenized hero becomes part of the process in which evolving local or regional social and political structures cloak themselves in the antiquity, authority, and universal claims of Islam. Just as Indonesia recast the Hindu Ramayana in its own molds, so did it modify such Islamic characters as Hamza (Wong Agung Menak) into the likeness of the Javanese culture hero Panji.[23]

Islamization and indigenization go hand in glove. One can distinguish three major types of evidence of the twofold dynamic: first, changes in the use and popularity of certain literary genres; second, the adoption of certain heroes and the rejection of others; and finally, the impact of heroic themes and portrayal on social systems.

Islamization and the Introduction of New Genres

A. Bausani offers a comprehensive explanation of how Islam and indigenous literary types have interacted. His basic premise is that, through a process of demythologization, the Islamic tradition has braided together elements of both high and folkloric strands of "epos" from across the world. Table 1 is a modified version of the chart by which he shows relationships among literary forms. As for content, Bausani suggests a much broader range of sources, recalling the global scope of human fascination with the hero discussed above. Bausani's model is not very specific as to precisely

Table 1. Genre and Islamization

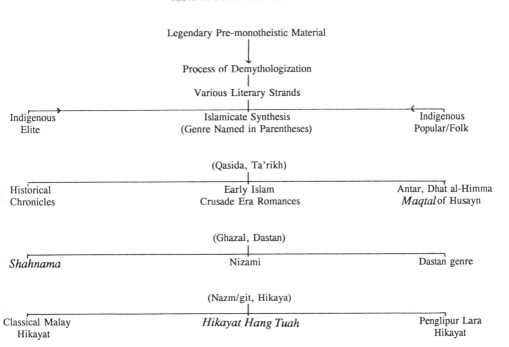

Legendary Pre-monotheistic Material

Process of Demythologization

Various Literary Strands

Indigenous Elite	Islamicate Synthesis (Genre Named in Parentheses)	Indigenous Popular/Folk
	(Qasida, Ta'rikh)	
Historical Chronicles	Early Islam Crusade Era Romances	Antar, Dhat al-Himma *Maqtal* of Husayn
	(Ghazal, Dastan)	
Shahnama	Nizami	Dastan genre
	(Nazm/git, Hikaya)	
Classical Malay Hikayat	*Hikayat Hang Tuah*	Penglipur Lara Hikayat

how the mechanism of demythologization works. It must suffice for our purposes to note that he regards the religious tradition as a kind of combination funnel and filter through which materials from both the Islamic heartlands and hinterlands were blended and rendered palatable to Islamic sensibilities.[24]

Picking up on a major element in Bausani's analysis, L. Brakel has studied the origins of the Malay genre called *hikaya*. As the survey of sources in the appendix indicates, several varieties of literature in other areas have gone by the same name. Brakel links the introduction of the genre to at least three changes in Malay society. First, Malay society became more integrated into "Mainland Asian Muslim culture." He theorizes that "a stage had been reached where, not any longer satisfied with the study of the sacred texts Qur'an and hadith themselves, Malay Muslims felt the need to subordinate their recreational and magically-inspired literature to Muslim values as well." Second, an emerging "cosmopolitan, international, post-feudal trading class" discovered that the new genre allowed them a much broader range of expression than either earlier Hindu royal cult-oriented literature or the sacral oral poetry of the Malay *penglipur-lara* ("dispeller of sadness") tales.

17

Third, though Malay culture had not welcomed a number of other significant Islamicate literary forms, the *hikaya* found a place because of the composite or "hybrid" structure of the earliest to gain popularity there, the *Hikayat Muhammad Hanafiya*. Brakel finds a connection between that dual structure and "certain features already present in Malay/Indonesian culture at the time." He explains that the story of Muhammad Hanafiya may have achieved popularity initially because, while its second half is a genuine *hikaya*, the first is a *maqtal* or "story of martyrdom." It may therefore have gained initial popularity through recitation at commemorations of Husayn's martyrdom (Karbala, 680). Brakel concludes that this work "contains two features which . . . must have been familiar to Sumatran culture prior to its introduction: its pronounced religio-Muslim character . . . and its function as a magical tale recited at ritual occasions, like the *penglipur lara* texts."[25]

W. Hanaway makes some interesting observations about the development of the Persian popular romance in relation to the gradual dominance of Islam over ancient Iran's Zoroastrian religious ethos. Noting that both "modes of thought" share the belief that good will ultimately overcome evil, Hanaway goes on to distinguish between the Islamic and Zoroastrian views of the role of the individual person in that struggle. He suggests that the characters of the Persian national epic, the *Shahnama*, seem "more real and human" than those of the romances, because Firdawsi's worldview still has the individual person acting as an ally of Ahura Mazda in the battle to preserve the world in its original, natural goodness. Even in the earliest of the romances, *Samak-i Ayyar*, Hanaway sees a "strictly Islamic" setting and perspective. Samak himself remains closer to the heroes of the *Shahnama* than do those of the later romances, and the romance contains far less of fantasy and divine intervention. Had the received text of the story derived from a later time, he contends, it would have featured a hero closer to a Hamza or an Iskandar, moving about in a world aflutter with *paris* and subject to constant divine manipulation.

Hanaway suggests that, in the Islamic view, the human person no longer functions as God's co-worker but takes an infinitely subordinate role. Whereas the Zoroastrian hero could still choose not to engage in the battle against evil, the Islamic hero is simply swept up into the melee and can choose either to accept his lot in faith or to deny God's sovereignty. Hanaway writes: "As the social and religious condition in Iran changed from the tenth century on, we see the popular heroes changing too. No longer is the hero of the romance a mighty warrior, defeating his enemies and gaining his ends by his own personal prowess. The hero slowly becomes a kind of strong, handsome innocent. He does not learn from experience or grow wiser with age, but maintains an eternal youth and freshness. His innocence is important, because he is the chosen one, the instrument of divine will by means of which evil is undone and injustice punished."[26] The romantic hero's guidance comes from others wiser than himself, but even their wisdom never raises them to heroic status. Because his success is foreordained, the hero needs no wisdom of his own; nor does he have Rustam's fearlessness born of self-confidence. The Islamized hero virtually floats along in a bubble of divine favor that no earthly force can puncture. Wielding only the divine names, in the direst straights the greatest name, the hero in his invulnerability no longer reflects actual human experience. The greater the divine protection, Hanaway argues, the more room in the story for the fantastic. Hence, the more pervasive the element of the miraculous in a romance, the greater the influence of an Islamic worldview. Following a parallel logic, Hanaway explains the heroic deterioration of the ayyar character from the fierce fighting companion of the earlier main figures to a type of picaresque or even buffoon. As the heroic portrayal declines in realism, so does that of the once credible sidekick.[27]

Association of Certain Heroes with Islam

Iskandar serves as perhaps the best example of a hero whose literary journey across the world from west to east found him serving to Islamize as he himself became more Islamic and to legitimate the royal claims of any king who could trace his lineage back to Iskandar. J. J. Ras discusses the role of Iskandar in the *Sejara Melayu* and the *Hikayat Bandjar*. He concludes that the authors introduced Iskandar not because of the desire to associate the Malay or Bandjarese kings with Alexander's glorious deeds as such, but "rather as a consequence of the need to give the old, essentially pagan, myth of their origin a 'decent,' quasi-Islamic, tinge, so as to legalize it and thus make it fit to be carried over into the new era, which was culturally dominated by the newly imported faith."[28]

It is most instructive to see which heroic characters different Muslim scholars are willing to identify as Islamic. I. Hamid does not so much as mention Hang Tuah—a hero many consider to epitomize Malay national spirit—in his Malayan perspective on *Arabic and Islamic Literary Traditions*. In his sections on "Malay Hikayats of Muslim Heroes and Pious Men," Hamid includes along with Muhammad such diverse figures as Hamza, Iskandar, Sayf ibn Dhi Yazan, and King Jumjumah (allegedly a pious Muslim and former ruler of Egypt and Syria).[29] Kassim bin Ahmad, on the other hand, devotes an entire short study to the story of Hang Tuah, which he calls a *sastera ke-pahlawanan* or heroic epic. Although Ahmad never mentions Islam, he notes that Hang Tuah regarded the Sultan as "God's shadow on earth," a standard Islamic epithet for the leader. Ahmad proceeds to challenge the traditional view that Hang Tuah is the quintessential Malay hero (and by association, perhaps, Muslim?)[30]

Another Malay study likewise challenges the received wisdom about Hang Tuah, but from a very different point of view. Hang Tuah represents not a good loyal Muslim but the antithesis of Islamic humanitarian heroism. In the view of Shaharuddin b. Maaruf, a major problem in his society is precisely the perdurance of the old feudal values he sees extolled in the epic *Hikayat Hang Tuah*, as well as in such other national classics as *Sejara Melayu*. Maaruf criticizes the tendency of contemporary Malay elite society to cling to the uncritical attitude that perpetuates the exploitative and inhumane mores embodied in the ancient texts. Hang Tuah's amoral loyalty to authority and Hang Jebat's unbridled violence are equally incompatible with Islam. As evidence of moral decadence, Maaruf cites several examples of wrongheaded interpretation of the heroes of classic literature.

Maaruf sees two trends in the literary criticism of the Malay elite. "Feudal romanticism" has five characteristics. First, it recommends passivity on the part of the masses; they must not presume to judge their leaders. Second, it applauds and finds much amusement in the debased morals of many alleged heroes, and claims that Hang Tuah was in tune with the needs of the people—whereas he actually cared only for his position in the court. Third, the romantic view glorifies all action done in service of the ruler, regardless of its ethical quality. The hero's apparently endless capacity for action, including all manner of bloodshed, is what makes him truly admirable. A character is heroic to the degree that he has allowed the voice of authority to drown out that of conscience.

Finally, the romanticizers portray the feudal hero as the epitome of the Malay spirit, as quintessentially Malay, and thus do a great disservice to Malays. The hero is unfortunately touted as a model of the good nationalist, but in reality those feudal values stand in the way of authentic development.

"Feudal Conservatism" on the other hand, does criticize the blind loyalty of the ancient heroes. It prefers to see Hang Jebat as the true hero, in opposition to Hang Tuah, for Hang Jebat exercised independent judgment in rebelling against authority. The problem here, in Maaruf's opinion, is that "The Malays are deceived into thinking that they have broken away from the feudal thinking, whereas in reality they have only substituted one feudal personality for another. Such a misleading innovation prevents the Malays from making a total break from their feudal past and to genuinely adopt the Islamic and modern humanitarian trend of thinking, more in keeping with contemporary challenges."[31] To those who would criticize him for inappropriately applying modern criteria to medieval feudalism and its most popular personalities, Maaruf replies that Islam was already the Malay creed in the fifteenth and sixteenth centuries. He is merely applying an age-old, but still vital, set of criteria against which one must judge both past and present Malay social values as seriously deficient. As examples of true Islamic humanitarian heroism, Maaruf proposes the second Caliph of Islam, Umar ibn al-Khattab (d. 644), Philippines patriot and revolutionary Jose Rizal (1861–1986), and Indonesia's nationalist general Sudirman (1915–1950).[32]

Heroes, Social Systems and Islamization

Two of the many relevant social issues one could identify are the incorporation of heroic values into formal religio-social organizations and the situation of women within the heroic milieu. Both matters are far too complex to discuss in detail here; but since they represent pervasive issues across the length and breadth of the Muslim world, they deserve some attention.

Chapter three will treat in some detail the code of heroic conduct that came to be known in Persia as *jawanmardi* and in Arabic as *futuwwa*. The latter connotes a pre-Islamic ideal of heroic conduct that then developed into the "chivalry" often identified with the horseman, who was in turn associated with heroic virtue. In time the notion lost its connection with horsemanship and became an exclusively religious term that characterized the spiritual charter of religious brotherhoods.[33] The heroic type known as the Ayyar, whom we shall discuss as a subset of the folk hero, embodied above all the code of "youngmanliness." The growth of organizations that identified themselves with the values of that code, at least in name, is too complex a phenomenon for us to explore here. It will suffice to note the connection between a certain type of heroic value system, not necessarily religious in inspiration, and later religiously oriented organizations that continued to look to heroic models such as Ali, who are of decidedly religious significance.[34]

Various theories have been advanced as to the relative fortunes of women before and after the coming of Islam. On the whole, it is impossible to make convincing generalizations as to how Islamization affects the lot of female characters in either literature or art across the Muslim world. It does seem that in general heroines enjoy loftier place and esteem in courtly or elite literature than in popular genres; but here, too, one needs to take sweeping characterizations with a grain of saffron. In the popular *Iskandarnama,* for example, one finds a thoroughly flippant and demeaning tone used toward women. In Nizami, on the other hand, women are much more noble and are treated as real human beings. Nizami's emphasis on Shirin's quiet, patient wisdom is paralleled, perhaps, by the portrayal of heroines in the Arabic *sira* literature as strong and brave. In the Antar and Hilal sagas, major female characters are warriors and earth mother types.[35]

Women in Kazakh Turkic epics possess idealized qualities like those of the hero, only slightly less advanced. For the most part, women are portrayed as intelligent and high-minded, though some epics do evidence a decidedly disapproving attitude. Even where the hero makes disparaging remarks about his wife, and about womankind in general, however, the principal female figure reasserts herself. Her wisdom and quick wit turn potential defeat into victory, and may even shame the hero into apologizing humbly. Some female characters model self-sacrifice, as in the case of the abducted wife and the mother who plead with the hero not to risk rescuing them from the enemy. Womanly beauty occasions some lyrical descriptions, but romance remains secondary to the theme of the hero's skill in battle.[36]

There is no question but that the male element dominates the heroic literature and art of Islamdom, in that the men occupy center stage far more often than the women. As we shall see later, however, a number of heroines are featured in ways that most readers will find quite surprising. One strong theme that may not be quite so apparent at first is that the women invariably function as links to the outside world, to the lands and peoples beyond those of the principal heroes. Whereas the heroes tend to relate to the outside in the capacity of conqueror, and to see the outsider as antagonist, it falls to the major heroines to form and/or to bring to light the more positive connections between inside and outside worlds. Heroes nearly always marry or pair up with women from national, ethnic, or even religious communities other than their own. Though they may do so initially as a way of taking possession of the outside world, the heroines frequently offer the hero the challenge of breaking down the psychic and cultural barriers that prompt him to envision the world as parcelled out. Thanks to the heroines, unification does not always happen through conquest.

Chapter Two

Issues in the Interpretation of Heroic Themes

Some literary critics have suggested that neither the classic texts nor the images that often accompany them ever quite succeed in developing a character fully. Some have been persuaded that the Islamicate world never produced a true epic hero. In both instances, critics have too frequently taken as their standards of excellence the modern novel, European portrait painting, and the works of Homer and Vergil. G. E. von Grünebaum has suggested that Islamicate literary characters had to be flat in order to function as models of behavior, lest too individualized a characterization render them inimitable. Thanks to a Catch-22, however, it was precisely because they were so underdeveloped that these flat characters could not serve as models. Unfortunately, it is all too easy to dismiss the classic heroic figures of the Islamicate world as flat and humanly negligible. Seen through our Euro-American filters, these characters lack that *sine qua non* of credibility—the verisimilitude of journalism or photographic realism; they do not develop according to our literary standards and tastes. Could the people among whom the stories and pictures of such characters have enjoyed truly immeasurable popularity have regarded these figures as mere decorative puppetry? Such a negative assessment has the hollow ring of cultural elitism and can shut the door to a fascinating avenue of understanding in the humanities. The crucial distinction here is not that between historical and fictional, or between round and flat characterization, but that between engaging and irrelevant.

We face a similar situation in respect to the visual illustrations of the stories. They may seem at first to lack the sort of depth and vivid characterization to which viewers of European and American art have become accustomed. If so, it is not because the miniaturists were incapable of making visible whatever meager psychological insight or affective subtlety the text could offer. We must develop new criteria for hearing and seeing. That is the subject of the present chapter.[1]

In terms of the broader study of the heroic themes as a global phenomenon, we need more data in two large areas. First, study of the relationship between literatures and visual arts in the various Islamicate traditions could provide more data on principles of visual exegesis as well as on how heroic stories function. Second, comparisons between studies of the first type and similar work in non-Islamicate traditions (e.g., illustrated Gospels, Jataka tales, and Hindu epics) would broaden our awareness of the vast range of meanings human beings have drawn from their heroic treasures. We must know more about motives for the visual interpretation of heroic themes and about the methods of interpretation suggested by relationships between text and picture. As further preparation for meeting the individual heroes in their Islamicate literary and visual settings, the present chapter seeks to articulate some major hermeneutical questions with which scholars of literature and the arts have wrestled.

We shall examine several approaches to three sets of such questions. We turn first to those literary studies that address the matter of the heroic personality as such, and to the ways its development within particular cultural contexts highlights important aspects of the Islamic world. Second, studies of the visual images of heroes likewise raise important issues. We will suggest some ways in which art historical studies can contribute to the investigation at hand. Finally, we shall look at potentially fruitful attempts to bring together the clues offered by literary and visual methodologies to formulate a visual/verbal hermeneutic. The numerous questions our survey poses about how to interpret the juxtaposition and/or blending of word-pictures and picture-words are indeed tantalizing.

Themes in Literary Approaches: Changing Character of the Hero, Literary Genres, and Cultural Values

One can identify several ways of looking at the material. First there are at least four approaches to the heroic character as such. One way examines the various types of heroes across a variety of cultures, as is done in the four chapters of part two below. Here we shall briefly outline three others. The second way studies such aspects as development in heroic moral capacity within a given culture over the centuries. A third looks at the values that heroes of a specific genre seem to embody for a culture during a single period of history. Finally, I shall suggest a way of looking at development using, not the model of the unfolding of a personality as individual lifestory, but that of growing into one's cosmos. Such a model situates the hero primarily in space rather than in time: change in the world rather than in the individual is the crux of the matter.

Hero as Index of Change within Culture and Society

M. K. Moghaddam relates major changes in the hero to the three periods of Iranian history—the pre-Islamic, the Islamic, and the Modern. He proceeds from the intriguing assumption that the stories of the heroes reflect a kind of evolution or maturation in the moral universe of the culture that has produced them. The heroes of the *Shahnama* represent and even epitomize the pre-Islamic moral universe. These first-phase heroes succeed admirably in encountering external evil and threat. Kawa the Blacksmith (a folk type who functions as a liberator of the oppressed), for example, responds to the external challenge of Dahhak's tyranny and its threat to Iranian national life. But he must enlist the help of the greater hero Faridun (a royal type who functions as a progenitor figure).

Rustam (a folk hero whom we shall call the lone knight type) represents some development in that he can face external evil alone: he boldly confronts the fatuous king Kay Kawus for his immorality and royal incompetence. But, ever the first-phase hero, Rustam remains incapable of dealing with more subtle, interiorized, spiritual and moral evil. So for example, when he meets his long-time friend Isfandiyar in a duel to the death, Rustam faces two unpleasant options. Now he must deal not only with an outside threat but with the inner evil as well, and he cannot cope. King Gushtasp has pitted one good man (his son Isfandiyar, a royal hero, the tragic prince) against another (Rustam). Rustam fails to convince Isfandiyar that he ought to reconsider his hopeless situation. Isfandiyar cannot win, for Rustam has a secret weapon he would rather not use. Unable to resolve the dilemma, Rustam must ultimately kill his friend. He can overcome external evil singlehandedly, but falters before inner evil.

In Moghaddam's scheme, the Taʿziya plays of the Shiʿi community, commemorating the martyrdom of Husayn (a religious hero related to the royal tragic prince type), sum up the plight of the second-phase hero. In this Islamic religious interpretation of confrontation with evil, the hero bravely stands up against incredible odds. He cannot win in the face of the external evil, but he has won the battle with inner corruption. In some ways the pre-Islamic hero Siyawush parallels Husayn, except that Siyawush avoids the inner evil symbolized by his seductive stepmother, only to be undone later by an external threat. Husayn resembles Suhrab (Rustam's son, who dies at his father's hand) a bit more, in that both call for a change within the world of heroic action. The difference here is that, though both are killed, only Husayn has the satisfaction of inner victory, while Suhrab merely dies in despair, unable to comprehend his fate within a larger scheme of things.

The modern-period hero, by contrast, sets out to conquer both outer and inner evil, that which exists in the world of the play as well as that which underlies his most profound inner conflicts. Moghaddam uses the example of novelist Chubak's Tangsiri character, a story with a less than glorious outcome, but one in which the hero faces all the hard issues and can in the end claim personal integrity.[2]

S. Idris pursues a similar line of questioning in the context of Modern Arabic literature. His investigation turns on the importance of understanding how different are the motivations of the classical hero from those of the modern hero, how varied are their respective ways of facing their worlds. Classical literature, he observes, depicts heroism as a movement toward the "world of the imaginary, the irrational, the extraordinary." In modern literature, heroism means "losing oneself in life, facing all its difficulties," refusing to take its blows passively, attempting to control one's circumstances. A major development seems to be toward more focused, less diffuse affect, together with a keener sense of suffering. The modern hero "discovers in the depths of his soul, despair, suffering and sadness; a profound anguish seizes him, which he takes on as a way of responding to the countless questions his life poses for him."[3]

In *Concept of a Hero in Malay Society*, S. Maaruf takes a slightly different approach while continuing to emphasize the values the hero embodies. Instead of looking at several heroes as representa-

27

tive of different ages, however, the Malaysian scholar discusses the problems inherent in trying to translate into contemporary terms the heroic values that won high marks in a bygone age. As we have just seen in the context of Islamization and indigenization, Maaruf discerns serious difficulties in transplanting the values of a medieval hero into modern circumstances, and cautions against a too-facile appeal to the imagined glories of the past.

Literary Genres and Cultural Change

A second approach to the character of the hero and its cultural relevance appears in J. S. Meisami's *Medieval Persian Court Poetry*. Three central chapters examine the genre of elite Persian romance in terms of the way in which its heroes enunciate changing values in medieval Iranian society. Underlying Meisami's analysis is the conviction that heroic figures in medieval Iranian culture did indeed function as exemplars and played a formative as well as descriptive role in the evolving value system. By no means merely a stick or cardboard figure, the hero exemplifies real human qualities and aspirations. Meisami writes that the "exemplary function of literature does not reflect a reductionary process by which the individual is deprived of value, but precisely the opposite: a conviction that the individual example validates the general principle, and, further, a belief in the human potential for both creativity and perfectability."[4]

Here, as in the first two approaches mentioned above, cultural change plays a part. Meisami focuses on how changes in the popularity of literary genres—and the kinds of heroic struggles that characterize the various genres—signal changes in values and ideals within a society. She identifies two literary streams that flowed out of the earlier "heroic epic": first, the "chivalric geste," recounting heroic deeds with a romantic and fantastic tinge; and second, the "romantic epic," whose plot turns on love rather than valor.[5] Meisami views the romance genre as inherently capable of communicating a weightier, more finely nuanced message. Romance delivers a more personal challenge, since, "In contrast to epic and *chanson de geste*, where the action is characteristically organized with reference to a larger, external design (such as the fate of a people), the romance plot is organized around the protagonist and his biography."[6]

Tracing the development of the romance in Arabic literature, H. Pérès finds a double cause, political and ethnic, rather than moral, as in Meisami's study. Under the Umayyad dynasty, urban poets talked of love as an alternative to expressing political dissent. Meanwhile, amid the harsher life of the Bedouins, there arose a kind of asceticism and mysticism expressed in the *hubb udhri* poetry. Among city dwellers, this new poetry was realistic; among the Bedouin, imaginative and platonic. Of these works, *Majnun-Layla* ranks high, along with the romances of Jamil and Buthayna, Qays and Lubna. Ethnic factors also played a part: in Abbasid Iraq, Persian Muslims took to translating into Arabic those works that "addressed the ethical imperatives of the new religion, and that could, at the same time, entertain with their accounts of wondrous happenings and enchanting description."[7]

On the origins of the genre called *maqama* (the "assembly" with its picaresque hero), Pérès refers to the "profound social inequalities" that gave rise to the roguish prankster heroes who lived as social parasites and preyed on the rich. He sees the hero as none other than the image of the "literary bohemian."[8] Of the more specifically epic works Pérès discusses, the *Sirat Antar* stands out for him as the epitome of the chivalric romance, in that its hero embodies most effectively both human weakness and brave nobility. This story of a Desert David exemplifies three most valued realities in the Arab world of the time: heroism, love, and poetry.[9]

Further analyzing the diversity of approaches to this same genre, the "Arabic popular epic," G. Canova finds the range quite broad. Purely literary investigations ask how the form relates to the broader history of Arabic literature. Some studies find evidence of "nationalism" and proof of the strength of Arab cultural patrimony. Others see the works as supporting a revolutionary spirit attempting to overthrow an invading foreign culture. Canova's own conclusions emphasize that the lack of authentically "epic" works in "official" (suggesting elite or more formal) Arabic literature is a result of a conditioning by religious leadership that had far less effect on the more popular levels of Arabic culture. What is most important here is the recognition that the genre represents a way of viewing the world, life, and history unique to a particular social group.[10]

Development in World Rather Than in Character

Perhaps what is needed most of all in the study of Islamicate heroic themes is a paradigm quite unlike those most western critics have applied, namely that of character development. In her study of the Malay epic *Hikayat Hang Tuah,* S. Errington has stressed the predominance of spatial organization and order over temporal or chronological continuity—and hence of character growth and change. The hero serves a far larger purpose than that of his personal evolution. He does not grow as an individual, but his life is integral to the unfolding of a cosmic story. This character succeeds as hero to the degree that he contributes to the fostering and maintenance of a divinely decreed order in the world.

In a study of a non-Muslim African culture's epics, Daniel Biebuyck has similarly noted "a key feature of Nyanga thinking: their preoccupation with space and place." He describes how the epic's structure and action correspond to the various levels and zones of Nyanga cosmology. In this approach the completeness of the cosmos rather than that of the hero supplies the "roundness" some critics find lacking in Islamicate heroic types. "The hero becomes, so to speak, a true hero only after he has successfully completed the whole cycle of events and deeds that put him through all the relevant spheres of the world."[11]

Using a variation on this model, H. Corbin has given great attention to the subject of * taʾwil* as exegesis of the inner meaning of non-sacred texts. According to Corbin, the Persian religious thinker Suhrawardi interprets the heroic patrimony of Iran within a cosmological-teleological framework. Suhrawardi finds development in the hero in relation to the hero's accomplishment of a goal that transcends human fulfillment or maturation in the psychological sense. Corbin's *Face de Dieu, Face de l'Homme* discusses Suhrawardi's view of the *Shahnama* within a continuum from heroic epic to mystical epic. At the heart of Suhrawardi's "Eastern Theosophy" stands the figure of Kay Khusraw, a royal hero from the *Shahnama* and son of the tragic prince Siyawush. As we shall see further in the chapter on heroic geographies, Suhrawardi envisions all significant action as occurring within a cosmological setting oriented toward a spiritual East that symbolizes the origin of light. Within that context, the life of the hero is as it were liberated from the confines of history, and heroic epic is transformed into what Corbin calls "mystical epic." In that scheme of things, the hero who has sojourned as an exile in the realm of history returns home to the "eighth clime." Kay Khusraw's mysterious deathless disappearance into the mountains thus makes him the epitome of the true hero, namely, the one who makes the transition to mystical experience.

Heroic fulfillment, therefore, depends on the successful navigation of the greater cosmos, the attainment of the spiritual summit at the center of the world, and the ultimate retirement into the mystical citadel (in this case, the fortress called Kang Dizh, built by Siyawush).[12]

Themes in Visual Approaches:
Iconography and Patronage

One would be hard pressed to find a more luxuriant outpouring of literarily oriented visual images and visually evocative literature than that of the Islamicate cultures we are studying here. Art historical studies of works that illustrate heroic themes (whether or not in direct connection with a written text) have too seldom discussed the precise relationship between story and picture. Most art historians begin with works as objects rather than with images as depictions of a given subject. Matters of style and connoisseurship often edge out issues of literary and more broadly cultural significance. Some work on formal characteristics and on specifically art-historical contexts can, nevertheless, contribute significantly to the interpretation of heroic themes. Without putting too fine a point on the matter, it is important to note the distinction between art historical approaches that seem to draw their conclusions without reference to narrative content, and those that clearly see the text as essential to their analysis. Here are some suggestions as to possible contributions to our topic from an art historical perspective.

Questions of iconography bear directly on the identification of a particular heroic character, but the implications can also be much broader. A number of recent studies contribute to interpretations of a range of heroic works, from Firdawsi to Hariri to the most sophisticated Nizami manuscripts.[13] Some of the questions they raise in the present context are these: Does the hero's or heroine's role in the image correspond to the text? How much additional detail has the artist introduced? Does non-textual detail suggest anything about the possible meanings the heroic story might have held for those who produced the image? How much detail has the artist left out? What is the physical relationship between image and text? How closely does the text included with the miniature (if any) correspond with the moment depicted? If the overall composition is largely formulaic (using more or less stock

31

items such as vegetation, terrain, animals, etc.), does its formulaic quality parallel that of the text illustrated? Are the characters' costumes inspired by fashions contemporary with the production of the manuscript and from the culture in which the work was produced?[14]

A number of recent iconographic studies treat important heroic themes. Particularly interesting among them are some that deal with the iconography of religious heroes, prophets, and saints. "The same characteristics that must have stimulated Muslim literary sources, vivid characters involved in vigorous action, with heroes usually triumphant over evil, were equally inspiring to early Muslim painters" and their patrons.[15] One study examines the development of visual imagery illustrating the story of Moses's battle with the giant Og, whom the prophet killed by whacking him on the ankle. Two questions concern the authors: why and from what artistic models did imagery from the Hebrew Bible appear in Muslim art, and through what literary channels did Jewish legend come to Muslim art and literature? Social-political and cultural forces at work during Mongol times explain both: Jewish converts to Islam, most notably the great patron Rashid ad-Din, brought the material to prominence.[16] Another study, dealing with three images—of Nimrod, Joseph and Jonah—unravels the literary and iconographic strands that have come together in those miniatures. The author concludes that "this iconography . . . reflects a new stage in Islamic painting, . . . expressing interest in different human societies and attempting to spread the message of Islam among its contemporaries."[17]

Studies that pay great attention to matters of patronage and to the overall historical setting raise further questions for us. Who paid for the illustrated version? From what segment of society did the patron come? Was the patron male or female? What was the patron's relationship to political or religious authority structures? How does the selection of scenes illustrated in one manuscript compare with the distribution of scenes found in other illustrated versions of the same literary work? Can one make any connections between apparently unique or otherwise idiosyncratic selection of scenes and events in history contemporary with the manuscript?[18] Is there any evidence that an actual historical personage—the patron—has been identified with the hero (Iskandar, Rustam, Yusuf, etc.) by having his image inserted into the illustration?[19] Is the artist possibly making allegorical or typological connections, either in a general way or between the classical narrative and major personages of his own time?

Discussions of iconography and patronage are essential for reconstructing the larger cultural contexts from which our heroic themes come. What is needed in addition are ways of further understanding how artists and patrons actually interpreted those themes, and why they proved to be of such great interest to them.

Themes in Evolving Visual/Verbal Hermeneutics

When all these questions have been addressed, what conclusions can one draw as to how the artist's work constitutes an interpretation of the story? The task of integrating the results of literary and art historical studies in a new synthesis poses a considerable challenge. In the original heroic materials, however, one can observe that integration at work in its original setting. Poets tell stories about heroes, in which other poets regale heroes with stories about other heroes. For example, Zal tells Rustam that now is the time Rustam should be enjoying life and "listening to lays of heroes."[20] In the romance of Hang Tuah, the heroes take courage from sagas of warrior heroes as they prepare to go into battle. Painters paint heart-ravishing pictures illustrating poems that tell of painters painting heart-ravishing pictures. The following are some marvelous examples. Rudaba's apartment walls are covered with pictures of heroes—something that must have stirred a twinge of jealousy in Zal as he climbed into her boudoir.[21] Bahram Gur steals into the forbidden picture gallery in the palace at Khawarnaq and falls in love with all of the women portrayed there. Khusraw has his painter put his portrait where Shirin will surely find it. Queen Qaydafa (alias Candace and Nushaba) has a portrait of Alexander that one of her courtiers had done while visiting in Egypt, and foils his ruse of disguise by recognizing him from the painting. Zulaykha plots to win Yusuf by planting around her apartment pictures of the two in amorous poses. Köroghlu forbids son Hasan Bey to enter a room in which hangs a portrait of a beautiful maiden.

On Relationships Between Story and Picture

In the search for fruitful hermeneutical models, scholars have proposed a number of interesting possibilities. A problem that seems to arise over and over is that attempts to approach literary and visual arts in an integrated way seem inevitably to lean toward linguistic models. Here are some of the more promising avenues of approach.[22] Images are principally of two types: those not physically related to a text, and those that occur with an inscription or on the same page with a text. Most principles scholars have teased out tend to be based on linguistic metaphors.

B. Connelly's suggestion about what one could call visual parataxis is a good example of the use of a linguistic model to describe the story-image relationship. A narrative that uses little or no subordination in sentence and thought structure (as might be the case in many oral performances) exhibits paratactic qualities. A picture that does not subordinate one action or figure to another is similarly paratactic, a visual equivalent to the words "and then and then and then." The organizational principle is that of simple oppositional or additive juxtaposition in an image. This may reflect the same phenomenon in the other medium, or it may be the artist's idiosyncratic touch or need for a simpler didactic mode in the illustration to a story being told to less educated folk.

Referring to under-glass paintings, especially of the Hilali saga, Connelly identifies visual parataxis as the pictorial equivalent of formulaic storytelling. "While the Hilali narrator juxtaposes narrative segments in a paratactic adding style . . . the glass painter employs a medium that knows no perspective, light or shadows. In its colorful dualistic disposition of motifs, the painted history serves to interpret the fdawi's tale and to draw out its basic terms." Glass paintings occupied pride of place in homes, and print reproductions of such paintings served as illustrations for live performances. Given that, Connelly explains further, "it may not be rash to assume that what the paintings depict summarizes and glosses the essence of the narrative versions."[23] More work needs to be done on parallels between oral and visual formulae. Just as the storyteller uses stock images, epithets, scenes, and so forth, so the illustrator draws upon a limited number of visual topoi.

D. Klimburg-Salter has contributed toward an understanding of the function of visual gloss as an interpretative device. As we shall see in detail in chapter nine, a manuscript of poems by Ahmad Jala'ir contains intriguing marginal illustrations. In form, the paintings represent "a typological link between miniature painting and illumination." Functionally, they allow a multiplicity of scenes to be associated with a text and give considerable space to the painter even as they remain clearly subordinate to the text. Too large and iconographically homogeneous to be mere decoration, the images do not simply "illustrate" the text as such. The poems are not narratives and "even the metaphors are too numerous and inconsistent to allow for direct pictorial representation. Moreover, each poem is short, and there is often more than one on a page . . . the paintings do not follow the text."

Klimburg-Salter calls the images "sympathetic visual idioms" whose style and technique, along with use of iconographic equivalents to various well-known metaphors from the lexicon of Sufism (journeyers, wisdom figures, lovers, birds) confer a pervasive "mystical mood." Taken together, the images affirm visually the poet's "spiritual yearning." Instead of "isolating dramatic moments in the text," the image serves as a gloss. Here pictures function much the way the marginal *text* of Attar's epic, *The Conference of the Birds*, functions in the early fourteenth-century *Anthology of Iskandar Sultan*, or the way other marginal texts serve to comment on main texts in many medieval manuscripts—subordinate but parallel.[24]

B. Connelly refers above to the use of pictures as "summaries" of a heroic narrative. M. S. Simpson has investigated a number of important heroic images found on objects other than manuscripts. Their apparent relationship to some heroic story parallels in part that of the North African glass paintings. Simpson suggests several helpful ways of naming other aspects of the text-picture relationship. First, an image may function as a metaphor for personal heroic attributes. Images independent of text may highlight a hero's importance as much for certain qualities as for achievement. For example, Faridun stands for noble lineage, Bahram Gur for royal enjoyment, and perhaps both stand for ideal royal behavior and power. Simpson sees in images of Dahhak and Azada (the harpist whom Bahram Gur trampled on the hunt) allusions to the struggle against evil.[25] If one can speak of "frame tales," why not also of "frame pictures," images that epitomize a whole story complex with its several sub-plots within sub-plots?

Approaching the matter from the other side raises this question: if images function as summaries or allusions to stories, heroic qualities, and so forth, might images not also have provided occasion or inspiration for the spinning of yarns to explain the existence of the image? One must distinguish between two possible dynamics here. In the first, the picture functions as *raison d'être* for narrative.[26] In the second, the image literally gives the storyteller an idea which he then translates into words and incorporates into his text. One study has suggested that Firdawsi may have gotten ideas for some descriptive passages from ceramic objects he had seen.[27]

Several interesting studies have recently pointed out the function of some images as illustrations not to a written text but to a recited heroic narrative. Some paintings have fold marks, suggesting that they were never part of books and that they were carried around by reciters and unfolded for small audiences.[28] Others are of larger format and on cloth, designed to be hung on a wall, or perhaps unrolled gradually as the narrator told the tale of the martyrdom of Husayn and other members of the family of Muhammad.[29] The former tend to be quite simple in composition. The painter has been careful to include only the bare minimum of characterization and setting, so as not to confuse the viewer and to provide as concentrated an illustration as possible. The latter are often quite complex. Since in the second instance only one image is used, it is up to the storyteller literally to point out which phase of the action he is now telling. The former are rather literal illustrations of an action that occurs in a simple space; the latter tend to show a highly symbolic spatial arrangement that suggests a world all its own into which the listener can travel in imagination.

We have thus far been speaking of images not integrally related to a text, or of images that seem to illustrate some text other than the one to which they are physically connected and to "comment" on the latter very subtly and indirectly. In his extensive studies of the illustrated versions of Hariri's *Maqamat*, O. Grabar has offered a number of useful distinctions among the various ways artists interpret their texts. The most obvious level is that of literal correspondence. If the text describes a plane tree in fall foliage, so does the miniaturist. If the narrator describes a knight dressed in leopard cap and tiger-skin tunic and mounted on a strawberry roan, so does the painter. At this level, one finds "visual puns" as well. The artist produces not a coherent visual interpretation but a book with pictures. Some illustrated versions of the *Assemblies* are marked by the use of rather arbitrary iconographic clues. The artist chooses some visual tag not mentioned in the text (a physical attribute, an item of clothing, etc.) by which a particular character can be identified throughout the manuscript.

A more descriptive approach pays greater attention to setting, thus providing less an illustration of the narrative's action than a commentary on the daily life and times of the artist. The hero and his sidekick are not essential to these scenes and do not appear at all in some miniatures. Another level of interpretation attempts a more intellectual or psychological analysis, sometimes including an element of satire. Hariri, for example, tells a story of how the hero wins a drove of camels and a singing girl. One witty miniature shows a handsome-enough drove of camels, but the "singing girl" next to them turns out to be a haggard old woman.[30]

In a similar move toward classification of images according to interpretative mode, L. Golombek distinguishes three types relevant here. First, the earliest direct illustrations of the text made explicit connection between text and image, but with image still subordinate. Gradually the image overcame the dominance of the text and, with less and less text physically present on the painting, eventually came to tell its own story. Secondly, some images function as visual metaphors on three levels (descriptive, abstract, and literary). In one image of Rustam's killing of Isfandiyar,[31] for example, the use of trees and bushes as a compositional device has more than merely formal significance. The dead tree describes the pathetic state of Isfandiyar as his fate overcomes him (descriptive). In addition, the image links the destinies of humankind and the natural world (abstract). Finally, the text describes the dying hero as "the straight-stemmed cypress bent" (literary).

A third type of image uses architectural setting as interpretation. The narrative moment is that of Zulaykha's attempted seduction of the prophet Joseph in the innermost privacy of her boudoir. Bihzad depicts the seven-room palace with its seven locked doors all clearly visible. This remarkable architectural structure seems to function as a mystical image—a symbol of the physical world with its seven climes, of God's beauty, and of the self with its struggles known to God no matter how far from the surface they occur. Like several interpretative types already mentioned, this image "transcends its literary model by suggesting themes that belong to the story as a whole."[32]

Another way of describing visual interpretations of text shares some features with Golombek's last type as well as with Klimburg-Salter's notion of visual gloss. It has to do with the relationships between pictorial space and narrative time, and involves a sort of

Table 2. Distribution of Major Heroic Sources and Settings

HERO \ REGION	Edge of World	Andalus Spain	North Africa	Sudan Egypt	East Africa	Arab MidEast	Rum Turkey	Iran	Central Asia	India South Asia	Southeast Asia	China East Asia	Edge of World
Abu Zayd of Saruj				S2P2		S1P1 A1	A3	A2	A2				
Abu Zayd al-Hilali			S2P1 A1	S1P2 A2	S3	S2P3 A2		A2	A2				
Ali			S2P3 A3	S2P3 A3	S2 A3	S2P2 A2	S2P2 A3	S1P1 A1	S3P3	S2P2	S3		
Antar			S2P2 A1	S1P2 A2	S3	S1P1 A2							
Bahram Gur						A2	S2P2	S1P1 A1	S3P3 A3	S3P3			
Hamza			S3	S3	S3	S2 A1	S3 A3	S2P3 A2	S2 A2	S2P1 A2	S3 A3	A3	
Hang Tuah						A3	A2			A2	S1 A1	A2	
Isfandiyar							S2P2 A3	S1P1 A1	S3P3 A2	S3P3			
Iskandar	A1	A2	A3	S3 A2		S2P3 A2	S3P2 A2	S1P1 A2	S2P3 A2	S3P3 A1	S2 A3	A2	A3
Koroghlu							S1 A2		S2 A1				
Rustam						S3	S2P2 A3	S1P1 A1	S2P3 A2	S3P2	S3	A3	

KEY: S = Story popularity; P = Picture production; A = Adventure setting. Number = relative importance; 1 = high conflation in that it brings together two scenes without actually depicting two separate moments in one frame (as some images do). As we shall describe in greater detail in chapter nine, one spectacular miniature shows Iskandar visiting a hermit living in a cave beneath a fortress whose inscription identifies it as the legendary columned city of Iram. But the poet does not describe Alexander's visit to Iram until much later in the narrative. Here the painter connects one architectural setting with another by a principle of analogy: both are reminders of mortality. The principle behind the allusion to another place and story may have something in common with the Rabbinical hermeneutical principle "Chayotze bo bemaqom akher" ("Just as it is in another text"), which uses the notion of analogy whereby the key to interpreting one text also unlocks another. The link between this scene and that of Alexander's later visit to Iram is that in both instances Iskandar learns about impermanence, transitory glory, and mortality.

This chapter has begun to touch upon a few of the many major hermeneutical questions one needs to address in order to appreciate the full cultural and religious significance of heroic themes across the world of Islam. Table 2 displays some more key relationships among heroic figures, geographical locations, story popularity, and the visual illustration of heroic stories. Subsequent chapters will reopen several of those questions and dig further into them insofar as they bear on our analysis of particular themes. The next four chapters will introduce the reader more thoroughly to some of the key characters as they appear both in literature and in the visual arts. Then in parts three and four, still further dimensions of their stories will come to the fore.

ISLAMICATE

HEROIC

FIGURES

PART TWO

Chapter Three

The Folk Hero

The adjective "folk" in this context requires some clarification. It refers chiefly, but not exclusively, to those heroic figures who (1) are of humble descent, and whose stories seem to originate most often among poorer and less educated people; (2) articulate and exemplify the aspirations of the masses, often getting away with deeds ordinary folks dream of doing but would not dare to try; (3) are to some degree anti-establishment and thus a threat to the status quo; (4) appear less frequently in visual art, and then most often in rather ephemeral pieces such as rarely survive long, or in works commissioned and paid for either by a middle class or by a princely class newly ascended to royal status; and (5) survive in literature either through unpolished (even crude) written versions of oral tradition or, though less often, in works crafted explicitly to tell the story in writing.

The Bedouin Ideal and Its Transformations

Chapter one's discussion of the functions of heroic themes and of Islamization hinted at the role of such values as bravery and honor in pre-Islamic Arab society. The typical Bedouin heroic figure was the man or woman of great courage, generosity, spontaneity, and loyalty, who put all his or her strength and virtue at the service of the tribe. The classic Bedouin heroic narrative served the people who produced it by fostering and even guaranteeing tribal unity, by preserving essential Bedouin values, and by serving as a link between the heroic figures as ideal types of Bedouin life and the audience assembled to hear the tale. The heroines usually exhibited courage in battle equal to that of their male counterparts, but they possessed in addition a measure of wisdom that counterbalanced the male tendency to swift and sometimes precipitous action.[1] Here we shall look at several examples of the Bedouin ideal and its transformations.

Most often of tribal, nomadic origin, the warrior and liberator of the oppressed types sometimes also appear in the guise of the

43

urban-based leader who goes on to become a major political figure. Three chief examples of the type occur prominently, and almost exclusively, in the literary genre known as *sira*. The first is purely fictional, the second an historical and dateable figure around whom much legendary material has collected, and the third, a man whose story consists of a substantial historical core embellished with some folkloric details. After the three *sira* personalities, we will look at a character who is very like the first three in many ways, but who seems to represent a clear Islamization of the type. We take our final example from Turkic popular epic tradition.

One of the earliest folk epics on the popular scene, the *sira* of the Banu Hilal, tells of (apparently non-historical) Abu Zayd, not to be confused with the picaresque Abu Zayd of the *Assemblies,* who will appear shortly. Son of a tribal prince, Abu Zayd eventually rises to leadership and ultimately comes to a tragic end when he is murdered. Abu Zayd's story brims with intrigues, including a father-son struggle of a sort that will find frequent parallels elsewhere, as the tribe battles its way toward conquest of the Maghrib. In the first of the three cycles, Abu Zayd also helps in vanquishing India. Not unlike the Persian hero Rustam in the *Shahnama,* Abu Zayd enjoys a life span of several hundred years. Abu Zayd dies more than once. Several important women play alongside the great Hilali hero. Most prominent among them is Jaziya (or Zaziya), who also has the starring role in at least one other narrative. She is the subject of several important glass paintings and shares the visual stage with Abu Zayd in numerous images in glass and print, often watching as the hero unhorses his opponent.[2]

Antar ibn Shaddad is a second important example of the Bedouin ideal. Antar's story claims a quasi-historical foundation in the life of a pre-Islamic poet (d. 615), the third and youngest son of Shaddad, belonging to the poor tribe of Abs, and of a black slave woman captured in a raid.[3] As a child, Antar must win his father's approval by slaying a dog at age four, a wolf at nine, and finally a lion. After successfully negotiating an arduous course of trials, he wins the hand of Abla. On his black steed Abjar, and wielding his thunderbolt-like sword Dami, Antar ranges far and wide defending the honor of his tribe, throwing banquets for the poor, and fathering children in clandestine affairs—twice with Christian women whose sons go on to become Crusaders. Here one finds interesting analogies with the seven marriages of Bahram Gur in far-off lands. Such elements in Antar are probably late additions, inserted to favor a peaceful climate after the first Crusades.

In addition to Antar's pre-Islamic and Christian connections, he also appears both as a precursor of Muhammad and as a Persian-style potentate, surrounded by the trappings of Persian courtly life. Moreover, Antar's overcoming the unacceptability of his blackness links him with the egalitarianism of the Kharijites, members of the early Islamic sectarian movement that refused to acknowledge Arab social privilege and insisted that leadership of the community was open to all authentic Muslims. As in the Hilali epic, the heroine is very much in evidence. In the Antar saga, two women stand out. Ghamra and Abla, both consorts of the hero, are fierce and able combatants who do not shrink from leading a cohort into the fray. Glass painted images of Antar and Abla are still popular in the Middle East, along with printed pictures in comic-book style. Some depict Antar alone, riding either his charger or a camel; some portray Abla alone in her camel-borne howda; still others show Antar with Abla riding together.[4] (See Figure 1.)

Finally, among heroes of the Arabic *sira* genre, comes Baybars I, champion of the common people, whose story is told from an urban middle-class perspective. Though he is an historical figure, Baybars's exploits are mingled with tales of magic and superstition. Middle-class folk and merchants emerge victorious, with his help, against the pretenses of the court; and popular religious elements of a rather intolerant Islam are prominent. I have not been able to turn up any significant visual interpretations of Baybars. Given the ongoing popularity of his saga, however, it is quite likely that some have been produced and are still in circulation. Stories of Antar, Abu Zayd, and Baybars continue to pass along the Bedouin ideals of heroic behavior for popular consumption all over the Middle East, especially in various parts of Egypt and North Africa. We look now at one excellent example of a transformation of the type under the influence of that process we have referred to as Islamization.

Perhaps no hero represents the Islamization of the pre-Islamic Bedouin ideal better than Miqdad, the Mikidadi of two popular Swahili epics, both by Al-Buhriy. One epic features Abd ar-Rahman, son of Muhammad's companion Abu Bakr, and the other centers around Miqdad and his beloved Mayasa.[5] Miqdad plays a swashbuckling hybrid of Robin Hood and Dartagnan, who appears

Figure 1: Antar riding Abjar.

out of nowhere when the last strand of hope seems stretched to the breaking point. I have included him here, rather than in chapter five among religious heroes, because he so clearly exhibits qualities of the folk hero translated into religious terms and can thus exemplify that process of transformation. One could say that in instances such as this, the Islamization of the hero-type does not occur at the expense of the hero's folk qualities.

In the Swahili epic *Utenzi wa Abdirrahmani na Sufiyani*, Abu Bakr's wayward son Abd ar-Rahman, under the evil influence of the villain Abu Sufyan, attacks a knight bound for Madina to visit Muhammad. The brigand takes the man's son hostage and demands a huge ransom. When the knight comes to Madina and announces his plight to the Prophet, Abu Bakr overhears and seeks to sway Abd ar-Rahman by sending his old friend Mora with a letter. Meanwhile, the captive son has won his freedom by impressing his captor that he should mend his ways. When Mora arrives he has little difficulty persuading Abd ar-Rahman to return to the Prophet's fold. His wife, a daughter of Abu Sufyan, then chooses to become a Muslim and go with her husband rather than return to her heathen father.

Needless to say, Abu Sufyan is thoroughly displeased with that turn of events. He immediately sets out to punish the turncoat. During a protracted struggle, Abu Sufyan inflicts a wound on his son-in-law, prompting a retaliation from his own daughter. Back in Madina, Gabriel tells Muhammad of the desperate scene. To the rescue he dispatches his five greatest heroes with Ali in the lead. Miqdad heads straightway to the side of Abd ar-Rahman's valiant wife as she holds off the foe, and tells her she can now retire from the field. At this point in the story, Miqdad comes into his own and wades into the enemy ranks alone. After he has hewn to pieces countless of the enemy, Kinana emerges to fight Miqdad. Kinana issues his challenge by asking Miqdad to tell him his (Miqdad's) name, a feature that occurs in many scenes of single combat. Kinana's brother warns that he is about to face the fearsome Miqdad, whereupon the infidel brothers accept Islam and change sides.[6]

Two traditions about Miqdad reveal other dimensions of his legendary character. The Iraqi tradition preserves traits and deeds of valor that link Miqdad with his pre-Islamic brethren who have much in common with Rustam, the Iranian Lone Knight whom we shall meet shortly. An Arabian tradition portrays the hero with features reminiscent of Bahram Gur, that outstanding example of the first sub-type of the royal hero, the romantic adventurer.

An Iraqi version sets the life of Miqdad during the reign of the second Rightly Guided Caliph, Umar (634–64). The young orphan is, like all the prophets, a herder of sheep. When he reaches sixteen his mother entrusts to Miqdad his father's armor along with enough gold to buy a good steed. He then sets off to do battle with the Sasanian Persians. As in the Arabian story, fortune soon brings the hero upon an ill-starred person in need of deliverance— in this case, a lad in chains deep inside a cave. No small challenge, even for a hero; for the cave belongs to a man-eating giant magician named Zoro who already knows that neither steel nor poison can do him in, but that a man named Miqdad might. The boy, whose name is also Miqdad, then explains that if the stranger assumes that name, the giant might merely imprison him rather than risk eating a poison that could kill him. Already the older Miqdad has run afoul of Zoro's magic when he tries to cut through a web to free the boy, and the web grows into serpents that entangle him.

That night Zoro returns carrying two dead children. Learning that his new guest is also a Miqdad, he chains the hero and sits down to a feast of young human flesh. He then consults his magic book as to when he will die; tomorrow, it says. Pressed further about how the giant will die, the book says it is not allowed to divulge that fact, but does proceed to tell the giant that on the morrow he will find plenty of dead bodies across the river on the Arab-Persian battleground. Once Zoro has gone out for food, the magical book speaks to the two Miqdads, telling them that God has already broken their chains and that tomorrow they will kill Zoro with fire. The book will shine its light at Miqdad, the hero, to give him a sign, the book explains. The hero later places the book on the giant's chest, and the volume bursts into flame.

From the ashes arises a woman who says she is Fatima, a jinn whose sin has condemned her to reside in a book until a hero releases her. Of course she then grants Miqdad three wishes. He chooses to be freed, to find his horse well, and to meet his deceased father. Miqdad then wisely declines her invitation to frolick in jinn-land with her, for duty calls him to return to battle. The grateful Fatima then bids them farewell with a promise to be ever at hand if only Miqdad will "whisper my name in the desert at midnight."

After a magical reunion with his father, Miqdad resumes his

combat against the Persians. Defeating all the shah's champions, Miqdad finally meets the king's daughter disguised as a warrior. Seeing each other up close, they fall in love at once. Not long after that, the Arabs defeat the Persians and the two lovers go off to live as leaders of the Qays tribe. Later, however, while off battling more heathen forces, Miqdad falls to the foe. Left for dead, the hero calls for Fatima, who obligingly appears, heals her man, and whisks him away to her father's kingdom.[7]

The Arabian story tells how Miqdad falls in love with Mayasa, who has sworn she will wed only the man who can defeat her in combat. Miqdad unhorses her and wins her heart; but her father, Miqdad's uncle Jabir, only grudgingly agrees to the match, and then only on terms of an exorbitant dowry. Miqdad resolves to journey until he has the wherewithal. His first obstacle is a giant who has taken a warrior named Qays and his lady prisoner and is about to kill Qays. Miqdad to the rescue. As the trio make their way, they encounter the deceased giant's three brothers, backed up by four hundred troops. Dispatching the giants and scaring off their minions, the heroes discover the giants' stolen hoard in a cave. Still Miqdad needs more, so he ventures on alone.

Near the border with Persia he routs the Persian king's guard, who has been instructed to seize Miqdad. Impressed at his valor, the king invites Miqdad to court, where he quickly becomes embroiled in royal intrigues, doing battle with various warriors, killing the royal lions, and finally eliminating a vizier whose bad advice has cost Miqdad the king's favor. The vizier's wealth falls to Miqdad, who goes off to recover his beloved.

Meanwhile, Jabir has given her to another, whose entourage Miqdad happens to encounter on its way out of Jabir's territory. After Miqdad has made short work of this new foe, he and Mayasa head for Jabir's estate. En route they meet Ali, who convinces Miqdad he should espouse Islam. With their new ally, the couple continue to Jabir's house. After Miqdad drinks himself asleep, Jabir has him sewn into a bull hide. Meanwhile, the suitor to whom Jabir has earlier given Mayasa takes possession of his bride, but not before Mayasa manages to inform Miqdad's aged mother to go get Ali. She flies to Makka and informs Muhammad, who immediately sends his premier hero to the rescue. Miqdad has twelve children by Mayasa and becomes Ali's lifelong friend.[8] I have found no references to visual interpretations of these Miqdad stories.

One final example of variation on the Bedouin theme comes in the form of a parallel from the Turkic tradition, whose name is Köroghlu. Like the Bedouin heroes, he champions the cause of the people; the socio-political system within which Köroghlu operates, however, is quite different. Son of a soldier in the Iranian cavalry, Köroghlu ("Blind Man's Son") becomes a vengeful rebel after the Shah blinds his father. The hero and his 365 men do battle from their forest stronghold of Chamlibel against the rich and powerful who oppress the ordinary folk. The epic character evidently derives from an historical figure who took part in Jalali raids against the Ottoman elite, from the sixteenth to the eighteenth centuries. In the west (Anatolian and Azeri versions), Köroghlu comes from humble circumstances and defends his own.

Further east, Central Asian variants raise the hero from the status of a Robin Hood to that of a legitimate leader of the people who defends them against Arabs and other external foes. Whereas the Anatolian version links the hero more directly to his father, the Central Asian emphasizes the wondrous quality of his birth in the grave from a mother who had been buried pregnant: his new name is Guroghlu ("Son of the Grave"). Despite the significant differences in the origins and social contexts of the two variations, both help to round out our picture of the character called here the warrior and liberator of the oppressed.[9] I have found no illustrated versions of the Guroghlu cycle.

The Hero as Possessor of Wit and Wisdom

All heroes exhibit noteworthy forms of cunning, and even the hero who earns a living by fighting only occasionally descends to an exercise of unalloyed bravado. One could say that most heroes show at least a modicum of practical wisdom, if only in knowing when to retreat and when to advance.[10] And in the end, as we shall see later, the hero more often than not learns something important about life. Some heroes, however, possess qualities of wit and wisdom that are not secondary but virtually essential. Among these types, some seem naturally endowed with that which others must acquire or receive as a gift. For all heroic figures of this kind, the possession, or acquisition, and judicious application of street-smarts, arcane wisdom, or magical power are a distinguishing mark. We look first at several examples of the naturally savvy character, the picaresque, and its opposite number, the trickster or buffoon. Several instances of the hero who learns or is granted special wisdom will follow that.

The picaresque/trickster hero (some would say anti-hero) is a roguish, sometimes buffoon-like, character. Although occasionally described with the attributes of a fighting Bedouin hero, he is urbanized and more sophisticated. Like the wily Odysseus, the street-wise picaresque hero lives not by deeds of physical prowess but by his dazzling eloquence and quick wit. Unarmed except for his rapier-like tongue, the picaresque hero charms and disarms everyone he meets. Hamadhani's vagabond scholar, Abu 'l-Fath of Alexandria, and Hariri's master of all trades, Abu Zayd, have their stories told in a series of vignettes narrated by a straight man (Isa ibn Hisham and al-Harith, respectively) who recounts his experiences of the unpredictable and sometimes embarrassing hero.

Clever plots and ornate language match the complexity of the hero's scheming motivations and ruses in an erudite combination clearly intended for the well-educated. Hamadhani's version apparently never achieved the popularity of Hariri's *Maqamat*. The latter has been preserved in a large number of illustrated versions, but I know of no extant illustrated versions of Hamadhani. During the thirteenth and fourteenth centuries, the stories gained great vogue in Baghdad and parts of the Mamluk realm. Miniatures sometimes depict scenes from the tales, capturing a high moment. Sometimes the image seems to relate quite indirectly to the story, and either serves merely to decorate the page or gives the viewer a glimpse into the daily life and times of the artist.[11]

Hariri situates the first story in a Basra mosque. A ragged old man claiming to be from Saruj arises to preach. He professes dire need in the wake of the Crusader invasion in his home town of Saruj, collects substantial alms, and then trundles off to a cave for a rich feast. When the narrator takes him to task for his mendacity, Abu Zayd explains lightheartedly that when times are hard one has to live by one's wits. All of Hariri's *maqamat* expand on that theme, with the crafty old man trying to sell his "son" as a slave at market, preaching (for money) at a funeral, and posing as a philosopher, among other brazen and outrageous exploits.

The heroes of the *Assemblies* belong to an extended family whose members are found throughout the Islamic world. One picaresque hero whose popularity has continued to our time, Khoja Nasruddin, has travelled under various names and in several guises all over the Mediterranean world and Arab Africa. He is the epitome of the wise fool, whose *raison d'etre* is to prove that persons and actions that appear simpleminded do not necessarily yield only folly. Nasruddin has no trade, although the honorific "Khoja" suggests the learning required of a religious scholar qualified to preach, lead prayer, teach, or even serve as judge. The Khoja has more than his share of human frailties, but always manages to land on his feet. Because one sees this character only in glimpses afforded by short anecdotes, his life story remains a puzzle with missing pieces. Individual vignettes focus on themes basic to the daily life of the folk who have kept the stories alive: food, borrowing and lending, the importance of cleverness, the acceptability of trickery. Miniature paintings and engravings of Nasruddin wearing a comically bulbous turban and riding his trusty donkey with enormous ears are among the most popular images of this thoroughly Turkified character.[12]

Jiha, an Afro-Muslim trickster, represents a major variant. Among the Muslim Ja'aliyyin of the Sudan, Jiha's popularity gives evidence of the process of Arabization of the Sudan as well as of the ubiquity of the character type. Sometimes transformed entirely into a religious figure and sometimes into a Robin Hood-like liberator, Jiha in general "draws certain traits and characteristics from the African trickster figure, modifies such features in accordance with the spirit and principles of Islam, and incorporates them into the Near Eastern Jiha."[13]

Other heroic types rely on different kinds of wisdom. Unlike the specifically religious hero, the sage or successful seeker after knowledge wields a weapon not explicitly associated with a divine presence or intervention. Some stories feature a pre-Islamic hero whose power, originally linked to a more diffuse mysterious or occult source, seems to be Islamized into a more avowedly religious phenomenon, such as blessing *(baraka)*, saintly wonder *(karama)*, or prophetic miracle *(mu'jiza)*. Often enough, the knowledge-hero appears to come out of a kind of shamanistic background, in that the special knowledge results from a "vision quest." Sometimes the character possesses wisdom innately. Our examples come from the full range of heroic traditions. From the Arabicate tradition comes al-Battal; from the *Shahnama*, Zal, father of Rustam; from the Turkic tradition, we have Dede Korkut; and from Southeast Asia, the Malay Hang Tuah.

Within the realm of Arabicate folk heroes, *Sirat Dhat al-Himma*'s al-Battal plays Oedipus to Abd al-Wahhab's Achilles. (Abd al-Wahhab, Dhat al-Himma's son, plays a major role on the side of the Kilab tribe, opposite the Sulaymite al-Battal.) Al-Battal's success derives chiefly from the endless intricate strategems and disguises hatched in the depths of his cleverness. Born lazy (his name can mean both "hero" and "sluggard"), al-Battal relies whenever possible on such machinations as drugs to help him kidnap the enemy, monkish garb to get him behind enemy (Byzantine) lines, and all manner of espionage. Though this man of many ruses does not want for physical prowess, he lacks the straightforward bravery of the warrior and avoids pitched battle. Al-Battal's knowledge of religious sciences and his ability to speak Greek and other languages belie his low birth. All in all, this hero is the perfect "fox," as one of his more formal names suggests (Ibn al-Husayn ibn Thaʿlab).[14]

Son of Sam and second of the three principal Sistanian heroes, Zal might at first seem better interpreted as a royal personage. As a character type, however, he seems to represent a wisdom figure— even down to his earliest physical appearance as an infant born with pure white hair, and to his name "Old Man." Thinking only that others will mock him for fathering such an ill-omened child, Sam rejects Zal and leaves him to die in the remote Alburz mountains. Thanks to the nurturance of the wondrous Simurgh bird, Zal overcomes the "trickery and enchantment" Sam has wrought upon him. Thanks to the Simurgh's gift of one of her magical feathers, Zal gains access to the special knowledge and aid that can effect the safe birth of his son Rustam by Caesarean section. Throughout his long career, Zal appears often as counsellor and confidant to several kings. His advice usually outweighs that of almost all other courtiers. In later chapters we shall look in greater detail at various key moments in Zal's life. Zal was also a favorite of miniature painters, not only because he was important as a character, but because his white hair provided a ready-made iconographic tag.[15]

From the Turkic tradition comes the multi-talented Dede Korkut. He functions as a repository for the collective wisdom of the Oghuz Turks. This hero-bard not only recounts the tales of heroes past, but stands ready to counsel the Oghuz nobility and invest newly matured future heroes with their weapons. He occasionally intervenes as negotiator as well. Perhaps most importantly, Dede Korkut is the bestower of names. When a lad has reached manhood, as indicated by his having shed blood and made heads roll, the sage steps in to confer an appropriate identity.[16]

Malaka, on the southwest coast of the Malay peninsula, entered history as the center of one of the first Muslim political entities in Southeast Asia. There the story of Hang Tuah ("Captain Luck") takes place. Hang Tuah's father brings his son to the new capital to provide him the best possible religious and cultural education. The boy grows up to enter the service of the raja (king) and soon becomes the only force that can separate culture from chaos. Hang Tuah's mission is to protect the central kingdom from the incursions of the barbarian (Javanese) "amoks," who threaten civilization when they "run amok."

Once a simple shopkeeper with no intrinsic connection to royalty, the hero achieves success by means of his superior knowledge. At first, his knowledge of magic allows him to gain the upper hand over enemy soldiers who have come to disrupt the life of the court on the eve of a royal wedding. By cunning, Hang Tuah wrests the magical *kris* (traditional Malay/Indonesian dagger) from the enemy leader. For that deed he receives the title "Laksamana," whereupon he and his four companions head off to consult a guru on a mountain, who can teach them what soldiers (and *hulubalang*, "local warrior chieftains") know. The teacher singles out Hang Tuah as the most promising, imparts all his *ilmu* ("knowledge" of warfare), and tells Laksamana he must not share this knowledge with anyone.

Each time the amoks attack, Hang Tuah prevails with his superior knowledge. At its source, such special knowledge is called *ilmu*, knowledge in its impersonal, pure, undifferentiated form. When the knowledge is put into action, the story refers to it as *tahu*—a more personal form of knowledge that implies deeper awareness. Hang Tuah's knowledge alone proves effective against the forces of chaos, in the face of which even royalty flee in panic. Still, the hero declines to arrogate the supreme place unto himself; for the power implied in royal dominion derives from a different form of knowledge, one that is hereditary and thus not available to a common person like Hang Tuah.

A second source of Hang Tuah's privileged knowledge is the ubiquitous Khadir, the archetype of the spirit-sage. Khadir imparts to the hero the secret of seeds that produce mangos immediately upon being planted. One of Hang Tuah's more amazing gifts is his fluency in many languages, including Siamese and Chinese. In one encounter with Khadir, the prophet-initiator touches Hang Tuah's lips and gives him a canteen of water to put on his ears and lips. In addition, Hang Tuah knows numerous charms and incantations, powerful enough to clog the canon of an enemy ship.[17]

Hang Tuah shares some characteristics with the Lone Knight, who makes his appearance shortly, in that Hang Tuah also serves a higher authority as court champion. Unlike the lone knight, however, this type actually acquires knowledge as an essential personal quality, so that he need never rely on sheer brute strength to win the day. Finally, whereas the long knight strikes one as more of a free-lance "Have Sword, Will Travel" character who serves in a variety of ad hoc capacities, Hang Tuah's destiny remains within the confines of a kingdom that requires his services for the cosmic purpose of fending off the forces of chaos.[18]

The Hero as Comrade in Arms and Champion

In this last variation on the theme of the folk hero, we examine those heroes whose principal characteristic is their relationship either to an ostensibly more important hero or to a larger authority or legitimizing power. The former type function as comrades in arms or sidekicks; the latter serve chiefly as champions to a court, although they also sometimes undertake adventures in their own right.

A class of characters known as ayyars (*ayyar*, pl. *ayyarun*)[19] plays a variety of roles in heroic accounts. The ayyar sometimes plays the comic figure, sometimes the trusted advisor to kings, sometimes the inscrutable wizard whose peculiar deeds conjure up a terrible power, sometimes the younger brother or half-brother who manages to talk some sense into a well-meaning but not very prudent older sibling. In one of its earlier Middle Eastern variants, the type derives from popular confraternities of persons (men or women). Bound by loyalty to a greater power, or acting ostensibly on their own authority, they swing into action to defend the royal court or to restore rights and possessions to the deprived poor.[20]

One early example of the ayyar type, who shares some features of the liberator of the oppressed, plays his part near the beginning of Firdawsi's *Shahnama*. Here is the setting. The evil Arab usurper Dahhak has managed to overthrow the fabled King Jamshid, who had weakened because of his loss of the *farr* ("divine mandate" or "glory"). Dahhak makes a deal with Satan (Ahriman) that in exchange for royal power, he will suffer two horrid serpents to sprout from his shoulders, each requiring as daily sustenance the brain of a young man. Dahhak's tyranny takes a grisly toll on the hopes of the people, when at last a humble blacksmith named Kawa stands forth to confront the evil power. Unwilling to lose the last of his own children to the evil tyrant, Kawa makes his move, even though he knows he is not quite the man for the job. Hoisting his leather apron aloft as a banner, he inspires what amounts to a revolution. Though he himself cannot bring the action to completion without the intervention of the powerful Faridun (who will appear in chapter four in the section on progenitor figures), Kawa's indignation at the ongoing slaughter ignites the spark by his heroic defense of the populace. Kawa remains a lesser figure within the vast sweep of the *Shahnama,* but he is one of the few from the Iranian epic to rate appearances in more than one visual medium—miniature painting as well as ceramic objects. Several plates evidently depict Kawa, banner ahoist, walking ahead of a figure taken to be Faridun as they lead Dahhak off to his punishment. I have included him here as a kind of proto-ayyar because of the role he comes to assume in relation to Faridun, the central hero of the piece.[21]

W. Hanaway's study of "Persian Popular Romances" identifies *jawanmardi* (the Persian equivalent of the Arabic *futuwwa*) as the code of conduct pursued by these ayyar characters. The urban-based, generally lower-class groups took the pre-Islamic Hatim at-Ta'i as their model of generosity, and Ali as the epitome of bravery. Though courtly personages in the romances often speak disparagingly of the ayyars as amoral low-life, the stories defend their standards, such as honor and sexual restraint, as lofty and worthy of emulation. Women in the romances frequently attempt to break into the tight circles of the ayyars. Virtually every princess would leave her palace by night, accompanied by a handmaid, to play the ayyar. The romances suggest strongly that women did gather in organizations paralleling those of the men, but little is known of their makeup and function.[22]

One fascinating character, explicitly referred to as an ayyar, also qualifies as a supporting figure, although one could easily argue that he, not the prince he serves, is the real hero. Samak-i Ayyar, in the Persian popular romance named after him, serves as alter-ego to Prince Khurshid Shah. Samak is of humble origin, as the narrator reveals in a very rare flashback that gives this character a personal history. His education and natural resourcefulness make Samak a perfect foil for the prince, whose heroic attributes of nobility, loyalty, generosity, and physical strength make him at least indirectly heir to the Bedouin ideal. Samak compensates for his lack of brute force by strategem and by the use of weapons that allow him to fight at greater distance than does the short sword. Most of all, Samak represents a heroic preference for values, truth, uprightness, and the kind of detachment that allows him great mobility. As Prince Khurshid Shah's role in the story wanes, Samak's waxes. The prince seems to function as a foil for the ayyar, a true folk hero who embodies high morals.[23]

Ayyar types appear far from the Middle East as well. In the early modern Indonesian epic *Hikayat Potjut Muhamat (The Story of Prince Muhammad)* we find an unusual but significant variation on the theme. Prince Muhamat, an historical figure of early eighteenth-century Acheh (in Western Sumatra), is the youngest of four brothers. As he watches his oldest brother, the Sultan, gradually losing his grip on the affairs of state, he tries in vain to persuade his other princely brothers to intervene. When they back down, Muhamat sees that he must take matters into his own hands for the good of the people. He knows that he must mobilize the local chiefs into a unified bloc in order to circumvent the Sultan and neutralize the threat of the former Sultan, whom Muhamat's father has ousted and who now seeks to return at the expense of Muhamat's weak older brother.

One especially powerful local chief has remained loyal to the dethroned Sultan, and Muhamat's journey and efforts to win him over fill a goodly portion of the story. Once Muhamat has succeeded through diplomacy and tact, his new ally swears his loyalty to the Prince, much against his mother's warning that by doing so the chief displays profound ingratitude to his patron, the dethroned Sultan. The local chief's change of allegiance brings to mind the conversion to Islam of Abd ar-Rahman, son of Muhammad's nemesis Abu Sufyan. In this case, however, the chief pays with his life, for the deposed Sultan is a *sayyid*—a descendent of the Prophet.

Meanwhile, the chief's support has given Muhamat the edge. Muhamat succeeds in shoring up his oldest brother's authority, and the Prince continues to support him. The prominence given to the local chief's ultimate ruin reveals the poet's ambivalence: he clearly praises Prince Muhamat's successes, but he cannot pass over in silence the evil of withdrawing one's loyalty, especially from an heir of the Prophet. Prince Muhamat functions in the story very much like the ayyars of Persian popular romance, except that he has outstripped his ruling counterpart in everything save the royal office itself. Unambitious for power, he remains content to play a supporting role.[24]

Trickster figures also sometimes appear as comic variants of the ayyar, in supporting, rather than starring, roles. Such characters belong to a larger group of personages who function as alter egos to the main heroes, especially in romances and post-epic developments of heroes like Alexander the Great. As we have seen in the case of Samak, an ayyar can serve as the king's vizier, the prince's squire, or the princess's handmaiden, and functions mainly to offer shrewd advice, skill, and even the cautionary warning. In their more explicitly Islamized and religious forms, these supporting actors exhibit primarily wisdom, insight, and knowledge of the unseen world and serve as guides. As we shall see later, for example, even a prophet so important as Moses pairs up with the enigmatic Khadir, who tells Moses he must not question Khadir's actions no matter how bizarre they may seem. In their more popular forms, however, the supporting characters can assume the comic role of jester, buffoon, or wisely foolish servant whose antics belie a surprising measure of astuteness.

Major identifying characteristics of the trickster type as it appears across the Indo-Persian (ayyar) and Malay (panakawan) regions of the Islamic world include the following. Tricksters can disguise themselves readily; they are sometimes associated with animals, especially the wolf. They often manifest some physical deformity and hence apparent weakness. The trickster frequently functions as initiator of the hero into life-mysteries crucial to the hero's success. Sometimes the character adds a note of comic relief, especially in its Southeast Asian variants. Finally, tricksters seem to echo the very ancient notion of the hero's divine origin, gradually degraded to the point that the hero requires the subordinate ayyar figure to remain whole.[25]

Two excellent examples of the trickster-ayyar are Amr ibn Umayya and Amr ibn Maʿdi Karib (greatest of the Yemeni heroes, who appears in numerous tales along with Ali).[26] They begin their literary lives in the Middle East as henchmen of Muhammad's uncle, Amir Hamza, and end their journey in Southeast Asia as Hamza's ever-faithful but club-footed clowns. In their Near Eastern forms, these characters still function in a serious mode, as potent warriors. Amr ibn Umayya, for example, receives considerable attention as Ali's capable right-hand—if not always entirely commonsensical—man in the Shi'i religious epic *Khawarannama* as well as in the Persian versions of the Amir Hamza story.[27]

As the story of Hamza moves to the Indian subcontinent, the characters take on a slightly more comical air.[28] In the Malay *Menak* (Hamza story) Amr ibn Umayya ad-Damri becomes Marmaya, and Amr ibn Ma'di Karib becomes simply Marmadi. Hamza remains vigorous and redoubtable, conquering unbeaten wrestlers even as a child, but his childhood mate Marmaya appears inept and silly and already launched at a tender age on a lifelong career of pilfering and bribery. By the time the two partners of Hamza appear in Indonesian versions, they have become still more comical and hapless. In the last phase, Malay literature provides the vehicle of transmission, and Indonesian popular theater effects the final transformation of the supporting character's tenor and function. But even when these characters seem reduced entirely to the role of comic relief, Amr ibn Umayya retains sufficient serious power to become a sage figure just long enough to perform a wedding ceremony.[29]

In Serbocroatian songs, too, one finds a variation on the clown/henchman theme in the person of Tale the Fool, "a curious hero whose attributes include miserliness, greed, and buffoonery used for comic effect, as well as extraordinary wisdom and strength." Tale's ragged appearance conceals "special, almost supernatural powers," and he "usually is responsible for directing military operations, dividing the spoils of battle, and executing judgment on the vanquished."[30]

Heroes who function chiefly in the context of a larger sociopolitical framework, such as the royal court, we shall call champions. Epic literature is full of such characters as Knights of the Round Table. Though heroes of this type usually serve a higher authority, the major examples manage to preserve a large measure of independence. Unlike their lesser counterparts, who tend to emerge from the crowd to fight and then dissolve back into the collectivity, these lone knights are always out in front and clearly set apart from the rest. They form a transitional type between the folk and royal heroes. Here we shall look at two examples, Rustam and Hamza.

In the Persian epic *Shahnama,* the horseman/hunter evidently reflects the interests of the cow-herding peoples of Iran, and the theme of the above-average herdsman eventually came to blend with themes from the royal court. The solitary paladin thus ceased to be a merely local or provincial favorite and was absorbed into a broader cultural milieu. Firdawsi, for example, seems to have stitched together preexistent local epics featuring a single unrivalled hero to fashion the *Shahnama.* It is surely no coincidence that the epic was commissioned by a Ghaznawid monarch, Mahmud, whose political ambitions were not limited to a given valley in Afghanistan. At the same time, as M. Hodgson notes, "urban and mercantile themes were strictly subordinated, despite the urban life of most of the more cultivated listeners."[31]

As the third in a trio of greatest heroes from a series of tales known as the Sistan Cycle, Rustam arrives early in the *Shahnama.*[32] It is true that in the Persian epic Rustam deals only with royalty and might not strike one at first as a true folk hero. However, Rustam's fame predates Firdawsi's poem, and in both pre- and post-*Shahnama* traditions he is very much a man of the people. Royal legitimacy is not uppermost in Rustam's ambitions.[33]

Rustam is easily the most prominent figure of this type, and perhaps of any of the types, with respect to the frequency of his appearance both in the *Book of Kings* and in manuscript illustrations of that text. He may also constitute the clearest example we have of a survival of the older, purely regional hero. Rustam makes his first appearance in the *Shahnama* just toward the end of the mythical Pishdadian dynasty, and remains an important figure well into the time of the legendary Kayanian kings of Persia. In his more developed form, Rustam appears to move in and out of the courtly sphere, so that he is neither explicitly identified as royal nor precisely at odds with the ruling establishment. He somehow transcends all that: he outlives many kings, survives even his own death, and takes center stage often over a span of several hundred years.[34]

Rustam's birth, as that of a number of the *Shahnama*'s heroes, attracts attention, but Rustam is a special case. His mother experiences a prolonged labor that jeopardizes the child. Father Zal (abandoned by own his father, Sam, then reared by the Simurgh— a mythical bird that sometimes functions as symbol of deity) recalls that the Simurgh had long ago given him a feather to burn in order to summon the Simurgh in time of trouble. The Simurgh then appears to heal the ailing Rudaba by revealing the secret of the Caesarean section. Upon delivery, the mother cries, "Rustam," meaning "I am free of pain."[35] Rescued by the Simurgh as his father had been, Rustam would go on to become the Islamicate world's preeminent rescuer of others. He is the Champion's Champion.

In many of his exploits Rustam's wondrous steed, Rakhsh, provides crucial assistance. The story of how Rustam found and captured the horse appears in numerous miniature paintings.[36] Viewers of miniature paintings can easily spot Rustam by means of his various iconographic tags: he wears his leopard-skin cap and carries his "mace of a single blow" and "lasso of sixty loops." M. Maguire has made a comparison and contrast between this hero's most celebrated set of adventures, the "Seven Courses," and the trials through which Rustam's royal counterpart, Isfandiyar, must pass. On the one hand, Maguire suggests, Rustam's trials formed the model for those of Isfandiyar. On the other, tighter narrative structure, a tendency to rely less on self and more on outside power, increased personal ambition, the function of religion as a source of continuity, and less naturalistic description, all mark the Isfandiyar cycle as a later development.[37] Mazaheri proposes another interesting interpretation of Rustam as Isfandiyar's culture-twin. He suggests that, in a medieval Iran divided politically east-west, the cow-herding Rustam (originally an adept of Mithra) defended eastern Iran, while Isfandiyar (a "Zoroastrian" Rustam, later supplanted by Muhammad's son-in-law Ali under the Shiʿi Buwayhids) reigned as hero over agricultural and anti-nomadic western Iran. This approach understands Rustam as the culture hero of eastern Iran, who would later give place to Ali as Isfandiyar had done earlier in the west.[38]

One might argue that the naturalistic, concrete, and easily identifiable exteriority of Rustam has made him a more popular subject of visual art than the more polished and interiorized Isfandiyar. Rustam does not, however, entirely lack a certain spiritual dimension, at least in his survival in later Islamicate tradition: the mystic Rumi, to mention only one among many possible examples, sees in Rustam a kind of spiritual paradigm, referring to the embryonic Jesus as a "Rustam hidden in Mary's womb." To call someone "a Rustam of his day" remains a high form of praise.[39]

Muhammad's uncle Hamza might seem at first glance to represent an obviously religious type of hero. A closer look, however, reveals that, apart from the hero's converting all those he vanquishes, the religious element in stories of Hamza has the feel of an afterthought. One does not get the impression that the hero functions primarily as the bearer and embodiment of essentially religious values. He speaks rather of a spirit of adventure than of a spiritual tradition or experience. Granted that Hamza, like Miqdad, bears a different stamp than such characters as Ali, Husayn, and Moses, one can take a closer look at how much Hamza has in common with Rustam. One could argue that Hamza, like Miqdad, also shares enough qualities of the liberator of the oppressed to be called a blend of the two types, especially since many of the adventures attributed to Muhammad's uncle Hamza appear to have originated with a Persian rebel of the same name. But for now it will suffice to relate Hamza to the lone knight type.

Van Ronkel has pointed out at some length the parallels between the adventures of Hamza and those of Rustam. Both heroes serve kings without actually belonging to the court; both often go off as knights to do battle against other kings; both fight demons (diws), in some cases in stories remarkably alike in such details as how the demon tricks the hero; in both cases a son (conceived under very different circumstances) is born after the hero has departed, and the sons both seek and find their fathers later (a feature found also, for example, in the Köroghlu cycle).

Few personages have been so popular for so long across so great a geographical expanse as Hamza. A combination of the range of his travels, his meeting several times with the prophet/guide Khadir, his symbolic association with the prophets Isaac and Solomon (he breaks Isaac's horse in Solomon's gardens and comes into possession of weapons and armor of other prophets), his wrestling skill and fearlessness in facing any challenger, and the comic relief his ayyars provide, all make Hamza's story appealing and colorful. Illustrated versions of his exploits, while not nearly as numerous as miniatures of Rustam's adventures, are still among the more important visual interpretations of a hero. One enormous manuscript provides most of our extant images of Hamza. The sixteenth-century Mughal monarch Akbar commissioned one of the most ambitious illustrated texts in the history of Islamicate art, the *Hamzanama*.[40]

The Survival of the Folk Hero

Does the folk hero survive in our time in the awareness of authors and readers in more traditional Islamic cultures? Medieval stories remain popular, but there has been much development in conceptions of the hero, especially in Arabic and Persian literatures. Literary characters capable of challenging, uplifting, and affirming the potential of real people populate the novels and poetry of numerous authors.

One knows heroism only by knowing first the fear beyond which the hero is called to advance. Heroes win admiration precisely because they are of human stuff, not because they laugh in the face of death. To the degree that modern authors consider the classical heroic mode as a flight from life into an imaginary world, they now describe the heroic as an immersion in life as it is, with all its suffering and disappointments. A threefold struggle emerges as the key idea in many modern Arabic novels: a nationalistic struggle against colonialism, a cultural and intellectual struggle of East versus West, and the struggle of social revolution.[41]

Scholars point to important continuities and changes in perceptions of the heroic in Persian literature as well. One critic suggests that modern literary heroes stand on the shoulders of heroic ancestors—Rustam's in particular. Anger at social and economic injustice now mirrors the classic hero's sense of challenged honor; prison recalls the underworld of the epics. Referring more specifically to the work of three twentieth-century Iranian novelists, D. A. Shojai draws these parallels: "Behind the father-son conflict of Esfandiary's novel stands the tragic clash between Rustam and Suhrab; behind the sociological conflict between individual and authority in ʿAlavi's work stands the catastrophic encounter between Rustam and Isfandiyar; and in the conscious making of a hero before he takes on any of these tragic actions, we have Chubak's *tangsiri* (man from Tangestan), a reflection of the conflict between Rustam and the Akvan Div."[42] One can see still another important classical folk hero reappearing in modern garb in the figure of Chubak's hero, the man from Tangestan. The blacksmith from

Islamicate Heroic Figures

Tangestan represents a development of Kawa the blacksmith. Like Kawa, Shir Mammad rails against an outside power (the British) symbolized by the Union Jack; unlike his predecessor, the modern hero also confronts the internal evil of Iranian acquiescence in the policies of the outsiders.[43] A similar parallel occurs in Mahmud E'timazadeh's 1977 novel *Kawa*. There the blacksmith plays the contemporary revolutionary who seeks to oust the tyrant (who like the ancient Arab Dahhak represents outside domination) and mobilize popular support for the Iranian Faridun (a classical progenitor who will reappear in the next chapter). Summing up his own role, Kawa says: "I am a blacksmith, a simple blacksmith. . . . They say that I attached a piece of leather to an arrow and called the people to rebel, and so they did. . . . Our problem was immense and we put a lot into solving it. Thousands like Kave and better than Kave worked themselves to death until they reached that tremendous moment in the story, but you only hear of Kave. What was Kave? The arm of the people. . . ."[44]

Finally, K. Markus has explored two Persian novels in which the hero-as-artist's life connects with the folk hero tradition in two ways. Formally the story recalls the structure of the classical hero's life: youth, the "journey" of growth beyond adolescence and of descent into an underworld led by a "psychopomp," and sojourn in a far-away land and culture. As for specific content, the stories make reference to the classical ethical tradition of *jawanmardi;* quote from the *Shahnama;* and allude to medieval folk heroes, to the leadership of Ali, and to Muhammad's "Night Journey and Ascension"—the latter two instances linking the protagonist to the tradition of the religious hero, on whom chapter five will focus.[45]

Alongside the more developed modern hero, folk heroes like Abu Zayd, Antar, and Baybars enjoy an ongoing popularity among storytellers in the twentieth century. Modern and contemporary equivalents of the classical warrior and liberator of the oppressed also appear in popular media from Morocco to Indonesia. A recent Pakistani publication intended for the education of children, entitled *Heroes and Heroines of Islam,*[46] includes along with a predictable roster of classical and medieval personalities a number of recent political figures. Mustafa Kemal Ataturk, Riza Shah Pahlavi, Muhammad Ali Jinnah (founder of Pakistan), and Indonesian "Strong Man" Soekarno top the list. Somewhere, no doubt, someone has composed epic commemorations of the deeds of these and other

64

personalities of their ilk. Had a revised and expanded edition of that work appeared in 1990, it may well have included Saddam Husayn of Iraq as champion of the poor and challenger of the Super Power. Here I shall mention very briefly one modern historical figure of Indonesian origin, whose story shares many characteristics of several of the classic types.

This fascinating character from twentieth-century Indonesia combines elements of the historical revolutionary, the liberator of the oppressed, the mythical/magical, and the picaresque. "The Scarlet Pimpernel of Indonesia" stars in a late 1930s five-volume novel of the same name *(Patjar Merah Indonesia)*, as leader in the fight to throw off Dutch colonialism and Stalinism. Tan Malaka, a leader of the Indonesian Communist party, is the historical figure beneath a heavy overlay of fantastic abilities to disappear, fly, and change appearance. As the more recent television clone of Baroness Orczy's original "Scarlet Pimpernel" was wont to say, "Sink Me!"[47]

Chapter Four

The Royal Hero

Royal heroes comprise a category of characters who do the things royalty do, and whose essential identity connects them with the life and values of the court. Although this fact does not necessarily imply that the literary and visual works that tell their stories derive exclusively from courtly circles, royal patronage did support most such works. By the same token, royal heroes have enjoyed popularity among more ordinary folk to the degree that stories often told in princely circles have made their way into, or perhaps even originated in, folk tales or popular romances. From that perspective, one could classify the Alexander of some popular works as more folk than royal. Here, however, we shall employ the criteria of function, lineage, and identity. A royal hero descends from royal stock and stands at the center of a socio-cultural system.

The present chapter examines five variations on the theme of royal hero: the romantic adventurer, the progenitor, the tragic prince, the heroine as warrior and lover/beloved, and the world-conqueror.

The Romantic Adventurer

We look here briefly at one minor example of the type, Gushtasp, and two major examples, Khusraw Parwiz and Bahram Gur. I have placed Khusraw Parwiz first, even though Bahram Gur appears in the *Shahnama* in his rougher, less developed state as a bit more of a swashbuckler (and thus more akin to the lone knight) than as a figure of lofty regal stature. J. S. Meisami has suggested persuasively that in Nizami's development of Bahram Gur and Khusraw, as well as of Alexander the Great (the last major royal hero considered here), one can see a progression in the relationship between the romantic and royal elements. Nizami describes Khusraw as lover-king, Bahram as progressing "to perfect kingship through love" with increasing emphasis on kingship, and Alexander as exemplifying the "two aspects of kingship—temporal and spiritual."[1]

Gushtasp, son of Luhrasp and father of Isfandiyar, represents the earliest example of the romantic adventurer in the *Shahnama*. Like the later Bahram Gur and Khusraw, he experiences some distancing from his father, wins the hand of fair maidens in far-off lands by proving himself in trials ordained by future fathers-in-law, and like Bahram Gur (at least in the *Shahnama* version) dies of natural causes. Gushtasp, however, never develops as fully as a character, or achieves as wide a popularity, as Khusraw or Bahram Gur. Gushtasp does make an appearance in many miniature paintings, principally in his role as adventurer. We find him most often in his sojourn in Rum (Byzantium) engaging in a range of ruses and exploits, from disguising himself as a smith to dispatching a dragon as a favor to a lesser hero who wants to claim the honor as his own. Later we shall encounter Gushtasp again in his role as disaffected father to Isfandiyar.[2]

Khusraw Parwiz represents a further remove from the adventurer toward the purely kingly figure. Nizami's romance *Khusraw and Shirin*, in J. S. Meisami's view, "focuses on the problem of the personhood of its protagonist Khusraw and the manner in which this is established (or revealed) in the course of his quest for union with his beloved."[3] Nizami tells the story the following way. Much-desired and long-awaited son of King Hurmuz, the young Prince Khusraw falls from grace temporarily for mistreating a peasant and his family.[4] Repentance brings his father's forgiveness, and a dream in which Khusraw's grandfather, Anushirwan, promises him incomparable royal power, a swift steed, and a beautiful wife. Khusraw sends his painter-friend Shapur (who functions as his ayyar) to fetch the lovely Shirin ("Sweet"), whom the painter says he has seen in Armenia. Shapur finds the lady and hangs a portrait of the suitor in a tree within Shirin's sight. With a single glance she falls in love and agrees to head for Persia on the incomparably swift steed, Shabdiz.[5]

Meanwhile, Khusraw's enemies have angered Hurmuz against him, and the prince flees to Armenia. On the way he spies a woman bathing. He suspects she may be Shirin, but she, not knowing the voyeur's identity, rides away before Khusraw can encounter her. This is one of the most often-depicted scenes from the romance.[6] (See Figure 2.) On to the Armenian court Khusraw rides, only to hear that Shirin is in Persia. Khusraw again dispatches Shapur (on the second fastest horse, Gulgun) to extricate her from the

Figure 2: Khusraw Parwiz spies Shirin bathing.

inhospitable palace-prison in which Khusraw's foes have seques-
tered her. Before Shapur can get Shirin back to Armenia, Khusraw
hears that his father is dying and returns to claim his kingdom,
barely missing Shirin once again.

One of Hurmuz's generals, Bahram Chubin, mobilizes popular support against Khusraw. Again the new king is Armenia-
bound on Shabdiz. Stopping to hunt, Khusraw at last meets Shirin
as she too hunts. Scenes of the royal pair's bucolic encounter have
delighted painters and patrons.[7] Shirin says she will be Khusraw's
only on condition that he regain his realm. In search of reinforce-
ments, Khusraw makes for Byzantium. The emperor offers fifty
thousand troops—but only if Khusraw will marry his daughter
Maryam monogamously. Khusraw agrees, defeats the rebel Bahram Chubin, and returns to Persia.[8]

Meanwhile, Shirin has acceded to the Armenian throne; but
when she hears of Khusraw's choice, she goes off to mourn in her
Persian prison-palace. Still playing the go-between, Shapur responds to Shirin's desire for milk from mountain herds by enlisting
the sculptor-engineer Farhad to dig a tunnel that can carry milk
to Shirin. Farhad, of course, is smitten at the sight of Shirin and
does an unrequited-love stint in the desert. Khusraw takes no delight in Farhad's affection for Shirin. He commissions the engineer
to cut a road through a stone mountain, promising Shirin as his
reward. Shirin goes out to encourage Farhad in his labor, raising
Khusraw's suspicions that the engineer may indeed see the job
through. The king sends word to Farhad that Shirin is dead, and
the disconsolate Farhad leaps to his death.[9]

Upon the death of Maryam, Khusraw takes a liking to a
woman in Isfahan named Shakar. He pursues her and eventually
makes her his queen. When his passion for the new wife cools,
Khusraw goes on a hunt that brings him to Shirin's residence. She
arranges a regal welcome in her courtyard, but herself remains
behind locked doors, telling Khusraw from the roof to go back to
his new lady—a very frequently depicted scene.[10] Shirin soon relents and goes after Khusraw. Concealed in a tent next to Khusraw's, Shirin hears the royal minstrel Barbad sing of the king's love
for her. In return, Shirin plants her own minstrel before her tent
to return the message. Lover and beloved discover each other,
marry, and prosper long.[11]

Enter the jealous son (by Queen Maryam), Shiruy. Khusraw is

apprised of his son's enmity but takes no action. At length, his son imprisons Khusraw. Shirin goes to stay with him, but one night while both are sleeping, a hit man enters and stabs the king. Khusraw dies, unwilling to disturb Shirin's slumber in his final agony. Like a character from a Freudian case-study, Shiruy pursues Shirin. She agrees to marry him after the funeral. But after saying she wishes to pay her final respects in the burial chamber, Shirin with a bare bodkin her quietus takes, and dies over Khusraw's corpse. Nizami has included many small details not mentioned by Firdawsi and has altered others significantly. For example, in the end Shirin enters Khusraw's tomb some two months after his death and there takes her own life by drinking poison.[12]

Khusraw and Shirin appear in scores of illustrated manuscripts, mostly of Iranian origin but with some important works produced in India and Turkey as well. A survey of nearly seventy illustrated manuscripts reveals that the most popular scenes are the following: Khusraw discovering Shirin bathing; the two lovers out in the countryside; Shirin visiting Farhad on Mount Bisutun; Khusraw and Shirin together amorously; and Khusraw entreating Shirin at her palace. Miniaturists have chosen to emphasize romance over adventure, but next in popularity come those scenes that portray the adventurous Khusraw: the king warring against Bahram Chubin; Khusraw confronting a lion; and Khusraw enjoying a royal soirée in the countryside. Scenes relating to the tragic subplot of Farhad's distant love for Shirin comprise a strong third grouping.[13]

Colorful and engaging as any of our heroic figures, Bahram Gur exhibits several features of the lone knight while remaining quite distinct from that paragon of lone knighthood, Rustam. Rustam began his literary career, that is to say, his history as a character in the entertainment business, as a cowboy and later made his name as a helper of kings. Bahram Gur entered history as an actual king of the Sassanian dynasty—Bahram V (420–38), called Gur (onager, or wild ass) because of his prodigious energy—later celebrated for his love of hunting, his amorous adventures, and his feats of bravery.

Unlike Rustam, Bahram Gur appears in only one section or story cycle in the *Shahnama* and stars in several later court romances. Still, Bahram's popularity as a subject for artists lags just slightly behind that of Rustam. His upbringing in the *Shahnama* clearly emphasizes his royal lineage. He deals with courtly figures such as nobles; he engages in regal entertainments; and he does not serve as a rescuer of the people as Rustam does.

Perhaps the most famous and frequently depicted episode in Bahram Gur's career finds the adventurer and his harpist slave-girl off on a hunt.[14] She antagonizes the hero with demands that he display extraordinary talent, and pays dearly for the proof. The basic story begins as Bahram's lady friend bets the hunter that he cannot turn a doe into a buck. He responds by planting a pair of arrows on the head of a doe. She bets he cannot turn a buck into a doe, whereupon Bahram shoots the rack off the head of a buck. Still not satisfied, his companion bets he cannot pin a deer's hind hoof to its ear. Bahram fires a shaft that just grazes the deer's ear and causes it to raise a foot to scratch the itch; then he lets fly another that pins the hoof at the ear. The lady's further response varies according to which version of the tale one is reading. Three major literary works develop the scene in slightly different ways, beginning with Firdawsi's unadorned version, proceeding to Nizami's less violent and more romantic retelling in the *Seven Portraits,* and ending with Amir Khusraw's further refinement of the feminine element in his *Eight Paradises.*

In the *Shahnama,* slave-girl Azada offends the proud hunter by refusing to praise his skills sufficiently, and pays with her life as Bahram Gur tramples her under his camel. Nizami's Fitna ("Rebellion") attributes the hero's skills to mere practice. Bahram Gur orders one of his men to kill her, but the henchmen instead gives her asylum. There she prepares to prove her point by carrying a calf up sixty stairs each day, growing in strength as the animal grows into a bull. When Bahram Gur later accepts an invitation to a party, Fitna puts on her show for him. The king relents from his earlier stubbornness and asks for forgiveness. Amir Khusraw has Bahram Gur simply abandon Dilaram ("Heart's Repose") after she belittles his hunting prowess and ascribes it to mere sorcery. A musician-farmer takes the girl in and guides her toward instrumental virtuosity. Her reputation prompts the hero to come hear this woman whose identity he discovers when they meet. Again he asks her forgiveness, but Dilaram does not resort to so splashy a display as that of Fitna.[15]

Bahram Gur's early career finds him engaged as much in adventure as in romance. He loves to hunt, but seems to prefer fiercer

71

game than deer. In order to claim his throne he must take the crown from between two wild lions. That whets his appetite for more action, so he orders a massive hunt for his favorite quarry, the wild ass (onager, *gur*). While on the hunt, he encounters a dragon and dispatches it; miniature painters have produced some striking depictions of that scene. In another of his more celebrated exploits, Bahram kills a ravenous wolf.[16]

Nizami shows his major development of Bahram Gur's story and character, however, in the cycle of seven stories in the *Seven Portraits*. Young Bahram's father, Yazdigird, exiles the boy to Arabia where Yazdigird's vassal, Nu'man, builds the prince a castle—the legendary Khawarnaq, about which we will have more to say later. Wandering through the castle, Bahram Gur finds a locked door, asks a servant for the key, and finds in the secret room a series of seven portraits, each of a princess from one of the seven regions of the world. The architect had done the paintings and placed a portrait of Bahram Gur among the seven.[17]

Some time later, after the hero has regained his rightful throne, a former assistant to the architect of Khawarnaq persuades the king to build a series of seven pavilions. With colors corresponding to days of the week, constellations, and zones of the earth, their decorative symbolism is designed to protect the king from the evil eye that threatens all who enjoy success such as his. As Bahram Gur revolves his way through the seven domes, each of the foreign princesses he has wed tells him a story intended to teach some key virtue, such as truthfulness and self-control. Miniatures of Bahram and his seven foreign lovers comprise the single largest cluster of visual images. (See Figure 3.) Only in relatively rare cases have painters gone beyond largely decorative purposes in their treatment of the theme. One can do just so much in depicting a woman regaling a king with her stories. On the whole, the miniatures are limited iconographically to indicating differences from one pavilion to another by the use of color schemes, but some miniatures depict scenes from the theme of the story told by the princess. The major exceptions are those delightfully elaborate images that embellish the pavilion setting with visual details not specifically mentioned in the text.[18]

Seven years of living in his astrologically coordinated chambers evidently leaves the king quite out of touch with the outer world. Emerging to set right the affairs of his realm, he remodels the

Figure 3: Bahram Gur in the White Pavilion with the Indian Princess on Friday.

pavilions into Zoroastrian fire temples and limits his royal pursuits
to hunting. At last comes the fateful expedition. Spotting a wonderful onager, the hero gives chase, follows the animal into a cave, and
is never heard from again. (Nizami observes that the word *gur* also
means "grave.")

In the *Shahnama* Bahram Gur simply dies of old age. Nizami's
tale highlights, according to G. Krotkoff, "the futility of astrological
practice and the need, in a successful life, for wisdom, justice, action, good deeds, and the acceptance of a higher order." For Nizami, the onager functions as a guide to the cave of ultimate
transformation.[19] Bahram Gur does not journey to an underworld,
but his life culminates in transferral to another level. J. S. Meisami
suggests that Bahram Gur undergoes the ultimate transformation
into the Perfect Man. (One might say something similar of the
gradual apotheosis of Alexander, to which we shall come shortly.)
Bahram Gur's vanishing into the cave gives him affinities with the
imam mahdi of Sunni Muslims and the concealed *imam* of Shi'i Muslims, as well as with their prototype, the Zoroastrian savior figure.[20]

The Progenitor

Progenitors are those heroes credited with the beginnings of
celebrated lines of heroes. The two best examples of the type appear in the *Shahnama,* but a variation became very important in
the development of religious heroes. Major and minor heroes alike
inevitably trace their own lineages back to some progenitor figure.
Occasionally a newly sprung dynasty might find it useful to claim
descent from a particular hero not otherwise noteworthy as a progenitor. So, for example, Malay kings found a special Islamic legitimacy in Iskandar because of his fame as one of God's prophets. In
Persia, the Sasanian dynasty was pleased to call Isfandiyar its prime
ancestor. In the next chapter we shall relate several religious heroes
to this royal type (especially Adam, Abraham, and Muḥammad).
Here now are two of the most important royal progenitors, Gayumart and Faridun.

Gayumart, the royal progenitor par excellence, inagurated the
mythical Pishdadian dynasty as the first of five culture heroes credited with structuring human society into civilization. He occupies
fewer lines of the *Shahnama* than any other major heroic figure, yet
artists and patrons have chosen scenes of his enthronement more
often than any I know of as the opening illustration to the epic.

(See Figure 4.) Gayumart presides as honorary father of the human race and giver of the arts of civilization. It was Gayumart who introduced the ceremonial throne and crown, clothing, and even food.[21]

For thirty years Gayumart ruled, "benevolent as the sun everywhere," attracting to himself all creatures, tame and wild, who came to take refuge with him, "bowing low before his throne. And so it was that he grew in majesty and power. All came to him in the attitude of reverence, and hence religion took its rise."[22] Firdawsi's verbal description reminds one of later paintings of Solomon presiding over his multi-level court.[23] Gayumart's three immediate descendents (Siyamak, Hushang, and Tahmurat) represent an evolution in the early institution of monarchy. Siyamak was the first example of the prince of tragic destiny, a type to which we shall come shortly. Grandson Hushang receives credit for discovering fire during his forty-year tenure. Great-grandson Tahmurat rules for thirty years, persuading the jinns and demons to teach him all languages and alphabets, so that he comes to command thirty tongues and wins the epithet "Demon-Binder."[24]

All in all, Gayumart leaves a legacy of civilizing and humanizing descendents. That first royal age both culminates in, and declines with the end of, Jamshid's reign of a thousand years. Jamshid, a culture hero like his predecessors, lives on in legend as a teacher of the civilizing arts. Numerous later heroes would pronounce the name of Jamshid in reverence, recalling the wisdom that his world-revealing cup afforded him, as well as the mortal failings that ultimately cost him the divine favor and doomed his millenial reign.[25] Taking advantage of Jamshid's disintegration, the Arab usurper Dahhak then initiates a millenium of tyranny that ends only at the instigation of the rebel Kawa and the rise of Faridun.

Faridun functions as Progenitor in a somewhat more symbolic fashion than does Gayumart. If Gayumart fathers all humanity, Faridun holds pride of place as the *paterfamilias* of Iranian heroes. A hero can make no nobler boast than to claim to be of Faridun's stock, and thus to inherit the patriarch's ox-headed mace (an important iconographic tag in many illustrations). A number of progenitor themes occur in this patriarch's saga. First, Faridun survives a much imperilled infancy, not unlike that of other progenitor types (e.g., Moses, Abraham, Muhammad). The usurper Dahhak dreams that a child will soon rise up and become the hero

Figure 4: Gayumart's Court.

who will dethrone him. Dahhak kills the child's father and later slaughters the wonder-cow, Birmaya, who had nursed young Faridun.[26]

Secondly, Faridun has a favorite son of whom the others are jealous (as in the story of Jacob). Faridun further resembles Abraham in that the sons of both are associated with either ruling or generating more than one major culture or ethnic group. Faridun, who is related only indirectly to earlier Iranian kings by his marriage to the sister of Jamshid, divides the world among his three sons. He sets Iraj over Iran (and the Arabs), Salm over Rum (Anatolia) and the West, and Tur over the Turks and China.[27] According to one strand of tradition, Abraham's son Isma'il (Ishmael) fathers the Arab race while Ishaq (Isaac) continues the Jewish line.[28] We shall return in later chapters to other aspects of Faridun's commanding role in the history of heroism.

The Prince of Tragic Destiny

Sometimes sprung from a progenitor type, sometimes not, the prince of tragic destiny recurs often in Islamicate heroic literature. This theme often occurs in tandem with the younger son motif: the father either as a deliberate act or as a result of some ruse bestows favor on the younger/youngest rather than on the first-born. The latter theme in turn frequently ties in with sibling jealousy stories (as in that of Joseph). Here we look at the three most prominent examples from the *Shahnama:* Iraj, Siyawush, and Isfandiyar.

Themes of the preeminence of the younger son and the resultant sibling jealousy occur in the tale of Faridun's youngest of three, Iraj. Faridun tests his sons by confronting them in the guise of a fierce dragon. The eldest, Salm, flees to safety; the brazen Tur charges too eagerly into the fray; but the wise Iraj tells the dragon that if it has any sense, it will vanish while it can, for it has dared to challenge the sons of Faridun! Daddy's doubts evaporate immediately. Iraj alone is worthy of command over the homeland. Salm becomes jealous and conspires with Tur to murder Iraj. True to another pattern (in which progenitor avenges son's death via grandson or great-grandson), Firdawsi has great-grandfather Faridun commission Manuchihr, the grandson of the innocent victim, to avenge Iraj's death. One can discern that pattern also in Gayumart's sending his grandson Hushang to kill the Black Demon, who had slain Gayumart's son Siyamak. Miniaturists have produced some marvelous images of Faridun's testing his sons, of Iraj's murder, and of Fridun's mourning. Pictures of the first scene usually manage to communicate something of the three sons' varied responses, while turning the father-dragon into a decorative tour de force. Images of the latter scenes capture moments of unsurpassed grief, as the father receives the decapitated corpse of his youngest child.[29]

Yet another prominent sacrificial son is Siyawush. Sudaba, one of the wives of his father, Kay Kawus, falls in love with young Siyawush. Unrequited, she falsely accuses the youth to his father. Voila! The Potiphar's Wife (Zulaykha or Wife of Pharaoh's Vizier) Motif! Twice Siyawush vindicates himself, once through trial by fire. He then wins permission to go into battle, accompanied by Rustam, against the Turanian King Afrasiyab. The warriors decide to negotiate with the Turanian, but Kay Kawus vetoes their decision. Rather than go back on his honor, Siyawush chooses to go over to Turan, where he marries Afrasiyab's daughter. The king's brother becomes jealous of Siyawush and incites Afrasiyab against him, whereupon Afrasiyab has Siyawush cruelly and unjustly killed.[30] Here again, but most ironically, grandson (Kay Khusraw) swears to grandfather (Kay Kawus) that he will avenge father's (Siyawush's) death.[31] Painters have two favorite scenes from this prince's short life: his riding unscathed through the fire, and the moment that Garuwy slits the youth's throat. Pictures of the first (See Figure 5.) emphasize Siyawush's triumph; those of the second, his agony.[32]

A final example is Gushtasp's son Isfandiyar. In this case the story rounds some unexpected turns. Isfandiyar's father tells him that he must avenge his grandfather if he wishes to inherit the crown. In addition, Gushtasp requires his son to enlist the submission of his long-time friend Rustam, from whom Gushtasp has become estranged. No great surprises so far. But then a remarkable series of encounters between the two young heroes culminates in one of the epic's most poignant scenes. In an earlier scene, Isfandiyar has killed a Simurgh (the magical bird who nurtured Zal and gave him the secret of the Caesarian section) by a series of ruses. As he drenched himself in the bird's blood, he closed his eyes. Now Rustam has learned that Isfandiyar's protection does not include his eyes; so, following the instructions of the Simurgh, Rustam fires a special two-pointed arrow to the eyes and kills his long-time

Figure 5: Siyawush's ordeal by fire.

friend Isfandiyar. With his final breath, Isfandiyar entrusts his own son, Bahman, to Rustam. After a while Rustam and Gushtasp are reconciled as well.

The battle between Rustam and Isfandiyar turns up among the most frequently illustrated of all *Shahnama* scenes. Isfandiyar appears often performing heroic deeds so that he ranks, along with Rustam and Bahram Gur, as one of the most popular subjects of illustrations that depict a single hero in action against the forces of evil. Like Rustam, Isfandiyar performs his seven feats or courses. The polished warrior meets almost every challenge, until he comes to blows with Rustam. Rustam, for his part, finds this victory most bitter, for fate has put him face to face with the mystery of evil. After doing everything he can to avoid this fight, Rustam must use a secret from the Simurgh to kill his friend. Miniaturists have produced several marvelous images of that tragic scene, as well as of Isfandiyar's moments of victory.[33]

The ill-starred prince of the epics seems to function as an intermediate prototype for the martyrs of later Islamicate religious literature and art. Earlier in the history of the type, one finds especially the imagery of the dying and rising divinities of the ancient Near East, particularly the fertility deity Tammuz. Later the type develops not only in religiously oriented imitations of the *Shahnama* but in passion plays mourning the death of Husayn and in the visual arts connected with them.[34]

The Heroine as Warrior and Lover

Dozens of noble and royal female characters play important roles in the heroic stories of the Islamic world. Although such figures almost never feature in their own full-length works,[35] and only rarely have the stage to themselves, they often share billing with their male counterparts. Some excellent examples of the pairings are found in courtly romances such as Gurgani's *Wis and Ramin*, Khwaju Kirmani's *Humay and Humayun*, Nizami's *Layla and Majnun* and *Khusraw and Shirin*, and Jami's *Joseph and Zulaykha*. In many ways these women develop more as characters than do the men, for they appear not only as young princesses and later as queens, but as mothers, lovers, warriors, and counselors. Here I have divided the subject of royal heroines into the not-very-comprehensive categories of warriors and lovers, since they suggest something of the range of the characters. Of the two types, the latter occur far more frequently. Similarly, the theme of loving dedication and loyalty more often forms a thread throughout the heroine's life, whereas the warrior theme typically remains more episodic or even limited to a unique incident. These royal personages are generally either queens or princesses. Other important women characters will appear later in the chapter on the heroic family.

While commoner women play an important role as fighting ayyars in the Persian popular romance entitled *Samak-i Ayyar*,[36] some warrior women also come from the ranks of the royalty. Two royal fighters in particular, one from epic and the other from popular romance, will give some sense of their function in the heroic traditions. First comes Firdawsi's Gurdafarid and then Purandukht from the *Darabnama*.

Gurdafarid is the daughter of Guzhdaham, an aging Iranian noble. She and her father await in the White Castle near the border between Iran and Turan, the first obstacle that Suhrab must overcome en route to meeting his father Rustam in Iran. Gurdafarid, whose name means "Hero-made," arms herself to fight Suhrab on horse. Knocking her to the ground, Suhrab tears her coat and knocks off her helmet, revealing her long hair. Needless to say, he who smites ends up smitten. Gurdafarid agrees to stop if he will keep her identity secret. She then promises him the castle and its inhabitants if she can first return there safely. He agrees, but she slips into the castle only to mock him from the ramparts, and then escapes with her father through a tunnel. Suhrab awakes next day to find himself in possession of a deserted castle.[37]

Gurdafarid's actions do not suggest a pattern in her behavior, merely an episode in which she rises to meet a challenge. The same holds true for many other warrior women in various types of literature (such as Gurdya and Jarira of the *Shahnama*, Mihr Nigar in the *Qissa-i Hamza*, and Ayn al-Hayat in the *Firuz Shahnama*, plus a few others.)[38] A class of women known generally as amazons, who make warrior activities virtually a way of life, appear in some popular romances.[39]

One individual character presents an exception by her ongoing warlike deeds: Purandukht of the *Darabnama*. Unlike the average princess whom poets praise for her lovely femininity, this daughter of the Persian Darab boasts "beauty, strength, fearlessness, and curiously, a moustache."[40] Just before her father dies at the hands of assassins from within his own ranks, he asks Alexander to promise he will marry his daughter Purandukht. Alexander agrees, but Purandukht suspects Alexander's complicity in the murder and swears to resist him with all her might. Intending ultimately to attack Alexander's capital, she wages several campaigns in Iraq and Syria. She loses near Baghdad but takes Aleppo, and, after killing her mother, manages to claim rule of Iran from her throne in Istakhr (Persepolis). In seesaw fashion, the fortresses of Istakhr and Aleppo change hands.

Here begins a series of incidents in which disguise and recognition are crucial, and from which even Shakespeare could learn a trick or two. Alexander and Purandukht finally join forces and fight together, with Purandukht extricating Alexander from a number of hopeless situations. In the end they part company, he to seek the water of life, she to return to Iran. On the whole, Purandukht comes off considerably stronger, shrewder and generally more competent than Alexander.[41]

From fighters to lovers we now turn. All of the heroic traditions have their prominent women. We have already met Abla, Antar's favorite, in the Arabic *sira*. Swahili religious literature gives important places to Fatima and the other women of the Prophet Muhammad's family, but otherwise to no royal types. The Turkic tradition has Banu Chichek, of whom we shall speak later, but she likewise is not precisely royal. From Southeast Asia comes a series of love interests—in the story of Hang Tuah, for example; but these women seem never to play such prominent roles as their sisters further to the west. The Persianate traditions boast perhaps the widest range of female stars. We earlier caught a glimpse of that marvelous character Shirin in her stormy romance with Khusraw. Speaking of Nizami's treatment of the principal characters, P. Chelkowski notes that "The contrast between Khusraw's weakness and Shirin's strength introduces a new dramatic dimension into the literature of the Near East in that it elevates the woman relative to the stature of the man."[42] Here is a brief look at several other strong, single-minded lovers: Rudaba, Manizha, and Zulaykha. The first two come from the *Shahnama*,[43] the third from court romance.

Rudaba is the daughter of Mihrab, a king of Kabul in the line of Dahhak. Zal, son of Sam and father of Rustam, leads an army to Kabul from Zabulistan. Mihrab likes Zal at first. Meanwhile Zal gets wind of a description of the king's daughter and forthwith conceives a desire to see Rudaba. Since the desire is quite mutual, Rudaba's maids seek to help her. They go to meet Zal near his camp to inform him that he is to meet Rudaba. When Zal comes a-courting, the princess lets her hair down and instructs him to climb up on it, but Zal declines to defile the "musky noose" and instead uses a lasso to scale the castle wall. (See Figure 6.)

Rudaba's father becomes upset at the thought of a foreign son-in-law. Both young lovers realize they face serious obstacles, but Sam has promised Zal anything he wants. Rudaba's mother, Queen Sindukht, tells her angry husband that Sam's sages have approved the match, thus cooling Mihrab's rage. Meanwhile back in Iran, Sam asks King Manuchihr's approval, but Manuchihr orders him to attack Kabul. Sam goes off on his mission, but Zal asks him to write King Manuchihr again, saying he will deliver the letter himself. After the king relents, Zal returns to Kabul. Royal nuptials completed, Zal succeeds his father as king of Zabulistan. Rudaba soon thereafter becomes the mother of the incomparable Rustam.[44]

As a preface to the story of Manizha, it helps to know how Firdawsi says he himself came to know the tale. One unimaginably dark night he was having trouble sleeping, so he asked his beloved to help him lose the night-terrors. She gladly poured him some wine, played him a tune on her lute, and told him an ancient story "full of guile and love, of magic and battle." "Once upon a time," she began. . . .

During the reign of Iranian King Kay Khusraw, an invasion of wild boars bedeviled the Armani forest people, so that they petitioned their king to destroy the beasts. Young Bizhan volunteered and headed off with the ill-intentioned Gurgin as his guide. After Bizhan dispatched the animals one by one, the envious Gurgin urged Bizhan to visit Manizha, daughter of the enemy Turanian King Afrasiyab, knowing full well that the king would not approve. Alone to Manizha's camp went Bizhan. Spying the handsome youth, Manizha sent her maid to ask his name, for she wondered whether he could be Siyawush come back to life. So enamored of Bizhan was she that she felt it could be Resurrection Day. Manizha then invited Bizhan in, drugged him, and spirited him off to her father's palace dressed in women's garb. When Afrasiyab heard of Bizhan's presence, he condemned him to death. Piran, a warrior sympathetic to the Iranian hero, intervened to persuade Afrasiyab

Figure 6: Rudaba unfurls her tresses for Zal to climb.

to imprison Bizhan in a pit instead. At the same time, Afrasiyab banished his daughter Manizha, who then began to beg food for Bizhan. Feeling the pangs of remorse, the dastardly Gurgin had returned to Iran alone. When Kay Khusraw and Bizhan's father, Giw, asked about Bizhan, Gurgin lied and so was imprisoned till Bizhan was found.

On Nawruz (New Year's), Kay Khusraw looked into Jamshid's world-revealing cup and there saw Bizhan languishing in his pit in Turan. He summoned the ever-vigilant Rustam, who entered Turan disguised as a wealthy merchant, along with his seven chosen fighters. Enter again the devoted Manizha. Rustam sought out Piran and gave him rich gifts, so that Piran's palace became a stopping place for caravans. Hearing of the activity, Manizha went to this "merchant's" storehouse in Piran's castle to ask him to seek help in Iran from the hero Giw and to beseech Rustam to come to Bizhan's aid. Rustam then gave Manizha some food, slipping his signet ring into a roast bird. When Bizhan bit into the fowl, he found the ring with Rustam's name and sent Manizha back to ask if this merchant were indeed the Lord of Rakhsh (Rustam's horse).

Finally Rustam divulged his identity to Manizha. They agreed that she would light a beacon fire at an appointed time to guide Rustam. With his seven warriors, Rustam arrived at the pit. After all seven failed to lift the stone, Rustam stepped in, saying he would liberate Bizhan only if he agreed not to seek vengeance on Gurgin. Rustam then put Afrasiyab to flight and sent Bizhan and Manizha back to Iran for a royal welcome by King Kay Khusraw.[45]

Finally, a passionate woman whose reputation underwent a dramatic transformation under the pens of several Persian authors is Zulaykha. I include her here as a royal character with some reservation, for she is the lover of the prophet Yusuf. However, she also comes from nobility and plays her most important role in literature and art produced by and for the court. Zulaykha's story tells how the lover's total attachment to the beloved can transform age into youth, lust into devotion, selfish attachment into salutary bewilderment.

Zulaykha enters Islamic lore in Qur'an Sura 12, as the wife of Pharaoh's minister who tries to seduce Yusuf after Pharaoh has taken him into his confidence and given him an administrative post. After the evidence of Yusuf's shirt (torn from behind) proves that Zulaykha initiated the attempted seduction, she attempts to exonerate herself. She invites all the noble women of Egypt to a banquet, and just as they prepare to slice into their dessert oranges, Zulaykha introduces Yusuf into the hall. One glance at Yusuf robs the women of their wits and persuades them that no one could hold Zulaykha responsible for her actions. Jami's story *Yusuf and Zulaykha* ends as the aged Zulaykha returns to Egypt and, after one look at the still youthful countenance of Yusuf, turns young again.

Dozens of miniatures celebrate many of these key moments in Zulaykha's career. Especially significant here are the scenes in which Zulaykha invites Joseph to her apartment. She has decorated the walls with pictures of herself and Joseph in amorous poses, hoping that he will take the hint. Perhaps the most compelling image is one (mentioned in chapter two) in which the master painter, Bihzad, shows the viewer all seven locked doors of the innermost palace, at the moment when Joseph seeks to break away from the seductress. Several images also capture the instant in which the women of Egypt cut their hands at the sight of the dazzlingly handsome prophet.[46] Mystical poets have often used the expression "to cut one's hand" as an allusion to the experience of sheer bewilderment in the presence of divine beauty.

The World-Conqueror

As world-conqueror, Alexander the Great surely stands in a class by himself. Poets, mystics, and historians alike have told, re-told, and embellished the story. In addition to occupying a signifi-cant portion of Firdawsi's work, Alexander emerges as perhaps the most widely celebrated of all the great heroes. He figures promi-nently in many historical and literary works, in Arabic, Persian, Turkish, and Malay, not to mention the earlier, pre-Islamic sources from which many of the stories derive ultimately.

Alexander seems to have developed into an amalgam of several heroic sub-types. He functions in the present typology as a transi-tional figure between the royal and religious types. As king he shows a remarkable willingness to seek guidance, accepting the advice of the sage Aristotle and the mysterious Khadir. As con-queror, he shows a compassion to the vanquished that brings him celebrity status. As world ruler, he becomes a model, so that a later leader can hope for no higher accolade than to be called the "Alexander of the Age." Traditions from a wide range of Islamic societies suggest that the Persians adopted Alexander as one of their own and that Iskandar even considered himself Persian.[47] According to one tradition, Alexander's father is Darab the Persian king, and his mother is given a Persian lineage via her father Fayla-qus—Philip—back to Faridun who had divided the world among his three sons. Beginning as warrior king and sage, Alexander grows into the very image of the "Perfect Person" and ultimately comes to be identified with the prophet-like figure Dhu 'l-Qarnayn of the Qur'an.[48]

Three main strands of Islamicate tradition provide the bulk of the materials in the Iskandar story. The first strand consists of sections of the Qur'an (Sura 18: "The Cave") that have come to be associated with Alexander, though the text does not name him; of Arabic histories, such as Mas'udi's *Prairies of Gold;*[49] and of Persian and Syrian folklore and legend. A crucial link in the Islamicate understanding of Alexander lies in his identification with the Dhu 'l-Qarnayn ("One with Two Horns") of the Qur'an (Sura 18:82ff.), and in the naming of Khadir as Moses' guide in that same Sura.

Combining that material with more from other lost Persian or Arabic sources, Firdawsi provides the second strand in the *Shah-nama,* the single most important literary account. Finally, a range of popular legends of Iskandar not found in either of the first two strands accounts for most of the remaining stories. Bits and pieces of the story then made their way to South and Southeast Asia, mainly by way of the Persian popular romance tradition. Let us take a brief look at some of the most important episodes in Iskandar's life story as it evolved across the Islamic world.

Firdawsi begins the story during the reign of Darab, star of his own Persian popular romance, the *Darabnama,* in which Alexander also plays a large part. Darab marries the daughter of Philip of Macedon, but then sends her back home (because of her bad breath!), unaware that she is with child. Philip protects his daughter by claiming that her child, Alexander, is his by a concubine. After the deaths of Philip and Darab, Alexander and Dara (Darius) ascend to the Greek and Persian thrones. Dara orders Alexander to pay tribute as his father had done. Alexander refuses and then sets out to see the world. After conquering Egypt, Alexander goes to Dara's court disguised as a messenger (the king as his own messenger is a recurrent theme in these stories), to assure Dara of Iskandar's peaceful intent. Recognized by one of Dara's messengers who has been to Alexander's kingdom of Rum, Iskandar makes his getaway and thus begins a series of battles that Alexander wins. In the last one, two of Dara's own men stab Dara, mistakenly thinking Alexander will pay them well. Dying in Alexander's arms, Dara reveals that they are half-brothers. Alexander agrees to wed Dara's daughter, executes the turncoat assassins, and assumes the mantle of the Kayanid dynasty as Dara's successor. Scenes of the two heroes' battles and of Dara's death have inspired many miniature paintings.[50]

Receiving the allegiance, daughter, and various gifts of King Kayd of India, Alexander further moves against Porus (Fur) of India and defeats him with wheeled iron horses filled with naphtha and ignited so as to breathe fire.[51] Once he has subdued India, the conqueror turns westward. Passing through Makka on pilgrimage, Alexander then sojourns for a year in Egypt, where Candace, the queen of Spain, has a painter do a portrait of Alexander for her. When Candace refuses his summons to Egypt, Alexander goes disguised as a messenger to her court. Responding to a touch of blackmail—she has the goods on him—Alexander agrees to leave her in peace, and then heads off to seek advice from the Brahmans.[52]

At this point, any sense of geographical continuity breaks down, and Alexander's wanderings in search of immortality take him into a world that clearly lies beyond ordinary experience on this earth yet without moving him definitively into the next life. He begins a voyage of discovery to strange lands and peoples, full of marvels and terrors. Now in Arab lands, now in Abyssinia, he encounters extraordinary forces, including black giants, Amazons, and monsters. Finally, he heads west toward the Land of Darkness wherein he hopes to find the Fountain of Life. Khadir the prophet, also associated with vegetation and fertility, guides him, but Alexander loses his guide and falls short of his goal. All along the way he sees such grim signs of his impending death as dead bodies on thrones and angels and talking trees that remind him of his mortality, but he refuses to believe them. Still his accomplishments do not cease. He continues to the East, where he builds an iron wall to keep out Gog and Magog, meets the Chinese emperor, conquers Sind, and receives the homage of the king of Yemen.[53]

Other approaches to the story of Iskandar emphasize different aspects of his person (e.g., details of his origins) and adventures. In the popular romance called *Darabnama*, for example,

Iskandar's mother abandons the baby on a mountain not far from Aristotle's dwelling. An old woman has her goat suckle the child and has Aristotle teach him dream-interpretation and wisdom till he is ten. Alexander eventually marries Dara's daughter (this time called Purandukht) but only after she brings an army against him several times and loses. Fantastic themes receive even greater attention. In his quest for immortality, Iskandar goes in the company of not one but three guides: Luqman, with a reputation for sagacity and lore; Ilyas, also known as Elijah, an alter-ego and brother of Khadir; and Khadir himself. His journeying follows a more whimsical course, and Alexander now has slightly more the feel of the romantic adventurer. In addition, one can see here many clues of a distinctive Islamic overlay. Along with stories of Muslim saintly personages, "a wonderful talking horse carries Alexander to the top of Mt. Qaf, where he sees bands of angels. The horse later brings him back down. This would seem to be a reference to the *mi'raj* of the Prophet Muhammad, thus identifying Alexander even more closely with Islam."[54]

Likewise far removed from the historical Alexander, the Persian popular romance *Iskandarnama* shares a number of major episodes with Firdawsi and includes numerous details from the first strand of tradition not found in the *Shahnama*. We find the conqueror early on involved in major intrigues in India, only the beginning of many episodes including disguise, attempted poisonings, marriages to foreign princesses, and other assorted weekend outings. Alexander has numerous encounters with fairy-like characters known as *paris,* who embody a kind of positive power constantly in conflict with the evil demons, the *diws.* Indeed the pari-diw tug-of-war seems to serve as an overall setting, constructing a cosmos as the stage for Iskandar's adventures.

Curiously enough, neither of these two major popular romances portrays Alexander as a truly great man whose virtue and skill elevate him markedly above the lot of ordinary folk. Perhaps "deliberately pictured as almost an anti-hero,"[55] Alexander fairly stumbles across the stage dragging a full complement of foibles and failings. Only his zeal for the spread of the true faith redeems him. W. Hanaway analyzes the situation this way:

> In both *Eskandar Nama* and *Darab Nama* we see an Alexander who is at once a famous world-conqueror and a bumbling,

> ineffectual leader beset by indecision, fear and lust for
> women. In other words, Alexander is reduced to the level of
> an ordinary prosaic human being. If we consider the creators
> of this literature and its audience, this change becomes easier
> to accept. Unsophisticated in both content and language,
> these romances were meant for the entertainment of people
> who were not educated. . . . Alexander represents the conflict
> inherent in the male-dominated, female secluding society of
> Medieval Iran. . . . The final irony . . . is that in both of these
> romances Alexander is given invaluable military aid by a
> woman.[56]

At the other end of the intellectual spectrum from the Alexander
of the popular romance stands the Iskandar of Nizami's two-part
Persian didactic epic, the *Iskandarnama*. Ever the king and the warrior, he now moves beyond these roles to the level of sage and
prophet. Son of Philip and schoolmate of Aristotle, destined from
birth to conquer the world, Alexander begins his global career by
delivering the Egyptians from a Zangi invasion. He founds the first
of many cities named Alexandria and returns home. Before long,
Dara goads Iskandar to a fight by demanding tribute. According
to Nizami, Iskandar colludes with two of Dara's men to have the
Persian king assassinated, but repents as Dara lies dying. Iskandar
then sets out to replace Persia's Zoroastrian faith with that of Abraham. And here begins the more fantastic segment of his globe
trotting.

   In Nizami's version, Queen Candace of Andalusia becomes
Queen Nushaba of Barda (somewhere nearer the Middle East),
who recognizes Iskandar from a portrait when he visits her disguised as a messenger. He will later rescue her from the Russians,
after first travelling to India and China. With the whole world
under his sway, the conqueror ventures into the Land of Darkness.
There an angel reproves him for his insatiable lust for empire.
Nizami closes his *Book of Nobility*, part one of the epic, with the
hero's returning home from a magically deathless city, whose citi-
zens wait to be summoned and then vanish beyond a mountain.
When God commissions Iskandar, now standing at the threshhold
of wisdom, as prophet, off he goes on another major journey that
will take him into landscapes of terrible majesty.

   In part two, the *Book of Wisdom*, Nizami's Iskandar expands as sage and prophet, surrounding himself at court with competing philosophers from the world over. Iskandar comes off as superior to many in knowledge, but the not-quite-self-effacing monarch still asks for advice from the Great Greeks. He then launches out on his new missionary journey carrying the books of wisdom that Socrates, Plato, and Aristotle have given him. From Alexandria to Jerusalem, from the world sea to the Nile, from Iram to India and China, Iskandar spreads the message of monotheism. Not long after he completes the wall against Gog and Magog, a voice tells Alexander to make his way back home to face death. Jami, the last of the great classical Persian poets, would recast the story once more, arranging many of Iskandar's wanderings (from Nizami's part one) in connection with the hero's love of wisdom.[57]

Stories of Alexander travelled nearly as far as the hero himself. In Malaysia and Indonesia, several significant works deal exclusively with Iskandar (the Malay *Hikayat Iskandar Dhu 'l-Qarnayn* and the Indonesian *Sirat Baron Sakender*). In addition, major elements of the Iskandar legend appear prominently in at least two other important Malay works (the *Sejara Melayu* and the *Hikayat Bandjar,* more crucially in the former than the latter). As we shall discuss further in a later chapter, the stories have played a very different role in Southeast Asia than they have further west. Suffice it for now to mention that Iskandar became associated with the establishment of Islamic and royal legitimacy.

Of the Iskandar elements in *Sejara Melayu* and *Hikayat Bandjar,* J. Ras observes that they reflect "the impact of Islam on a society the members of which were still used to thinking within a magical frame of reference." The works integrate two Islamic characters especially, Iskandar and the prophet Khadir, into the "Malay conception of the way in which a royal dynasty comes into being."[58] Here we find the invincible world ruler Iskandar inserted as a solar figure on the male side of the royal genealogy, identified as the heavenly father of a mortal king (Surjanata or Bitjitram Sjah). Meanwhile the prophet Khadir plays Iskandar's counterpart on the female and aquatic side of the genealogy.[59] In the two Southeast Asian works devoted almost exclusively to Iskandar's adventures, we discover various tales from Persian sources blended with indigenous myths, tales, and historiography. Alexander remains the world-traveler, but the emphasis falls on his role as the missionary who brings the true faith of Abraham.

91

Miniature painters have often shown Iskandar, slaying dragons and assorted monsters and marching against a variety of foreign powers from Egypt to India, and living as a journeyer and a seeker. Illustrations to the various works that tell his story depict Iskandar as he makes pilgrimage to the Kaʿba, enlists the help of wise guides, ventures into the land of darkness, seeks the Water of Life, and encounters a Talking Tree that informs him he will soon die.

Although artists have often painted the deaths of heroes as well as villains, they have far less often depicted scenes of grief at such losses. Alexander has the distinction of joining the company of Iraj and Isfandiyar as a hero whose passing is mourned in pictures, not remarkably often, but quite noticeably. The range of texts about Alexander that a patron might pick out as suitable for illustration, and of specific scenes that an artist and/or patron might choose to illustrate, is such that one can venture an estimate as to the overall tone of interpretation of a work (e.g., the degree to which the overall subject matter has been spiritualized, or to which its more nationalistic or militant aspects have been emphasized, etc.) on the basis of the Alexander images alone.[60]

Chapter Five

The Religious Hero

Joseph Campbell has made a distinction between tribal or local heroes and universal heroes. Among the former, he includes Moses and Huang-Ti, who are sent to a particular people. He calls this the fairy-tale type, who achieve a microcosmic triumph. As an example Campbell cites the despised or youngest child who masters great powers to overcome personal oppressors. Universal heroes achieve broader victories that afford human society as a whole the possibility of rejuvenation.

Classical Islamic thought makes a roughly analogous distinction. To every people on earth, God has sent a prophet *(nabi)* with a message suited to its specific needs, bringing the sum total of prophets, in round numbers, to 124,000. In addition, the Lord of the Universe has sent to all humanity chosen messengers *(rasul,* pl. *rusul)* who bear a communication of universal validity. In other words, every *rasul* is a *nabi,* but not vice versa. Here we shall consider religious heroes as either microcosmic/local or macrocosmic/universal. This distinction does not correspond neatly with that between *nabi* and *rasul,* but it does offer some indication of the relative significance of major religious characters within the Islamic tradition.

An interesting dynamic begins to emerge from a study of these religious figures. Islamicate heroic narratives and the artists who have illustrated them have transformed and adapted for specifically religious purposes the literary imagery and iconography of heroes not explicitly religious in origin. One finds among religious heroes strong echoes of the major types, such as warrior/liberator, tragic prince, and progenitor. The same dynamic appears also to work the other way around. Action, motivations, and settings (temporal and geographical circumstances, persons to whom they relate) of originally non-religious heroes begin to take on an identifiably Islamic cast. In the story of Antar, for example, one can see both phenomena. On the one hand, characters and scenes in the *Sira* of Antar clearly suggest Qur'anic models. Battle scenes recall those of the prophet, especially those of Khandaq (627) and Khaybar (629); images of pillared cities, darkness, and serpents abound. Nimrod and Pharoah are types of the tyrant; Solomon and Sheba, of the royal couple. On the other hand, the prophet/sage Luqman of the Qur'an appears as an Ethiopian slave who becomes a Bedouin wanderer in the Antar tale.[1]

Here we shall look at three major types of microcosmic or local religious heroes before considering the universal figures. Those three types are the minor prophet, the sage or spiritual guide, and the more generic holy personage to which the notion of saint provides a very loose analogy. Table 3 provides an overview of how Islamic tradition views the interrelationships of the major religious heroes and heroines.

Microcosmic/Local Heroes

To certain particular tribes or peoples, God sends warning figures whom we shall call minor prophets. They sometimes deliver a specific, if not ultimate, scriptural revelation and thereby bring into being a People of the Book. The hero's role in forming a people is of particular importance. Stories of this type occur mostly in the two important literary genres mentioned in the appendix as "Tales of the Prophets" and "Universal Histories," although several of the prophets (most notably Joseph) also play prominent roles in the romance or mystical epic forms. In this category I would include the following, but will mention only the most important, especially those whose stories have provided material for the visual arts. Major examples include Adam and Eve, Noah, Abraham and his two sons, Jacob and his son Joseph, and Moses. Several other lesser but still important pre-Islamic prophets are Jonah, David, and Solomon.

Adam, a progenitor type, occasionally appears in pictures along with Eve, usually in a Paradise setting. As in the story of the loss of royal glory (farr) by the early Persian King Jamshid and his ouster by the evil Dahhak, Iblis (diabolos, Satan) makes his influence felt in the story of Adam and Eve. The primordial couple enjoy a place of prominence in various quasi-historical works in Arabic, Persian, and Turkish. Miniature paintings often depict the couple standing in the Garden, flanking the central tree from whose base the rivers flow and surrounded by their immediate descendents.[2] Another favorite scene shows the two expelled from Paradise, as

Table 3. Genealogy of Religious Heroes and Heroines

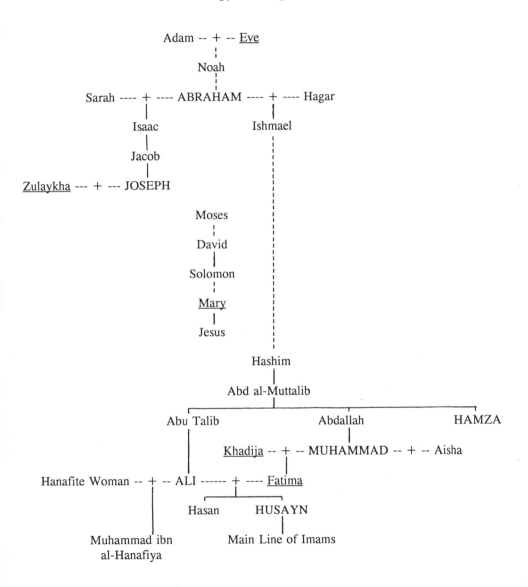

Key: + = Married to
      Upper case = Major male figure
      Underscoring = Major female figure
      Solid vertical = Immediate descent
      Broken vertical = Remote or collateral descent

Eden's bouncer, the angel Gabriel, bites the finger of astonishment.[3] According to Shiʿi lore, Adam bequeathed to posterity several items of cosmic prophetic significance, all of which he brought out of Paradise with him. The most important are, first, the Ark (of the Covenant); second, his own sarcophagus; and third, the fork-tipped sword, Dhu 'l-Faqar. All three became the heirlooms of a succession of prophets.[4]

The original couple's story occupies at least two entire Swahili poems, the *Epic of Adam and Eve* and the *Life of Adam*. I have turned up no other literary tradition that has accorded the first prophet such prominence. In the former work, it is not Cain's jealousy but Abel's desire to marry Cain's twin sister that leads to the murder of Abel. In the latter, Adam decides to eat the forbidden fruit, not because of Eve's invitation, but out of heroic idealism. Before coming to Paradise, Adam had spent a time on earth and is thus familiar with the harshness of life there. Now Eve has sinned and lost the privilege of Paradise. Because she will need protection and help on earth, Adam selflessly follows her down. These and other Swahili religious poems generally treat women in a harsh manner that shows little sense of their nobility. With the notable exception of Job's wife, only the women around Muhammad (his wife Khadija, his mother Amina, his daughter Fatima) merit praise in Swahili poetry for their personal strength.[5]

Noah's (Nuh) story revolves almost entirely around one major episode, that strange journey without readily traceable itinerary that occurred during the Flood. Only the ark's circumnavigation of the Kaʿba from above stands out as a landmark with which Muslim lore locates the odyssey of Noah's vessel. Muslim miniaturists have painted a significant number of images of that curious voyage, especially in the context of universal history and tales of the prophets. Only in Swahili tradition, evidently, does the prophet occupy his own epic work.[6]

Abraham (Ibrahim), likewise a progenitor figure, comes within a ram's nose of sacrificing his only son, who is unnamed in the Qurʾan, but whom most of subsequent tradition identifies as Ismaʿil rather than Isaac (Ishaq). Once Abraham has given proof of his unstinting devotion, God grants a reprieve. The scene of Abraham's near-sacrifice of his son has inspired a few (mostly Turkish) miniature paintings, most of which include the barest details of the narrative—the two principals, angel and ram. In a variation on the theme of the division of the world among the progenitor's sons, Abraham's two offspring become the fathers of the children of Israel (Isaac) and the Arabs/Muslims (Isma'il). Isaac also becomes curiously connected with warrior traditions. The prowess and success of Muhammad's uncle Hamza gains an immeasurable boost when Hamza comes to own Isaac's horse and bow.[7]

Like all the prophets, Abraham had his implacable enemy. Probably the most illustrated scene in the tale of Abraham shows the patriarch either being catapulted into, or sitting safely in the midst of, Nimrod's fire. Such images appear most of all in illustrated versions of tales of the prophets and in universal histories.[8] Abraham's role as progenitor also extends symbolically through his position as the first seeker after the One God (hanif). He was thus the father of subsequent prophets, and ultimately of Muhammad, whom the Qur'an likens to Abraham more than to any other prophet. As a spiritual progenitor of Muhammad, Abraham functions chiefly as the builder of the Ka'ba, and secondarily as the proprietor of the seventh heaven, where Muhammad meets him during the celestial journey of his Ascension (to which we shall return shortly).[9]

Jacob (Ya'qub), also a progenitor, weeps himself blind at the loss of his second-youngest son, Joseph. Later the aroma of Joseph's shirt restores the old man's sight. Jacob's twelve sons inherit leadership of the twelve tribes, but none of the twelve achieves the popularity and religious stature of Joseph (Yusuf). To the contrary, the others go down in history as wolves who sought the blood of their own brother. Because Joseph suffers as a result of his brothers' jealousy, we may compare him to the tragic prince type among the royal heroes. Yusuf does not end up a martyr, however. Instead he achieves a position of authority over his brothers. A more important theme in the Joseph story, that of preference for the younger son, links him in part with other heroic characters, such as Faridun's son Iraj.

Joseph's brothers' jealousy prompts them to throw the youngster into a pit, which in turn becomes a symbol (or literary topos) among Islam's mystical poets, a sign of the dire straits from which God delivers his own. In an analogous development, the pit to which Afrasiyab consigns Bizhan becomes a symbol of political oppression.[10] Miniatures of Joseph's rescue from the well appear relatively often in illustrated texts, especially of the Persian romances of Nizami and Jami, but also of several versions of *Stories of the Prophets*. These images usually emphasize God's solicitude for the young prophet by depicting the angel Gabriel in the pit with him. Sometimes the attending angel's comfort is likened to Father Jacob's tearful love for his son. In the next frame, we find the Ishmaelite traders discovering Yusuf in the well, also a favorite scene of miniature painters.[11] (See Figure 7.)

As suggested in the last chapter, Joseph's story also includes a strong romantic element. Whereas the *Stories of the Prophets* and universal histories tend to emphasize the explicitly scriptural aspects of the story, the didactic and mystical poets lean more toward features of the story that lend themselves to allegorical interpretation. Yusuf's fascinating relationship to Zulaykha begins with the prophet's deliverance from the test of her wiles and culminates much later in the restoration of Zulaykha's youth at the sight of Joseph. In addition to major literary interpretations in Persian, a substantial Swahili epic also tells of Yusuf and Zulaykha's happy marriage and three children.[12] Artists delight in creating scenes of various facets of this complex romance—from Zulaykha's failed attempt to seduce him, to the scene in which the women of Egypt "cut their hands" in bewilderment at the sight of Joseph's staggering comeliness, to the couple's "mystical marriage."[13]

Moses (Musa) exhibits some of the characteristics of the lone knight and liberator of the oppressed. As a reflection of the lone knight type, Moses and his sidekick Aaron (Harun) confront no less than the supreme monarch. Moses wields a miraculous staff for a weapon and rescues the daughters of Jethro from the Midianite bullies. Miniatures show Moses, sometimes with brother Aaron, unleashing his dragon-staff against Pharoah's magicians. That scene has provided a model in recent times for vivid color posters depicting the late Ayatullah Khumayni unleashing the dragon against Shah Muhammad Riza Pahlavi, a modern pharoah who can no longer depend on foreign powers to prop him up. The imagery clearly puts the religious hero a notch above his folk and royal counterparts. Religious heroes not only vanquish dragons but transform them into their servants.[14]

Another popular scene, from a story that made its way into Islamic lore via Jewish midrashic or legendary sources shows Moses engaged in single combat against the giant Og (Aj or Uj). Moses's staff barely reaches as high as the behemoth's ankle, but the

Figure 7: The Prophet Yusuf (Joseph) in the well, ministered to by Gabriel while Midianite traders camp above.

prophet leaps into the air and delivers a crippling whack to the shins. Og falls all the harder because of the mountain he wears like a collar: he had hefted the mass intending to drop it on Moses and his people, but God caused a bird to peck a hole in the mountain so that it fell around the giant's neck. A number of charming miniatures illustrating the story, mostly in historiographical sources, depict Og's ignominious defeat.[15] Shiʿi lore places Moses's staff among the prophetic heirlooms that Adam took out of the garden with him. Like Faridun's ox-headed mace, this wand and weapon makes its way down the generations until the Arabian prophet Shuʿayb (often identified with the Biblical Jethro) gives it to his son-in-law, Moses.[16]

Of the more than two dozen prophets popular in Islamic lore across the world, several others deserve notice by virtue of their appearance in a variety of literary and visual sources. Jonah (Yunus), sharing the stage with a large fish in a number of miniature paintings, relies only on God in the darkness of the whale.[17] Swahili lore calls the whale "the moving tomb" God employs to test Jonah, as He tests all prophets.[18] The whale represents the underworld into which many heroic characters make a perilous descent, thence to return with some special boon or knowledge. Jonah's experience teaches him what the pit teaches Joseph: total surrender and trust in God.

King David (Dawud) resembles most of all the royal adventurer, famed as a heart-stealing singer, warrior, and maker of chain mail. Widespread tradition has it that David's coat of mail became one of the prophetic heirlooms, handed down to Muhammad himself. Miniatures of David are very rare, but he makes an appearance in the Ottoman *Subhat al-akhbar* holding the chain mail that made him famous. David's song could melt mountains and turn iron to wax in his hands.[19]

David's son Solomon (Sulayman) appears more often, usually enthroned in regal splendor. (See Figure 8.) Sometimes he reigns over a court crowded with every conceivable form of life, from angels and jinn (whom he had commandeered into building his temple for him) to the Simurgh and all other birds (whose language Solomon speaks) and animals. Sometimes Solomon presides over ranks of prophets, kings, and warriors. Such images characterize Solomon not only as the chief of monarchs, but as preeminent among a broad range of heroic types. In other scenes he sits oppo-

Figure 8: The Prophet Sulayman (Solomon) and his court. Note the presence of Jinns, all animals, and the Simurgh above.

site an enthroned Bilqis, Queen of Sheba. Solomon has something in common with Alexander as a fellow world conqueror. Solomon's dominion never reaches the actual geographical extent of Iskandar's, but none can claim a more far-flung spiritual or mystical sovereignty than the Son of David.[20]

In the genre called "Tales of the Prophets" and an important group of Persian folktales derived largely from it, Solomon represents the ultimate in both valor and splendor. Solomon's image as king has mingled in Iranian tradition with that of Jamshid, whose world-revealing goblet expanded his knowledge of all creation. As suggested earlier when we saw Hamza break Isaac's horse in Solomon's garden, Solomon also represents prowess as a warrior. In those folk tales that make Solomon, Rustam, and Ali contemporaries, Solomon's qualifications and fame give even Rustam cause to seethe with a desire to outdo Solomon. So imposing is Solomon that even Ali is content to serve as one of the king's champions.[21]

Salih appears very rarely in miniatures, and then typically in the scene where he brings forth a camel from the great stone mountain. Jesus (Isa) and his cousin John the Baptist (Yahya) seldom show up in the visual arts, and then mostly in images apparently produced by Turks.[22]

We have already encountered the fascinating and mysterious character called Khadir (Khizr). Virtually every explicitly religious hero—and more than one not so obviously religious—who ventures off on a journey either meets him in a dream or enlists his services as guide. Khadir's place among the minor prophets, according to some listings, may result from his identification and sometime-confusion with Ilyas (Elijah). In any case, Khadir represents a second local type of religious hero, the sage or spiritual guide, and as such recalls the folk hero who possesses special knowledge. In addition, Khadir combines the mobility and ubiquity of the lone knight with the ability of the picaresque trickster hero to get away with a variety of deeds that would land anyone else in serious trouble.

Khadir serves as guide to Moses on his search for the confluence of the two seas, and to Alexander in his search for the Water of Life, where Khadir pairs up with Elijah as they discover the fountain forbidden to Alexander. In both instances Khadir and his charges end up going separate ways. Moses loses the services of his guide because he insists on asking Khadir to defend his bizarre actions after Moses has agreed not to do so. Iskandar misses out on the Water of Life because, in one account, he is too eager for it; Khadir finds the spring precisely because he is not seeking it for his own ends. Khadir is the type of spiritual guide *(pir, shaykh)* whose tutelage the seeker must accept blindly, in simple and utter trust, regardless of how irrational the guide's instructions may seem. Almost all of Khadir's appearances in the visual arts occur in the context of his relationship to Iskandar, and most of those illustrate texts of Nizami's *Iskandarnama.*[23]

Holy persons comprise a third type of local hero. Their stories are told in the hagiographical genre described in the appendix as "recollections" *(tadhkira).* One of the most famous holy persons, Hallaj, suffers martyrdom and becomes a model of spiritual constancy and courage. Ibrahim ibn Adham's conversion story evidently follows the pattern of the Buddha's great renunciation. Holy persons appear in miniatures less often than prophets, but we have some extant images of many renowned figures, such as the Sufis Jalal ad-Din Rumi; his father, Baha' ad-Din Walad; and Ayn al-Qudat al-Hamadhani. Abd al-Qadir al-Jilani, founder of the earliest formally constituted Sufi order, appears in more-popular arts such as the glass painting of Tunisia.[24] He is also a favorite comic-book character in Malaysia and Indonesia.

Perhaps more significant within the present context—and certainly easier to associate with their non-religious counterparts, especially among the type of the folk hero—are the warrior-saints of Java. Javanese tradition extols the nine holy persons *(wali songo)* as the first to bring Islam to the island. Several achieved fame for their involvement in the fifteenth-century overthrow of the Hindu kingdom of Majapahit. Muslims of course regard them most favorably, whereas those who consider Islam and Javanese tradition radically incompatible dismiss the saints as villains. Even in the clearly pro-Javanese *Sirat Dermagandul*, with all its antagonism to the Muslim saints responsible for the Islamization of the island, one can discern in reverse the very characteristics for which Muslims still venerate these saints. They are willing to fight even their own fathers if they remain infidels, they lead the faithful against infidels, and they perform miracles. Ironically the *Sirat Dermagandul* has the mother of one of the saints chide the Muslim saint for his inability to perform miracles, and she uses Muslim stories against him to convince him that only punishment awaits those who fight their fathers.[25]

Another holy figure associated with warrior-like heroism lived in the Middle East but became especially popular in Southeast Asia. Shaykh Wali Raslan of Damascus (d. ca. 1145) actually lived in a mosque; however, tradition places him in a *ribat,* a frontier outpost, originally set up for the defense of the fringes of empire and eventually given over to the waging of the "greater jihad" of self-conquest. As his story travelled eastward, he gained fame as a warrior of the spirit and as a preacher who counselled combat against the Crusaders. According to one medieval source, Shaykh Raslan wielded the sword "with consummate mastery, for defence and protection, in both military and spiritual warfare, until the achievement of the purge he was hoping for."[26] An analogous development seems to have occurred in the story of the Turkic dervish-warrior Sari Saltuq.[27]

A number of holy women not only stand as heroines in their own right, but share in and amplify the heroic sanctity of the prophets and saintly men to whom they relate. Along with the Egyptian Asiya (Pharaoh's wife), Khadija, and Fatima (see below), Mary the mother of Jesus ranks as one of the four perfect women.[28] As mother of a prophet, Mary had to hold firm against criticism resulting from the unusual birth of Jesus and to endure the general climate of unbelief among the people to whom God had sent her son. When Moses stood before Pharaoh to deliver his message, he found only obstinacy. In Pharaoh's household, only his wife Asiya believed the word of the prophet. For that, she has found a special place in Islamic tradition. These women appear only infrequently in visual productions, and then only in historiographical works.

Macrocosmic/Universal Heroes

In the Islamic tradition, the Prophet Muhammad and his immediate Family are the principal macrocosmic or universal heroes. Muhammad is the Messenger of God, who delivers the universal and ultimate revelation, the Qurʾan. Stories of the Prophet, told and pictured in several illustrated versions of literature that represents a development of the *sira* genre (such as the *Siyar-i Nabi* and the *Miʿrajnama*), include his entire life-cycle from wondrous birth to peaceful death. Along the way, he does battle with evil nemeses and replaces the Black Stone in the Kaʿba—thus becoming clearly associated with Abraham, who is said to have built the Kaʿba originally.

Perhaps most prominent among Muhammad's heroic adventures is his guided cosmic odyssey through the heavens and hells, during which he proceeds even to the throne of God. Expanded versions of the tale of this "Night Journey and Ascension" experience also include Muhammad's visitations to various far-flung places both in this world and the next. Qazwini's account of the "City of Equality" (Miqyarat) in the Sahara, for example, has replaced Iskandar with Muhammad as the city's most celebrated visitor.[29] Muhammad's journey experience becomes the theme of numerous separate works across the Islamic world. Mystical poets regularly include a lengthy adversion to it in the opening encomia of longer poetic works. Miniatures of the journey cycle appear in many manuscripts and are among some of the most intriguing in the Islamicate repertoire. Muhammad's transformation into the "Perfect Person" (al-insan al-kamil) or homo caelestis is the ultimate manifestation of this heroic theme. Here are some of the high points of Muhammad's heroic career.

From a spiritual perspective, Muhammad functions as the progenitor par excellence, for God created him first of all creatures. Mystical poets call him the final cause of creation, the reason behind it all, quoting the sacred tradition, "But for you, I would not have created the universe." From the Shiʿi perspective especially, Muhammad begins a new branch of sacred genealogy, that of the Family of the Prophet. To Ali he bequeaths his ring and weaponry, including the sword Dhu ʾl-Faqar, which stays in the family right up to the twelfth Imam. More importantly, Muhammad passes on special knowledge and light.[30]

National literatures across the whole of the Islamicate world boast many tales of Muhammad. Swahili literature includes one of the most extensive collections of Prophetic heroic memorabilia. Of seventy-two presently known Swahili epics of the utenzi form, at least twenty-seven feature the Prophet.[31] In that vast panorama of Swahili epic literature, Muhammad often plays the role of director of the action from the sidelines. God alone, of course, can effectively direct earthly affairs, but insofar as any human being can participate in that, the Prophet does. No ordinary mortal, Muhammad has privileged access to God and special knowledge of things occurring many days' journey away.[32]

In the *Epic of Heraklios,* for example, Muhammad's presence alone proves sufficient to give the outnumbered and poorly armed Muslims victory over the vastly superior Byzantine forces, even though Muhammad is long dead by the time the action takes place. Even the redoubtable generals Khalid ibn al-Walid and Amr ibn al-As, who have covered themselves with glory in their exploits, here run for cover behind Muhammad and Ali. And thanks to Muhammad's sagacity, the champion Ali manages to arrive on the scene in the nick of time. Knappert explains the Swahili story's embellishment and historical inaccuracy: "If Mohammad was there, then history becomes meaningful: God helped him to scatter the unbelievers before him. But it is not only the romantic longing for a beautifully constructed narrative, it is also the distance in time that made the turbulent events of ten years of war merge together into one story."[33]

The Prophet's wives, also known as Mothers of the Faithful, come next in the heroic hierarchy. Muhammad's first wife, Khadija, enjoys considerable attention in the Swahili version of the *Hamziya.* A favorite story tells how she meets and falls in love with Muhammad. As she sits on the roof of her father's home, she looks across the sand toward Makka and spies a caravan coming southward led by a young man. A small cloud seems to follow him, keeping the handsome chap ever in the shade, but that shade actually comes from the wings of two angels. Khadija knows, in addition, that without some special blessing from God, she would be unable to discern such marvels, and she takes it as a sign of divine destiny that she and Muhammad are meant for each other.

Gabriel comes to visit Khadija. Once she has overcome her initial terror at his appearance, the angel convinces her that Muhammad is indeed "the hidden treasure she had wanted" and the "elixir" she needs. She proposes marriage to Muhammad. The legend suggests that Muhammad exercised an irresistible attraction on Khadija and that the Prophet possessed healing powers.[34]

Among the prophet's wives, apart from Khadija, only Aisha occupies a significant place in literature. Because Aisha alone among his wives remained childless, Muhammad's daughter Fatima has overshadowed her in the literature. To Fatima we shall return shortly. The only other woman directly related to Muhammad who has gained some fame is his mother, the faithful Amina, whom tradition holds up as the model for all expectant mothers.[35]

Aisha is a daughter of Abu Bakr, father of the troublesome son Abd ar-Rahman who appeared in chapter three. Muhammad marries her when she is only ten years old. One story of Muhammad's marriage to her comes from the Swahili tradition and includes an element common in heroic literature, namely, first recognition of a beloved through a picture brought before the eyes of the soon-to-be lover. An angel painted a picture of Aisha, and Gabriel brought it to the recently widowed Prophet. The text of the story goes on to describe a conversation that Abu Bakr carries on with Muhammad via messages sent with the young Aisha; it tells how Muhammad proceeds to treat the girl as only a husband may, even though she has not yet been informed that they have been married. When Muhammad makes advances, Aisha responds angrily, as any woman of integrity would under the circumstances. Of course, Muhammad approves of her behavior, since he expects such integrity of any woman who would be his wife. Aisha thus becomes, in a roundabout manner, the paradigm of the woman who knows her rights and stands up for them.[36]

Shi'i Muslims regard Muhammad's son-in-law Ali and his descendents as the legitimate heirs to authority and leadership. In the stories of these Imams, we find several elements reminiscent of the royal hero, especially of the progenitor (in this case Muhammad), of the tragic prince (especially Husayn), and of the world-conqueror (notably Ali). Three major illustrated manuscripts evidently produced entirely under Shi'i inspiration and patronage are the key sources in this instance: the Persian *Khawarannama* (*Book of the East,* or *Glory*), a late imitator of the *Shahnama;* the Turkish *Maqtal-i Al-i Rasul* (*Martyrdom of the Messenger's Family*); and the Turkish *Hadiqat as-Su'ada* (*Garden of the Felicitous Ones*). Prominent images in the first show Ali performing feats of bravery, slaying dragons and demons; associating himself with prophetic and royal legitimacy by removing the pillar of Solomon and releasing a spring from the floor of the Temple; and having Gabriel indicate to Muhammad that Ali is indeed his spiritual heir. The latter manuscript shows Ali several times receiving the fealty of the Muslims who acknowledge his leadership, and depicts a number of scenes of death and martyrdom.[37] (See Figure 9.)

One of the most fascinating works in which Ali gets top billing

Figure 9: Husayn at the deathbed of his brother Hasan.

comes from the Timurid court of Herat in the early fifteenth century. In the *Khawarannama*, perhaps the earliest of the truly Islamic epics, Ali and four fellow heroes (especially his ayyar companion Amr-i Umayya) do battle against all manner of kings and dark forces. Their mission of liberation to the East leads them across a fantastic landscape in which they beseige a series of seven fortresses bearing the names of various metals (copper, bronze, etc.) and set free the Muslims held captive there.[38] In the end the victorious heroes return to be with the Prophet in Madina.

Some stories place Ali in the company of characters who in no way are actually contemporary with him. These are mostly non-literary accounts or folk tales, although such anachronisms occur in the literary sources as well. His two most famous pseudo-contemporaries are Rustam and Solomon, sometimes both in the same story. Sometimes Ali goes up against the formidable Rustam. Rustam hears of the magnificence of Solomon and sets out to humiliate him, but encounters Solomon's champion Ali along the way. Rustam eats dust and becomes a Muslim.[39]

In the Swahili epic about the Byzantine king Heraklios, Ali plays a prominent role as the hero who rushes in from the wings to save the day. To heighten the dramatic tension, God instructs Muhammad to leave Ali at home. Muhammad advances toward Tabuk to confront the enemy, covering a thousand miles in two days. Successful as they are in battle, the Prophet's forces cannot quite turn the tide; they must have Ali. At God's direction, Muhammad calls to Ali. Hearing with no trouble, the hero makes the scene in an hour, humiliates the foe, and returns home. As always, Ali stands head and shoulders above all other heroes, for he is the lion of God, the sword of Islam.[40] Muhammad's son-in-law shows another side as well; he is not merely a violent force against enemies. Ali's ability to heal wounds of fallen warriors with his mere touch provides an additional reason for his celebrity status.[41]

A common theme in stories that feature Ali is that the Prophet calls on God to send him in just when all hope seems lost. Muhammad withdraws from the heat of battle to find a respite in which he can pray for deliverance. Ali, says the Prophet in the Swahili epic of Amuri, "causes sharp blows to rain down on all (his enemies) ending their thirst (for fighting)." Ali's swift appearance on the scene testifies both to his intimate friendship with Muhammad and to God's power to effect a happy resolution for the Muslims.[42]

Several tales recount another dimension of Ali the hero, with greater emphasis on the explicitly religious aspects of his character and on his willingness to die to advance the cause of the faith. A young man of low degree once asked a king for the hand of his daughter in marriage. The king agreed on condition that the suitor bring him the severed head of that greatest of champions, Ali. Undaunted, the youth approached the hero in Madina and explained his dilemma. Without hesitation Ali consented to have his own head lifted if the youngster would embrace Islam immediately. When the young man expressed reservations, an incensed Ali bested him in a brief duel. Again the hero offered the youth his life and help in defeating his beloved's father in exchange for a profession of faith. The young man and his Muslim bride lived, of course, happily ever after.[43]

Once there was a Queen of South Arabia named Manaya, who worshipped an idol. Her minions displeased her by becoming Muslims, so she cut off their hands and noses. The unfortunates sought healing from Muhammad, who not only restored their mutilated bodies with a splash of ablution-water but sent Ali off to redress the injustice. Two of the queen's henchmen intercepted Ali; when they divulged their plan to behead Muhammad, Ali dispatched one, and the other converted to become Ali's spy. With help from spies, Ali made his way to Manaya's castle. Once inside the idol temple, he decided to assuage his hunger by lopping off a piece of the statue, made of honey and dates. Enter the queen, who upon witnessing her idol's impotence became a Muslim. Just after Ali had gone, however, she reneged and repaired the idol. After learning of her treachery in a dream, Ali again penetrated the castle with the inside help of one of his converts, there to compass inexorably the downfall of the infidel monarch. In the process, Ali exhibits a wide range of heroic strengths: he catches in mid-air a convert whom the queen found out and had hurled from the ramparts; kills by his sheer weight an enemy giant who overexerts trying to lift Ali; and allows himself to be chained and taken prisoner inside the castle, only to break his chains and lead the final fight.[44]

Three other stories showcase Ali's unselfishness. One centers on Ali's decision to fast for three days, eating only after sundown, in order to speed the healing of his two ailing sons, Hasan and Husayn. Each of the three nights, as the family prepares to break the fast, a group of hungry people pass by—prisoners of war being repatriated, blind beggars, and homeless orphans. Each night Ali's family opts to go hungry in order to share its food.[45]

Another tells of his struggle to liberate himself and his new bride Fatima from penury. Travelling as far as Syria to return with only three pieces of silver, Ali encounters three people more unfortunate than himself en route home again. His last coin he gives finally to a woman who approaches him at the gate of Madina. Just then a man offers to sell Ali a camel on credit; while Ali is walking the camel home, a merchant offers him a bag of gold for the beast. All three unfortunates are, it turns out, God's messengers sent to verify Ali's generosity. The wondrous camel is none other than the same that God had created from stone for the pre-Islamic prophet Salih, and Gabriel is the merchant. After paying for a suitable wedding feast, Ali and Fatima give the leftover cash to the poor.[46]

In the third story, Ali goes a step further in his willingness to sacrifice himself for the less fortunate. This most selfless deed then provides the prologue for a series of tests that Ali wins with little effort. Sent off by Muhammad to rescue a Bedouin shaykh's daughter from the king of spirits, Ali is not long on the road before he meets a poor Bedouin begging for food. Since Ali relies always on God and carries neither money nor provisions, he offers to become the Bedouin's slave—Ali would fetch a handsome sum on the market. A Zoroastrian king named Abd an-Nar, "Servant of the Fire," buys Ali. His devoted service wins for Ali the king's affection, as well as the envy of the king's minister. At this point the jealous vizier becomes the instrument through which the storyteller sets up the three trials Ali must pass. Thinking to undo Ali, the minister proposes what he thinks will be an impossible task: creating a tunnel through rock for a water channel. In a deed of strength reminiscent of Rustam, Ali powers his fist through the rock with such precision as to accommodate precisely the proper flow of water.

For his second test, the minister tells Ali to rid the realm of a troublesome dragon—a simple task that only increases Ali's esteem in the eyes of the royal subjects. At this point, the king's daughter falls prisoner to the same evil spirit, Wahash, who had earlier abducted the Bedouin's daughter. Again the minister has Ali sent off to the forbidding Lion Castle. Wahash he kills handily, and those of his minions he spares become Muslims, as do the grateful Abd an-Nar and his family.[47]

Even when he knows for certain through a dream of the Prophet that he is about to die, Ali does not flinch. In simple acceptance of God's immutable will, he faces his would-be murderer, tells him he is aware of his hidden dagger, and begins his prayer ritual. Once again, the tale situates the murderer's motivation in a romantic setting: Ibn Muljam is said to have agreed to pay as part of his beloved's dowry the head of Ali. His bride-to-be hates Ali, for he had killed her father and brother in the battle of Nahrawan.[48]

Several major themes appear throughout the tales of Ali. One is that he, like Rustam, often receives calls for help from those who know he can rescue them. Unlike Rustam, Ali covers great distances in the twinkling of an eye, sometimes borne by a flying horse. Like Rustam, Ali is enormously powerful, quells dragons, and is fiercely loyal. Unlike Rustam, Ali is also the model husband and father, and he nearly always converts to Islam either the people he goes to aid or those he comes to conquer. Ali's wife Fatima sometimes teams up with him in the less violent moments of the tales.

As with all that happens on earth, Ali's marriage to Fatima came to pass by Divine Decree; and from their union come Muhammad's two grandsons. Hasan's descendents still refer to themselves as Sharifs; Husayn's line go by the title Sayyid. Here begins the long story of heroic redemptive suffering around which the Shi'i interpretation of human experience revolves. To our next section, on martyrs and mahdis, we leave the stories of the children of Fatima, and focus here on their mother.

The Swahili epic of Fatima stands out as one of the most popular works devoted exclusively to this favored daughter of Muhammad. One of only four perfect daughters of Eve, Fatima epitomizes all that is beautiful, radiant and strong—and dedicated to her father's values. As many male heroes must grow up without benefit of father, so Fatima's story emphasizes how her mother Khadija orphans her into the sole care of Muhammad. Her father struggles to make time to be with her in the midst of all his cares. When she has grown, her legendary comeliness makes her the desire of royalty the world over. None can match Ali in worthiness. And Ali has the added advantage of having lived in the prophet's house ever since Ali's own father died.

Ali is penniless, but Muhammad cares only that God has decided Ali should marry his daughter. For this marriage literally made in heaven, Ali is represented by Gabriel, and Fatima by God himself. As her dowry Fatima prefers to all the riches that myriads of angels could bring down, the granting of one simple wish: that at the Judgment she have leave to intercede for the forgiveness of all Muslim women, and thus to secure Paradise for them. Her golden necklace is to be the symbol of her intercessory role.[49]

On his own deathbed, Muhammad assures the grieving Fatima that she will follow him in six months. On the fated day, she falls faint while grinding grain. In her weariness an angel comforts her with the news that she will join her father the next day. Recovering her strength, Fatima finishes the grain and bakes the cakes that guests at her wake will eat. For one last time she sits down to fix the hair of her daughter Zaynab. But she begins to feel feverish and asks Ali to go out for the one thing that might relieve her: pomegranate juice. All over he searches until at last he finds an old Jewish merchant who gives Ali his solitary remaining pomegranate.

Returning home, Ali meets a poor blind beggar who laments that he has searched everywhere for Ali, the only man wise enough to suggest a cure. Ali gives the beggar his only pomegranate, where-upon Gabriel comes down with a basket full of the fruit. Recovering enough to continue her minstrations to Zaynab, Fatima bequeathes to her daughter her greatest treasures. First, she gives her a tooth still bleeding that an enemy had knocked out of Muhammad's mouth with a stone. Then she gives Zaynab the seal-ring with which Solomon himself had ruled the four kingdoms of humanity, animals, jinns, and devils, instructing Zaynab to pass it to her nephew, Zayn al-Abidin, destined to be the fourth Shi'i Imam. Finally, Fatima gives her a vial of dust (ambergris) from the ground of Paradise; it would turn red at the moment of Husayn's death. Fatima dies in peace that night.[50]

Martyrs and mahdis (guided ones whose return in the fullness of time is awaited) are two final religious heroic types. In both Sunni and Shi'i tradition, important personages have witnessed to their faith by giving their lives, and the hope that the end of time will see a reestablishment of justice on earth is embodied in various mahdi figures. (The term mahdi is used in a more generic sense by Sunni Muslims; for Shi'is, the last of the legitimate spiritual successors to Muhammad—for example, either the twelfth or the seventh Imam—is called the Mahdi.) We look here at one example

113

of a martyr from Sunni tradition, then at three examples especially prominent in Shiʿi lore.

Muhammad's cousin Jaʿfar appears to have been considered the first of the Islamic martyrs, though the slightly later Shiʿi martyr Husayn treated below has far greater notoriety. In the Swahili epic of Heraklios, Muhammad in Madina hears that Jaʿfar was the first to die (followed soon by Muhammad's adopted son Zayd ibn Haritha) in fighting against the Byzantine foe. Jaʿfar had been close to the Prophet and had carried the Muslim standard into battle. In Swahili lore, Jaʿfar embodies the willingness to fight for the faith even to the death. As standard bearer, legend has it, Jaʿfar suffers the loss first of his right arm; then he hoists the escutcheon with his left, only to lose that hand as well. Not to be undone, he catches the falling flag and carries it by pinning it between his leg and his horse. Never does he lose the banner, and for his troubles God rewards him with martyr's wings.[51]

Ali's descendents are the suffering family and the martyrs par excellence. Beginning with Ali himself, who endures the indignity of having his right of succession denied by those who came to be called Sunni Muslims, the story of redemptive suffering encompasses Ali's wife, Fatima, and their sons, Hasan and Husayn. One scholar notes that popular tradition makes an interesting connection between the Shiʿi Imams and Iranian monarchy. According to S. Soroudi, "Shiʿa Imams beginning with the fourth down to the twelfth . . . inherited *khvarna* (the special light or aura of kingship) through the marriage of Imam Husain . . . to princess Shahrbanu, the daughter of the last Sassanian king, Yazdagird III."[52]

Son of Ali and grandson of Muhammad, Husayn shares with his brother Hasan miraculous powers as a child. One story tells how the mere touch of the children healed the singed wings of an angel; another how Gabriel himself had avuncular feelings for them, rocked them to sleep when their own parents were too fatigued to do so, and brought them fruit from Paradise, and even clothes (for their family was too poor to afford good things), suits of red and green. But not all Gabriel's gifts were happy: the boy who chose the green, Hasan, would die by poison; the one who chose the red, by the sword.[53]

Hasan's death, by treacherous poisoning, legend ascribes to his second wife, Jaʾida. One version says she wrapped him, as he slept, in a sheet soaked with an undetectable poison that his skin absorbed. Another claims she left a pitcher of poisoned water by his bed. In a dream Muhammad had warned him, but Hasan knew God had unalterably willed his departure in any case. When Husayn, also aware of the poison, came to him and offered to drink with him, Hasan reminded Husayn of his destiny to die at Karbala.[54]

Husayn is the protomartyr whose story is linked to the suffering of all the prophets of old in the "passion play" accounts. It is the same tale upon which the storytellers base that of Muhammad ibn al-Hanafiya mentioned below. Perhaps more poignantly than any other, the epic of Husayn drives home the tragic destiny of the hero confronting raw hatred and evil. Husayn shares something of the fate of the royal hero we have named the prince of tragic destiny, but several distinctively religious elements significantly shift the burden of the story. Here is a brief summary of the tragedy of Karbala.

The short Swahili "Epic of Husayn's Death" and the longer "Epic of the Killing of Husayn" are among several documents that narrate the tale of the battle of Karbala in 680, in which Husayn and most of his immediate family were slaughtered. As J. Knappert observes, the poet goes to great lengths to capture the sense of sheer mindless and undeserved hatred that possess the forces of the Umayyad Caliph. He speaks of entanglement, intrigue, rottenness, intense hostility, and jealousy of the sort Cain felt for Abel. Like his father Ali, Husayn hears a call to aid victims of oppression and injustice.

In one of the stories, Husayn pays a courtesy call to the court of Yazid in Damascus and discovers to his shock that the caliph makes a mockery of Islam. He and his family then return to settle in Madina for a quiet and non-revolutionary life. As the tale unfolds, Husayn becomes aware that it is his responsibility to act against the Umayyad caliph's tyranny and increasingly godless ways. Responding to a letter from the people of Kufa pleading for help against the brutal Umayyad governor, Ubaydallah ibn Ziyad, Husayn sends Muslim ibn Aqil to be prayer leader in Kufa. As troubles mount in Kufa, Husayn resolves to go himself and informs his followers that they may choose whether or not to join him in the combat. With seventy-seven stalwarts he departs for Kufa.

On the way Husayn refuses both the help of angels who offer him the hope of conquest and the obeisance of jinns who promise him a kingdom over them. Further temptations assail him: armies of lions, snakes, birds, ants, and porcupines one after another offer him sure success. Husayn sends them all away with his gratitude.

As a religious leader, and *imam*, first of all, Husayn begins by preaching the word; but he does not take refuge in the word, for he knows he is destined to die. When news comes that the Umayyads are moving toward Kufa, Husayn leads his band toward Karbala. Cutting off their access to the river Euphrates, the enemy army decides to see if Husayn's people might not die of thirst. When Husayn carries his suffering child Ali Asghar to ask the enemy for water, they refuse and then shoot the baby as Husayn cradles him.

Gradually the enemy tightens its grip, and the band of Shi'i believers begin to lose hope. Husayn offers flight by dark as an option, but all prefer to remain till the end. Gravely wounded, Husayn withstands the jeers of the enemy; instead of shouting back, he prays, "I give thanks to Thee, our hearts are rejoicing! We are not sad at all! We hope for Paradise, we long for death rather than to kneel for them." Against the two thousand Umayyad troops, Husayn bravely fights on for ten agonizing days, until the tenth of Muharram, the first lunar month of the Islamic liturgical calendar.

In an ever-tightening noose, the enemy kills Husayn's supporters, his family, until only the hero and his youngest son remain. With his sword, "Rapid Lightning," Husayn cuts down hosts of enemy. In one version, Husayn carries the child toward the river, fighting on as he goes, to meet his end. Another has him returning to rescue the women in camp, only to face ambush there. At that point he has a vision of Muhammad—as in the Shi'i passion play— who encourages him and promises Husayn he will be allowed to mediate for his people in Paradise. Another vision, of his mother Fatima, follows as Husayn nears death.

Pulling an arrow from deep in his throat and wounded by thirty-three spears and thirty-four swords, Husayn expires, and his mother accompanies his soul to heaven.[55]

A fascinating character in many ways peripheral to mainstream Shi'i martyrology, Muhammad ibn al-Hanafiya, the youngest son of Ali's second wife, has proven nevertheless a major figure in the heroic tales of South Asian Islam especially. Because he was the half-brother of the protomartyr Husayn, Muhammad has taken his place among the major religious heroes. How this happened in a region that has never been strongly Shi'i is discussed in the appendix.

The historical Muhammad ibn al-Hanafiya apparently had no desire to become embroiled in the family battles against the Umayyad caliph Yazid. In the legend, however, he hurriedly leaves celebrations for his daughter's wedding upon receiving a letter about Husayn's hopeless plight. On the way toward Karbala, he and his men meet up with Umayyad forces. Like a true hero, Muhammad challenges them to a single combat. After dispatching the only serious contender, Muhammad wades into the Umayyad ranks barehanded and tears apart 40,000 men so that their blood fills a nearby wadi.

Encountering a fresh Umayyad contingent, Muhammad ibn al-Hanafiya again faces their champion, Shimr, who had earlier murdered Husayn. Shimr dies an ignoble death, and half of his million troops bite the dust. Again Yazid musters a million cavalry and eight million archers and mounts a hundred thousand ropes-men atop forty thousand elephants. It takes seven hundred lassoes to slow Muhammad down enough to allow an enemy leader to cut off his arm. Amazingly, Muhammad's troops rally, surround the Umayyad hosts, and free Muhammad.

That night Muhammad the Prophet appears in a dream to his nephew and namesake, who asks only that he might live long enough to rescue Husayn's son Zayn al-Abidin, now imprisoned in Damascus. The Prophet tells Muhammad to have a friend go search for his severed arm on the battlefield. Ibrahim Astar manages to find it and returns it in his turban. The younger Muhammad replaces the arm into its socket and touches it with the Seal of Prophethood his uncle had loaned him in the dream. His arm fully healed, Muhammad sets off for Damascus.

God sends a cloud to hover over the hiding place of the evil Yazid. The terrified caliph runs crazily about and, as only true justice would have it, trips into the very grave he has dug for Husayn's survivors. The cloud, which identifies itself as the spirit of Husayn, then leads Muhammad to the imprisoned family of Husayn. There Muhammad anoints and crowns Zayn al-Abidin caliph and becomes his military commander. Later, while out in the desert, Muhammad thinks an enemy is hiding in a cave. He enters, only to have the opening seal up behind him. He then hears God announce to him that he will be the Hidden Imam who will one day emerge to fill the world with justice once again.[56]

Recognition of the Imams' heroic status has been evident in miscellaneous manuscript illustrations, as well as in the two Shi'ite texts mentioned above. An example of such an image is the visual metaphor of the "Ship of Shi'ism" in the *Shahnama* created for Safavid Shah Tahmasp. Even though the text of the epic nowhere mentions the scene depicted, the artist, working for a Shi'ite patron, has seen fit to paint a boat whose chief passengers are the Prophet Muhammad, Ali, Hasan, and Husayn. There are literally scores of miniature paintings of these religious heroes—many dozens, indeed, of the Prophet's Ascension alone. The iconography features a wide range of easily recognizable clues as to the heroes' identity. Muhammad rides the winged steed with human face, Buraq, and Ali has his famous mule, Duldul. Muhammad typically, but not always, wears a green robe, and Ali carries the twin-pointed sword, Dhu ʾl-Faqar (the "Cleaver"). Nevertheless, the visual and verbal affinity of these religious types with the folk and royal types is unmistakable and, quite likely, deliberate on the part of authors and artists.

A number of important folk and royal heroes we have looked at, including those not depicted explicitly as Muslim believers, have exhibited some awareness that their power ultimately derives from a source beyond themselves. Rustam, for example, seems a surprisingly pious chap; he prays often, and the Deity is not loathe to respond to him. In addition, countless extraordinary or fantastic events take place in the sagas of many of our heroes. Such occurrences do not all belong to the same category. It may help to think of these events as transpiring within several different orders or planes, as drawing their power from different sources. The following stratification does not depend on any particular succession of these levels, but merely suggests they are different.

On the more mundane level, one can attribute the cleverness of an Abu Zayd of Saruj or the prowess of an Antar to native talent. At a level above that, the power that allows a villain to get the upper hand temporarily over a good hero might originate either in the hero's momentary carelessness or, more ominously, in the inscrutable dictates of impersonal Fate. At still another level, we find protagonist and antagonist contending within the arena of the opposing but sometimes playful, quasi-personal forces called fairies

118

and demons (*pari* and *diw* in Persian), or the mischievous creatures of smokeless fire called *jinn*. Here the hero's fortune depends on his or her sealing an allegiance with the more positive forces. Moving up a notch in the multi-level cosmos, the forces take the more personalized shape of devils and angels.

On the next level up in the exercise of power, Islamic tradition makes a distinction among three sorts of extraordinary events. First comes sorcery or magic (*sihr*), such as Pharaoh's courtiers conjure up in transforming their rods into serpents. Over against that, the prophets exercise an option called the evidentiary miracle (*mu'jiza*), by which God provides proof of the prophet's authenticity. Hence, Moses's staff/dragon devours those of Pharaoh's magicians. Finally, saints enjoy the ability to perform wonders (*karamat*). In kind these do not necessarily look so different from the wonders prophets work; the difference is one of degree, and theologians developed the distinction perhaps out of a desire to preserve a hierarchy or gradient of power. God permits magic only as a test for believers, but actually causes miracles and wonders through the intermediacy of the prophet or saint.

In the adventures of religious heroes, God's power ultimately wins the day. Marvels and miracles point not to the hero's prowess but to God's transcendence and sovereignty. Whatever the hero's need, God provides. That does not preclude the possibility of tragic endings, as we have seen in the case of Husayn and the other martyrs. It does mean, however, that whatever the immediate outcome, evil will not win final victory. To the villain, the hero may cede a battle here or a skirmish there, but in the end, the spoils of war go to the faithful.[57] Before discussing some of the thematic elements in the lives of the heroic characters described in these last three chapters, we turn to some of those villainous and evil powers against which our heroes are at their best.

Chapter Six

Villains and
the Forces of Evil

Villains generally serve a fairly clear basic purpose: they provide resistance, a force against which the hero must exert himself. Bad guys vary in potency. They usually increase in vigor and ferocity to build tension and underscore the principal hero's prowess. Several sorts of villainous powers range across the heroic landscape. Here we shall describe some major examples of three types: non-human, super-human, and human forces. This brief chapter will close with a look at the mystery of evil as impersonal and at the phenomenon of moral ambiguity in the villain.

Non-human Personifications of Evil

Iblis (from the Greek *diabolos*) or Shaytan (Satan) ranks as the prime nemesis in many heroic narratives, but is especially prominent in tales of religious heroes. In Swahili Islamicate epic literature, which treats religious themes almost exclusively, Iblis plays the role that made him famous. A Swahili epic of Adam and Eve takes its cue from the Qur'an as well as from later popular interpretation. Iblis becomes the villain when he refuses to pay homage to the newly created Adam, pleading that Adam's mere clay scarcely merits a bow from Iblis' fire. (See Figure 10.) The poet describes the archenemy as egotistical, intellectually subtle and sophisticated, refined in manner, and ironically, suffering from worry and second thoughts. Here the poet uses the word *wasiwasi*, a term the Qur'an uses to describe the very means Satan uses to afflict his targets: whispered temptation, insinuation. God engages Iblis in conversation as to why the rebel has chosen to balk over so easy a command. When Iblis persists in his pride, God expels him from Paradise, forever to live as an outsider. But God grants Iblis's parting request to remain a thorn in the side of humanity by planting the seed of rebelliousness.[1]

Two of Iblis's most famous appearances as enemy are his ap-

120

Figure 10: Angels pay homage to Adam and Eve. Note Iblis (Satan) with gray face at upper left.

parent success with Adam and Eve and his failure with Job. Satan approaches Eve not in the form of a serpent but evidently in human guise, as in many other Islamicate stories of his encounters with people. He takes Eve into his confidence as though he were a "friend of the same sex." The poet describes in rich detail how Eve becomes the tool of Iblis, and how Adam counters every argument thoughtfully. Meanwhile, Iblis continues to play on Eve's fears of losing Adam to other women, an unlimited supply of whom grow on the girl-tree. In the end, the hero's compassion does him in: he will eat the fruit only because Eve has already done so and condemned herself to a life on earth. Adam will heroically effect his own expulsion in order to go with Eve, for she will be unable to cope by herself on earth.[2] In the Swahili *Epic of Job (Utenzi wa Ayubu)*, Iblis reappears in his attempt to seduce a religious hero known for his patience. By God's leave only, Iblis goes about his grim business; but because Job is under God's protection, he endures in fidelity.[3]

A variation on the Satan theme appears in the story of Ra's al-Ghul (literally, "Head of the Ghoul"), an astonishingly ugly demon-like creature.[4] Like other works of the *maghazi* type, it features the Prophet's companions, with Imam Ali as the hero who arrives just in the nick of time. In the story a South Arabian king keeps an idol's head in his palace and worships it, for Satan makes it speak to him. In a Swahili version called *Utendi wa Rasi ʾl-Ghuli*, a Yemeni king kills a Muslim woman's eleven sons to punish her for her fidelity to Islam. The woman seeks help from the Prophet, who, after curing Ali of a fever, sends him to the rescue. The poem was apparently once recited at Swahili weddings.[5] Some modern North African glass paintings depict Ali doing battle with the demon-king of horrific visage.[6]

Ahriman is the Persian counterpart to Iblis. In the *Shahnama*, Ahriman plants the seeds of several major disasters. Early on, he leads Dahhak astray (more on that shortly). Later, Ahriman persuades King Kay Kawus in a fit of hybris to attempt a flight to heaven on an eagle-powered throne. Firdawsi uses the story as an example of human greed and corruptibility, though the king does repent after this and several other celebrated falls from grace. Miniaturists have delighted in experimenting with various ways of illustrating Kay Kawus's airborne misadventure.[7]

An enemy of Kay Kawus, the king of Mazandaran, is actually a diw. When the Iranian monarch has had enough of the diw, he sends his champion Rustam off to bring him to heel. After acquitting himself creditably in the "Seven Feats" on the way to Mazandaran, Rustam accosts the pesky king. Just as Rustam is about to gain the upper hand, the Mazandarani turns himself into a boulder. Some of the most charming miniatures depict the moment of petrification, showing the diw in various stages of transformation: entirely in boulder shape, entirely in stone but more or less resembling a mounted horseman, or midway through the process.[8]

On the way to Mazandaran, Rustam must do battle with the even more formidable White Diw. In a scene frequently chosen for illustration, Rustam corners the foe in his cave and does him in.[9] Later under King Kay Khusraw, Rustam finds himself pitted against one of the wiliest of diws. Appearing first as a wild ass (onager, *gur*) in a herd of horses (an often-illustrated scene), Akwan eludes capture. When Rustam lies down to sleep, the protean diw transforms itself into a storm-wind, digs up the patch of earth on which Rustam lies and heaves the hero into the sea. Painters have generally opted to show the diw as monstrous but otherwise anthropomorphic, rather than attempt to depict a storm-wind. When Rustam and the diw meet again, Rustam has had enough and removes the villain's head.[10]

At the end of the Akwan episode, Firdawsi inserts one of the clearest examples of how one teller of heroic tales understood his own material. The poet gives a forthrightly allegorical exegesis of the story: "You must recognize the demon as the man of evil, he that displays ingratitude towards God; for you must reckon anyone who transgresses the ways of humane conduct as a demon rather than a man. If your reason refuses to believe these tales, it may be that it has not accurately understood this inward significance."[11] If Firdawsi can be so unambiguously articulate about the underlying meaning of this series of encounters between hero and villain, one can hardly doubt that he held similar opinions about the whole scope of the heroic experience. Firdawsi's interpretation is rooted in his fundamental concept of human nature and its moral limitations under divine dominion. To forget those limits, to be so full of arrogance that one knows no fear or sense of shame, is to slide over the edge from humanity into the demonic. Diws like Akwan

123

personify baser tendencies gone awry. The hero, by contrast, embodies contained, focused power—energy that remains (if only just barely) within the boundaries of propriety.[12]

Super-human Villains

Lines between the human and the non-human grow fuzzy in the realm of heroic struggle. Here we shall use the term "superhuman" to refer to such characters as giants and ogres, even though the narratives may also refer to them occasionally or interchangeably as either demons or human beings. In the Antar saga, Ghawwar ibn Dinar of Sudan exiles Antar's consort Ghamra and appoints the giant Saʿiqa ibn Andam to rule there. The giant makes camp at the Trail of the Gazelles.[13] Saʿiqa is but one of many enemies described as giants in the Antar *sira*. Sometimes the term "giant" seems to designate merely a man whose great strength and size underscore his worthiness as an adversary for the hero. Sometimes, as in this instance, the enemy evidently springs from something other than a purely human genetic pool.

Such characters appear more often in folk or popular material than in courtly or elite literature. In the Hamza stories and in various tales about Iskandar, the hero often encounters the forces of evil as grotesque and beyond human scale. Artists who created the *Hamzanama* of exceptionally large format for Akbar were particularly fond of portraying the enemy as gigantic. Many of those miniatures are very successful in communicating a sense of evil as an overwhelming presence capable of virtually engulfing all in its path.[14]

Giants occur in Turkic narratives as well. The story of Basat and Tepegöz in *The Book of Dede Korkut* tells how an Oghuz leader adopted a child who grows up to be big trouble. Uruz and his men happen one day upon a strange mass of protoplasm quivering on the ground. The throbbing egg splits and out comes a one-eyed boy, fruit of an illicit union between one of Uruz's shepherds and a fairy he had bedded against her will. Uruz decides to bring the boy home to raise him with his son Basat, who as a child had been lost during a hasty move by the tribe and reared by a lioness. As Tepegöz ("Top-Eye") grows, he takes to eating the ears and noses of his playmates. Since the boy resists correction, Uruz sends him away. Shielded by a ring from his fairy mother, Tepegöz marauds the land from his mountain stronghold, devouring shepherds and sheep. For a long time, the indestructible cyclops[15] decimates the population and beats up on one Oghuz hero after another. Even Dede Korkut's shrewd arbitration secures only a slowdown in the carnage. In order to avenge the death of his blood brother Kiyan Seljuk and to help the tribe, Basat finally decides to confront his giant step-brother. In spite of his parents' pleas, Basat goes off, only to be quickly captured and stuffed into the giant's boot. Basat manages to cut himself out and blinds the cyclops. When Tepegöz asks the challenger his name, he realizes they are half-brothers and tries to play on Basat's sympathy. Basat remains resolute and cuts off the giant's head.

In its unfolding of the resolution of a terrible evil that has befallen the Oghuz people, the story of Basat suggests the primal struggles between individual and group, father and son, brother and brother, as the good and evil sides of the self. Father loses second son (Basat) but later regains him; father adopts third son (Tepegöz) but is forced to disown him. Second son wins a name upon his reintegration into the tribe; ostracized son never wins a name other than the descriptive Tepegöz; second son avenges death of older brother by killing half-brother. Basat must pass three tests posed by his evil half-brother, and in so doing he neutralizes the evil power. In the end, the giant has no recourse but to appeal to sympathy; again Basat passes the test and overcomes. Here the villain personifies an evil of which society must be purged, even though the shepherd, not his progeny, is ultimately responsible.[16]

Human Villains

Among the principal varieties of human villain, one can single out the evil king, the mass murderer, the infidel, the outsider, and the traitor. The enemy's knights, of course, always merit a large dose of vilification, but for present purposes the designation "enemy knight" seems too inclusive to be very useful.[17]

A standard villain type is the wicked despot who tyrannizes his own people, along with as much of the rest of the world as he can grab. Some kings seem to be inherently perverse; a few start off with as much chance of becoming decent human beings as anyone else, but make a disastrous choice somewhere along the way. A common device for setting the scene is the revelatory dream in which the tyrant sees his imminent demise, engineered by a hero or prophet soon to be born. Celestial portents often include the rising of a new star or similar startling phenomenon. Astrologers divine the portents reluctantly, for they know that the truth will likely hurt them before it hurts the king. The revelation also frequently prompts the despot to order a wave of futile infanticide. Stories shared by Biblical and Islamic traditions include those of Pharaoh and baby Moses, and of Herod and Jesus. Islamic tradition has developed further the story of how Nimrod responded to the expected birth of Abraham. One of the most colorful evil kings in Islamicate heroic literature and art is surely the Arab Dahhak.

Dahhak is a man originally of noble-enough descent who becomes a villain by making an irrevocable deal with the devil. He gains power at the cost of having sprout from his shoulders two serpents, each of which requires the brain of a young man daily. Like Pharaoh and Nimrod, Dahhak has a dream of his infant avenger, Faridun. His reign of terror finally leads to a rebellion (mentioned in chapter three) incited by Kawa the blacksmith and brought to completion by Faridun. The loathesome usurper who had dethroned the spiritually bankrupt Jamshid gets his just deserts when Faridun chains him forever to Mount Damavand. Dahhak ends as did Prometheus, but the deeds that set the evil Arab on that path smack not at all of Promethean altruism.[18] One of the most intriguing features about Dahhak's role in the *Shahnama* is that, in spite of his heinous crimes and personal hatefulness, he remains an indirect ancestor of some of the greatest heroes, most notably Rustam. Illustrators have often chosen scenes from the Dahhak cycle to enliven their visual commentary.[19]

Enmity between Iran and Turan provides the single most important motive for ongoing conflict in the action of the *Shahnama*. Though Iranians and Turanians alike traced their ancestry to Faridun, Tur's murder of brother Iraj opened a wound that would fester for generations. No character better personifies the bitter feud than the Turanian king Afrasiyab. At the end of Shah Garshasp's reign, Afrasiyab launches the first of many attacks against Iran. Under Garshasp's successor, Kay Qubad, Rustam leads the Iranians on counterattack. Through nearly a quarter of Firdawsi's poem, and several Iranian regimes, Afrasiyab and Rustam continue their see-saw struggle. To Afrasiyab goes the dubious distinction of seeking to pit Suhrab against his father, of plotting the death of Bizhan, and of having Siyawush murdered. Nearly successful in his attempts to make Iran his own, Afrasiyab is capable of considerable duplicity to get what he wants. That trait apparently runs in the family, if his brother Garsiwaz represents the line faithfully (as we shall see shortly). Two of Afrasiyab's daughters, however, represent redeemable qualities even in the house of an evil king. Afrasiyab appears in a relatively large number of miniature paintings, most often in court and battle scenes.[20]

Another sort of human villain, the loose cannon, is the very embodiment of chaos. The Southeast Asian character Hang Jebat provides the best example. Of the many major sequences from the Malay *Hikayat Hang Tuah,* the story best known and most popular as a theme of contemporary movies and plays revolves around the conflict between Hang Tuah and his opposite number, Hang Jebat. Hang Jebat suddenly breaks into a rage and begins killing, in a scene redolent of a mass murderer's rampage. Much of the episode's interest for modern Malaysians derives apparently from a highly politicized interpretation: the tension between civic duty and the demands of friendship. According to that reading, one can offer some justification for Hang Jebat's actions. We discussed the implications of such interpretations in chapter two. In the present chapter we focus our attention on the original context and possible traditional explanations for Hang Jebat's unexpected violence and mayhem.

As S. Errington indicates, Hang Jebat does not act like a usurper, for the havoc he wreaks cannot possibly help him establish a base of power from which to take the throne. Nor do Hang Jebat's actions suggest a concern for redressing some injustice suffered by a friend or royal subjects. Even the villain himself admits to having no lofty motive. More than once he says, "If you are going to be evil, don't go half-way." His friend Hang Tuah is framed and condemned to death, and he does not resist. Hang Tuah's willingness to die for a crime he did not commit, merely because the raja has ordered it so, stands in stark contrast to Hang Jebat's unvarnished defiance. A court minister then spirits Hang Tuah away to a hiding place, lest the people rise up against an official who would permit the execution of a clearly innocent man. One cannot therefore interpret the story as recommending rebellion against a corrupt regime.

A simpler and more frightening force seems to have launched Hang Jebat on his rampage. The phrase "to run amok" explains it all. A kind of temporary insanity begins with some insult or humiliation, grows into a dark amnesiac brooding described as "heart [liver] sickness," which in turn bursts into open rage. Hang Jebat runs amok, as do all the outsiders who represent the forces of chaos surrounding the Kingdom of Order of Malaka.[21] Speaking of another figure who runs amok, Tameng Sari (one of the invaders, not an insider like Hang Jebat), Errington describes the resulting bedlam: "people scatter in all directions . . . hiding on rooftops and under houses, each looking out only for himself. The scene images a condition of the world which is like a more extreme form of the world without rajas in it . . . . But the disruption is so extreme and so vital that it is not enough to dismiss it as merely the absence of the raja. Tameng Sari seems a vehicle for a sort of energy unleashed into the world."[22] What makes Hang Jebat's rampage more terrifying is that it can happen even from within the safe, protected world of royal order.[23]

One characterization of the villain that rarely allows of individualized description is that of the "infidel." Swahili literature tends to emphasize the enemy's mendacity, irascibility and irrational qualities, and tendency to drunkenness. Christian bishops exemplify extremes of all these vices. One particular Christian tactic always proves to be a serious miscalculation: attacking just when the Muslims are at ritual prayer only stirs the latter to a more vigorous response.[24] Turkic tales likewise revel in descriptions of the infidel hordes with a few choice epithets. They are "bloody dogs" of "savage religion and intemperate speech," but that does not deter the heroes from lusting after their daughters.

Infidels wear all black clothing and have black blood. To add insult to injury, they frequently consign any captured Muslim to the pigsty. Turkic heroes rarely excoriate the enemy for drunkenness, since they themselves often get roaring drunk not long after they have engaged in the ritual prayer—clear evidence that the Islamic elements were simply overlaid on tales told before the Turks were Islamized. So too, apparently, the term "infidel" came to replace some more generic term for enemy.[25]

Sometimes the infidel has a name, especially in stories of Muhammad. One of the Prophet's toughest enemies is Abu Sufyan. This villain even has his name on a famous Swahili poem, the *Epic of Abd ar-Rahman and Sufyan*. He represents the potential for hybris and invincible ignorance in an unbeliever. But as the story recounted in chapter three suggests, the children of stubbornness are not beyond redemption. Abu Sufyan's own daughter, not unlike Afrasiyab's two noble daughters, finds her way to goodness and truth.[26]

Hostile intent toward the unbeliever is a relatively concrete and, at least on the surface, well-defined and easily justified frame of mind for the hero with a religious mission. Often, however, the embodiment of evil takes the more diffuse form of "the outsider," the other person from elsewhere. Mere otherness sometimes emerges as an explanation for the existence of evil in the world. One of the best-defined outside powers is that of Turan in the *Shahnama*. Implacable enemies, the Turanian Hatfields and the Iranian McCoys wage an ongoing feud over several centuries and many kingly reigns. The enmity carries none of the religious overtones one finds in the relations between Muslim heroes and infidel outlaws. A somewhat similar tone characterizes relations between Arabs and Abyssinians in the *sira* literature; like Iranians and Turanians, they are blood relatives going back many generations. These longstanding divisions, however, generally do not inspire the storyteller to describe the outsiders as something other than human.

Perhaps no story symbolizes the fear of the outsider better than that of Iskandar's building the wall to contain Gog and Magog. In this instance, the villain is a hybrid of the fearsome unknown and the malevolent foreigner whose expansionist proclivities must be checked. Gog and Magog bear the additional heavy burden of eschatological doom-terror, for their appearance on the scene signals the victory of chaos over cosmic order. To Iskandar falls the task of overcoming the unspeakable threat and delivering the world from "evildoers and tyranny." The inhabitants of a beautiful city at the foot of a mountain describe to Iskandar the ever-present danger posed by the creatures "through whom our lot becomes one of sorrow and suffering. Their faces are those of camels, their tongues are black and their eyes the colour of blood. In their black faces are teeth like boars' tusks and none dares to encounter them. Their bodies, covered with bristles, are the colour of the Nile; their chests, bosoms and ears resemble those of elephants . . . . In the Spring, when the turbulence from the clouds arrives, that green sea is stirred to effervescence, the clouds raise up serpent-like creatures out of the waves, and the aether roars like a lion."[27] Employing a hundred thousand smiths and masons, the world-conqueror virtually welds the outsiders into their mountain, never again to threaten the world's repose and tranquility. Several marvelous miniatures show Iskandar's workers laboring at their massive project, with the misshapen denizens of the outer realm looking on in stunned amazement.[28]

Now and then an otherwise good knight turns bad, out of spite or envy. Gurgin son of Milad stands out as an authentic traitor in the *Shahnama*. King Kay Khusraw sends Gurgin off with Bizhan to help in the extermination of the wild boars plaguing Armenia. Gurgin, smitten with jealousy at Bizhan's prowess and unmitigated success, decides to set up the hero so that he can be taken captive and thereby run afoul of the Turanian King Afrasiyab. The story has two happy endings, however. Rustam sets Bizhan free, and he marries Manizha; and, at Rustam's insistence, the repentant Gurgin receives pardon for his treachery.[29]

In other malevolent characters, treachery runs much deeper. Afrasiyab's brother Garsiwaz plays the Iago of the *Shahnama*. Always lurking in the wings and ready to do his brother's dirty work, Garsiwaz epitomizes spite and envy. Garsiwaz plays crucial roles in the episodes of Siyawush and Bizhan. He manages to poison even his wicked brother's already venomous mind with plots against the innocent. To Garsiwaz Afrasiyab assigns the grim tasks of murdering the king's own daughter Farangis and executing Bizhan; of seeing to it that his other daughter, Manizha, is thoroughly disgraced; and of having Siyawush murdered. Thanks to Rustam's timely intervention, Garsiwaz fails in the first instance and succeeds only partially in the second. Garsiwaz is entirely successful only against Siyawush, the prince of tragic destiny. The Turanian's envy is such that he will stop at nothing to do away with the Iranian youth. The heinousness of his slander and betrayal make Garsiwaz the most despicable of villains.

The Mystery of Evil and Moral Ambiguity

Heroes rarely lose, except to suffer temporary setbacks. When a hero does sustain a truly crushing blow, it often comes not at the hand of evil personified but out of the inexorable turning of fate's inscrutable wheel. When a young hero dies before his time, as do Suhrab and Siyawush, all concerned can only shake their heads in disbelief and bow to a superior power. As we shall see later, in the chapter on the humanity of the hero, the experience of icy-fingered evil and death often occupies the storytellers' attention. In religious narratives, fate or destiny takes on the more personal aspect of divine will. Harsh though its decrees may appear to the outsidcr, God's will ultimately envisions a positive outcome. From the religious perspective, evil finally yields to good, even if along the way the innocent must apparently pay the ransom of the guilty, as in the death of Husayn. A major difference between the concepts of destiny and divine will is that, while both are inscrutable, the latter is at least not so stark as to leave earthly players without a sense of purpose and hope for some sort of future. The hand of fate rearranges with a steely cold grip. In either case, only the fool dares rebel.

Most of the villains one meets in heroic stories appear, unlike the cartoon characters Boris Badenov and Crabby "Rotten to the Core" Appleton, thoroughly detestable and devoid of redeeming features. Several of them, however, have another side. As we have suggested in chapter two, popular Malay interpretations of Hang Jebat have not always come down hard on the man whose claim to fame is that he ran amok. An ongoing debate among modern Malay commentators evidences a split opinion as to whether Hang Jebat models reprehensible and irredeemable conduct, or whether he deserves praise and emulation for his willingness to revolt against a corrupt system.

A still more arresting example of such ambivalence occurs in the development of Iblis's personality and plight over the centuries, especially in Arabic and Persian mystical literature. In a variation on the theme of sympathy for the devil, Sufi authors have seen in Iblis the epitome of a lover who finds himself in an impossible dilemma. God has willed that he should worship none but God, but has commanded Iblis to pay homage to the newly created body of Adam. To paraphrase the mystical poet al-Hallaj, God has said to Iblis, "Jump into the water, but don't get wet." Iblis has suffered from bad press, when all along he merely tried conscientiously to do the impossible, and got caught in the middle.[30]

131

ELEMENTS OF THE HEROIC CYCLE: NARRATIVE AND ICONOGRAPHIC THEMES

PART THREE

Chapter Seven

Heroic Identity and Legitimacy

Various facets of heroic identity and legitimacy constitute an important complex of themes.[1] Here we shall discuss the following: unusual circumstances surrounding the hero's birth and infancy; elements of parent-child conflict; intimations of destiny; the hero's emblems of identification and the related iconographic tags that appear in illustrations; and the phenomenon of mistaken identity.

Special Circumstances of Birth and Childhood

Circumstances of a hero's birth are nearly always unusual. Portents and dreams vouchsafed to mother, father, or grandparent often announce the child's coming, and the signs are frequently associated with light imagery (sun, moon, stars), as in the stories of Kay Khusraw and Muhammad. Hang Tuah's father has a dream in which the moon hangs over the infant hero's head, presaging a leadership role for his son.[2] Forewarning sometimes comes to the future hero's nemesis as well, so that the child's mother must take him away to safety (Moses, Abraham, Faridun, Jesus). Great physical obstacles sometimes stand in the way, such as Mary's virginity; Rudaba's need for help in delivering Rustam; or advanced age, infertility, and childlessness (for example, of several major Turkic epic figures).[3]

In two of the great Arabic *siras,* the savior-like births of Abu Zayd and Antar are quite similar in detail, with marked interest in the mystery of birth and growth.[4] In utero and as infants, the heroes are often described as unusually large, heavy, and possessed of prodigious appetites (e.g., Zal and Rustam).[5] Pregnancy tested the mother of a hero beyond ordinary limits. As a child, Turkic hero Alpamysh could fling an enemy, shoot a large bow, and kill a playmate even with an unintentional blow. Baby Sajn, hero of another Kazakh epic, had nearly as enormous an appetite as little Rustam. Every three days he consumed one large mare's marrow

135

and fat. Alpamysh's childless parents prayed to a saint and received the child as a gift, and a holy person foretold in a dream that Sajn's parents would be similarly blessed.[6]

Orphaned Heroes, Oedipal Conflict, Exposed Child

Several important themes surround the youth of many heroes. The importance of relationship to the father, or lack thereof, leads to variations on the theme of the fatherless hero. Heroes are sometimes born in the apparent absence of a father-figure (Muhammad) so that in later years they must inquire about their own identities (Faridun, Darab). Miqdad's father died when Miqdad was very young, as did Muhammad's. Iskandar was unaware of his father's identity until he fought his half-brother Dara, whom he had not known was his half-brother. Faridun's renegade son Tur refers to Shah Manuchihr, who would later kill Tur to avenge his grandfather Iraj, as an "unfathered boy-king"[7] because Manuchihr's link to Iraj is via Iraj's daughter rather than through a son.

A fine example of the son who grows from infancy in his father's absence, and is later reunited happily with the father, is that of Salur Kazan in the Turkish Dede Korkut cycle. Uruz grows up thinking his grandfather, the great Bayindir Khan, is his father. Uruz's mother does not tell her son of his father's whereabouts for fear she will lose him as well to the infidels who are holding her husband in far off Tomanin Castle. Discovering the truth almost accidentally, Uruz sets off to free his father. When the infidel king hears of the approaching Muslim force, he promises to set Kazan free if he will get rid of the attackers. Kazan swears to do so.[8]

Kazan confronts the first of the Oghuz heroes, Bamsi Bayrek, and clubs him with Bamsi's own mace. Bamsi manages to utter a boast that his leader is none other than Uruz son of Kazan. Without divulging his own identity, Kazan calls for the attackers' leader to come forth. But first, in a standard narrative tactic to heighten tension, the storyteller brings forth two other major knights whose losses serve to emphasize Kazan's prowess. At last Uruz approaches and slashes his father's shoulder. As the youth prepares to charge again, Kazan reveals his own identity and says: "Summit of my black mountain, my son! Light of my dark eyes, my son! My hero Uruz, my lion Uruz, spare your white-bearded father, son!" They reunite joyfully and return home.[9]

Unmistakable suggestions of Oedipal conflict are nearly universal. Sometimes the theme combines with that of the "exposed child." The albino Zal's father Sam rejects him and abandons him in the wilderness to perish, a fate similar to that of Oedipus. Three moments from the story of Zal's troubled early relationship with his father have inspired numerous miniature paintings. One shows the fabulous Simurgh swooping down to carry the abandoned waif to her nest. The second shows a group of caravan travellers noting the odd sight of an albino child sitting in the nest among the Simurgh's young and learning how he got there. They pass the word along to Sam who, in the third scene, eventually repents of his deed and goes to retrieve the boy and be reconciled with him.[10]

The late medieval story of Arabian hero Sayf at-Tijan ("Sword of Crowns") tells how the child's father Sharahbil leaves the boy's mother, "Thunderbolt of Wars," and abandons the infant to be adopted, first by a gazelle and later by a prince.[11] An important but rather unusual variation on this theme is abandonment by the mother. It occurs twice in the Persian popular romance *Darabnama*. Darab's (Darius) mother, Humay, fears that she will lose her throne to the youth. In a variation on the Moses story, she sets him adrift in a trunk on the Euphrates river. Iskandar's mother also abandons her son, half-brother to Darab.[12]

Some sons are sent away to be educated in the traditional courtly and fighting skills. Bahram Gur's father sends him to Arabia, where king Nuʿman builds him the castle of Khawarnaq.[13] Some part company with the father in anger. Gushtasp, eager for dominion and dissatisfied with his father's inattentiveness to him, leaves first for India and later for Rum (Byzantium). He returns eventually when his father abdicates in his favor. Gushtasp's own son Isfandiyar in turn poses a threat by his desire for the throne. In this instance, father sends son away ostensibly to capture Rustam; but Isfandiyar suspects his father's motives, interpreting his orders as a rebuff even though Gushtasp has promised his son the throne should he manage to bring Rustam back in chains.[14]

Kay Khusraw, greatest of the Kayanian line, is born after the murder of his father, Siyawush. One of the portents that attends his birth is the appearance of Siyawush in a dream to Piran, commander of the Turanian army, announcing the arrival of the child. In a variation on the theme of the exiled son, grandfather Afrasiyab, who orders Siyawush's death, has Kay Khusraw sent to live with shepherds to prevent the boy from discovering either his own true identity or Afrasiyab's complicity in the death of his father. The king later has second thoughts, wishing he had done the boy in to preclude any future threat to his throne. Summoned back to court, Kay Khusraw saves himself by feigning insanity. Afrasiyab is satisfied that the youth is incapable of exacting vengeance and sends him off to genteel retirement (or so the king hopes) in the city of Siyawushgird.[15] Still another variation on the theme has the hero spending time as a shepherd boy as an essential part of his education.[16] Among religious heroes, the notion that all prophets begin as shepherds is an important aspect of their identity.

As suggested above with the story of Uruz and Kazan, a major device is father-son combat, usually with neither aware of the other's identity. This type of encounter builds to a height of pathos few other scenes can generate. Most father-son engagements, like that of Uruz and Kazan, do not end in tragedy. Abu Zayd, hero of the Bani Hilal saga, effects a reconciliation of two tribal groups. Abu Zayd has been sent away from the Hilali and ends up in the protection of the enemy Zahlan harem. He grows to become the champion of Zahlan and is sent out to exact tribute from the recalcitrant Hilali, whose representative in battle is Abu Zayd's father. B. Connelly explains that "the myth of the birth of the hero is the myth of the origins of strife *within* the community . . . [and] can be heard as a tale of oedipal conflict with a strong mother-son incest component. It lends itself easily to a reading on the universal level as a myth of the primal horde killing off the father and absconding with the mother—or, at least, as a tale of all this narrowly averted."[17] Antar fights his disapproving father, Shaddad, and the father wins because the son decides not to put up a serious resistance.[18]

Of those conflicts that end tragically, none surpasses in poignancy Rustam's fight with his son Suhrab. Firdawsi introduces one twist after another in the combat scenes. However often one reads the narrative, its masterful suspense keeps one hoping that it might yet end happily. From the outset, the poet counsels his audience not to judge Rustam too harshly, for a force greater than individual moral weakness has determined events. Firdawsi sees the father-son conflict and the death of the son as part of a much larger picture: "The beasts know their young: the fish in the sea, the zebra in the field. But man, blinded by wrath and greed, cannot tell his son from his foe."[19] Here we have a reflection on death and on the virtual inevitability of conflict even between the nearest of kin. Scenes of the several-day contest and of the boy's death have made for some exquisite miniature paintings.[20]

A variation on the theme has the hero's son murder his father. The Swahili medieval *Utenzi wa Liongo Fumo* (*Epic of King Liongo,* written down finally only in the 1930s) exemplifies this theme. Liongo can be killed only by a copper needle in the navel (a secret only his mother knows). The mother of Liongo's son, herself daughter of the enemy King of Galla, tells her son he must discover the secret of his father's vulnerability. He must pretend he wants to know only in order to be able to protect his father better. Aware of his son's wiles, the father decides to tell the secret anyway. In this rather unusual situation, the son knows the identity of the father and deliberately seeks to kill him. As in the tragedy of Suhrab and Rustam, the son here takes his mother's side.[21]

Sometimes father sets son at odds with a third party so that the son must gain his father's acceptance by winning a contest. Antar and other low-born heroes must face the enormous consequences of the father's ill-concealed shame at the son's social unacceptability. In the case of Faridun's sons, the father himself becomes the third party in the guise of a fierce dragon who tests the mettle of the three youths. This last conflict is related in turn to sibling-rivalry stories (Jacob's sons, Faridun's sons). The theme exists in tension with the absolute importance of being able to account for, and boast about, one's lineage. Only the son who passes his father's test is worthy to claim his proud ancestry, but only the son who responds by claiming a noble descent can hope to pass the test. To that idea we shall return when we consider the hero's family dynamics.

The Sense of Destiny

Heroes vary in the degree to which they are free to choose their own course in life. Oddly enough, it appears that the freest is the picaresque type, for he is by nature protean and almost by definition free of ordinary societal constraints. Among the other types, one finds that a Rustam is less bound by some image of what he must become than are such royal figures as Isfandiyar and Gushtasp, who are driven by a desire to accede to the throne. In addition, the portrayal of the royal hero seems to have developed more under the influence of Zoroastrian tradition and is thus suffused with a stronger sense of direction by a greater power. The

Shahnama often tells of kings visited by a divine presence called the *farr* (or *khwarna*).[22] Lives of religious heroes whose stories have evolved directly under Islamic influence exhibit still more clearly a sense of outside direction and purpose. The death of one good hero, Isfandiyar, at the hands of another good hero, Rustam, remains predominantly tragic and inscrutable. The rejection, suffering, and martyrdom of the prophets and of Muhammad's family, however, occur within the context of a larger design. Folk and royal heroes tend to face their destiny rather stoically, once they realize its inevitabilility, but they rarely grasp the broader implications very clearly. Martyrs know precisely why they live and die, and seem drawn to their fulfillment.

Emblems of Identification, Identity, and Authority

Several identifying features play major roles. Especially important are the names bestowed on a hero, the heirlooms passed down from one hero to another, certain physical traits, and implements or weapons used by specific heroes. One story that links names explicitly with the hero's destiny occurs in the early pages of the *Shahnama*. Iranian king Faridun postpones giving his three sons names "out of delicacy" and "so that no one shall have been able to discuss them." When Faridun does name the three, he chooses names that correspond with aspects of the character and destiny of each. As Faridun sends his servants forth in search of suitable mates for his three sons, he gives instructions that, in addition to being like triplets in physical appearance, the maidens also must be as yet unnamed.[23] The story of how Zal receives his special name from the Simurgh, who cares for him after Zal's father abandons the child on Mt. Alburz, also links name with destiny and experience. Says the wondrous bird, "I bestow on you the name of 'Dastan-i Zand,' because your father practised *dastan* ('Trickery') and enchantment on you. When you return to your own place, command the warrior who will be your counsellor to call you by that name."[24] The youth's father also later gives him the name Zal (Old Man).

Knowing the name of the hero or the enemy can work both good and ill. For the hero who can strike fear into the heart of the foe merely by declaring his identity up front, the name is a potent weapon. For the foe who finds the name itself daunting, certain defeat is imminent. Knowing the enemy's name also gives a warrior an edge. Kinana asks Miqdad's name as a challenge;[25] Puladvand, a Turanian knight, asks Rustam's name on the verge of single combat. When Antar discovers he is not sure of the identity (i.e., name) of the knight he is about to face, he withdraws. The foe, Suwayd, seems to have the upper hand, for he recognizes Antar by his blackness, size, courage, and skill.[26]

In the Turkish story-cycle of Dede Korkut, naming constitutes a very specific function that only the wise Korkut can perform. The tale of Bamsi Beyrek explains, "In those days, my lords, until a boy cut off heads and spilled blood, they used not to give him a name."After the son's initiatory heroic experience, some merchants whose goods the hero has restored to them pay the youth homage in his father's presence. Father asks, "Has my son cut off heads and spilled blood?" They reply, "He has indeed cut off heads and spilled blood and laid men low." "Enough to give the boy a name?" asks the father. "Enough, lord, and more than enough," the merchants respond.[27] Ironically, the criterion of feeding the hungry and clothing the naked later occurs side by side with that of head-lopping as a standard of one's worthiness to sit among the heroic nobles.[28]

Narrative and iconographic conventions link nearly all the great heroes with some specific emblems of identity. One of the several types of emblem is the heirloom, a kind of heroic hand-me-down. Usually the hero comes into possession of such an emblem by sheer serendipity. He either practically stumbles over it, or wrests it from a rival, or simply inherits it from an earlier hero. In the first category, we find Hamza and his sidekick Amr ibn Umayya entering a garden, which turns out to be Solomon's, where they find all sorts of prophetic memorabilia waiting for them—Isaac's horse and saddle, among other useful items. Such prophetic inheritances form a separate category to which we shall return shortly.

Some items mysteriously disappear into the heroic underworld, are lost for a while, and are later rediscovered and reclaimed by a hero. Sometimes the rediscovery happens only after a lengthy search. Jamshid's cup, analogous to the Holy Grail of Arthurian legend, and the thrones of Iskandar and Kay Khusraw are examples.[29] In the case of Kay Khusraw's throne, the heroic object serves to create a virtual pilgrimage center. Iskandar goes to pay respects to the throne in the palace of Sarir.[30] Heirlooms of this sort sometimes undergo various metamorphoses, as in the case of Jamshid's throne, which successive monarchs have remodelled or otherwise modified.

Heroes often inherit special weapons, such as the fork-tipped sword called Dhu ʾl-Faqar, passed down from Muhammad to Ali and so on through the Family of the Prophet. Most miniature paintings of Ali display the famed blade prominently. Faridun is one of the earliest heroes to design his own characteristic emblem. He tells his two older brothers to have smiths make him a heavy mace shaped as an ox head.[31] Faridun's ox-headed mace becomes a symbol of authority and legitimacy as it makes its way down the generations of heroes. In miniature paintings the mace stands out as one of the more obvious iconographic clues as to which figure is the hero. We shall discuss particular qualities and functions of heroic weaponry in greater detail in chapter eleven.

Turkic and other epic tales with a distinctly Shiʿite tinge emphasize the hero's links with Ali or with other members of the Family. Abu Muslim, perhaps best known as the "ax-wielder," receives the black robe and turban of Ali along with the sword of the early mystic-type Salman the Persian.[32] Sayyid Battal receives Husayn's turban, Ali's standard, and the sword of Muhammad al-Hanafiya. Abu Muslim and Sayyid Battal's heroic descendent Malik Danishmand in turn has for his emblems of authority and legitimacy Sayyid Battal's banner and Abu Muslim's black standard. Ali's spiritual successors, the Imams, are said to bear the attributes of Ali—namely, his mule Duldul and his sword—within themselves.[33]

Another distinguishing feature is the set of physical attributes more or less specific to one character. Sometimes these marks furnish artists and viewers with iconographic tags, as in the case of Antar's blackness or Zal's whiteness. But since physical characteristics as such are in general not a primary concern of miniature painters, these qualities as a rule serve a purpose internal to the story: that is, they are mentioned as allowing characters in the narrative to recognize each other but seldom appear as identifiable marks in visual interpretations. Birthmarks discovered or uncovered just in time to avert disaster are one example. Another, more subtle and less frequently used, is the perceived likeness of one hero to another. Kay Khusraw is a good example. He has gone into exile to escape the wrath of his grandfather Afrasiyab, murderer of Kay Khusraw's father, Siyawush. The Iranian nobility, convinced that the reigning king, Kay Kawus, is no longer capable of governing, send the warrior Giw to find the exiled prince. When Giw happens upon the youth, he recognizes him both by the birthmark he inherited from his ancestor Kay Qubad and by his likeness to Siyawush.[34]

More often than not, the male hero's physical characteristics are of minor concern to the narrator. In fact, there seems to be a striking emphasis on the hero's rather ordinary appearance, even his lack of comeliness, especially in the case of the black men. Appearance is decidely subordinate to strength and bravery, for these confer honor. In some stories, it is the hands that figure significantly. The hero's hands are large, surprisingly delicate but very strong, and white, perhaps an allusion to the potent white hand of Moses.[35] Villains are often more readily identifiable by their physical appearance in miniatures than are the heroes: Dahhak with the two snakes sprouting from his shoulders, demons and jinns of strikingly ugly countenance.

A third type of identifying emblem is the implement, such as a weapon or an article of clothing, for which a particular hero is most famous. Rustam's lasso of sixty loops, while difficult to depict in miniatures, often occurs in literary descriptions of him. The son of Zal wears a sort of tunic made of tiger (sometimes leopard) skin, and a helmet decked out with the skin of a leopard's head. Rakhsh, Rustam's rose-colored steed—along with Khusraw Parwiz's black stallion Shabdiz and the rose-hued Gulgun, second fastest horse on earth, that he loans to Shirin—is consistently identifiable in miniatures. Khusraw Parwiz appears most often in red. Bard-hero Dede Korkut's *kopuz* (lute) also falls in this category, although I know of no images that depict him. In the story of Ushun Koja's sons Egrek and Segrek (retold in greater detail in chapter ten), the lute appears without explanation in the possession of Segrek, who has gone to find his long-lost brother. When Egrek comes to fight the sleeping Segrek, unaware that he is his brother, he picks up Segrek's lute. Segrek awakens and is about to run Egrek through with his sword, but stops out of respect for Dede Korkut's lute in his brother's hands.[36]

A few other items facilitate identification of a hero in miniature paintings, but they are generally specific to a particular story. These include such things as settings in which only one hero could be situated—the seven domed palaces of Bahram Gur, Alexander's talking tree, Joseph's well, Jonah's whale. In this category, one could also include the elaborate spiked chariot which Isfandiyar devises to kill the Simurgh, and the vulture-powered throne on which Kay Kawus attempts to fly to heaven (although one could mistake it for a similar device employed by the evil King Nimrod).

Among religious heroes, several identifying items appear regularly. Muhammad's green robe becomes, by association, the garment of choice of a number of other prophets. That robe is one of relatively few specific items in the heroic religious iconography of Islamicate painting. Muhammad's vesture approaches the status of an heirloom in that one or another earlier prophet wears green also, as do members of the Prophet's family on occasion. Numerous other heirlooms, however, occur in stories of the religious heroes. Some have already been mentioned; others include Adam's sarcophagus, Moses's staff, and Joseph's shirt.

A standard device for recognition of one character by another is the amulet, usually a gift from some important relative like the mother or father; a talisman, sometimes a direct gift from God that protects the hero; or a birthmark that the hero does not ordinarily leave open to view, but which becomes visible during the course of a fight or revelatory conversation. In one of the best-known and most ironic cases of recognition come too late, Rustam's son Suhrab wears an amulet Rustam himself had left with the boy's mother, Tahmina, to give the child so that his father might later recognize him. In their battle to the death, Rustam sees the sign after he has mortally wounded Suhrab. A Turkic variation on that theme has Köroghlu leave an armband with the mother of his son Hasan Bey. After the boy has grown up, he sets off to find his absent father. The two meet and wrestle, until Köroghlu spies the band and recognizes Hasan.[37] In *Sirat Antar* we find Antar's son Ghasub preparing to behead ad-Dahmar. Just in time ad-Dahmar spots an amulet on Ghasub and asks whence it came. Hearing of its origin, ad-Dahmar reveals that he wears its twin on his own shoulder. Antar spares him and is reunited with a whole clan of long-lost relatives.[38]

Talismans are both protective and indicative of the hero's status. Swahili tradition includes one epic composed entirely around the theme of a talisman granted by God, a valuable stone wrapped in green silk with a name of God known only to Solomon and Muhammad. Related thematically to Solomon's famous seal-ring, which once fell into the hands of a demon, the Swahili talisman is transferred by angelic messenger from the neck of the villain to that of Ali, who then slays the villain. The equal-opportunity device protects and empowers villain and hero alike.[39]

Disguise, Mistaken Identity, Recognition

Finally, the theme of deliberate disguise and/or mistaken identity appears often. One must distinguish between disguise employed for strategic or tactical purposes and those kinds of masking, denial, or failure to identify that result from some human deficiency in a character. This theme ranges from simple disguise to the much more subtle and heart-rending problem of father and son failing to recognize each other. Examples of the strategic or tactical device might include the following, among others. Several of our heroes go off in disguise to another royal court, posing as their own ambassadors. Alexander goes thus disguised to Dara, to the Emperor of China, and to Qaydafa (alias Candace, Nushaba), Queen of Andalusia, who recognizes Alexander from a portrait she has had made before the king arrives in her land. Disguise as merchant provides another relatively common device. Rustam tries this ploy successfully when he goes to Turan on behalf of Kay Khusraw. In the Antar story, the invaders pose as merchants to get past the tree known as the Mistress of Fires and Lights in the Land of Ensigns. The Turkic hero Uruz, son of Salur Kazan, and his men dress as merchants as they enter infidel territory to rescue Kazan; their disguise apparently lacks credibility, for the Christians immediately spot the ruse and call the outsiders liars.[40]

Women sometimes dress in men's clothing to effect some ruse. In *Sirat Antar,* Ujubat al-Anam dresses as a man and lures Safwan and Antar to her father Hammam's castle in the Land of Flags and Ensigns.[41] A Serbocroatian epic tells how the woman betrothed to Djerzelez Alija disguises herself as a warrior to carry off the queen of Baghdad.[42] In the story of Umar an-Nu'man in the *Thousand and One Nights,* the hero Sharkan confronts an army of Amazons disguised as Christian men. Once he realizes who they are, he stops short of killing Abriza, and they join forces.[43] Occasionally the disguise is reversed, with a man putting on women's clothing.[44]

Questions of heroic identity are more complex and subtle than the relatively simple surface indicators might lead one to believe. If it is true that the heroes of the older epics and romances are simpler, less self-possessed and enjoy less self-knowledge than those

145

of later works, especially of the romantic epics, it is nevertheless equally true that their identity as characters is far narrower than their meaning as heroes. A poet like Firdawsi had few illusions about the underlying complexity of human experience. The directness and apparent simplicity of the storyteller's art is a thin veil over a deep reflection on things human. We run the risk of missing out on that fact if we apply uncritically the canons of twentieth-century psychological insight. Firdawsi's understanding of personhood and human development (and that of other writers as well) may not seem at first to be at the center of his concerns, but that is because his mode of expression is so different from what the contemporary reader has come to expect.

J. S. Meisami makes some helpful observations on the matter of identity in the context of Persian courtly romances. Without suggesting that her observations are transferrable whole-cloth to other genres and cultural settings, one can profitably take from them some hints as to how to formulate related questions in the broader context of the present survey. Meisami analyzes how Nizami's *Khusraw and Shirin* "focuses on the problem of the personhood of its protagonist Khusraw and the manner in which this is established (or revealed) in the course of his quest for union with his beloved."[45] A key motif in the process is that of disguise or non-recognition. One of the most-often depicted scenes illustrates Khusraw's discovering Shirin as she bathes in a stream. Neither knows the other is the beloved. Khusraw, in disguise, wonders what harm there would be in possessing this woman and her fine horse (actually the one he has lent her). Though he has already fixed his heart on Shirin, he allows himself to covet this woman as well. Shirin, naked, senses that this must be her beloved. Nizami contrasts the king's guile and mixed motives with the Armenian princess's simplicity and transparency. Shirin in turn contrasts sharply with the outwardly deceitful Shakar, for whom Khusraw falls and who claims she does not deserve her reputation for loose morals.

Khusraw's ambivalence raises the larger question of whether he can choose to change from a self-centered to a genuinely loving individual. As king, he believes he can have whatever he chooses to possess; as lover, he leaves much to be desired. Farhad the sculptor models the kind of single-minded and selfless devotion Shirin deserves in a lover. Meanwhile Khusraw refuses to realize that Farhad poses no threat to him, for Shirin has professed her love for Khus-

146

raw alone. As lover, Khusraw wrongs Shirin by infidelity; as king, he does Farhad the ultimate injustice of plotting to precipitate his death. At length Khusraw's choice of justice, as king, and of care, as lover, evidences change and growth in his self-awareness and identity.[46]

Applying some of those suggestions to the broader range of heroic themes, it is useful to think of identity as directly related to the choices one makes. Among the options offered our heroes, we find the following, expressed here as dyads or dichotomies: dominion or contemplative withdrawal, exercise of brute force or attentiveness to the demands of statecraft, great wealth or modest sufficiency, honor by death or shame by retreat, amoral adventurism or interpersonal responsibility, violence or love, loyalty or treason, veracity or treachery, spontaneity or caution. Heroes, of course, almost always choose what we would expect a hero to choose, even if only in the end. Heroes do err, and, except in the often unbuttoned cosmos of the popular romance, they usually exhibit some capacity for learning from the patterns of their choices.

Some heroes neither agonize over their choices, nor face a particularly challenging array of subtly variegated options. In many instances, that fact is a function of the limitations of a genre rather than an indication of the storyteller's (or his original audience's) lack of insight. Most heroes face turning points and must make momentous decisions. In the more refined literature of the court, there is often greater scope for nuancing the moral values demanded of an authentic hero. In the rough and tumble universe of the folk warrior, ethical junctures frequently appear in the form of external obstacles to be overcome. In the words of H. T. Norris, "As each obstacle is cleared away on the route of his onward march, so an obstacle is removed in the mystery of his birth and true origin and lineage. Hence, the conflict without is also a conflict within. The discovery of the uttermost parts of the earth is at the same time the self-discovery of the hero."[47] In chapter eight we turn to the hero's mandate to discover both outer and inner worlds.

Chapter Eight

Journey as Context of Quest and Test

Reading between the lines of Islamicate heroic stories, one can argue persuasively that the search for identity ultimately motivates all heroic human striving. As for expressed motives for undertaking journeys, our sources describe a relatively limited range. Heroes most frequently set out to intercept and vanquish some foe whose advances threaten the peace of the realm, or whose adherence to an alien creed affronts the ruler's need for conformity among his subjects. These include, for example, Rustam and Hamza, and perhaps Hang Tuah in his capacity as royal emissary. Others bivouac their way across the known—and unknown—world in hope of global conquest. Alexander stands out most prominently here, along with several famous monarchs of later history, such as Sulayman the Magnificent and Akbar, each of whom commissioned major works to chronicle their own world-grabbing travels.

A motive rather common especially for several of the folk hero types is a gallant willingness to undertake a rescue. Champions march off to respond to a cry for help from outnumbered forces, or to liberate someone held hostage. Antar, Ali, and Miqdad are among the best examples of this motive. Perhaps next in frequency come journeys to win the beloved. In most cases, such motivation remains secondary to some larger purpose, often appearing as a subplot, as in Antar's adventure to the Land of Flags and Ensigns ostensibly to unite Safwan, son of Lawn az-Zalam, with his beloved Uʿjubat al-Anam. However, the romantic motive does come to the fore as in the cases of Nizami's Bahram Gur and Khusraw Parwiz.

An urge to defend challenged personal honor spurs some heroes on. A somewhat less differentiated search for truth or sanctity or immortality drives still others. Hang Tuah and his companions head for the mountains, where dwells a guru who can impart to them both the martial arts and a deeper, almost mystical knowledge. Of course, some heroic figures journey for a combination of these reasons. Sometimes—as in the case of the Prophet's Hijra, his Night Journey and Ascension, and the Pilgrimage—journeys become paradigmatic for a people traveling both as a community and as individual seekers. Finally, picaresque heroes usually travel out of more spontaneous, ad hoc motives. They move about because a particular place or setting suits their immediate, and probably ephemeral, purposes.

Journey in this context becomes a metaphor for the larger picture of the hero's life. In a later chapter we shall explore some possible ways of understanding what such explicit motivations might suggest or allow of deeper interpretations. First, some sense of the more obvious aspects of the journey theme, and its numerous sub-themes, will be helpful. These will include the necessity of guidance and the various types of guides, the revelatory function of dreams and omens, other worlds and faraway lands, trials and ordeals, the romantic element, and the return home.

Need of a Guide

A special guide or authority figure often leads the hero on the journey. Guidance is personified or embodied in a number of different forms, corresponding more or less to the geography within which the journey takes place. Some guides function rather like scouts or trackers, interpreting some earthly landscape. Others use ordinary signs as clues to the extraordinary or lead the journeyer across the divide between two worlds. Still others show the way in oracular fashion but do not actually accompany the pilgrim on the road. Guides can be either human or not, anthropomorphic or zoomorphic, even dendromorphic, as in the case of Alexander's talking tree, and so forth. Here are some major examples of the various types.

Living human guides who know the earthly terrain play a fairly basic role as pathfinders. Even Rustam, who accomplishes his first five trials without guidance, eventually receives help. That he accomplishes the first five solo may be a clue that the stories are less polished than the accounts of Isfandiyar's seven courses, for the latter has a guide in all of the seven.[1] In his fifth feat, Rustam overcomes Awlad, a warrior sent to do him in, and coerces him into acting as his guide. In his march to the west, Antar consults his brother Shaybub. With his firsthand knowledge of Sudan's harsh wastes, Shaybub claims he can lead the warriors through with con-

149

fidence.[2] This kind of trailblazer plays the least significant role within the larger scheme of the heroic endeavor.

The second major function of the guide is to point out inner meanings of things, to initiate and to instruct in a spiritual or otherwise arcane and inaccessible tradition—either a body of doctrine or a more generalized knowledge about the underpinnings of human life and such mysteries as death, evil, and power.

In the Javanese *Hikayat Shah Mardan,* a kind of Indo-Muslim romance, the hero returns to his home country after studying abroad. After he encounters the denizens of at least two well-guarded palaces and marries a princess, Shah Mardan continues his journey. Two significant spiritual guides figure in his quest. The first, Shaykh Salam ad-Din, instructs the hero in *ilmu hikmat* ("wisdom," a Javanization of two Arabic terms) and leads him through forty days of asceticism.[3] His second guide is of a different sort, as we shall see shortly.

Our discussion of heroic geography will deal with an important goal of, or way station on, several heroic journeys: the City of Brass. In the present context, the *Thousand and One Nights* story of the City of Brass offers an interesting connection. A pious shaykh guides an expedition to the West in search of Solomon's fabled brass bottles that imprison the Jinn (more popularly known as the Genies in the Lamps) who once worked for the king. At one crucial juncture, the shaykh identifies the Black Castle after the band has wandered through a desert. He then cautions the travelers not to let the gossamer enchantments of the place lure them over the walls to their deaths. The shaykh penetrates the sheer deception of the place, manages to enter, and opens the gates from within.[4] He demonstrates a type of spiritual guidance, even though his counsel does not contain explicitly Islamic religious teaching. The burden of his guidance concerns the need to distinguish appearance from reality, form from meaning *(sura, maʿna).*

Several major heroes seek counsel from sages, hermits, and ascetics of various kinds. Dwelling typically in caves, in huts, or on mountains, these guides offer advice about a range of issues. A key theme is the impermanence of human existence and the vanity of power. Scenes of "Prince with Holy Man" abound in miniature paintings, especially of the Mughal dynasty. Royal heroes seem to seek out these usually aged oracles more often than do other heroic types. One of the most-often depicted is Iskandar's consultation with the hermit who lives in a cave beneath Mount Alburz.[5]

Another type of guide to whom only royal heroes have recourse are philosophers. These are urbanized, court-based counterparts of the hermit figure. Unlike the guides heroes meet along the way, the philosopher does not typically freelance, but rather functions as part of the royal retinue. The philosopher is a character type most famous in connection with Iskandar. Aristotle, Iskandar's teacher, joins the not-always-congenial company of several other philosophers in Nizami's two-part *Iskandarnama*. In all of the Iskandar narratives, the king employs a coterie of philosophers as part of his entourage and brings them out to render opinions on all that he encounters. Sometimes traveling with the king, they form a phalanx of wisdom around the knowledge-thirsty monarch, making him the beneficiary of their sagacious testaments.[6] A second type associated mostly with the court is the astrologer. Always consulted at moments of crucial decision, the astrologer pronounces on the auspiciousness of particular times and places in relation to the expressed designs of his patron. Astrologers also judge the potential of infants destined for either the success or the downfall of the royal house. Non-royal personages occasionally enlist the astrologer's services, but with somewhat less frequency. A careful look at some miniature paintings of court scenes may reveal a magus or astrologer off to the side, taking a reading on a brass astrolabe in preparation for delivering advice to the sovereign.[7]

Sometimes the hero enlists the aid of a guide to cross over from one world to another; sometimes the guide simply appears unsolicited to offer timely counsel. In some cases, the wanderer enters the other world alone but has gone there precisely to find guidance from among the shades. In other instances, the guide comes to the seeker from beyond the grave (or in the case of a guide who never died, from beyond the ordinary world) to bestow important knowledge. Here we shall include angelic guides, the spirits of prophets and other deceased persons, and that remarkable phenomenon called the Simurgh.

Angelic guides make frequent apparitions. Several times in the *Shahnama*, the angel Surush materializes to give some guidance or warning to one of the heroes. Surush intervenes, for example, just as Faridun prepares to deliver the final mace blow to Dahhak, and tells the hero to remove the villain and chain him to Mount Damavand. Royal hero Khusraw Parwiz likewise benefits from Surush's felicitous arrival. During one of his skirmishes with the usurper Bahram Chubin, Khusraw retreats up a mountain with the challenger in hot pursuit. With a sword at his back and granite ahead, it appears Khusraw will be overcome. He utters a fervent prayer. Surush drops in on a special horse, gives the hero a lift, and delivers him to the other side of the mountain. Somewhat after the manner of a Gabriel figure, Surush reveals to Khusraw that he will become king and must hold to the faith. Surush functions as more than a mere *angelus ex machina,* for the messenger clarifies the hero's mission and his appearance marks a downturn in Bahram Chubin's fortunes. Both scenes have inspired some delightful miniatures, usually fairly literal in their interpretation.[8]

Such occasional guidance is also the province of Gabriel in more explicitly religious narratives. An important player in Swahili epic literature in particular, "Jiburili the Teacher" silently "slides down" just when the going is roughest. First, God instructs the archangel, then Gabriel delivers the crucial instructions to Muhammad, who alone sees the apparition, though others may notice a heavenly aroma.[9] As God's messenger to Muhammad, Gabriel mediates divine guidance. One predictable message: now is the time to call in super-hero Ali to save the day.[10]

Gabriel's most celebrated and extended stint as guide finds him squiring Muhammad from Makka to Jerusalem (*Israꞌ,* "Night Journey"), through hell and the various heavens and back to earth (*Micraj,* "Ascension"). A popular Swahili version based largely on the hadith found in the *Mishkat al-Masabih (Niche of Lamps)*[11] is still recited on the evening of the Ascension, the 27th of (the lunar month of) Rajab. Muhammad makes intermediate stops in Madina and Bethlehem. Along the way, the archangel gives Muhammad instructions on how to deal with each situation. He explains what they are witnessing and introduces the Prophet to the various figures they encounter. Gabriel opens the gates at each level of heaven, for he knows the password needed to answer the questions of several of the gatekeepers.[12]

In his role as chief angelic guide, Gabriel appears in many miniature paintings. Most important are those illustrating Persian and Turkish versions of the Micraj such as typically occur either as prefaces to lengthy works of didactic or mystical poetry or as separate works devoted entirely to the Prophet's Journey. Painters depict Gabriel leading Muhammad, astride Buraq, through a firmament crowded with lesser angels and through scenes of hell's utter horror and torment. Toward the higher rungs of heaven's ladder, Gabriel has to retreat from God's presence and leave the Prophet to take the last steps alone, in keeping with the Tradition: "I have a moment with God in which no one comes between me and my Lord."[13]

Two prophets who enter the hero's space and time from another dimension and who are associated particularly with wisdom and access to the realms of spirit play important roles: Khadir and Luqman. In chapter five, we described the general background and development of a fascinating figure called Khadir (usually pronounced "Khizr"), especially in relation to the prophet Moses and as a key spiritual initiator in the Islamic mystical tradition. Here we shall look at Khadir's role as Iskandar's guide as the world-conqueror sets aside his usual pursuits to search for the Water of Life. For all of Khadir's vaunted skill in guidance, his success rate is not impressive, but that failing appears not to be his fault. The storytellers seem to be suggesting that some goals simply lie beyond human capability regardless of how clearly the path is indicated. Firdawsi has Iskandar meet Khadir when the king and his men, already headed for the Land of Darkness, come to a vast city in the West, and Iskandar goes about it looking for a guide. Surrendering himself at first unreservedly to Khadir, the *Shahnama*'s Iskandar produces two seal rings that will provide light for himself and for Khadir. Three days on, the path diverges, and Iskandar strikes off on his own, while Khadir takes the right path, bathes in the Water of Life, and returns to God.[14] (see Figure 11)

According to several versions of the popular romance *Iskandarnama*, only Aristotle, Iskandar, and Khadir know of the existence of the Water of Life. A Persian variant has Khadir appear and offer his services just when the king asks the people who live at the edge of the world how they became believers. They tell him Khadir taught them, whereupon the guide materializes and asks Iskandar whether he intends to go to the Land of Darkness. During the course of the journey, Khadir guides the army by day and vanishes at nightfall. A series of intermediate territories provide the storyteller an occasion for talking about how the true faith is

Figure 11: Khadir (Khizr) and Ilyas (Elijah) at the Water of Life. Note Alexander in the background.

spread through prophets God has sent there. In this version, Khadir goes ahead, discovers the spring, and returns to inform Iskandar; but when the two retrace Khadir's steps, the spring has vanished.[15]

The Malay *Hikayat Iskandar* further Islamizes the story. God intervenes in the life of Iskandar and saves him from Iblis's temptations to haughtiness by sending Khadir to set the king straight. Quite smitten by Satan's wiles, Iskandar does not take kindly to the guide's interference. A battle ensues. Khadir wears the king down, and he submits. In exchange for their becoming Muslims, Iskandar and his troops will be given leave to conquer the whole earth. Khadir's much expanded role in the Malay story has him guiding Iskandar from the outset of the king's travels, and only at the end does Khadir lead Iskandar into the Land of Darkness. As in Firdawsi's rendition, the two become separated, and the guide alone finds the spring.[16]

Of lesser importance but still significant is Luqman. We spoke above of the journey of the Javanese hero Shah Mardan. As he continues his odyssey, the young prince meets the prophet and sage Luqman. They engage in lengthy discourse about a wide range of Islamic religious and mystical subjects. Their discussion reads like a Javanese Muslim catechism, including everything from the basics of Qur'an recitation and ritual prayer to the more subtle matters of self-knowledge and the interrelationships of the "four paths," *shari'a* (religious law as a whole), *tariqa* (the mystical way), *haqiqa* (the innermost or ultimate reality), and *ma'rifa* (the final goal of intimate knowledge of God).[17] Shah Mardan's guidance is episodic rather than continuous, and the guides function more as stations along the way than as providers of a map. In this case, Luqman performs a function related to that of Khadir in the stories of many saints and mystics. Khadir often appears to such religious heroes and initiates them into the religious order, sometimes investing them symbolically with the patched frock of the *faqir* ("mendicant"). Suhrawardi describes another variation on the theme of wisdom as guide. He speaks of a "Castle-fortress of the Soul" at whose door stands a young spiritual guide called Eternal Wisdom, who journeys incessantly without ever leaving home.[18]

Zal and son Rustam have a special mentor in the Simurgh, the fabulous bird who dwells in the distant Alburz mountains and appears occasionally to advise them. The bird has formed a special bond with Zal, raising the infant after his father Sam abandons him in the wilderness. At the birth of Rustam, the Simurgh responds to the burning of one of its feathers by bringing the secret of Caesarian section to Zal. When Rustam falls from battle wounds at one point, Zal again enlists the Simurgh's knowledge of healing to repair Rustam. And in the fateful moment of his clash with Isfandiyar, the Simurgh tells Rustam the secret of his adversary's vulnerability. You may recall that Isfandiyar had killed a Simurgh and become invulnerable by bathing in its blood, but Isfandiyar had closed his eyes and so was not shielded there. The Simurgh has provided miniaturists with a special opportunity to display their imagination and palette in creating the extraordinarily decorative creature.[19]

Iskandar's Talking Tree both reinforces and breaks out of the pattern of the king's sources of guidance. The world-conqueror finds the Tree's utterances just as hard to hear as those of his other oracles. He almost always seems to wish he had never asked. Beyond that, the Tree is strikingly novel and imaginative. In a letter to his mother, Iskandar describes how the Tree's male heads told him by day that he would soon die, and how the female heads informed him by night that he would not return home.[20]

Revelatory Dreams and Omens

Among the more important interpretative devices the stories use to describe the journey are dreams and omens. Ability to interpret dreams is one of a guide's most important qualifications, especially in connection with a court setting. Most heroes have dreams now and then. Dreams are especially common in the popular romantic epics, but are more abundant in the later works. Even in earlier literature, such as the *Shahnama*, royal figures tend to have dreams more often than do warriors or knights. An example from a courtly romance is Khusraw Parwiz's grandfather Anushirwan's appearance in a dream to promise Khursaw a horse, a throne, and a wife.[21]

According to W. Hanaway, dreams in Persian popular romance literature perform several functions. They can serve to articulate motives for new action, to warn in time to avert a disaster, or to provide instructions on proper action. Hanaway suggests that the use of dreams in the romances results from a blend of older Iranian literary themes with a "general Islamic fund of Popular lore, partly Persian and partly Middle Eastern."[22]

Dreams sometimes include the occurrence of omens. Before venturing off into the Sudan to avenge the honor of Antar's consort, Ghamra, both Antar and his brother Shaybub have dreams. Antar dreams a black animal issues from his loins, becomes a bird of prey, and attacks him viciously. As it is about to lift him skyward, he awakes in terror, convinced the dream foretells his imminent death. Shaybub tries to persuade Antar that he was merely suffering from indigestion, offering as proof an account of his own dream: a bird of prey attacked him but then changed into a gazelle and "a jesting human." Their cousin Urwa offers interpretative advice, warning them to be careful, for eagles and the like portend war.[23]

Other Worlds and Faraway Lands

Specific details of the places in which heroes travel will occupy chapter nine, on heroic cosmologies. For the moment it will suffice to mention but briefly the principal conceptions of place as it relates to the heroes' experience. Journey motifs frequently wear a cloak of mystery. Sometimes a hero's full name includes an epithet that suggests how central to the character's image the journey theme is. Antar's *kunya* (a kind of honorific name), for example, *al-mughallis,* can be taken to mean "traveler in the darkness." With or without such an epithet, heroes almost always go to a far-off land, often described as some other world or realm beyond ordinary human experience. Alexander goes to the Land of Darkness and seeks the Water of Life; Bahram Gur travels the seven climes; Joseph goes unwillingly into Egypt, whither Moses too accepts a mission; Hang Tuah acts as royal emissary to the far corners of the globe; Hamza wanders the length and breadth of the known and unknown worlds; Muhammad embarks on a many-leveled tour through the hells and the heavens.

In non-religious tales, the journey may be simply one of conquest for the glory of the tribe. But the goal of the religious hero often expands into one of more cosmic dimensions, so that the journey becomes paradigmatic for believers: the Prophet's leaving home (the Hijra), his farewell Pilgrimage, and his Ascension are all to be emulated. In brief, three sorts of goals correspond roughly to the three kinds of guidance mentioned above: destinations on earth, places at the edge of this world, sites beyond this world. Our next chapter will provide details as to some of the principal places in each of those levels. Here we shall focus on some of the major happenings along the road.

Trials and Ordeals

Among the numerous difficulties a hero faces in transit we find a surprisingly broad range, from clear polar oppositions of obvious good against obvious evil, to a sense that one must often choose between or among more than one good. The heroic struggle, on which we will focus more sharply in chapter eleven, assumes a variety of outward shapes; it is essential to the larger metaphor of journey. There is never a shortage of dragons, demons, villains, untamable seas and uncharted wastes, sirens, riddle-mongers, and martyr-makers standing between mission and fulfillment. But the often fantastic outward manifestation of the trial masks the deeper issues of the mystery of evil, human mortality, the enormous power of nature, and fear of the unknown.

Tests take several forms. Sometimes conflict emphasizes physical prowess, bravery and skill in battle. Other trials address the hero's moral fiber, virtue, or strength of religious commitment; still others his wit, judgment, and political savvy. We have already described Faridun's test of his three sons as a guage of their aptness for leadership. As to specific themes, several types of test predominate: single combat against an enemy of unimaginable strength and fury; struggle against the elements and the forces of nature; conquest of a reputedly impregnable stronghold; killing a force of evil, as embodied in either animal or demonic form; winning the hand of a coy beloved. We shall treat the theme of single combat in greater detail in chapter eleven. Here are some examples of the other themes.

Sometimes the trials occur in stylized sets of three or seven, as in the Seven Feats of both Rustam and Isfandiyar. In a helpful comparison and contrast of the seven-fold tests, M. Maguire concludes that the Isfandiyar cycle is modeled on that of Rustam, but that several differences suggest a development in characterization. Both heroes must pass through the trials on the way to fulfilling a greater mission. Rustam takes a dangerous shortcut to Mazandaran to rescue Kay Kawus, held captive by the White Diw; Isfandiyar heads for the Brazen Hold (no relation to the City of Brass in

Arabic lore) in order to kill the Turanian Arjasp, who had killed his uncle Zarir.[24] Beneath the surface, however, differences abound.

Rustam's actions evidence little complexity in motivation, whereas Isfandiyar's deeds occur in the context of what Maguire calls a "religious, intellectual and conscious Zoroastrian ideology" and as a result of both religious fervor and the desire to get his father Gushtasp to abdicate. Rustam engages the forces of nature and malevolence because they occur in the ordinary course of a lone knight's existence. For Isfandiyar, life is more complex. His actions fit into a more coherent whole that relates to his royal destiny. When Rustam does battle, he fights, so to speak, bare-fisted and at close quarters. Isfandiyar employs strategy and special devices, such as the spiked chariot with which he ensnares the Simurgh or the magical chain which he receives from Zoroaster in Paradise. Of their seven trials, the only one the two heroes have in common is the fourth, the killing of the witch who appears first as a lovely woman who offers the hero a picnic lunch. As Maguire points out, the heroes both discover the ruse by uttering the name of God; but Rustam says it accidentally, whereas Isfandiyar's authentic devotion prompts him to say that he would prefer God as his drinking companion. At that moment, the woman reverts to her true appearance, and the hero slices her in two. (Here is the theme of woman as temptress, to which we shall return in a moment.)

Few sequences of action have captured the attention of miniature painters as the Seven Feats have. Virtually every large-scale illustrated manuscript of the *Shahnama* includes images of all fourteen scenes. (See Figure 12.) But as Maguire suggests, the painters rarely attempt to express the major differences in the underlying meanings of the two heroes.[25] One major exception occurs in some illustrations of the single combat between Rustam and Isfandiyar, and to that we will return in the context of the larger category of struggle.

Trials typically unfold episodically in the process of journeying, rather than in more organically integrated sequences. Still, the trials are never purely isolated, *ad hoc* adventures; at some level or other they connect the hero to a larger scene. Alexander conquers a monster dragon on an island in the western ocean; here the dragon is the ocean, so that one can see Iskandar as "representative of the divine subdual of the ocean."[26] His is a constant strug-

Figure 12: Isfandiyar battles a dragon.

gle against forces of evil and chaos that situates Iskandar as guardian of cosmic integrity. Hamza seems to function in a similar way, though perhaps on a less lofty plane. For Hamza, too, every new scene brings its confrontation with the bizarre and terrifying. The very fabric of his daily existence is made of the extraordinary.

Heroic trials can stand between the hero and a special destiny. Royal heroes must sometimes remove certain obstacles to their achievement of the throne. Bahram Gur, for example, has to fight two lions that stand guard over the crown. Siyawush has to convince Afrasiyab that he can hunt and play polo with the best of princes. A frequent theme in the male hero's quest to establish himself as a man and dependable ally is the storming of a stronghold to release someone held captive there. Antar goes to the Hisn al-Uqab ("Fortress of Eagles," so lofty is it) to release his two sons.[27] Numerous Turkic heroes must prove themselves to their fathers, as do the sons of Faridun. Of this we have already seen examples in chapter three, and more will follow in later chapters.

On his mystical journey to the world beyond, Muhammad must pass several trials in the form of small tests. On their way through hell, a voice calls Muhammad from the right. Had he responded, the Jew calling would have turned all Muslims into Jews. From the left calls a Christian; Muhammad is silent, or his community would become Christian. Before them stands a beautiful woman, but Muhammad resists the temptation, for within, she—the world—is emptiness and misery. When the travellers arrive at Jerusalem, Muhammad asks for something to drink. Angels present three bowls (two or four in some versions) from which he must choose: wine, water (honey in one version), or milk. He passes the test by choosing milk, which is neither too rich nor too abstemious. As in Iraj's steering a middle course between rashness and cowardice, Muhammad wins through balance and moderation. In every instance, the integrity and welfare of the Muslim community depend on Muhammad's successful completion of the trials.[28]

Some stories cast women in the role of temptress. Several heroes' trials occur when a woman tries either to seduce them or to get them to make an unwise choice. Afrasiyab's wife Sudaba falls in love with her step-son Siyawush. When the youth refuses her advances, she poisons the king's mind against the prince, so that Siyawush must prove his innocence by riding through a bonfire. He passes the test, but the aftermath of the event eventually leads to the prince's murder and to renewed hostilities between Iran and Turan. The prophet Yusuf meets his biggest test when Zulaykha tries to seduce him. He too pays for his virtue with emprisonment, but their story ends more happily than Siyawush's. Both Rustam and Isfandiyar survive one phase of their complex trials by seeing through the false appearances of a demoness who offers a free lunch.[29]

Romantic Elements: Marriages Fated and Forbidden

Romantic elements abound. They include the following, to mention only the most important. Hero wins the beloved by passing tests, usually set by the father/king, as with Antar and Abla; or by getting around obstacles, as when Zal climbs to Rudaba. A marriage can symbolize world conquest through marriage-alliance. Mystical marriage can suggest a spiritual fulfillment, as in aged Zulaykha's return to youth at the sight of Joseph, and their subsequent union.

In the story of Umar an-Nuʿman in the *Thousand and One Nights*, the hero Sharkan heads for Christian territory to fight the infidels. Before he can fulfill his duty, however, he meets Abriza the Amazon and falls in love with her. After the two engage each other in combat, Sharkan abducts Abriza, who then agrees to become a Muslim. Unfortunately, when Sharkan's father, Umar, tries to seduce Abriza by using a drug, the woman manages to flee the palace only to die at the hands of her guide. V. Christides enumerates the following subordinate motifs in the story: a duel between hero and woman warrior, hero's fight with Amazon band, hero's love from afar, kidnapping of foreign princess, resistance from woman's parents, use of narcotic to seduce, conversion to Islam, father-son rivalry, and hero of mixed descent (Arab and Greek).[30]

The stories of Rustam and Tahmina, Bizhan and Manizha, Zal and Rudaba, Khusraw and Shirin show several more key romantic motifs. In each instance the woman is an outsider; the hero who virtually personifies Iran marries a non-Iranian woman. The parents of Rudaba and Manizha protest vehemently at the prospect of their daughters' marriage to foreigners. In the romance of Bizhan and Manizha, the abduction and seduction with the aid of drugs works the other way around: Manizha waylays Bizhan and has him spirited away to her palace.[31] An important metaphor for the heroic romance is the hunt. Both in literature and in the visual arts, storytellers have exploited the rich possibilities of this image to describe the complexities of the hero and heroine's mutual pursuit. We have already spoken of how the hunt can destroy a potential relationship, as in the case of Bahram Gur and his lady friend Azada. Perhaps the best examples of the role of hunting in the unfolding of the romance come from Nizami's tale of Khusraw Parwiz and Shirin. With consummate delicacy, the poet transforms the chase after game into an image of courtship.

Finally, the hero must return home with the prize of his quest, to continue his role among ordinary mortals. Sometimes the return is the most challenging part of the journey. In religious material especially, heroes become newly aware of the call to serve humanity, to teach, to share a revelation, to govern with new wisdom. Princes return from exile to the throne, kings return from campaigns, Alexander emerges from the Land of Darkness, Ali comes to Kufa to claim the allegiance of all Muslims, Muhammad descends to earth again. With the following sample of heroic itineraries, we turn to a more detailed look at the terrains and worlds through which the heroic journey leads.

Samples of Heroic Itineraries

Iskandar: Rum (throne)—conquers Egypt—Iran as own messenger—Euphrates to defeat Dara—Persepolis (throne)—India via Oman to defeat Porus (Kashmir, Sarandib/Sri Lanka the capital of Kayd, Island of Devalpas, India, Kashmir by sea)—Makka (pilgrimage) via Oman—attacks Egypt—Yemen—Iraq—Armenia—Andalus (Spain)—Sarir—India—China—Transoxiana (fights Russians)—back to Andalus—searches for Water of Life (through various enchanted or bewitched places to Mt. Qaf and Land of Darkness)—crosses China Sea (wall against Gog and Magog)—from China via Siyawushgird to Sind and Yemen—dies in Babylon, whence his body is carried to Alexandria (Egypt).

Hamza: Born in Makka—Yemen—Makka—Ctesiphon (historic Sasanian capital)—Sri Lanka (first by land, then by sea, meeting Khadir several times)—Ctesiphon—Rum—Egypt—Ctesiphon—carried by his horse, wounded, to Makka—

Golden City on Mt. Qaf—various sailing adventures, shipwreck, returned by Paris to Qaf—Tangiers—Aleppo—castle in Turkistan—Makka . . . (similarly varied travels continue).

Rustam: Royal capital—Mazandaran and his "Seven Feats" (just south of Caspian)—China to rescue shah—fights Turanians (northern Iran)—Samangan and romance with Tahmina—Sistan—kills Suhrab in Iran—Sistan as exile—Hindustan—returns to fight Turanians—Zabul and encounter with Akwan diw—Khotan, where he saves Bizhan—Sistan—fights Isfandiyar at River Hirman (east-central Iran)—Kabul to hunt—dies in trap set by king and Shaghad.

Chapter Nine

The Geography of Quest and Conquest

Landscape and geography play a significant role in many heroic narratives, both literary and pictorial. Their importance varies a great deal in literature as in the visual arts. In heroic literature, one finds a spectrum of interest in geographical setting stretching from the merely incidental and often imprecise mention of a place-name, to extended and detailed descriptions of natural and constructed settings.[1] The more detailed type tend to be depictions of fantastic lands and celebrated buildings.

Most narratives at least reflect some notion of the structure of the world; some represent variations on a well-known cosmological theme; a few virtually construct a version of the cosmos from the ground up. In the visual arts, concern for place manifests itself in an equally broad variety of narrative devices. Settings range from the merest hint of groundline or architectural feature, through moderately detailed spatial arrangements, to exquisitely elaborate images of interior decoration and architectural and landscape composition.

Difficult questions of the relationship between a given narrative and its historical context lie beyond the scope of this survey. Crucial as historical criticism may be to the study of all literature, we must leave to others the precise determination of how historically and cartographically precise the sources are. Here we focus on how setting abets the narrator's purposes. We shall, however, observe some distinctions in the ways the stories approach and construe the world of heroic experience.

World-construction operates on at least three levels. First, actual places (specific cities, prominent structures, climes, natural features such as special trees, mountains, rivers, etc.) often serve to mark the hero's whereabouts. Whether or not a narrator locates a particular item with geographical accuracy and consistency, we will

165

refer to such more or less precise references as constituting an earthly landscape.

Those landscapes whose descriptions shade over into the fantastic we will call imaginary. They show the hero wandering far beyond the known world in search of destiny or adventure, or clearly employ spatial reference in a symbolic rather than truly geographic sense. The latter would include dualistic analyses of the world as inside/outside, order/chaos, and so forth. Finally, some heroes journey across a terrain that is definitely not of this world, known or unknown. These are especially, but not exclusively, religious heroes whose sojourns may take them to either inner or outer space, across what we shall refer to as landscapes of the spirit.

Rarely, if ever, can we discern an obvious line of demarcation between one level and another, and it could be argued persuasively that some settings here identified as imaginary can as well be called spiritual. I propose the distinctions as a way of organizing the material and do not mean to suggest they represent discrete categories in the minds of narrators or listeners.[2] The present chapter seeks not to debate whether the traditional cultures that produced the narratives regarded their world as a unity or as a plurality, but to hint at the breadth and diversity of human experience the heroic themes represent.

Earthly Landscapes

Some storytellers take great care to transplant into a local geographical situation narrative material that originated in a foreign setting. They reconstruct the place so that their audience will be able to identify more readily with the action.[3] Here we shall be more concerned with how narratives describe and measure the world of the heroic action by using both constructed and natural markers. Legendary architecture evokes a sense of place and conjures up images of lands and peoples; special trees can likewise create a feeling of locale with overtones of antiquity and mystery.

Heroic narratives sometimes make symbolic use of actual landscapes and terrains in relation to territorial sovereignty. One of the principal means of locating, identifying, and describing the nature of the place (or perhaps as Christian Norberg-Schulz puts it, the *genius loci*) is architecture. Arabian tradition tells of numerous fabulous architectural works, mostly pre-Islamic in origin and mostly associated with the civilizations of Yemen and Hadramawt. King

166

Solomon is said to have had his Jinn build three palaces for Bilqis, the Queen of Sheba (Saba): Ghumdan, Salhayn, and Baynun. Tradition attributes more than a few wondrous citadels to Solomon, and the search for the bottles in which the king contained his Jinn-builders provides one motive for certain heroic journeys.

The Qur'an associates several pre-Islamic peoples with structures that have taken on symbolic significance in various heroic narratives. The people of Ad, for example, to whom the Prophet Hud was sent, built royal dwellings famed for their loftiness and luminosity.[4] Qur'an 89:5–7 also links a fantastic city, Iram of the Columns, with the Adites. The scripture uses Iram as an example of divine power: unbelief can bring to ruin even so magnificent a foundation as many-columned Iram, which King Shaddad boasted was the paradise on earth that rendered faith obsolete. M. J. Rubiera explains the persistence of stories of such places as reflecting "an aesthetic conception of a very unusual urbanism." Such is the power of these archetypes in the Arab view of the world, that they continue to be recalled in literature long after they have been reduced to ruins.[5]

"Deserted wells" and "lofty palaces" often mentioned in *sira* works are hard to locate specifically because they are so common. But the columned city of Iram is easier to locate because it was overturned. H. T. Norris observes that "An upturned city, palace or human habitation and a well or water course which retreats deceptively [a mirage or a "well of receding water"] from the approacher until vanishing point, only to fill once more as the approacher withdraws, are notions capable of symbolic, psychological or mystical interpretation." He associates such imagery with an illusion of "many a horizon in a shimmering haze," "a symbolic portrayal of treasure, death or renewal of life."[6]

Several heroes visit lofty-columned Iram in the course of their peregrinations. Most notable among the ancient city's later guests is Iskandar, whose visit both the popular romances and the last book of Nizami's *Khamsa* describe.[7] Iram's relatively rare appearance in miniature paintings usually shows only either a nondescript structure or walled enclosure, or the tomb of the city's founder, Shaddad. A few illustrations of Iskandar's visit to a garden depict a setting indentifiable only with accompanying text, and two or three others show the monarch in front of the tomb of Shaddad.

One exquisite illustration to a *Khamsa* of the Timurid era

makes a significant point in this context, even though it does not explicitly depict Shaddad's city. Chapter two has already offered a suggestion about the level of interpretation the painting seems to represent. The image employs a composite architectural and natural setting in which Iskandar visits a cave-dwelling hermit who lives beneath the walls of a city-fortress. On one of the bastion's turrets and above its main gate, the painter has inscribed a Qur'anic verse (89:7) that refers to "Iram of the lofty columns / the like of which has not been raised in any land."[8] The miniaturist evidently wants the viewer either to understand that the walled city is Iram, or to take it for a structure whose symbolic function is like that of Iram. In either case, the message probably relates to the futility of thinking a stout fortress can insure one's longevity. This indeed is the burden of the text of Nizami that the miniaturists have included in the frame. Iskandar describes the stronghold controlled by a cohort of thugs. The "world-possessor" asks the "world-seer" to use the "key of prayer" to open for him the mountain stronghold, for the sword may well prove ineffective. The old ascetic obliges, and the king manages to take the fortress.

Several clues suggest that the structure functions as a "type" of Iram. First, in Nizami's narrative Iskandar's visit with the hermit (the bottom half of this miniature) does not occur in the vicinity of Iram. Secondly, the painter's building is inhabited by an unsavory band brandishing weapons upon the ramparts, apparently prepared to defend their stronghold, and representing the crew of highway robbers described in the text. Third, an entirely different text in Nizami later describes Iskandar's visit to Iram explicitly.

One popular version of the Iskandar romance notes that on the front gate of Iram, at whose stairs its proud builder Shaddad had died just after completing the project and boasting on it, Iskandar reads the inscription: "Life in these lands is not for all eternity. Think not thy realm will last. Prepare to die."[9] Evidently the painter has brought together here two scenes linked by a common theme, that of the acknowledgement of mortality. The hermit, as all the other oracles Iskandar consults on his search for immortality and dominion, gives the king the same bad news that the inscription on the gate of Iram delivers.[10] Babylon, where Iskandar dies, is an image of Paradise as well. Murals on the palace walls show battles of Afrasiyab and the portrait of Khusraw. There is no dust or earth in the city. But in this instance, the earthly city becomes a place for the king's transition to the next life, something more than a mere reminder of Alexander's morality.[11]

One of the most influential geo-political metaphors in both Arabic and Persian literature is that of the global sovereignty claimed by the Sasanian King of Kings from his fabled palace at Ctesiphon.[12] With its massive *iwan* (a vaulted hall), the palace gained a reputation for magnificence, inimitability, and, ironically, perishability. One of the marvelous circumstances attending the birth of Muhammad was the rupture and near collapse of Khusraw Anushirwan's proud arch. The demise of the Sasanian symbol of royal power thus became a hallmark of a new hero's rise.

Another aspect of this use of earthly landscape involves references to buildings constructed by famous kings of old who left a moral legacy more positive than that of Shaddad. For example, the *Iskandarnama* has the king's retinue point out to him as an example of how a good king treats his subjects a caravanseray built by Siyawush and Kay Khusraw.[13] Sometimes the architectural works of former royal heroes function as places of pilgrimage for later kings. Nizami has Iskandar make pilgrimage to a castle of Mt. Alburz— not far from the fortress beneath which he consulted with the ascetic—built by Kay Khusraw to house his throne and the world-revealing cup inherited from Jamshid. Iskandar also pays his respects at Siyawushgird, the retreat and burial place of the tragic Prince Siyawush.[14] K. Markus mentions in this connection a tradition that links the phenomenon of architecture as geographical marker with that of special trees, a subject to which we shall return shortly. According to Markus, "To express acceptance or continuity of the ancient tradition in the teaching of Zardusht, King Gushtasp built a palace *(kakh)* by the side of the venerated cypress of Keshmar (which was planted by Zardusht himself) where the painted portraits of the primordial holy kings, among them Jamshed and Faridun, were kept."[15] In a similar vein, *Sirat Antar* describes the "Castle of the Clouds" as a "ruin from the age of Noah" (actually since Ham's time) in which there is a throne said to have belonged to Iskandar.[16]

The Arabic *sira* of Antar shows considerable interest in place. On the macrocosmic level of the story as a whole, the hero's adventures unfold in a quadripartite world, each quarter of which constitutes the realm of an integral monarchy. The four realms are Byzantium; Sasanian Persia, with its capital at Ctesiphon (Mada'in);

the region of Hind and Sind, located, rather vaguely, along the shores of the Indian Ocean; and what one might call "greater Ethiopia." Within this larger structure lies a set of smaller ones. H. T. Norris observes that "Under each of these supreme rulers is a series of lesser rulers who need to be defeated or won as allies before confrontation with one of the rulers of the quarters of the world. This idea is Persian. It is combined with the tales of Islamic conquest found in the *Pseudo-Maghazi* literature."[17]

Recalling the Qurʾanic "Verse of Light," with its cosmic "sacred olive tree neither of East nor West" (Qurʾan 24:35), in some heroic narratives wondrous trees create a place for the action. In sometimes grim depiction of the harshness of enemy territory, the narrator of Antar calls Sudan the "Land of Fear." More importantly, the story locates a number of significant episodes by reference to special trees. The "Tree of Silent Barter" is the key feature in a rare episode of respite for the hero's people en route to Sudan. Antar's consort Ghamra tells of a tree nearby that contains a secret. Whenever merchants pass this tree, they leave samples of their wares beneath it and withdraw for the night. Next morning, the merchants return to discover items of commerce placed among their own, each new item wondrously and inexplicably suited to the merchant's own climate and people. If a merchant likes the proffered trade, he leaves with the new goods; if not, he simply removes his own original offering.[18]

Another tree marks a yet more mysterious, and this time also dangerous, locale. Antar takes a detour from his larger purpose, to avenge Ghamra's honor in the Sudan, and sets off for the Land of Flags and Ensigns to rescue the beloved of Safwan, the son of Lawn az-Zalam, an enemy knight who has now sworn allegiance to Antar. The Land is neither in Africa nor in Yemen as such, but is described as having some qualities of both places.[19] A tree called the "Mistress of Fires and Lights" stands between Antar and the *Hisn al-Uqab* ("eagle's fortress" or "castle") where King Hammam keeps a jealous eye on his daughter, "Wonder of Humanity." After telling of the awesome powers the tree will unleash against any who approach without proper ceremony, the story describes a strangely pilgrimage-like ritual. In order to pass safely, one must approach the tree as a merchant wearing blue clothing, rub antimony on the left eye, and fast for three days. The story then digresses into an aetiology and resumes without saying whether Antar actually fulfills the tree's requirements.[20] In addition to such major tree markers, each segment of the *sira* needed a city, palace, castle or magic source at its climax, according to Norris.[21]

J. Knappert describes the geography of Swahili Islamic literature as "entirely Arabo-centric," with Makka and Madina as the dual navel of the universe. Beyond live the Byzantines, the Turks and Persians, the Chinese, and the Indians.[22] Swahili epics may describe nature's beauties, but the larger purpose of landscape in the epics is "the expression of man's smallness in the setting of huge mountains and vast valleys, and of course for their use by a pastoral society."[23] Here we have begun to move across the thin line between descriptions of the physical universe and a religious cosmology that locates its center at some sacred *axis mundi*. We find ourselves now walking amid landscapes of the imagination and of the spirit.

Landscapes of the Imagination

In the realm of cosmology, the journey takes the traveler to the very boundaries of both map and mind, and then beyond. When the narratives follow the hero's itinerary out toward the fringes of the known world, both reader/listener and traveler find themselves pushing past the limits of actual geography into the landscapes of imagination. Often the "round earth's imagined corners" (John Donne) are marked by natural or constructed features that clearly function as boundaries. Certain actual sites are described as existing at the marge of the earth. By virtue of the aura of danger and inaccessibility such places evoke, they take one over the line between actual and imaginary landscapes. Among sites of this sort, the ancient garrison city of Qayrawan (in Tunisia), for example, stands out in the *Thousand and One Nights*.[24]

At this point, descriptions even of actual landscapes begin to sound suspiciously lacking in factual underpinning; but compared to some of the truly imaginative settings of popular romance, they seem positively photographic. One of the most important medieval Muslim descriptions of the structure of the known world shows the inhabited climes encompassed by ocean and by a circular mountain range called Mt. Qaf. One could travel either east or west and ultimately reach that mysterious realm. We shall return shortly to the larger, spiritual significance of Mt. Qaf. Other sorts of natural boundaries, legendary for the difficulty travelers experience in get-

171

ting to or beyond them, often become transformed into the quasi-fantastic. One such feature is the "river of sand" in the Sahara, said to be an ever-flowing, shifting obstacle to travelers.[25]

The importance of the larger cosmological setting increases as one moves deeper into the terrain of the imagination. S. Errington observes in her study of the Malay *Hikayat Hang Tuah* that the story takes its shape rather from its geography than from a sense of history or chronology. "The narration moves from a raja in heaven to the Malay world; then expands to the Far East (India, China, Siam) and returns to Melaka; then stretches to the Levant and Istanbul and returns to Melaka, and finally ends." Coinciding with a "depletion of the world's potential," the movement "parallels what may have been an expanding geographical consciousness in the historical experience of Malays." According to Errington, the story "talks" with images of the world.[26]

A Malay work about an explicitly religious hero, Muhammad ibn al-Hanafiya, makes more schematic use of a cosmological structure. The action, historically limited to central Iraq, expands into a cosmic battle. Muhammad and his eight brothers and allies, who are a mix of historical and fictional figures, form five groups and fan out to engage the global enemy. The cosmic battlefield is structured like an "X," with the hero at the center and his four groups of allies engaging enemy forces at the four intermediate directions. In the center Muhammad ibn al-Hanafiya confronts the principal villain, the Umayyad caliph Yazid. In the Northwest, Masib Kaka fights the "Farangi" (Franks, Europeans); in the northeast, the three Ali's take on the Chinese; in the southwest, the Turks encounter the Abyssinians; and in the southeast, Ibrahim Astar battles the dark skinned Zangi. The central hero stands at the *axis mundi,* where he maintains contact with the unseen world through dream messages from the Prophet Muhammad. Four subordinate groups of warrior heroes represent the positive forces that defend the four quarters of the cosmos. The outsiders represent the forces of demonic destabilization with their threat to cosmic harmony.[27]

No genre of heroic narrative surpasses the popular romance for sheer fantasy in constructing settings for the central action. Of those romances, the *Iskandarnama* and the story of Hamza in its Persian and Urdu versions present excellent examples of magical setting. Geography as such is of little concern, as the hero darts about improbably from one far-flung region to another. Emphasis is on the hero's virtual mastery of the world, even to its remotest and most inaccessible corner.[28] Nothing epitomizes the magical land better than the Island of Sarandib, or Serendipity, often associated with Sri Lanka. On one of their several landings there, Hamza's ayyar Amr dreams of four prophets, each of whom bestows a gift on him. From Solomon, he gets a sack of gems; from Adam, a bag of wishes. Isma‘il and Abraham confer on him the ability to change shape and to speak three hundred languages, and to run like the wind.[29] Serendipity is the essence of these and other magical landscapes. Miniaturists in Persia and India especially have excelled in their ability to suggest a sense of magic, both in their landscapes and in their use of architectural setting. Akbar's grand and heavily illustrated *Hamzanama* includes several superb examples.[30]

As in descriptions of actual earthly landscapes, so in the land of imagination, celebrated cities and palaces provide the most important device for setting. We shall look here at two major examples of the former (the City of Brass or Copper in its several variations, and the City of Gold) and two of the latter (the palaces of Khawarnaq and Shirin). The city no longer functions as an architectural archetype, but still serves as a moral exemplum from the past. The palaces in the land of imagination, unlike those mentioned in the context of earthly landscapes, function neither as architectural archetypes nor as didactic devices, but as settings in which the heroic characters act in the "present." They are the places of enchantment and mystery.

Solomon's jinns built the City of Copper in the west—Andalusia, according to some accounts—near the Sea of Darkness. The bastion resisted all attempts by explorers to ascertain what lay behind its walls. Various versions of the same story describe how every person brave, or perhaps foolish, enough to venture over the top of the parapet, dissolved into laughter and disappeared forever behind the walls. The legend grew that the city was inhabited by the dead and that explorers were lured over the wall by lovely maidens. Night 574 of the *Thousand and One Nights* tells how Musa ibn Nusayr penetrated the defenses of the city and described its fabulous riches and arsenal of finest weapons.[31] The City of Copper has also been associated with adventist or "messianic" themes in Iranian Islamic thought, for it is there that the *mahdi* ("guided one yet to return") resides and waits for the destined moment of his reentry into history. One tradition identifies that figure as Bahram Chubin, the rebel Sasanian general who sought to usurp the throne and whom Khusraw Parwiz had to defeat in order to claim his royal succession. In this context, the city takes on a decidedly apocalyptic significance, very remotely parallel to that of the Heavenly Jerusalem. This tradition situates the city or fortress in either Central Asia (Transoxiana) or perhaps a bit further east, in the land of the enemy and of exile, thus making the hero's eventual return all the more dramatic and poignant.[32]

The Shi'i religious epic *Khawarannama* features the exploits of Ali, with emphasis on his conquest of the Seven Fortresses, each made of a particular kind of metal and other precious substances, on his way to the City of Gold. According to G. Calasso, the geography of the marvelous that unfolds in the story is an attempt to express in spatial terms a continuity between a heavily Arabized Islamic tradition and an Iranian past. The story therefore develops the theme, begun in the story of the City of Copper (or Brass), into an extended geography that serves as a backdrop for the deeds and religious mission of a more-and-more Iranized Shi'i hero. Accompanied by his ayyars (the "ayyarest" being Amr-i Umayya, whom we have mentioned in chapter three), Ali takes the fortresses of steel, mineral, magnet-stone, copper, brass, silver, and gemstones. Siyawush's Kang Dizh, to be discussed shortly, had seven walls, each of a different metal; and Kay Kawus built seven palaces for himself on Mt. Alburz—one of gold, two of silver, two of steel, and two of crystal. Each episode showcases Ali's talents as well as those of particular heroic companions. Special attention is given to scenes at the Crystal Mountain and the fortress of the Talisman of Dal. One could interpret the conquest of the various strongholds as a symbolic movement from exterior to interior, from appearance to inward meaning.[33]

Persian heroic literature's two most celebrated palaces are the one made most famous by Nizami's *Haft Paykar*, Lakhmid King Nu'man's Khawarnaq (near Kufa in present-day Iraq), and that of Shirin, queen of Sasanian monarch Khusraw Parwiz. The Lakhmids were Arab clients of the Sasanian dynasty of Persia, and Nu'man was an historical figure among them. According to one story, a Byzantine architect named Sinimmar (Simnar) is said to have constructed the palace for Nu'man over a span of seventy years. That version has Nu'man toss the builder from the pinnacle to prevent him from ever divulging the secret of the one piece whose removal would bring down the entire edifice.[34]

Another version of the story has the Sasanian King Yazdagird "The Sinner" commission King Nuʿman to construct the palace so that Yazdagird's sickly son Bahram Gur can live in a more healthy climate. After Sinimmar constructs a building at which all marvel, the architect unwisely boasts that, if the king had paid him the wages he deserved, he would have made a palace that would turn and follow the course of the sun. Because he has not done so, Sinimmar meets his death by freefall.[35]

Nizami's *Haft Paykar (Seven Portraits)* develops the imagery of Khawarnaq, and the seven pavilions related to it, most extensively. In Nizami's version of the story, King Yazdagird, fearing for his throne, suspiciously sends his son Bahram Gur away to live with Lakhmid king Nuʿman. There, Bahram Gur enters the one off-limits room in the palace of Khawarnaq and discovers the portraits of the seven princesses, with his own portrait in their midst. After his father dies, Bahram Gur returns to claim his throne. His architect, Shida, an apprentice of Simnar, suggests that the king construct seven domed pavilions as an astrologically correct protection from the evil eye. The poet transforms the motif into a metaphor for the cosmos by paralleling the seven pavilions and their inhabiting princesses from the seven climes, with the seven planets, the seven colors in the traditional *haft rang* ("seven colors") system, and the seven days of the week, the four elements with three spirits, and so forth. G. Krotkoff has studied the interrelation of the various levels of imagery, including in some detail the numerological connections among the various stories on the basis of numbers mentioned in the stories told by the princesses.[36] J. S. Meisami takes the significance of the two structures, Khawarnaq and the seven domes, still further: "These buildings symbolize the contrast between temporal and spiritual kingship: the material achievement of Khavarnaq is transcended via the passage through the domes to the final, spiritual edifice of the fire temple."[37]

Shirin's palace has taken on somewhat less symbolic value than that of Khawarnaq, but it still bears mentioning here. According to tradition, the great royal hero Khusraw Parwiz built the palace for the lovely Shirin between Baghdad and Hamadhan. Shirin liked fresh milk, but because her palace stood high in the mountains (according to Nizami's version) and far from pasture, the sculptor-architect-engineer Farhad was enlisted to dig a tunnel to carry the milk through the rock mountain.[38]

Probably the nearest thing to an epic underworld one finds in the non-religious Islamicate sources is the fabled Land of Darkness. Iskandar's foremost goal as a world conqueror and traveller is to reach the legendary Mt. Qaf by marching through that *terra incognita.* Mt. Qaf is at the very end of the earth. As H. Corbin notes, "To reach it, it would be necessary to walk for four months 'in the Darkness'; that is why Alexander's progress through the region of Darkness is that of the archetypal spiritual hero."[39] At this point we find ourselves crossing over into landscapes of the spirit.

Landscapes of the Spirit

Corbin provides one possible way of understanding the significance of imaginary and spiritual landscapes. His term "psychological geography" will serve us as an apt summary of both aspects of the subject. Corbin's approach attempts

> to discover the psychological factors that come into play in the conformation to a given landscape. The phenomenological presupposition implicit in research of this kind is that the essential functions of the soul, the *psyche,* include the projection of a nature, a *physis;* conversely, each physical structure discloses the mode of *psycho-spiritual* activity that brings it into operation. In this sense, the categories of the *sacredness* "which possesses the soul" can be recognized in the landscape with which it surrounds itself and in which it shapes its habitat, whether by projecting the vision on an ideal iconography, or by attempting to inscribe and reproduce a model of the vision on the actual earthly ground.[40]

We shall apply some of Corbin's theory indirectly in this final section of the chapter.

One can distinguish between at least two major contexts for describing the world of spirit. The first produces a more conventional view of the Paradise that awaits all faithful Muslims beyond death. The other deals rather with a transition from one state to another that seems not to depend on actual passage from mortality to immortality. Such imagery is deliberately ambiguous and far more subtle.

Heroic narratives provide a number of conventional descriptions of the next world—a place to which martyrdom promises a direct route. A Swahili story of Sunni Islam's proto-martyr in the *Epic of Heraklios* occasions a description of Ja'far's life in Paradise. There is, of course, a celestial mosque from whose minaret the original muezzin, Bilal, summons all to prayer. Ja'far delightedly flits about on the wings God has given him as a much-improved replacement for the arms he so valiantly lost in battle; now he can go from one end of Paradise to the other in a single day, whereas others may live here a thousand years and never see it all.[41]

In the case of Muhammad, the hero's journey takes him far beyond this world into the many-tiered realm of spirit—first, according to Swahili versions, into a world between heaven and earth and then into hell and heaven. In the intermediate space, he has a series of peculiar encounters, each of which J. Knappert sees as a "parable, a symbolic *tableau vivant* painted in vivid colours, like the paintings of Hieronymus Bosch."[42] As Muhammad proceeds to hell and the heavens, the terrain is again described in fairly conventional terms. First he gets a sample of infernal punishments. At the end of his Night Journey, he comes to Jerusalem, whence he ascends heavenward. (See Figure 13.)

Like the phenomenal universe, Paradise is stratified into between seven and ten levels (hell often into seven), each named after some Qur'anic reference. In each of the celestial tiers, the spiritual traveler meets certain other prophets assigned there. Each level has its distinctive topography, marked by wondrous rivers, mountains, and trees. The seventh heaven, made all of gold and ruled by the prophet Abraham, is the Celestial Paradise (the first is the terrestrial) whose mosque sits directly above the Ka'ba in Makka. Rivers (usually four, but sometimes six or eight) of water, milk, honey, and wine flow through it from beneath the central tree. Two flow into Paradise, and two flow out and into Egypt. As in some descriptions of earthly landscape, the tree is a key topographical feature, a cosmic axis that leads to the highest level of Paradise whither Muhammad alone may climb.[43]

The function of this level of cosmology differs considerably from that of the types detailed earlier. Here the hero's purpose is not conquest or rescue, but discovery and the quest for the most useful knowledge of all. From these climes the hero must return with a message both of hope and of caution. Experience of the

Figure 13: The Prophet Muhammad's Ascension (Mi'raj) astride Buraq.

world beyond provides the hero with the credential of spiritual prowess.[44]

E. Waugh describes stories of the Prophet's Ascension as "reflections of spiritual values which took root in the primitive ummah and which bore fruit in the creation of a religious world consonant with the needs and moods of some elements in the Muslim community."[45] He further observes that the legends of Muhammad's other-worldly journeying gradually evolved by two modes of expansion: the Prophet's interviews with various personages at each level of heaven, and the description of a celestial geography marked by sacred places that parallel those on earth. The journeyer thus discovers the "heavenly counterpart to concrete geographical locations." Waugh relates all the major features of this sacred geography to more ancient shamanistic traditions.[46] For the community at large, the stories have a kind of geo-political significance; certain specific sites need to be defended. For the mystics, who "internalized the ascension and spatialized inner experience into qualitative values in ascending order of importance," the stories have more personal than communal implications.[47] With that, we come to the second major dimension of landscapes of the spirit, the inner journey and spiritual transformation.

According to J. S. Meisami, Nizami's imagery of the seven climes in the *Haft Paykar* serves as a vehicle for Bahram Gur's inward journey "from temporal to sacred kingship symbolized by a movement from garden to garden." Tales one, five, and seven, she notes, "are set in gardens, while the interlude as a whole is framed by the two gardens of the narrative: the garden in winter . . . from which Bahram takes refuge to feast . . . and to order the construction of the seven domes, and the royal pleasance in spring, described in imagery of Paradise, rebirth and resurrection, where the action leading to the restoration of order is set in motion."[48] The contrast between appearance and reality, barrenness and fertility parallels that between ignorance and enlightenment.

Nizami links all three gardens with that of Iram. The first *is* that magical and unattainable Paradise; the second, illusory and dream-like, excels Iram in every way; the third, planted firmly on earth and within reach, only resembles Iram. Rather unexpectedly, perhaps, it is the last that represents both attainable reality and transcendence. The realm of the spirit exists neither beyond space and time, nor in the insubstantial realm of dreams, but in the here

179

and now. The first two gardens may tempt with their appeal to fantasy, but they ultimately elude the journeyer. Only in the last can the sojourner dwell, and in the *Haft Paykar* it opens into Bahram Gur's spring garden, at the opposite end of the reality spectrum from the artful contrivance of the winter garden with which the garden imagery begins.[49]

In traditional Iranian cosomology, the seven earthly climes continue into another world, the eighth clime. Here, according to Suhrawardi interpreter H. Corbin, one has left the realm of the heroic epic for that of the mystical epic. The heroic experience is that of a passage to the East. In that realm, the Orient as source of illumination encompasses the greater sphere of the highest angelic intelligences ("the world of Power," *jabarut*) and the lesser sphere of other angels and heavenly souls ("the world of majesty," *malakut*). Corbin would include here not only the more obviously religious or mystical heroes, but a number of major characters of epic stature, to the degree that their experience transcends history. To go beyond this world is also to go beyond history: mystical epic is a history that shatters history—it is metahistory. Heroic epic stands between the prehistoric and the metahistoric. Mystical epic is the product of a further passage beyond mundane experience in which the hero accomplishes his "oriental finality" by breaking free of all earthly causality. The hero thus becomes the embodiment of *ta'wil*, "not merely the interpretation of a text that reveals its true meaning, its inner esoteric sense, but a hermeneutic of the human that guides one back to one's true being, one's origin, one's 'orient.'"[50] Hero has become pilgrim.

It is in that spirit that Suhrawardi interprets the mysterious and prophet-like disappearance of Kay Khusraw at the end of his life.[51] Suhrawardi gives surprising attention to Firdawsi's Kay Khusraw, whom he seems to have regarded as a forefather of the Ishraqi (Illuminationist) school. Much of Suhrawardi's interpretation focuses on the wondrous cup of Jamshid, the castle Kang Dizh (Iranian counterpart to the Arthurian Grail and Grail castle) and Kay Khusraw's sojourn in the eighth clime. This superb example of a "landscape of the spirit" merits at least a bit more detail.[52]

Kay Khusraw's father, the tragic Prince Siyawush, had built the fortress called Kang Dizh, which Corbin says "illustrates the theme of mysterious dwellings built by sovereigns and heroes, and whose fundamental significance is eschatological. To repair to this mystic palace is to hide oneself from the eyes of the world."[53] Kang Dizh exists in that uncharted world of the "extreme north," the heavenly pole where the eighth clime begins, at the top of the Alburz mountain (the place where Sam had abandoned son Zal and the abode of the Simurgh). One must pass through the "middle clime" en route to this *axis mundi,* also called Mt. Qaf. Seven walls, each of a different metal, surround the fortress with its fourteen mountains and seven navigable rivers. Each of its fifteen gates is some 2,400 miles from the next. Thither, says Suhrawardi, does Kay Khusraw escape after questing far and wide to rid the world of his evil maternal grandfather, Afrasiyab, to live as one of seven royal figures in the presence of a Zoroastrian messianic Saoshyant. On his journey into the mountains, Kay Khusraw is accompanied by eight loyal knights. He bids them go back, for they will not survive the harsh environment; Gudarz, Zal, and Rustam take his advice. The other five insist on remaining with their sovereign. They come to a spring, and again Kay Khusraw begs them to turn back while they can. He then bathes in the spring, the Source of Life, and disappears from their sight. After looking for the king in vain, the five knights perish in a snowstorm—a poignant scene often depicted in miniatures.[54]

Landscape of the spirit appears in another important context, where it serves not to illustrate the text as such, but to provide a unique key to the text's meaning. D. Klimburg-Salter has made a fascinating connection between the dominant metaphor of Farid ad-Din Attar's *Conference of the Birds,* that of a perilous mystical journey through seven valleys, and a collection of mystical poems called the *Diwan of Sultan Ahmad Jalaʾir.* In Klimburg-Salter's interpretation, the painter has used images of six of the seven valleys to "comment on" the poems. By superimposing, so to speak, scenes in which the birds of Attar's mystical epic are paired with visual metaphors from human experience (scholars, lovers, travelers, and so forth), the painter offers a hermeneutical device that presupposes a familiarity with the Attar's spiritual landscape. Why only six of the seven valleys? Perhaps because, as Attar suggests, the seventh transcends the imagination and defies visualization. Klimburg-Salter argues that a resurgence of interest in Attar around the time of the manuscript's production suggests a diffusion of the poet's geographical allegory sufficiently broad to support such a visual interpretation of Sultan Ahmad's verses.[55]

The Heroic Cycle: Narrative and Iconographic Themes

We have already begun to cross the fuzzy boundary between what we have called the narrative and iconographic dimensions of the heroic cycle and the symbolic dimensions. The next three chapters will address the latter more directly but will never leave the former aside entirely.

ELEMENTS OF THE

HEROIC CYCLE:

SYMBOLIC

DIMENSIONS

PART FOUR

Chapter Ten

Relational Motifs:
The Hero and the Human Family

Two large questions concern us here. First, how does a heroic figure function as hero in the various familial roles of father and husband, mother and wife, child and sibling? What of the hero as mentor, as friend and peer? In other words, are some specific qualities to be sought in a heroic father, mother, and so forth? Second, what does the interaction of the different roles suggest about the storyteller's insight into the human condition? Since the hero is in some ways larger than life, this chapter extends the notion of the human family. The hero belongs to, and is often seen as an essential link with, the broader family of humanity. To have a hero tucked away somewhere in one's genealogy can boost not only one's self-esteem, but one's political or religious legitimacy as well. Beyond that, Islamic tradition has developed the concept of the hero as a kind of corporate personality, one who sums up and embodies the best in humankind. That is the hero as perfect or cosmic person. Strictly speaking, of course, one ought to study this kind of theme, as all the others, by first attending directly to cultural context and literary genre. Our purpose here, however, is simply to provide some sense of the range of relational motifs that have engaged readers and listeners across the Islamic world. The reader may find Tables 3 (p. 95) and 4 (below) helpful in tracing key relationships.

The Hero as Father

Father-son relationships clearly rank among the most important family issues depicted in heroic literatures the world over. Rarely are they without serious difficulty, and in general, heroes do not appear to make ideal fathers. Various sub-themes emerge on closer look. First, some stories come to a tragic resolution of the tension, ending in the violent death of either father or son. Second, a father sometimes becomes disaffected with a son who defects to the enemy (political, religious, or both). Sometimes the son repents

Table 4. Genealogy of Heroic Figures of the *Shahnama*

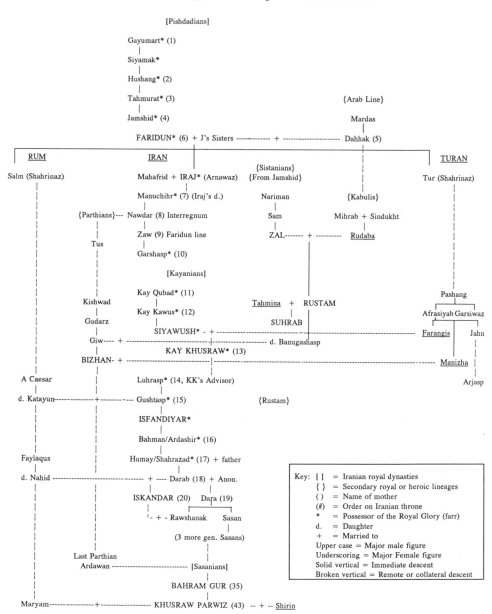

Key:
[ ]	= Iranian royal dynasties
{ }	= Secondary royal or heroic lineages
( )	= Name of mother
(#)	= Order on Iranian throne
*	= Possessor of the Royal Glory (farr)
d.	= Daughter
+	= Married to

Upper case = Major male figure
Underscoring = Major Female figure
Solid vertical = Immediate descent
Broken vertical = Remote or collateral descent

and returns; sometimes his actions ignite an enduring hostility. Third, the theme of early rejection through no deliberate fault of the son can end in an eventual reconciliation, usually one of two main types. Resolution turns typically either on the father's admission of unjust treatment of his son, or on the son's ability to persuade his father by heroic deeds that his father has reason to claim and be proud of him. Finally, there are stories in which one son either stands out from the start as daddy's favorite, or emerges from among his siblings to garner the paternal favor that hinges on the successful passing of a test. To the last of these we shall return shortly when we consider sons, daughters, and siblings.

One way of analyzing the stories that end tragically looks at the outcomes of the prominent father-son struggles and divides them into two basic types, with some variations. In the first type, the prince is in the words of K. Markus, "crushed to death by paternal authority and falsehood." Suhrab's death at the hands of his father, Rustam, provides the prototype of the theme and the only example of a direct filicide. (See Figure 14.) More indirect examples of the death of a prince as a result of paternal animus occur in the struggles between Kay Kawus and Siyawush, and between Gushtasp and Isfandiyar.

A second type of story features usurper-sons who overthrow their fathers. Gushtasp dethrones his father Luhrasp peacefully. After Dahhak makes his deal with the devil, he ousts his father Mardas. What Khusraw Parwiz does to his father, Hurmuz, Khusraw's son Shiruy later does to Khusraw.[1] Between these two types falls the case of Nushzada, son of Anushirwan. Nushzada does not attempt to win the kingdom by heroic deeds as Gushtasp and Isfandiyar do; nor does he kill his father, as Khusraw Parwiz and Shiruy do; neither is he simply innocent as are Siyawush and Suhrab. Instead, Nushzada becomes Christian, to his father's considerable pique.[2]

In the Javanese *Sirat Dermagandul*, the issue of disparity between religious allegiance of father and son comes to the fore. The work uses the example of past heroes to extol the necessity of a Muslim son's remaining loyal to his father regardless of how shabbily the infidel father treats him. Hamza maintains his filial piety even when his father plots to have his princes do away with Hamza. A son must take responsibility for inviting his father to Islam, as Moses, Abraham, and Muhammad had done (though it is actually

Figure 14: Rustam kills his son Suhrab.

his uncle and guardian, Abu Talib, whom Muhammad had tried to convert). And a prince who goes against his father for any reason will surely rue the day, as does David's son Absalom.[3] Later, however, the document says, Abraham, Moses, and Muhammad succeed even though they did rise up against their fathers. Here the point is that, serious as enmity with one's sire may be, it is still forgiveable—unlike falling out with one's teacher.[4]

On the whole, father-son relationships are fraught with tension. When a father like Rustam does manifest some growth into that familial role, it is too little too late. When Rustam realizes he has killed his own son, his grief surely equals David's when he laments so touchingly the death of his son Absalom. Rustam even attempts suicide but is dissuaded from the act. Thereafter he pays more attention to his son Faramarz. Curiously enough, Rustam's relationship with his own father, Zal, stands out as one of the more amicable. Zal, who knows what it is like to be rejected by a father,[5] not infrequently shows up as Rustam's companion, especially in the role of ambassador. Zal seems to know his son better than most heroic fathers do, and the pair appear together in miniature paintings more often than any other father-son duo.[6]

One of the best vignettes of a Turkic hero's relationship with his son occurs in the *Book of Dede Korkut*'s story of "How Prince Uruz Son of Prince Kazan Was Taken Prisoner," not to be confused with the story, mentioned earlier, of how Kazan is taken prisoner and how his son Uruz frees him. The bard describes how the feasting father looks to his right and laughs, to his left and rejoices; but when he looks forward and sees his sixteen-year-old son Uruz, he weeps. Son Uruz wants to know why his father is not pleased with him. Kazan explains that he has not become man enough to inherit his father's power. Uruz chides Kazan boldly: "Does a son learn skills by watching his father, or do fathers learn from their children? When have you ever taken me to the infidel frontier, brandished your sword and cut off heads? What have I seen you do? What am I supposed to learn?"[7]

Uruz's response pleases Kazan, who then proposes to take the boy on a hunt and to the infidel frontier. On the way, Kazan answers Uruz's questions: what is an enemy, and will the enemy demand the blood of their own from one who kills them in battle? Suddenly the infidel host approaches, tipped off by a spy that Kazan is off his guard. Kazan sends the boy off to the mountain to observe the fray. "In those days a son did not go counter to his father's words; had one done so, the father would not have acknowledged him as his son."[8]

Watching from a safe distance, Uruz decides his father is being too easy on the infidels. He hastens to the attack and falls prisoner. Not finding the boy among his men, Kazan is at first furious that the youth has run home to his mother. But when Kazan's wife sees that Uruz does not return with Kazan, she rails at her husband for allowing harm to befall her son. Kazan, mad with grief, returns to the scene of the attack with ninety thousand men. As he approaches the infidel stronghold, the captors inform Uruz that they are about to take his father. He asks for mercy, and they let the boy run to wave his father off. He fails, of course. Kazan proceeds to subdue the enemy—with a little help from his wife, who tears down the infidel escutcheon—and forms a procession of victorious single combatants that is a veritable who's who among Oghuz heroes.[9]

Two other heroes whose fathers play notably positive, if only brief or occasional, roles in their lives are Hang Tuah and Miqdad. Hang Tuah's father puts in a brief appearance at the outset of the Malay epic. Unlike most heroes' fathers, his chief concern is to see to it that his son gets a proper education and a chance to serve the crown. Miqdad's father visits from the land of death to teach his son how to be a warrior.[10]

Among religious heroes, the picture of fatherhood is decidedly different and altogether felicitous. Ali and Muhammad are veritable paragons of fatherly devotion. Shi'ite tradition especially notes the familial virtues of the two major male figures of the House of the Prophet. Jacob, too, expresses great care for his sons, and for Yusuf in particular. In his grief at Yusuf's loss, the old man weeps himself into blindness. The return of his sight through the scent of Yusuf's shirt is among the more touching images of father-son relationship.

Closely related to the hero's role in relation to his son is the less prevalent but still significant function of mentor or foster parent. We shall mention only one major example and one lesser parallel. Perhaps seeking to make up for his failures as a father, Rustam functions as one of the most important mentors in the *Shahnama*. There is a certain irony here, so great are this champion's difficulties in raising his own children. (Perhaps he is like the cobbler whose children went barefoot?) Because of his unrivaled talents as a horseman and warrior, royalty seek him out as the ideal tutor for the prince in the manly arts. So Kay Kawus has Rustam serve as Siyawush's guardian and chief of staff. Rustam becomes angry when the king suggests that Siyawush must go back on his word to Afrasiyab. As a reward for his his integrity, Rustam is banished to Sistan, and the disillusioned innocent Siyawush defects to the side of Afrasiyab, who ultimately has the prince murdered and incurs Rustam's unquenchable wrath and vengeance.[11]

How Rustam comes to be the mentor of Isfandiyar's son Bahman is a moving story. As Isfandiyar lies dying from the arrow Rustam shot into his eyes, the prince begs Rustam to take care of his boy. Rustam agrees and thus becomes the tutor of Gushtasp's eventual successor, Bahman, also known as Ardashir.[12] An interesting analogy to this story occurs in that of Hang Tuah. When Hang Jebat goes mad and begins to run amok, his old friend Hang Tuah is called in to stop his rampage. Hang Jebat explains that he behaved badly because Hang Tuah has been treated unjustly—the Javanese ruler of Majapahit has put out a contract on him. As they prepare to fight, Hang Jebat asks Hang Tuah to adopt the son he hopes will be born to one of his consorts; and as he dies in Hang Tuah's arms, he asks again.[13]

The Heroine as Mother

Women in the *Shahnama* are nearly always selfless and generous. As mothers, they are utterly devoted to their children. As heroic figures, the role of the major female characters is no less crucial than that of their male counterparts, even though they appear in the foreground far less often. In the cases of Faranak and Mahafarid, for instance, the entire destiny and hope of the nation depends on their negotiating most difficult circumstances in bringing forth and rearing two early kings, Faridun and Manuchihr.

Firdawsi explicitly says that when a son kills his father, one must look first to the mother to discern the reasons for the violence. His explanation of the source of the problem may result from a basic insight into what modern psychology calls the oedipal conflict, as well as from the pervasive fear of women one finds in the *Shahnama*.[14] In the case of Christian convert Nushzada, for instance, the prince's mother is Christian and represents a foreign element. Son takes mother's side here, with disastrous consequences.[15] Mothers not infrequently represent an alien element, in that they often descend from non-Iranian stock. This last feature definitely serves to cement alliances and aid the hero in the conduct of foreign affairs, but it can also pose a threat to family stability.

Two of the more important mother figures of the *Shahnama* are Faranak and Tahmina. Faranak is the daughter of a Scythian king and the wife of Jamshid's descendent Abtin, whom she met when he traveled to her father's court. Most significantly, Faranak bears the great Faridun. The story of Faridun and his mother begins before Faridun's birth when the villain Dahhak has a dream revealing that—according to the interpreting sages—the child will dethrone him. Dahhak then dispatches soldiers to kill the child and his family. Faridun's father flees home, only to be killed by the foe and become another in a long line of "missing fathers" in heroic literature. Faranak takes her child to the desert where she sees the wondrous cow Birmaya, whose owner allows Birmaya to nurse Faridun and becomes his guardian for three years. Fearing Dahhak, Faranak then takes Faridun to the Alburz mountains, where a holy man accepts Faridun into his tutelage. Later, an enraged Dahhak slaughters Birmaya and burns Faranak's palace. At the age of sixteen, Faridun is reunited with Faranak and vows vengeance. Kawa the Blacksmith rebels and, once Faridun has joined his cause, succeeds in securing Dahhak's demise. Faranak, in gratitude to Ahura Mazda, devotes her life to service of the poor.[16]

A tragic figure among the heroine-mothers of the *Shahnama*, Tahmina is a princess of Samangan (east of Balkh) who falls in love with Rustam when he visits her father's court. Rakhsh, the wonder horse, has wandered off while Rustam is napping, so Rustam walks the remaining distance to court. The king likes him immediately, and Rustam falls in love with his daughter. After drinking too much, Rustam asks for her hand in marrige. Next day he hears the call of adventure and decides to return home with Rakhsh to Zabulistan. Before departing, Rustam gives Tahmina an amulet to put on the arm of their yet-unborn son. In due course, son Suhrab is born, grows up, and becomes restless for his father. He sets out on a horse of Rakhsh's breed with an armed band to fight King Kay Kawus and find Rustam. Tahmina sends along with Suhrab a certain Shanda Razm, whom Rustam knows. Turan's ruler Afrasiyab sends an army to help Suhrab, so that Kay Kawus will need to call on his champion Rustam, and contrives to keep Rustam's identity from Suhrab. Suhrab captures the White Castle on the border between Iran and Turan, and Kay Kawus calls for Rustam. Rustam kills Shanda Razm in the enemy camp without letting him speak to identify himself. In his first combat with Suhrab, Rustam loses, but mortally wounds his son in the second. Hearing of the tragedy, Tahmina loses her mind in grief, tears her hair, gives her jewels to the poor, and dies broken-hearted a year later.[17] A number of miniature paintings show the moment of Tahmina's first romantic encounter with Rustam; much rarer are scenes of the mother telling her son about his absent father.[18]

In the *Sirat Dhat al-Himma* we find a most interesting relationship between mother Dhat al-Himma and son Abd al-Wahhab. The heroine's cousin seduces her with the help of a drug. Because of the unusual circumstances of his conception, the resulting child is black—a fact that eventually enables him to command the allegiance of the black troops who fight with the Kilab tribe. Amira ("Madame Commandante") Dhat al-Himma is a redoubtable warrior as well as a devoted mother. Unlike most other heroes, Abd al-Wahhab learns the martial arts from his mother rather than from a male mentor. When his mother meets her match in single combat (about half the time), it is often Abd al-Wahhab who comes to the rescue. Eventually the son steps into his aging mother's place as principal champion, much to Dhat al-Himma's jealous chagrin. In any event, mother seems to have raised her boy well; for he turns out to be all a Bedouin-style hero should be: brave, generous, and thirsty for justice.[19] Before turning to images of the hero as son, daughter, and sibling, we look briefly at heroic spousal relationships.

The Heroic Marriage

As chapter eight has suggested, romantic elements abound in heroic tales. The relationship itself usually takes second place to the process of courtship, which is typically fraught with difficulties and contests. Surprisingly, perhaps, the hero very often chooses a woman from outside his own tribe or nation. One Turkic story that describes the interesting beginning of a marital relationsihp is that of Kan Turali in *Dede Korkut*. The hero goes off to win the lovely daughter of the infidel king, for he has heard of her surpassing beauty and must have her. He must first defeat the bull, lion, and camel that stand between him and the girl's hand. He does so and takes her away.

Meanwhile her father the infidel king has second thoughts, wishes he had not let her go with Kan Turali, and sends his warriors off to bring her back. The princess alerts her sleeping hero that her own father has come, and while Kan is performing his ablutions before prayer, she goes off to fight the warriors. They are her own people, so she lets some escape and has mercy on those who plead for their lives. Meanwhile, Kan Turali's parents arrive at the camp to find their son missing, and they hold the princess responsible for their son's absence. She rides off to find Kan temporarily at the mercy of the infidels. To the rescue she goes and routs her own people, unwittingly threatening the virility of Kan Turali, who tells her he must kill her lest she embarrass him in public. She declines to boast, for boasting is not a woman's natural inclination, and asks him to spare her. He insists they battle, so she removes the heads from two arrows and bids him shoot. He says that girls get to go first. When she fires a shot that knocks the lice out of his hair, Kan Turali can no longer resist, and the two reconcile.[20]

One obviously needs to tread lightly in the area of cultural and societal models of desirable family relationships, avoiding as much as possible the use of one's own norms of acceptability. Still, it seems not unreasonable to make at least a few tentative suggestions. As wives, major heroines show a tolerance for their husbands that seems limitless. Only now and then, as in the Swahili story of Fatima and in various Turkic narratives, does the female spouse show very strong negative affective responses toward her husband. Husbanding as such receives relatively little attention in heroic literature. Perhaps the Swahili tradition comes closest to describing heroes in terms of their domestic connection. Recall for example the Swahili storyteller's attention to Ali in relation to Fatima (see chapter five). Even the more-developed romantic spouses, such as Khusraw Parwiz, are depicted as having a long way to go toward willingness to settle down and direct some attention homeward. In general, one can conclude that as husbands, heroes simply do not count for much. The role of husband is not a critical ingredient in the image of the authentic hero. Images of the male heroic figure tend to focus almost exclusively on how he makes his mark on the outer world rather than on the home. In that respect, the heroine's role is quite different, emphasizing the functions of mother and wife, and only on occasion spotlighting her warrior skills.

Nizami, no doubt an experienced marriage counselor in a previous incarnation, tells a tale that would surely delight the heart of many a family-systems therapist. The poet has the princess in the *Haft Paykar*'s yellow pavilion entertain Bahram Gur with a story of how Solomon and Bilqis had a child paralyzed and seriously ill from birth. They pray that God will heal the infant. The response comes that if they wish the child to be restored to health, they must divulge their innermost secret to each other. Bilqis admits that she harbors a desire to trick her husband. Solomon confesses that, for all his wealth, he nevertheless covets more of the same. With their dark secrets out in the light, their child begins to improve.[21]

The Hero as Son, Daughter, Sibling

We have treated above the theme of the father's preparing the son for his future role as head of the family or tribe, and as hero. The other side of that coin is the theme of the son's struggle to grow into his father's boots in due course. Several stories from *Dede Korkut* deal with the main facets of the theme. Two pertinent tales in the cycle are those of Yigenek Son of Kazilik Koja and Emren Son of Begil. Yigenek, who is either unborn or one year old when his father departs (both circumstances are mentioned in the story), learns some hard realities at age sixteen. He has never met his father and has thought all along that his father is dead. He now discovers that infidels have held his father captive for sixteen years, and resolves to free him. Kazilik's brother (Yigenek's uncle) has tried unsuccessfully six (or seven) times and seeks to dissuade the boy. Yigenek goes anyway, and after the tribe's twenty-four most valiant heroes have failed to best the infidel king, the son succeeds.[22]

In a variation on the theme, the aging hero Begil laments that he has no grown son to carry on for him, no brother to keep him company. Begil breaks his leg in a freak accident while hunting and must take to bed for an extended recuperation. King Shökli the infidel hears from his spy that he would do well to strike the Oghuz while their leader is out of the picture. Begil laments further that his scrawny boy Emren is not yet a man, but consents to have the youth don Begil's armor and ride to battle on his horse. When the infidels realize the Oghuz defender is not Begil, they become overconfident. In response to Emren's prayer, God gives him the strength of forty men. Emren drives the infidel king to his knees, Shökli converts and becomes a good Muslim, and the boy become a man saves the father's honor.[23]

One of the commonest themes is that of the youngest son's gaining his father's favor and/or outperforming his older brothers. Faridun is an excellent example of the younger-son theme. When he resolves to go against the tyrant Dahhak, he informs his two older brothers that he can see the crown about to descend on his own head. As the three go off to the tyrant's lair, a lookout reports back to Dahhak on the approach of three men—in the middle of whom stands the youngest, but he is clearly superior to the others in every way.[24] Faridun's own three sons in turn reinforce the theme, in that the one who wins Faridun's favor is the youngest, Iraj. Miniaturists have often depicted Faridun's strained relationship with the two older sons after their murder of Iraj.[25] In the story of Umar an-Nuʿman, the hero Sharkan leaves home because "he cannot tolerate his father's love for his brother Dhu ʾl-Makan."[26] Among religious heroes, Joseph (Yusuf) represents the best example of both sub-themes. As second-youngest of twelve, the prophet is the apple of his father's eye and a source of endless jealousy to his older brothers. A major feature of the Joseph story, however, is that the brothers are eventually reconciled in an exceptionally moving scene, when Joseph reveals his identity to them.[27]

A good example of the hero as brother is that of the story of Segrek in the *Book of Dede Korkut*. It tells of how Ushun Koja's older son, Egrek, is captured while raiding an infidel compound. Years later, after his then-unborn brother, Segrek, has grown into a "good, brave, heroic, reckless warrior," Segrek learns that he does indeed have a brother. Furious with his mother, Segrek vows to find Egrek. Their father tries in vain to prevent Segrek from re-opening an old wound. Let him not cause his parents grief; word of his brother is only a false rumor. His parents try unsuccessfully to stall Segrek by marrying him to his betrothed, but he refuses to rest until he finds his brother. Assaulting the stronghold of the infidel, Segrek dispatches dozens of enemy knights.

Dozing off to sleep later that night, the infidel king conceives a plot to kill the interloper while saving his own knights. He gives the prisoner Egrek arms and a horse and sends him out to kill the "crazy warrior" wreaking havoc in the neighborhood. Promised his freedom in return for this service, Egrek agrees. He approaches the sleeping Segrek and picks up the lute on the ground near him.

As Egrek asks the musical question "Why do you sleep, young man?" his brother awakes with a start, prepares to slash the stranger, sees the lute of Dede Korkut in Egrek's hands, and stays his sword out of respect for the lute. They discover their brother-hood in the charming exchange that follows, teach the infidels a lesson in swordsmanship, and return happily home.[28]

Antar's brother Shaybub plays a less inimical role, but functions still as a kind of foil to Antar. Antar's stature as hero depends on his prowess in battle, his honor, and his eloquence. But because Antar is perhaps a bit too wild and unpredictable to lead the entire tribal host, his brother Shaybub comes to the fore. Shaybub's main heroic virtues are his swiftness, cunning, cool bravery, and ability as a guide. Whereas Antar (like Rustam) fights with the sword, a weapon that requires more sheer strength in close struggle, Shaybub (more like Isfandiyar) uses the smart hero's weapons, the bow and arrow.[29] Shaybub functions not only as brother but as ayyar to Antar.

The sub-theme of adoption plays a minor but interesting role, as does that of the half-brother relationship. Köroghlu is perhaps the most famous father to adopt two sons.[30] As suggested earlier in the chapter on villains, Uruz Koja's well-intentioned adoption of the misbegotten offspring of his shepherd (by the fairy he had raped) causes enormous suffering for the tribe and comes to a salutary but unhappy resolution. His actual son Basat has no choice but to kill his own adopted half-brother to rid the world of a chaotic force that represents, or at any rate has resulted from, a moral lapse in the community.[31] Enmity between some half-brothers reaches terrible proportions, as in the case of Rustam and Shaghad. Rustam's half-brother so envies Rustam that he agrees to become an accomplice to murder to be rid of his rival. Shaghad knows where Rustam is to be hunting and has a booby-trapped pit dug and camouflaged. Rustam ignores Rakhsh's protestations at the aroma of newly turned earth and plunges into a nest of spears. In his dying moment, Rustam convinces Shaghad to string Rustam's bow so that the latter can defend himself against a wild beast. Shaghad then positions himself behind a tree for safety. With his last scintilla of energy, Rustam raises the bow and pins the traitor Shaghad right through the tree. A number of marvelous minia-tures have captured the doubly grim moment.[32]

Several important heroines play their principal parts as daughters. Farangis is daughter of Afrasiyab, the king of Turan and implacable enemy of Iran. Siyawush goes to Afrasiyab's court for refuge from his stepmother, Sudaba. Piran, a member of Afrasiyab's court, tries to make a match between Siyawush and Farangis. Afrasiyab agrees and appoints Siyawush ruler of Turan-to-China. Siyawush proceeds to build Siyawushgird palace (which will later become a place of pilgrimage for all who mourn the martyr-like death of the young prince—pilgrims who will even include Alexander, in one of his stories). Afrasiyab's brother Garsiwaz envies Siyawush and convinces Afrasiyab that Siyawush is plotting against him with help from Iran. Garsiwaz persuades Siyawush to flee to Iran for his life. Afrasiyab apprehends the escaping prince and has him killed. Farangis's bootless pleas land her in jail, and Afrasiyab then orders her killed when she curses him. Fortunately the wise Piran intervenes because Farangis is pregnant. Piran takes her home, and she bears Kay Khusraw. Kay Kawus sends Giw to bring her to Iran where she marries, reluctantly, Kay Kawus's son Fariburz. Khusraw becomes king after Kawus dies. Thus does another royal daughter serve a noble purpose, this time, ironically, giving birth to a child who will come to rule the land of her father's rivals. Farangis appears rather rarely in miniatures.[33]

Katayun (also called Kitabun and Nahid) is the daughter of the king of Rum who marries Gushtasp (son of Luhrasp, successor to Kay Khusraw). Fearing Luhrasp will not yield the throne to him, for Luhrasp says his son is too young, Gushtasp leaves for Rum. Katayun dreams of a youth among her suitors and chooses him, but upon awaking she can see no such youth among the princes. The next day when the king gathers the wealthy nobles, Gushtasp comes under the assumed name of Farrukhzad, whereupon Katayun chooses him. The king, angry at his daughter's choice, threatens to behead both, but his minister intervenes and persuades the king merely to banish them to live on Gushtasp's hunting and her few gems. Later Katayun's two sisters are wooed, one by the Rumi chief, Mirin. The king agrees on condition that Mirin slay the wolf. In his horoscope Mirin sees a bond with a warrior from Iran. He enlists the services of Gushtasp, who then slays the wolf, but Mirin claims the credit and wins the hand of Dilanjam. A second Rumi chief, Ahran, seeks the king's youngest daughter, but is told she will be his only if he can slay the dragon of Mount Saqila. Ahran then also goes to Gushtasp and asks him to slay the dragon. Gushtasp obliges, removes the monster's teeth, and gives the carcass to Ahran. Later, when Gushtasp joins in polo and archery, King Afrasiyab wants to know who he is. Gushtasp reveals himself as the one Afrasiyab had driven away. He produces the dragon's teeth, still not entirely convincing the king. At length, Luhrasp sends his other son, Zarir, to bestow the throne on Gushtasp. Gushtasp and Katayun leave for Iran, and Luhrasp retires to solitude. Gushtasp later becomes the "Constantine of Zoroastrianism."

Gushtasp and Katayun had two daughters, Humay and Bihafarid. With Isfandiyar in prison and Gushtasp gone to Sistan for solitude, the Turanian Arjasp attacks Iran for the fourth time, wins the conflict, and kidnaps Humay and Bihafarid. Gushtasp asks his vizir, Jamasp, to solicit Isfandiyar to free his sisters. Isfandiyar agrees reluctantly and decides also to avenge uncle Zarir, who died in Arjasp's first attack. After reconciling with his father, Isfandiyar goes to Turan disguised as a rich merchant, Kharrad, to do business. Humay and Bihafarid, sent to fetch water, pass his shop. Isfandiyar hides his face as they enter to plead their cause with him. When Isfandiyar answers, Humay recognizes his voice. After the daughters return to the palace, Isfandiyar persuades Arjasp to hold a feast on the ramparts, saying he promised God a feast in thanksgiving if he is delivered from a storm and taken safely to Turan. At the feast, Afrasiyab's men become drunk, and a smoke signal alerts Isfandiyar's forces to attack. Rushing into the palace, sometimes called the Brazen Hold or Iron Fortress, Isfandiyar tells his sisters to go to the warehouse and then he kills Arjasp. The story has features similar to those of the rescues of Shahrinaz and Arnawaz by Faridun, of Rama's wife Sita, and of Helen of Troy, and recalls Rustam's use of the merchant disguise in an attack on Turan.

Finally, heroines are sometimes featured as sisters. Shahrinaz and Arnawaz—the first women one encounters in the *Shahnama*—are the two princess sisters of Jamshid, whom Dahhak had killed. When Dahhak seizes the murdered shah's sisters, Faridun vows to rescue them (according to the Avesta), and in a dream-like vision a maiden reveals Dahhak's location. Faridun crosses the river Dijla (Tigris) in Baghdad on horseback and makes for Dahhak's noble castle with its threat of untold dangers. Faridun approaches, tears down Dahhak's protective talisman, and enters. Inside he discovers the two women, who inform him that Dahhak has fled to Hindustan. Dahhak soon returns in a rage, only to encounter Faridun, who is more than ready for him. Faridun marries both Shahrinaz, who becomes the mother of Salm and Tur, and Arnawaz, who gives birth to the tragic prince Iraj. The story emphasizes the heroines' devotion to each other and to the values their father had espoused.[34]

Peer relationships and friendships among heroes receive surprisingly little attention. Loyalty is surely a major heroic virtue; but it is generally loyalty to family, tribe, nation, or supreme authority. As peers, heroes allow few equals. And friendships can be sorely tried—and fail in the end, as in the case of Rustam and Isfandiyar, or Hang Tuah and Hang Jebat. Heroes meet at the peer level sometimes as boon companions, bending the elbow as they listen to stories of bygone heroes. Sometimes they collaborate as brothers in arms against a common enemy. Occasionally one hero will arrive on the scene of conflict in time to extricate his equal from embarrassment and defeat. On the whole, however, friendship seems to take second place to larger purposes and commitments. Heroic narratives and images seem less interested in the intricacies of peer relationships than in family dynamics.

The Hero in Relation to a Larger World Scene

Two final relational motifs connect the hero to a world beyond that of blood and marital ties. The first casts the hero as a crucial link in royal genealogy. Numerous dynasties in Islamic history have felt it critical to their claims to legitimacy to establish the heroic origins of their lineages. One could say that, in a sense, virtually all of the major heroes, both those well-attested historically and those still largely legendary, have functioned as progenitors. Although motives for such connections are always complex, the linkage seems at times more prominently to serve political ends; at others, the design seems more suited to enhancing ethnic or cultural prestige. Some examples from medieval Iranian history include the following. The tenth-century Saffarid dynasty, founded by Ya'qub ibn al-Layth the Coppersmith, traced its lineage back to the first Iranian king, Jamshid. The ninth-century Tahirids boasted descent from Rustam. In the tenth century, the Samanids harked back to the late Sasanian Bahram Chubin, as did the Ziyarid dynasty. And in tenth-century Baghdad, the Buwayhids claimed the famous Sasanian Romantic Adventurer, King Bahram Gur.[35] As mentioned earlier, Malay legends go to great lengths to associate the royal family with Iskandar.

An intriguing Ottoman Turkish work entitled *Subhat al-akhbar,* or "Rosary of World History" as the German facsimile edition puts it, shows in text and pictures how important the heroic figures of the greater Islamic world were in the lineage of an Ottoman Sultan of the eighteenth century. Beginning with Adam and Eve, the genealogy proceeds gradually to trifurcate into columns of (1) heroes and kings of the past, (2) religious heroes through the family of Muhammad and the Imams, and (3) the caliphs and Sultans. It apparently suited the Ottoman patron to cast himself as a descendent of the great heroic figures, royal and religious, and as a perpetuator of their line. That many of the heroes are Iranian makes no difference.[36]

A similar message is communicated by several miniatures in which King Solomon is depicted as presiding over the ranks of kings and heroes well back into history. Rustam stands out prominently, as do other Iranian heroes.[37] Such concern with locating heroes in one's past is paralleled by the interest in portraying certain heroes as descended from major religious or prophetic forbears. Antar traces his lineage back to Noah, via Shaddad to Shem.[38] Manuchihr says his lineage will become evident when he fights; everyone will know that he is of the line of his grandfather Faridun.[39] A common related theme is the rediscovery of one's lineage in the unexpected meeting of long-lost relatives. In both the Antar and Dhat al-Himma stories, the amulet or talisman is a device used often as a means of later recognition. Antar's half-brother Shaybub meets his maternal aunt, who tells him of his heritage, of how anguished his father had been when Shaybub was captured, and of how the aunt had left distinguishing marks on his body—a white mole on his shoulder "and other black marks and signs." After doing battle long and hard, Antar discovers that he is the uncle of Hammam and the cousin of Ghawwar, his erstwhile enemies.[40]

The second world-expanding theme describes the hero as well beyond the merely human. Some heroes are so much larger than life that they develop into literally cosmic figures and corporate personalities. The hero's apotheosis into the "perfect person"—or, as H. Corbin puts it, "Man of Light"—is a feature especially pertinent to religious characters. We have already seen, however, that an analogous development can occur in other heroes as well. J. S. Meisami observes that Bahram Gur's journey from temporal to spiritual kingship "incorporates the dual functions of priest and king, echoing both an ancient Iranian ideal of kingship and the Islamic concept of the king as Perfect Man."[41] The concept of the perfect person places even some originally non-religious figures in the line of the greatest of religious heroes, including the Prophet Muhammad. The theme is vast and leads off in several important but, for present purposes, tangential directions. For the moment, it must suffice to note that Alexander the Great is probably the finest example of this sort of elevation, a process that has been called "Euhemerization," after the Greek Euhemerus, whose legend elevated him far above the realm of the merely human. As we mentioned in chapter four, Alexander developed from a pre-Islamic foreigner, to a heroic world-conqueror, to a prophet, sage, and "perfect person."[42]

Growing into well-integrated members of their own families, as well as of the larger human family, is only one dimension of the struggle that heroes must face courageously. The next chapter discusses several other aspects of the heroic struggle, both internal and external.

Chapter Eleven

The Two Struggles and the Enemy's Many Faces

Struggle forms a major theme in the life of the hero. As suggested in chapter six (on villains and evil), the cause of the contest can assume a variety of guises. In the more traditional villains, one sees personifications of various negative forces as well as reminiscences of historical enemies, Muslim and non-Muslim. Evil as an abstract concept or vaguely mysterious power for seduction or destruction rarely plays a role in the classic heroic narratives, though it does begin to emerge as part of the modern hero's world.

In the present chapter we shall discuss some of the fundamental heroic attitudes toward struggle and the principal characteristics of the hero's encounters with the enemy. The term "two struggles" refers to the classic Muslim understanding of the two aspects of *jihad,* "struggle" with a variety of connotations, not merely "holy war" as it is so often rendered. The "lesser" struggle is that against the external enemy, the infidel or outside aggressor. Some major folk heroes especially are often associated with that outer dimension and do not appear deliberately to take up arms against their own inner demons. As we shall see, however, the same Islamicate cultures that produced and cherished stories of such spiritual extroverts as Antar and Rustam also developed highly sophisticated interpretations of the struggle's implications for the hero within. "Greater struggle" describes the battle against the inner nemesis of one's baser human tendencies, recalling the saying of Muhammad, "Your greatest enemy is between your two sides." Not surprisingly, some religious heroes concern themselves with the interior struggle to a greater degree than do others; but now and then, a royal type can approach overtly the level of sensitivity and self-awareness requisite for the "greater *jihad.*"

A number of themes emerge from a look at heroic struggle. First, when confronted with serious danger, challenge, or aggression, the hero expresses a willingness to risk death, whether in

hopes of winning the paradise of martyrs or as a way of maintaining honor and avoiding the shame of a cowardly withdrawal.
Second, when advancing to the fray, the hero often packs weapons
that become identifying marks, and frequently rides a horse whose
fame nearly equals his own. Third, both outer and inner struggle
are part of every heroic life, even when the narrative does not
strike the present-day reader as psychologically insightful. Fourth,
military engagement, with special emphasis on the virtually man-
datory episodes of single combat, and confrontations with the
"Beast" are two of the chief metaphors for struggle. Finally, two
important social dimensions of struggle emerge: the round table or
fraternity of warriors takes several forms in the various Islamicate
cultures; and relationships between the sexes, both as allies and as
antagonists, are a striking feature in many stories.

The Willingness to Die for a Cause

Media coverage of recent developments in the Middle East and
elsewhere in the Islamic world has often left the non-Muslim public
convinced that Muslims are everywhere eager to fling themselves
upon the pyre of martyrdom. But even in the traditional accounts
of the great religious heroes, the main character is rarely hungry,
much less crazed, for death. Ja'far, the first martyr according to
popular Swahili traditions, does not "go gentle into that good
night"; he does not wish to die or to suffer multiple wounds. He
is, however, willing to pay a price to support a just cause. So are all
heroes, in varying degrees, but especially religious heroes.

The story of the Shi'i protomartyr, Husayn, has been widely
told and been popular as far east as Malaysia. This Shi'i variation
on the theme of the tragic prince has rated more versions of his
epic in more different languages than almost any other religious
hero. Martyrs are the ultimate warriors for principle, standing up
against astronomical odds when a more pragmatic person would
long since have called for arbitration or surrender. Death *is* victory,
both in itself and its immediate consequences, and in the fact that
it leaves to the cowardly perpetrator only the bitterest dregs of
indefensible aggression and atrocity. Of Husayn's struggle J. Knappert observes, "Like Roland, Husein finds his strength in the fact
that he is fighting the enemies of his faith and, like Roland, he has
a long battle to fight before he is allowed to die."[1]

In the *Shahnama*, the major heroes are "protectors of the Divine-human (in Iranian context that is, royal) order against both human and supernatural menaces."[2] Heroes like Rustam, Faridun, Isfandiyar, and a score of others, are willing to put their lives on the line in service of a greater good. When Kay Khusraw decides to go into a mysterious self-imposed exile, the Knights of his Round Table follow him. Even after the sovereign tells his paladins to return lest they be caught in the approaching blizzard, several stay out of sheer loyalty and die in the storm on the mountaintop. Hang Tuah serves his ruler in a similar capacity and would give his life to preserve order at the center of the realm. Most often, of course, the willingness to face the threat of death comes to the fore when each hero marches out to do battle with an enemy of towering size and strength. To such direct encounters we shall return shortly. First we will look at two symbolic aspects of the hero's approach to certain danger—namely, arms and mount.

The Symbolism of Weaponry and Horse

Multiple issues appear in the naming and description of weaponry and horses. According to H. T. Norris, for example, "The occult side of the Arabian hero's personality, his sword and his amazing horse are to be observed in the inter-relation between medieval star names, swords and a mighty hero (*jabbar*) who is one of two brothers and one of three royal children."[3] Some of the more famous swords in the Arabic *sira* literature are these: Antar's sword called Dami, made of meteorite; Abu Zayd Hilali's sword named Shahman, one blow of which can cut two mounted camels into four halves; Amr ibn Maʿdi Karib's (called Knight of the Arabs) sword Samsama, traditionally believed to have been handed down to the Abbasid Caliph al-Mahdi (775-785). Weapons in the Arabian romances are described as quite similar to those of the early Caliphate. David's mail and hauberks are much in demand in the popular Arabic epics.[4]

Rustam's description of his own armor is as vivid as any. His sword he calls "a cloud which has the luster of water (tempered steel) but which rains blood." He, along with other heroes, needs a mace as big as a chunk of mountain.[5] At one point after a period in retirement, Rustam bestirs himself to do battle against Isfandiyar. He goes to his armory and, with great feeling, calls on his weaponry to serve him well in the coming encounter; the weapons have, after all, enjoyed sufficient rest of late.[6] But the Persian hero's arsenal never vies with the hero for the audience's attention. In at least one other epic tradition, the tools of combat step into the narrative foreground almost to the point of becoming characters in the story. In Turkic epics, armor and weapons frequently utter words of wisdom to the hero. For example, Sajn's "white armor" exhorts the warrior on the verge of battle: "Be not afraid, oh hero Sajn. Speak no other words. If you do not destroy the ranks of the enemy, it will be your fault. If ninety arrows come and penetrate me, it will be my fault. May Heaven protect you."[7]

Though the Swahili historical chronicles tell of many battles on land and sea, they never mention horses or camels; but Swahili epic literature revels in detailed descriptions of both, as well as of the weaponry used.[8] Swahili epics parallel the hereditary aspect of the hero's weapons with that of the villain's. Just as Muhammad's armor of chain mail was originally fashioned by David, the master armorer, and handed down through Solomon, so the enemy's weaponry and armor have come down to him from the arch-enemy, Pharoah. Ali arms himself with a staff made of wood from Noah's ark.[9] A variety of weapons that once belonged to prophets become great prizes for the heroes who manage to take possession of them. One of the clearest examples is that of Hamza, who discovers in Solomon's palace a treasury whose contents include the Ishaq's sword Samsam, belt Kamkam, and saddle; Isma'il's armor; the boots of Salih; and the helmet of Hud.[10] As chapter seven indicated, some weapons of non-religious characters also take on the status of heirlooms. Most notable is the ox-headed mace Faridun had forged for himself, which becomes both the symbol of authority and identifying mark of subsequent heroes. Among Faridun's less noble descendents, the sword of rebel son Salm plays a similar role.

Certain specific weapons are of such fame and importance as to warrant particular and more detailed attention. Although bow and arrow are also significant, we must leave them aside for now and consider only blades and other hand-wielded tools.[11] Two such weapons play prominent roles. The first, Dhu ʾl-Faqar, appears in a wide range of religious heroic traditions; the second, Hang Tuah's dagger, is distinctively Southeast Asian.

Ali's sword, Dhu ʾl-Faqar, originally belonged to Muhammad, who, according to one version, had found it at Badr. Like many ancient Arab swords, it has a double point. At Uhud, Ali fights in the front line. When his sword breaks, Muhammad gives him Dhu

ʾl-Faqar. At first the Prophet worries that Ali will have trouble handling the blade; but he wields it deftly, prompting Muhammad to exclaim, "There is no sword like Dhu ʾl-Faqar, and no hero like Ali!"[12] The crux of the matter is that the hero receives his sword from another whom he admires or who wins or captures it in a battle.[13] The sword, whose name means "The Cleaver" (or, metaphorically, "The Discriminator"), is said to be longer than any other. One etymology explains that the name derives from grooves or notches (fuqra) in the blade. Dhu ʾl-Faqar appears in a fairly large number of miniature paintings and functions as a convenient iconographic tag, but typically without showing grooves or notches. The forked tip, for blinding an enemy, evidences the weapon's magical quality. Miniaturists often emphasize the forked tip by equipping Ali with an identically shaped scabbard.[14]

In the story of Hang Tuah and in other Malay heroic tales, the *kris* is the weapon of choice. A short blade, somewhat longer than a large dagger, the kris's physical appearance is hardly sufficient to strike fear into enemy hearts. But there is more to this weapon than meets the eye. According to S. Errington, the kris functions as a "repository of a sort of free-floating energy from the world."[15] Individual blades vary in potency, and only the greater hero can manage the more powerful weapon. In the hands of a warrior not possessed of the requisite special knowledge (tahu)—hands such as Tameng Sari's (an invader intent on destroying Malaka), or Hang Jebat's (insider though he was)—a powerful kris spells destruction. Only the proper knowledge, gained through focused attention under the tutelage of a guide, can control the blade and prevent it from possessing the one who wields it and causing him to run amok. When warrior and weapon are a perfect match for each other, the blade can even warn its master of impending danger.

In Hang Tuah's hands, the kris becomes an instrument for maintaining the order of the cosmos, in service to a king. As suggested in chapter three, Hang Tuah initially relied on his special knowledge to gain possession of the weapon. Now his *tahu* serves to fashion the kris into a force for good. The kris functions as a mark of office and authority, and symbolizes the very force that undergirds the power of its possessor and those he serves. When Hang Tuah dives to retrieve the Sultan's crown, lost overboard as the Sultan gazes down at a golden fish, the hero loses his kris to a

207

white crocodile. Thereafter the fortunes of the Sultanate of Malaka take a steady downward turn; both sultan and Hang Tuah suffer constant illness. The loss of crown and blade thus portend the victorious Portuguese invasion.[16]

Horses, like weapons, often boast a distinguished lineage or history of ownership. Hamza finds a steed descended from that of Solomon; Miqdad's wondrously fast horse Rishan is identified as a foal of the Prophet's mare.[17] A hero's horse is particularly important in the various branches of Turkic epic. Dede Korkut often likens horses to falcons and describes them as plumed, clearly linking them to the phenomenon of the flying horse of shamanistic origin, of which Muhammad's mount Buraq is a relative.[18] Köroghlu's mount Kyrat and Bamsi Beyrek's Bozat (both names meaning "Gray Horse") are endowed with such extraordinary powers as speech and flight. Sometimes the hero's best advice comes literally from the horse's mouth.[19] The bond between hero and horse figures quite prominently in Turkic stories. Central Asian Kazakh hero Targhyn (of the epic by the same name) on his deathbed sings to his horse, Tarlan, a farewell song that would surely have inspired jealousy in the hero's wife: "Your ribs please me, they are like a fortress built from stone. Your hips please me, they are like the smith's anvil," and so on. Seldom has a beloved heard more glowing praise from a lover.[20]

No horse is more legendary than Rustam's Rakhsh. As in many heroic narratives, the storyteller gives considerable attention to the process by which the hero chooses his mount. Rustam needs a steed of sufficient durability to carry its master's prodigious bulk. Every time Rustam put his hand on a horse's back to test its strength, its belly dragged the ground. With vision keen enough to see an "ant's footprint on a black cloak two leagues away," Rakhsh is one of a kind; she and Rustam were destined for each other. The owner's price for the rose-colored mare: the restoration of justice to the Iranian fatherland. Rakhsh is as ready for the challenge as the laughing paladin who alone can ride her. Several miniature paintings have depicted the scene with wit and charm.[21] Other famous steeds from the *Shahnama* are Bizhan's horse, Shabrang ("Night-hued"), and Khusraw Parwiz's two horses: the world's fastest, Shabdiz ("Midnight"), and the second fastest, Gulgun ("Rose-hued"). The many illustrations to the romance of Khusraw and Shirin that expand on Firdawsi are usually faithful to the text in their choice of the horses' colors. Depictions of the scene in which Khusraw spies Shirin bathing typically offer good examples.

Two major religious heroes have especially famous mounts. When Muhammad is introduced to Buraq, the human-headed winged quadruped assigned to bear him aloft on his Night Journey and Ascension, the hybrid creature declines to carry the Prophet and has to be cajoled into doing so. She has in the past served Abraham and other prophets.[22] Buraq thus takes her place in the tradition of prophetic heirlooms. The second most famous animal associated with a religious hero is Ali's mule Duldul, easily identifiable by its exaggeratedly long ears and sometimes by a pinkish, speckled coat.[23]

The Greater and Lesser *Jihads*

Swahili heroic literature deals with the subject of the lesser *jihad* perhaps more than any other Islamicate tradition. J. Knappert observes that "The fundamental theme in the Swahili epic is the war against the infidels, be they undefinable demoniac enemies like Ra's al-Ghul, intractable pagans like King Katirifu, or Christians like the Greek emperor or the nineteenth-century Germans, about whose attacks several epics were composed in Swahili in about 1910."[24] The archetype of the outward *jihad* in Islamicate heroic literature is surely the Herekali epic. Religious polemic suffuses much of the narrative and appears in such details as the Byzantines' temerity in launching their fourth attack during the ritual prayer and the centrality of martyrdom as motive for the Muslim fighters. In one curious scene, the Swahili epic describes how one of the spies of Heraklios is brought before Muhammad. Captivated by the Prophet's goodness and light, the spy wants to tell all; but when Muhammad asks him to reveal the number of Byzantine troops, he declines for fear of the emperor. Umar threatens to kill the spy, but Muhammad orders him released. When the hapless Byzantine reports back to the emperor, the latter executes him for singing Muhammad's praises. As the spy's head rolls away, it professes itself a Muslim.[25]

The "greater struggle" occupies the attention of some of the more sophisticated religious heroes, although in general the stories of such popular holy persons as Abd al-Qadir al-Jilani and Sunan Bonan include a generous measure of miraculous swashbuckling. It is more difficult to describe the inner contest in vivid terms than to paint a picture of armed contingents clashing amid clouds of sun-blotting dust across battle fields strewn with severed limbs. But though saint and prophet are often associated with conquest, they remain first and foremost warriors of the spirit and only secondarily combatants in the arena of the lesser struggle. As noted above, tradition sometimes links religious heroes with heirloom weaponry. Nevertheless, even when the prophet or saint ostensibly battles an outward foe, enemy and weapon are also allegories of the interior struggle.

Images of Struggle: Battle and the Beast

The grand melee is stock in trade for virtually all epic narratives, as well as for the artists who have illustrated them. Storytellers delight in describing how the thundering of the troops raises such dust that day turns to night, how the earth shakes, how blood runs like a river, and how the clash of arms can be heard for miles. Miniaturists, especially in Persia, India, and Turkey, have found in such scenes the greatest challenge to their compositional skills. They have usually met the challenge by packing their picture frames to the point of bursting with seething tumult and eye-popping panoply. Just as the narratives often use a formula to describe battle scenes, so do the painters. One can easily spot visual quotations, not only of overall compositional schemes and landscape settings, but of individual characters and figures (horses, elephants, and other animals) as well.[26]

According to W. Hanaway, battle scenes in the popular romances usually follow a pattern that includes seven elements. At dawn the drums call the two sides to the battle lines. There follows a description of the principal hero's horse and accoutrements. Prelude to single combat includes challenge and boasting, followed by single combat itself recounted in minutest detail. Then the battle at large commences, often described in but a few lines of text. Another drum signals a moratorium at dusk. The last element involves the sending out of the night patrols.[27]

We have already described some of the more famous scenes of single combat, including those between Rustam and his own son Suhrab, Rustam and his friend Isfandiyar, and Hang Tuah with his long-time companion Hang Jebat. They are more famous perhaps because of their poignancy and tragic dimensions. Precipitated by destiny or fate, such encounters raise thorny questions of human freedom and responsibility, as well as of loyalty and love. More often, of course, scenes of conflict pit unambiguously inimical forces against each other. Here are some of the principal elements that emerge from a study of scenes of single combat.

A common theme is that of the chief knight on one side scouring the enemy ranks in search of their most celebrated champion. The challenger inevitably has trouble locating the object of his rage. As one thing and another postpones the champion's appearance, the challenger has to settle for dispatching any number of lesser, but by no means lightweight, warriors. Meanwhile, the champion's ire only increases as he watches his fine young soldiers go down in death or into captivity. At length, the hero breaks through all restraints to take the field in a clash of titans. Says Antar to al-Abd Zinjir, "Woe to you, by God the Judge. I only stood aside in this combat on account of my contempt for you and those like you who count as nothing in my eyes. Were it not for the fact that you have slain my men and captured my cubs I would not have come forth against you."[28]

Next to his battle with Hang Jebat, Hang Tuah's most important contests are with the guru of the Javanese soldiers and the amok Tameng Sari. A number of hit men are sent against Hang Tuah by the rival Sultan of Majapahit. They try all sorts of ruses to do him in, including attempts to make him so drunk he cannot fight, but Hang Tuah overcomes all threats and grows in his stature as principal champion of the Sultan of Malaka. Tameng Sari's violence arises from his being amok and possessing the magical kris, which he loses to the shrewd Hang Tuah. It is interesting to note that both of his main single combats occur before he and his four colleagues head off to Wirana Pura mountain to study the arts of war with the guru Sang Persata Nala. Thereafter, emphasis seems to fall on the combat of the group rather than on that of Hang Tuah alone, until he is forced to face his friend Hang Jebat, who has run amok in the palace.[29]

In *Sirat Antar,* the giant Suwayd ibn Uwayd, lord of the Banu Tamim, goes up against Antar at the request of the usurper Ghawwar ibn Dinar. As prelude to the fight, Ghamra spends the night telling stories of the giant's callous might. Next morning Antar meets the foe without knowing he is Suwayd, but suspecting so on the basis of Ghamra's account. Later in the same battle, Antar fights the champion Lawn az-Zalam ("Color of Darkness") and

bests him without breaking a sweat.[30] The hero unhorses both chal-
lengers using the butt of his spear, so as to capture rather than kill
them. He refrains, not out of compassion, but as a way of proving
how little concern such upstarts cause him. To Antar's considerable
displeasure, his overzealous son Ghasub later kills the captive giant.
Lawn az-Zalam goes on to become one of Antar's staunchest supporters. In the Arabic tales, even the most sanguinary combat often
ends in the hero's gaining new allies from among his former enemies. In addition, as suggested earlier, he often discovers that the
enemy are actually his own kin from some long-separated ancestor.[31]

Probably the most unusual scene of single combat occurs in
the Swahili epic of the Battle of Uhud. There we find the Prophet
Muhammad responding to the challenge of one of his adversaries
of the Quraysh tribe, Ubay ibn Khalaf. Mounted and brandishing
a long sword, the enemy boldly seeks the honor of killing Muhammad. The Prophet's companions immediately gather around to
protect him. But to their great surprise Muhammad has decided
to face the challenger alone, armed with no more than a small
dagger. In the ensuing engagement, the Prophet hits the enemy
with the flat of the blade. Though he has barely nicked the
Qurayshi, the wound proves fatal several days hence. The poet delights in recounting how the big bad challenger whimpers and how
his own people mock him. They do not understand that even the
slightest wound from Muhammad can wipe out a world of evildoers. Ubay explains, "By God, if this pain had been divided and
everyone had been given even a little of it, all the people, everybody
in the world . . . . If everyone had got it, all the people on earth
. . . would have passed over (to the next world)." The poet insists
that Muhammad "during the whole of his life killed nobody whatever by his own hand. The Prophet did nothing at all like this
except in the case of this evildoer . . . ."[32]

Depictions of scenes of single combat provide a major visual
theme in illustrated manuscripts of all kinds. One miniature even
shows Muhammad on the verge of engaging a challenger when
Gabriel intervenes to prevent the fight. Most popular are scenes
from the *Shahnama* in which the various Iranian champions take
on the toughest of the Turanians. We have already mentioned some
of the encounters of Rustam and Antar. Unlike scenes of mass
battle, which draw the viewer's eye hither and thither across the

field of action, those of single combat challenge the miniaturist to focus on a dramatic moment and rivet the viewer on the central action. Sometimes the artist will take the opportunity to make a thoughtful statement on the nature of human life and mortality, as in the scene of Rustam and Isfandiyar described in chapter two. Some scenes offer a chance to parade a few satisfyingly familiar iconographic tags before the viewer, while including some action readily identifiable from the text at hand, such as Rustam's hoisting Ashkabus (or Afrasiyab) high out of his saddle. (See Figure 15.) Many are rather generic and, like all formulae, virtually interchangeable with other scenes of the type. Painters insert them to vary the visual rhythm and add a dash of drama.[33]

In chapter six we mentioned a number of forms that evil and the enemy can assume in heroic narratives. The single most prominent non-human shape which sinister power can take was left for the present context, owing to the important metaphorical and/or allegorical dimensions associated with it. Monstrous beasts of various types play a very important role in the process of heroic coming of age. We have already seen how Firdawsi regarded the demon as an allegory for the godless, amoral person. Dragons, lions, wolves, the occasional rhinoceros, and other hybrid wild things seem to represent not merely forces that threaten the world externally, but those within the hero as well. Several aspects of this theme are especially important.

First, Islamic tradition has long identified the baser human tendencies, referred to collectively as *nafs*, with wild beasts such as the dragon or the wolf. *Nafs* has also been described in martial terms, with the troops of *nafs* joining battle with those of heart or spirit—*qalb* and *ruh*. Mystical poets like Rumi and Attar speak of Moses overcoming the dragon of *nafs* when he throws down his staff, and of the jealousy of Joseph's brothers as the real wolves in that story, against their claim that an actual wolf has devoured their brother. Among religious heroes, Ali and Muhammad are the most important who confront the beast—Ali especially in the Shi'i *Khawarannama* and Muhammad in the expanded version of his biography that gained popularity particularly in Turkey. Second, human beings are referred to as dragons rather frequently in the *Shahnama*. When Faridun sets out to test his three sons, he assumes the form of a dragon. Dahhak, with the two serpents sprouting from his shoulders, is the human dragon par excellence. Among

213

Figure 15: Rustam lifts Turanian king Afrasiyab from his saddle.

the other villain-dragons are Afrasiyab, so described nearly a dozen times; Iskandar's Indian opponent Porus; Ardawan, who murders Ardashir to end a dynasty and start another; and Rustam's enemy Puladwand.

Third, beasts such as dragons and wolves appear as forces that terrorize the land. Only the best of the heroes can rid the earth of such menaces. Bizhan saves the Armani people from the scourge of the wild boars; Isfandiyar slays the dragon of Mt. Saqila; Iskandar frees the Arabs from the dragon that has plagued their land. Fourth, these beasts often stand between the hero and the accomplishment of a task essential to the hero's destiny. Antar comes of age by wrestling a lion. In the *Haft Paykar*, Bahram Gur must win his crown by snatching it from between two ravenous lions; he must kill a dragon who guards a treasure in a cave, and he faces the dreaded rhino-wolf. (See Figure 16.) Nearly all of the major Arabicate and Persianate heroes fight at least one dragon, and some of the most strikingly beautiful miniature paintings depict those scenes. The dragons, usually Chinese in style, writhe sinuously across the picture frame, adding a note of graceful terror to the image.[34] Farther to the east, where the dragon is regarded as a benevolent creature, other beasts fill the role. Hang Tuah confronts a warrior who has the power to become various animals, including a tiger. Our hero responds by becoming a still-larger tiger. One way of interpreting the confrontations with fierce animals sees them as manifestations of the darker side of the self as well as of external negative forces. Whichever power they represent, the important issue is that the hero is the one who summons up the courage to deal with them over and over again.

Social Dimensions of the Struggle

Heroic struggle occurs in a variety of social contexts as well as within the individual. Here we shall mention two such contexts. First, heroes sometimes belong to brotherhoods of knights or warriors; and second, friction and outright conflict can occur between masculine and feminine elements, either literally between man and woman or more symbolically between the masculine and feminine aspects within every human being.

One can find fascinating parallels between the Arthurian legend of the Knights of the Round Table and the inner circle of Kay Khusraw's paladins. Along with Rustam and Isfandiyar we find, for

215

Figure 16: Bahram Gur kills the rhino-wolf.

example, Gudarz, Giw, Bizhan, Tus, and Gustahm.[35] In the story of Hang Tuah, one finds a similar squad of *hulubalang* ("warriors") engaged in the service of the Sultan of Malaka. Hang Tuah and his four companions form a redoubtable fighting force, embark on several journeys together, and most notably enlist the services of a guru in the mountains to teach them the martial arts. The group breaks apart eventually and tragically, but the phenomenon of the warrior gang is unmistakable. Still another round table appears in the confederation of early fighting heroes gathered around Muhammad. The most prominent circle includes, in a Swahili version, Ali, Umar, sometimes Abu Bakr, Khalid ibn al-Walid, sometimes Amr ibn al-As, sometimes Zubayr, and Miqdad.[36]

As mentioned earlier in the section on warrior women, a number of important female characters appear prominently in scenes of war and conflict. Ghamra, consort of Antar, leads her own cohort, and the narrator describes her as "a wonder in the eyes" of all the rest.[37] A number of the major narratives offer an important insight into some of the critical gender issues under consideration among the peoples that created and reveled in the stories.

Some North African variations of the Bani Hilal story emphasize the role of women more than others. The Tunisian version of Zaziya in Bani Hilal is a true earth-mother type who wades into battle and does not hesitate to ensure the tribe's survival by entering a distasteful marriage to obtain needed food. Several versions describe women as both creators and solvers of problems, associating with them highly stereotyped feminine wiles, eroticism, and martial skills. There women appear as both a major source of conflict and a critical resource for its resolution.[38]

Among the scenes most frequently depicted in North African reverse glass painting and their printed counterparts are those which show either Antar or Abu Zayd conquering an enemy, with the beloved Abla or Zaziya seated to the side in a howda. Some similar scenes make a set of conflicting values still clearer: Bedouin woman on one side, verdant urban setting of the settled people on the other, and in the middle, combat between the nomad and the city-dweller. According to B. Connelly, both the paintings and the tales exhibit three recurring themes: "(1) arrival in a place, (2) confrontation ensuing from the boundary transgression, and (3) the sacrifice of a nubile, marriageable female in recompense for that encroachment."[39]

In addition to their roles as warrior-women, women sometimes go into battle disguised as men. One could take this as a sub-theme of the motif of disguise and mistaken identity. We have already mentioned Suhrab's single combat with Gurdafarid at the White Palace. In the Bani Hilal story, Zaziya, who has become a judge in Andalusia, advances as a knight against troops who carry parasols. Their ninety-five-year-old leader fights Zaziya to a stalemate and asks whose son his worthy opponent is. She reveals herself, whereupon her former husband and murderer of her brothers (the ninety-five-year-old Dhiyab) kicks her to death. This and two related incidents suggest, according to Connelly, "a hidden, underlying discomfort with the relationship between the sexes—perhaps a discomfort with marriage and the penetration of boundaries, both personal and group, that coupling implies."[40]

Still another variation on the disguise theme in relation to that of male-female combat appears in the story, from the Turkish *Book of Dede Korkut,* of Bamsi Beyrek's efforts to win the hand of Banu Chichek. While off on a hunt with other princes, the hero comes upon the encampment of the girl he is destined to marry. She approaches disguised as one of her own nurses and challenges him to a contest of hunting, shooting, and wrestling. Banu Chichek assures him that if he can beat her, he will also be able to overcome her mistress. After winning the first two tests, Bamsi summons all his strength to throw the girl in wrestling. Then she divulges her identity.[41] In some instances, male-female combat occurs between the hero and a woman destined to become partners, and without the device of disguise. For example, in the Antar story, the hero and his consort Ghamra first become a pair when Antar rapes her after defeating her in single combat.

In his psychological analysis of the *Shahnama,* A. Shariati discusses the poet's apparent fear of the feminine. The hero Isfandiyar, among others, utters advice such as "Never divulge your innermost secret to a woman, or you'll find it all over the street; don't follow a woman's orders, for you'll never find a woman whose advice is sound." All sorts of problems come from associating with women, says the poet. Most telling of all, Firdawsi likens a woman to a dragon, for the two share the qualities of treachery and danger. Shariati sees here evidence of the poet's fascination with, and fear of being devoured by, the feminine—specifically, his mother. In the person of Siyawush, one can see the clearest instance of the poet's projection of his own fears onto one of his characters. Siyawush flees his step-mother, Sudaba, preferring to endure exile rather than give in to desire. Some of Shariati's analysis presses his point too far, but it does offer a good example of a contemporary psychological perspective on the theme.[42]

Heroes have this in common with more ordinary folk: struggle. Perhaps more than any other single aspect of heroic experience, it is this one that makes a hero heroic. Struggle also forces heroes to deal, eventually, with their ordinary human limitations. To that subject we now turn in chapter twelve.

Chapter Twelve

Rediscovery of Authentic Humanity:
The Heroic Mind and Heart

The prize of the hero's quest is sometimes quite other than was anticipated or desired at the outset. What the authors and artists so often seem to communicate is that one cannot ultimately escape from one's humanity. One of their key insights appears to be the need to accept one's mortality and to go on in the face of it. A powerful motive in some heroes' quests is the thirst for immortality, to be achieved indirectly, through power or fame or descendents, or more directly, through the literal avoidance of death.

Iskandar may be the only major hero who sets out explicitly to find the Water of Life. Still, he enjoys the company of numerous other heroes in his efforts to outflank the grim reaper. Throughout the Islamicate materials, one sees a constant tension between the recourse to physical prowess or personal cleverness on the one hand, and the appeal to a superior power or force as means to gaining immortality on the other. Generally speaking, heroes who are more consciously aware of their own contingency and of their existence within a larger web of forces and relationships are ultimately the more credible. In other words, the hero must come to terms with the limits of his power; he must meet his match. In the words of Joseph Campbell: "the first work of the hero is to retreat from the world scene of secondary effects to those causal zones of the psyche where the difficulties really reside, and there clarify the difficulties, eradicate them in his own case (i.e., give battle to the nursery demons of his local culture) and break through to the undistorted, direct experience and assimilation of what C. G. Jung has called 'the archetypal images.'"[1] That task calls for considerable self-knowledge, certainly more than many critics are willing to attribute to medieval Islamicate literary characters.[2] We shall see to what degree our heroes live up to the demands of the "examined life."

The Notion of a Heroic Biography

Islamicate heroic types exhibit a broad spectrum of human qualities. They vary in the degree to which the accounts of the hero's exploits approximate a life story. Not all heroes fit neatly into any scheme or cycle as the one proposed here. Some, like the picaresque and the ayyar, rarely if ever model a life as such. Instead they stand for certain desirable traits or virtues. I do not suggest that their cleverness, faithfulness, bravery, wit, and spontaneity are lacking in heroes who are born, grow older, and die. It seems, rather, that a biography is less crucial to some types of characters than to others. It is true that even so salty a rogue as Abu Zayd of Saruj ends up as an older man who mellows as he reflects on his life of quackery and skullduggery, but he does not precisely grow old: he merely becomes old, rather suddenly. Heroes of his type function as selective personifications of positive or enviable aspects of human experience, sometimes more seriously, as in the earlier ayyar figures, and sometimes humorously.

Most villain types seem to share the truncated existence of these characters *a la carte.* Their roles depend little or not at all on genealogy, except to accentuate their bizarre origins, or on the manner of their exit from the stage, except to emphasize the horror of their crimes or the strength of the hero.[3]

Among those heroes whose stories develop into a more or less coherent biography, some seem to manage a kind of perpetual youth, perhaps because the audiences to whom they most appealed never clamored for heroes with realistic life cycles. These are for the most part among the characters we have termed folk heroes. They are born, grow rapidly into adulthood, often skipping an identifiable adolescence, and die. Some, like Antar and Rustam, have the equivalent of several lifetimes in which to complete their labors. Death is always sad, often tragic, and sometimes works a great hardship on survivors. Only in rare cases, however, does the folk hero reflect articulately on his approaching demise, either in advance or in the final scene itself. In modern Islamicate literatures, one could argue, the folk hero has evolved into a more integrally developing character who struggles through the rigors of human growth.

221

The Heroic Cycle: Symbolic Dimensions

Other heroes age before one's eyes, as it were, but those tend to be the royal types whose very existence is bound up in an historical process of power and succession. As we shall see shortly, the romantic version of Bahram Gur's life has the hero disappear mysteriously in the end. In a similar final scene, Kay Khusraw evaporates with the mountain mists. On the whole, however, the royal heroes come closer to passing through identifiable life stages as they ride toward eternity on the steed of impermanence. Fate, destiny, remains the one implacable force to which every wise person must ultimately bow.

Fully developed religious heroes are at once closer to the fact of mortality, or at least slightly less uncomfortable with it, and paradoxically insulated from it because of their conviction of a life beyond death. Some predominantly religious characters who retain major features of their folk prototypes, such as Ali for example, recklessly scoff at death as they wade into the fray. Confidence in their own strength lies just beneath a thin varnish of trust in God's power. But the more refined religious types seem to regard death as part of a larger picture. That fact applies to the martyr and the prophet types perhaps most of all. Religious heroes' lives have their meaning in the context of a divine plan, in which the individual plays but a miniscule part.

One might think of heroic biography as a vehicle for expressing the experience and aspirations of a people. A protracted life span, such as those of Antar and Rustam, becomes almost a metaphor for the life story of a nation or culture. S. Hanna, for example, uses such a model to interpret the Antar story. Hanna sees Antar's adventures as a summation of experiences of the Arabs in the earliest centuries after the coming of Islam. Antar's life addresses the issue of Arab superiority over both Byzantine and Persian, and criticizes the Shuʿubiya movement's refusal to acknowledge Arab social privilege as superior to that of non-Arabs.[4]

Hang Tuah's life story seems to function in a similar way in relation to the early history of the Malay Peninsula. In the *Sejara Melayu* (ca. 1536), Hang Tuah, an historical figure who died around 1500, appears as a prominent noble in the sultan's court at Malaka. There he distinguishes himself by his loyal service to the crown. The chronicle depicts Hang Tuah as a talented but altogether human figure, given to ordinary failings, whose death attracts relatively little attention. Within the next hundred and fifty years or

222

so, Hang Tuah develops into a larger-than-life personage whose adventures mirror the fortunes of his people.

In the romantic epic treatment of his story, the hero takes on a very different cast. Instead of practically growing up in the palace, the hero begins life as the son of a poor woodcutter who brings him to the city in the hope of giving him a good education. During Hang Tuah's meteoric rise in service of royalty, he accumulates power through arcane knowledge and invulnerability through his magical kris, racking up accomplishments and traveling the world from Rum to Siam. After 110 years of public life, Hang Tuah disappears with his beleaguered sultan into the country's interior. As the identity of his people is eclipsed (only temporarily, the story suggests), so does the already superannuated hero go into a kind of Imam-like concealment. Someday—perhaps—he will return as Malay fortunes rise again.[5]

Here are some of the thematic elements of the heroic rediscovery of humanity, with examples of how several major heroes deal with the human condition—what questions they ask, what they love and fear, and how they view the ultimate purpose of life.

The Message of Faridun's Iwan: *memento mori*

Heroic personages, especially of the royal type, serve one of the storyteller's didactic purposes by embodying and exemplifying attitudes toward mortality. Persian wisdom writer Saʿdi's *Gulistan* opens with a story that features a poetic inscription allegedly written on the main gate of Faridun's palace: "The world, my brother, stays around for no one; bind your heart to the World-Creator and it is sufficient."[6] Another tradition, from the same writer's *Bustan*, attributes to Faridun's predecessor, Jamshid, similar reflections. A miniature in an album of Mughal emperor Jahangir shows royal hero Jamshid writing his meditations on mortality upon a boulder. Jamshid was, after all, the king whose magic cup afforded him a glimpse of the world and life in its full sweep.[7]

Firdawsi likewise reflects on mortality by recalling heroic kings who are no more. During a respite in his battle with son Suhrab, Rustam asks his brother Zawara to go console their mother and father about his death, which he fears is imminent. Remind them, says Rustam, "If you remain on earth a thousand years, You shall meet death, this common end. Observe Jamshid, the mighty sovereign, and Tahmurat, the slayer of giants. There was no king like

223

them in the world, but they at last went to their Maker. The world they owned passed to other hands. . . . Young or old we belong to death; none remains in this world forever."[8] A related tradition in the theme of *memento mori* associates Jamshid with the Garden of Iram. Though Jamshid possesses a magical world-revealing cup, he fails to be aware of his approaching demise. Surprised by a destructive whirlwind—which, according to the Qur'an, destroyed Shaddad, builder of Iram—the once powerful and wealthy king can take with him only the "tale of the cup."[9]

Even characters who are not famous for their powers of introspection get reminders of their impermanence. Antar has a dream that makes him fear "the cup of death will touch my lips." He sees a portent of wars to come and dangers to himself, but he declines special protection and shortly thereafter moves off on a journey to avenge Ghamra's honor in the Sudan.[10]

An intriguing feature of several stories of the Dede Korkut cycle is that the bard ends them with a formulaic reminder of life's transience. The stories of these bold heroes seem to have as a major purpose a pointed warning not to forget one's mortality:

> Where now are the valiant princes of whom I have told, Those who said "The World is mine"? Doom has taken them, earth has hidden them. Who inherits this transient world, The world to which men come, from which they go, The world whose latter end is death?[11]

Dede Korkut himself is said to have lived three hundred years by artful dodging, but he too eventually runs out of places to hide. Tradition has it that wherever he traveled, the sage would encounter gravediggers and ask them whose grave they were digging. They had heard, the diggers would reply, that a certain Dede Korkut was searching for this very grave, and Korkut would flee again. At last he dies near such a plot, and to this day a tomb with his name inscribed on it is maintained in Kazakhstan.[12]

At the end of the Turkic *Danishmandnama* the storyteller offers a retrospective of the full range of heroic characters, from Gayumart to Rustam to Iskandar and beyond, as a reminder of transience. Where are those who have preceded us? he asks again and again in a litany of the great who have left only a fading memory of their deeds. Let the recollection of the great heroes whose sword and crown the wind has borne away serve to lessen one's attachment to the world below, he counsels. And let this tale of Malik Danishmand's struggle for the faith stand as a reminder that only the battle fought in the path of religion can help keep life in perspective.[13]

No major figure hears the warning *memento mori* more often than Iskandar. Few have greater difficulty heeding it. The Iskandar of popular romance is far more obstinate than the Iskandar of the *Shahnama*. On virtually every leg of his far-flung wanderings, the world conqueror encounters some vivid, stark reminder. In one instance he meets a people who have their graves in front of their houses so as to have the fact of mortality ever before them.[14] All along his itinerary, Iskandar faces dead bodies on thrones and various sage figures who tell him he will not return home. One wise old man tells Iskandar in the *Iskandarnama* that he has invested too heavily in this world. The sage conjures up images of kings and prophets past—Jamshid, Dahhak, Kay Khusraw, Solomon, Shaddad of Ad, who built Iram of the Lofty Columns—as examples of mortality. Iskandar agrees that the burdens of kingship are more trouble than they are worth, but persists in concern for his reputation: what a shame it would be "that men after me should read the *Iskandarnamah* and the wonders that I have seen and of which I have written, and then say that Alexander was defeated by the fairies, or, still worse, by a woman."[15] Nizami (and at least one Southeast Asian derivative) has Iskandar's life take a different turn after he accepts the inevitability of death. The world conqueror accepts a mission as a prophet sent to help people put life—and death—in a religious perspective.

Attitudes toward death in the heroic literature reflect, on the one hand, prevailing values in the culture that produced them, and on the other, the storyteller's views on the matter. A. Shariati suggests that one can understand the *Shahnama*, and Iranian culture in general, only if one appreciates the poet's own experience of death. He sees in the death of Firdawsi's young son a source of such profound grief as to suffuse the entire epic with a sense of loss. Characters of the great poem enunciate the poet's tragic view of life and death. According to Shariati, a certain oedipal element in the mythic prehistory of Iran gives rise to a spirit of revolt characterized by narcissistic retreat (which liberates both the poet and the listener to escape into the world of imagination), depressive grief, and a fear of the feminine. Though Shariati's analysis seems to rely too heavily on the shaky concept of a "national mentality," it does exemplify a significant attempt by a contemporary Iranian to make sense of the deepest human concerns treated in a literary classic.[16]

Associating the idea of death with another cultural setting, that of Arab North Africa, B. Connelly describes the death of the central figures in the *Sirat Bani Hilal*. Dhiyab murders Abu Zayd al-Hilali, along with Zaziya and Hasan, after which their orphans kill Dhiyab. Death and the fear of death in the saga Connelly relates to the fear of incorporation, of being "eaten" by outsiders. The death of the hero becomes a metaphor for the danger of loss of corporate identity.[17]

Swahili epic literature seems surprisingly optimistic about the subject of death. The violent deaths of the early caliphs do not receive so much as a mention. Even Muhammad's death does not give cause for great sorrow, for the Prophet had reached an advanced age, and went, one can rest assured, to Paradise. The passings of Muhammad's daughter Fatima and wife Khadija have no tragic aura about them. Outside of Africa, many epic heroes die young and tragically (Suhrab, the Serbian Prince Marko, Heracles, Achilles).[18]

Heroic Death

Antar's death at an advanced age is a protracted affair. Five months and five days elapse, from the moment an enemy wounds him with a poisoned arrow to the day he dies sitting on his horse in an attempt to draw the enemy off and give his people time to flee in safety. He may have been old in years, but Antar never really ages in the story. He remains vigorous and potent till the end. He is aware of his impending demise, but he does not dwell on it. His main concern, as a good liberator and leader of the tribe, is for the continued safety of his people.[19]

Hang Tuah's story exhibits another interesting side of this theme. The Sultan of Malaka, desirous of knowing what lies beyond this life, asks for a volunteer to be buried alive and report on the experience. Hang Tuah agrees. In the grave, he holds a string; when he tugs on it, the Sultan exhumes him. Hang Tuah then reveals that two erupting volcanoes accosted him. He found a ceramic vessel and managed to fight them off, but because the pot was cracked, their fire slipped through and burnt off all his clothes. As the hero who has tried out death, Hang Tuah is the one whom popular belief allows also to escape it. Tradition says that he retired to a life of saintly asceticism and lives on near the source of the Perak River. As suggested earlier, his withdrawal from view functions in a way analogous to the concealment of the Shi'i imam. The legend of Hang Tuah's imminent reappearance gained new vitality for a while during the mid-1950s, when Malaysia was looking forward to independence.[20]

"The Story of Wild Dumrul" in *The Book of Dede Korkut* portrays something of the picaresque attitude toward death. Wild Dumrul one day makes fun of some warriors who are mourning the death of one of their own. When they tell Dumrul that Azrael, the angel of death, has come and that none can stop him, Dumrul boasts that he will defeat the angel in single combat. God, who is not amused, sends Azrael to give Dumrul notice. Azrael is about to take Dumrul, that "crazy pimp," when the wild man confesses God's unity and receives leave to find someone willing to give his or her life in exchange for Dumrul's. Dumrul goes to his father and mother, pleading that it would surely be preferrable for one of them to die than to live to mourn the loss of their beloved son. Neither wishes to part with life, so Dumrul asks for time to make a testament to a wife of his, not of his own tribe. To this mother of his two sons he says, "Go marry another lest you be without a protector." She replies that she will gladly give her life for Dumrul. When Azrael arrives to do his work, Dumrul pleads that his wife not suffer the loss of her husband; let Azrael kill them both, or let both live. God is pleased with Dumrul's continued praise and decides to take both of the crazy one's parents, allowing Dumrul and his wife another hundred and forty years together. The moral of the story: you cannot outrun death, but faithful acknowledgement of God's unity can buy you a little time.[21]

Among the great heroes of the *Shahnama*, one finds several extraordinary examples of the level of maturity and humanity Joseph Campbell would require of an authentic hero. These characters all had their major Islamicate literary debuts in the *Shahnama*, but all came to occupy roles in Islamicate thought transcending those that they play in Firdawsi's epic. Kay Khusraw, Bahram Gur, Alexander, and Khusraw Parwiz all face the prospect of death in very different, and clearly individualized, ways.

227

Kay Khusraw makes his peace with Zal and the nobles, recalling his lineage and rule. Weary of empire, he will go into self-imposed exile. He recalls that thus Kay Kawus and Jamshid had done; and, by identifying himself in passing with the evil Dahhak and Tur, he implicitly acknowledges his need for forgiveness. Then he vanishes into the mountains. Later tradition would place him among those who departed this world without dying, journeying to the "eighth clime" at the summit of the Alburz mountains.[22]

Bahram Gur, incomparable as romantic adventurer, enjoys somewhat less success in his role as king. Rallying toward the end, he regains lands he had once lost, but goes on spending the treasury bankrupt. Finally he realizes it is time to abdicate. Setting aside world affairs, he turns his attention to worshipping God. To his prime minister he says, "Resign the world to Him that created it; it is through him that this revolving wheel is made manifest. The wheel goes on, but God remains in his place as my guide and yours to what is good."[23] In Firdawsi's account, he dies in his sleep at age sixty-three. Nizami's *Haft Paykar* interprets Bahram Gur's departure very differently. Out on a hunt, the king spots a beautiful onager. He leaves his party and pursues the animal. When it enters a cave, Bahram follows, never to be seen again. G. Krotkoff observes that "the description of the final chase is not couched in terms of impending disaster, but on the contrary, it is made clear that Bahram is following a leader ('angel, four-winged messenger'), and that when both enter the cave, the life of the hero reaches its highest fulfillment. There is no commiseration of his fate."[24]

Alexander the Great is perhaps the most broadly and richly developed of the heroes. Though he did not live to be forty, his career spans a wide spectrum of literary works from Firdawsi to Jami and beyond. He links Greece to the Middle East and to South Asia and brings Aristotle with him as a kind of culture-hero from afar. Iskandar's death and the obsequies are a relatively frequent subject of miniaturists. Dramatic images, of the monarch lying on his shield or of his survivors' intense grief over their loss, are among the more moving illustrations in manuscripts of both the *Shahnama* and later romances. (See Figure 17.) More importantly, Alexander's story is punctuated with dramatic reminders of mortality: the Talking Tree, his failure to arrive at the Water of Life, the warning of the astrologers. According to Firdawsi, Iskandar finally faces his mortality squarely. Aware of his imminent death,

228

Figure 17: The death of Alexander. A tree once warned of his imminent death; here a tree mourns in flame.

the man who has fallen short of immortality while gaining the length and breadth of the world writes to his mother, who appears in at least one painting of Alexander's funeral: "Without any doubt my spirit will behold yours when the appropriate time arrives. Endurance is a nobler virtue than love; the impatient are men of a lower degree. Your love watched over my body for years; now pray to God for my pure soul."[25]

Khusraw Parwiz gets much good advice from the wise Shirin; some of it concerns this life's transience and the importance of preparing for the next world. She recalls how King Jamshid had to face his end. Later Khusraw Parwiz remembers his old dream: "He knew that all from earth and water made, though prospering, at last in ruin is laid. The new moon, while it waxes, grows in light; when past the full, then wanes its lustre bright."[26] Shirin persuades the king to take a new approach to life, but his new search for wisdom weakens his grip on the scepter and hastens his fall from power. Dying from a stab wound inflicted as he lies sleeping in his dungeon, "Khusraw performs his first selfless and spontaneous act of concern for another. . . . he wakes to find his life's blood draining away but refrains from waking Shirin for fear that she will be distressed beyond measure at his state."[27]

Death in our heroic stories is clearly more than the mere cessation of biological function, for none of these great works envisions the human person as a machine. Human life is multivalent and many-faceted. Beneath the surface—and not far beneath, at that—the hero searches for enduring values. However fatalistic a character may appear in the face of mortality, death remains the ultimate mystery whose depths none may plumb utterly. In the story of the City of Brass in the *Thousand and One Nights,* spiritual death results from failure to store up provisions for the heart. The tale progresses from the Black Castle built by an egotistical person, to a city in which a good and just queen sits dead on the throne, to Karkar, whose walls are bathed in light and whose inhabitants were initiated by Khadir, all strongly suggesting that the true life is that of the spirit.[28]

Explicitly religious images of death, of course, tend to describe the hero as ever aware of the presence of death and, accordingly, preparing to face it. This does not mean that the hero can or should confront death stoically. Far to the contrary. The death of a religious hero is as sad as that of a royal or a folk hero, even if the heroes' mourners believe they will soon rejoin their dear departed one. Among Islamic religious heroes, Husayn stands out as the one most often and deeply lamented. His was a martyr's death, perhaps less a reminder of mortality than a testimony to human treachery and a tribute to the redemptive quality of suffering, when the suffering is that of a sacred personage. There is clearly much more to say on the subject of death and the hero.[29] For the moment, these few remarks must suffice as we take up another side of the heroic acknowledgment of human limitations—namely, the recognition that it is preferable to make peace before one's time is up.

Forgiveness and Reconciliation

Need for forgiveness and reconciliation are evident at every turn in the lives of the great heroes. Perhaps that is because the acceptance of mortality requires an admission that things cannot go on indefinitely as they have. Storytellers often concern themselves with the heroes' hunger for rapprochement and some semblance of social equilibrium. Even an Antar, the very embodiment of eagerness for the fray and new adventure, delights in confirming the identity of a long-lost branch of the family among his erstwhile foes. Recognition of one's own humanity in that of the other is the stuff of reconciliation. B. Connelly locates the dynamics of one facet of human reconciliation within the context of insider-outsider interaction. When Abu Zayd, hitherto identified with the Zahlan group, does battle with his father, he brings about the rejoining of the Zahlan with the Hilal: "The boundaries of the inside and the outside of the two groups expand and collapse as the family reconciliation mirrors the merger of groups into one large united community. This merger of the in-group and the out-group recurs over and over in the spiraling cycles that comprise the *Hilaliyya*, the greater, total tale that exists only in the heads of the tradition's adherents (poets and patrons alike) and that is metonymically implicit in each episode."[30]

One of the more poignant examples of father-son reconciliation occurs in the tale of Boghach Khan, son of Dirse Khan, in the *Book of Dede Korkut*. Dirse Khan and his wife suffer from failure to have a son, but after their fervent prayers, God grants them a boy. Dirse Khan's forty warriors become fiercely jealous of the youth, who gains repute by besting a raging bull. The warriors poison Dirse Khan's mind against Boghach ("ox-man"), telling him that the youth has turned malicious and will rouse the wrath of the other khans against Dirse. They hatch a plan whereby Dirse Khan will take his son hunting and then kill him at the opportune moment.

On the hunt Dirse shoots his son with an arrow and, in fear of his own forty warriors, pretends to feel no remorse. When he tells his wife what he has done, she goes off in search of Boghach. Meanwhile, Khadir has appeared miraculously, touched the wound, and told the hero that mountain flowers and his mother's milk will provide a healing balm. Boghach's mother arrives, makes the medicinal mixture, and applies it. In the interval, Dirse's forty warriors decide Dirse Khan must not reunite with his son, so they take the Khan hostage to infidel land. Boghach's mother pleads with her son to reconcile with his father: "Take your forty warriors, deliver your father from those forty cowards . . . if your father showed no mercy to you, do you show mercy to your father." The boy responds and rescues his father; the two embrace tearfully as they tell each other their stories.[31] Few stories of father-son conflict are clearer and end in so forthright a reconciliation initiated by the son. Here Dirse's warriors play the part of the jealous siblings of other stories.

Deathbed confessions fall from one or two heroic tongues. Heroes like Rustam do not spend a great deal of time in prayer during the ordinary course of events. But in his final moments, as he manages to kill his own treacherous brother, Shaghad, Rustam seeks forgiveness of God and recalls that he has always been a godly man: "Praise be to God—for I have ever been a man who has known God—that, when my spirit reached the point of departure from my lips, day had not turned to night before I exacted this vengeance. Now, O God forgive my sins and take me unto Thyself."[32] Occasionally the death of another impels implacable enemies to be reconciled. Variations on this theme are evident in later Islamic religious literature as well, on down to the Shiʿi passion play at whose ending Grandfather Muhammad persuades the martyred Husayn not only to forgive, but to intercede on behalf of, his murderer.

Heroes as Human Beings

We close this chapter, and our entire survey, with a few reflections on a facet of the hero that we twentieth-century Euro-Americans have come, for a variety of complex reasons, to associate with authentic humanity. I refer to what one might call a character's affective range—the capacity for self-expression in general, but especially the ability to communicate feeling or emotion. Few characters in world literature or art have communicated more successfully than some of those we have met in these pages, and one can learn a great deal from them. Much of what they express may not strike the contemporary reader as particularly sophisticated. But if this is so, it is because we have not learned how to read the characters and their stories for their central messge.

If heroes sometimes appear to be rather one-dimensional, it is more likely because certain aspects are emphasized to the point of exaggeration than because the hero simply lacks range altogether. (*A la carte* or cartoonish figures such as the rogue are obvious exceptions here.) It is certainly true that many heroes seem to lack subtlety of emotional expression even when their range spans the affective gamut, from fairly spontaneous joy and wonder to intense fear, anger, and grief. That fact ought not, however, to diminish the significance of the breadth portrayed.

Even Sir Macho himself, Rustam, gets his emotional pigmentation from a remarkably variegated palette. At the murder of Siyawush, whom Rustam serves as a mentor in the heroic arts, the older hero is stricken with grief for seven days. Rustam roars off on a rampage of unparalleled vengeance. Rustam laughs a lot, and he is not immune to fear, as when Akwan the Diw raises him aloft before tossing him into the sea. He is capable of feeling betrayed, as when his half-brother Shaghad compasses Rustam's ruin and Rustam manages to terminate the traitor before himself expiring. Most of all, Rustam's sense of grief and utter despair when he realizes he has killed his own son reaches an extraordinary peak of emotional intensity. Here is naked rage every bit a match for that of Achilles.

Rustam's responses are indeed always larger than life, but he does respond in ways that surely reflect the affective needs and capabilities of his creators and his fans alike. The same could be said for most major heroes, with the greatest sophistication to be found in more elite literary and visual creations. In general, folk and religious heroes seem less refined and flexible than many of the royal types—allowing for the fact that some folk and religious types appear in works created for better educated constituencies, and that some royal types star in more popular works.

The Heroic Cycle: Symbolic Dimensions

To enter into the worlds of these many classic heroic figures is indeed a challenge. It is also an invitation to reflect on our own humanity in all its fragile beauty and imperfection, all its potential for the noble and the perfidious alike. Our heroes and heroines may seem impossibly far away in time and spirit. Yet to their mysterious venues in antiquity and in cultures very unlike our own so many great works of art and literature invite us. Any time one can spend enjoying their hospitality holds the promise of an unexpected homecoming.

Sources of Heroic Imagery:
*The Major Literary and Artistic
Traditions*

A vast array of heroic themes and characters emerge from an equally broad range of literary and visual sources. A brief survey of the materials according to literary and artistic traditions will provide necessary background for a further study of some key themes. The following attempt to delineate the sources into traditions will be to some degree artificial in that, first, one cannot draw very neat lines between either literary or artistic schools and, second, a given artistic tradition does not always quite correspond to a particular literary tradition. In short, the boundaries are a good deal fuzzier in reality than they appear in the present survey. In addition, the survey has left out much important data and does not attend directly to such complex issues as influence, authorship, transmission, and patronage. Material has been chosen so as to include examples of representative works, prominent literary types, themes, and characters, as produced in a variety of ethnic, geographic, and cultural settings.

Three ways of characterizing the interrelationships among the sources are useful here. First, one can speak of traditions on the basis of the way material (characters, themes, story lines, levels of iconographic sophistication, etc.) from one ethnic source shapes that of another ethnic group. So, for example, it is possible to speak of an "Arabicate" tradition, including literature in Arabic, visual arts created to illustrate those works, and similar materials produced under the significant influence of Arabic language and Arab culture. Specifically, the Arabicate tradition would encompass: (1) stories of pre-Islamic Arabian origin that made their way across North Africa; (2) originally non-religious characters who have found a place in Islamic Arabic material; (3) religious themes and personages of Islamic and Arabic origin that have developed into major elements among peoples and in literatures decisively influenced by Arabic language and culture (Swahili is a prime example here, though one might also include, for rather different reasons, other Afro-Islamic groups such as the Berber and the Sudanese); and (4) the visual arts, especially of Iraqi, Syrian, or Egyptian origin, or the popular arts of North Africa, such as reverse glass painting.

Secondly, one could describe a tradition as growing, not only by way of political and cultural dominance, but also through the agency of linguistic affinity. For example, one can speak of a Persianate tradition that developed in connection with related Indo-Aryan languages of the Subcontinent, as well as through the importance of Persian itself as a language of diplomacy and trade. Within such a Persianate tradition, one would find: (1) pre-Islamic stories of Iranian origin that supplied a large portion of the subject matter for Persian heroic literature and visual art after the Islamization of Iran; (2) pre-Islamic themes and characters of non-Iranian origin that have become important parts of Iran's cultural heritage (e.g., Alexander the Great); (3) Islamic religious themes that, while not uniquely Iranian, have become heavily identified with Iranian Shiʿism (e.g., the suffering of the Imams and the prowess of Ali); (4) both religious and non-religious themes that achieved wide popularity and importance first under Persian influence, and then rose to equal pride of place in the largely Persianized courts and cultures of South Asia (especially as evidenced by works in Urdu, Sindhi, and other languages spoken by Muslims, and by numerous translations from Persian and imitations of Persian works in the various other languages of major significance within Islamdom); (5) the visual arts produced to illustrate many of the above themes.

Thirdly, one can describe the sources in terms of their relation to the religion of Islam. One could characterize as Islamicate the materials produced in the various Turkic languages on the one hand, and in the several Malayo-Polynesian languages on the other. These two Islamicate traditions exhibit the influence, in varying degrees, of both the Arabicate and Persianate traditions. The term "Islamicate" applies equally to much of what I have called "Arabicate" and "Persianate" material, and the rather arbitrary relegation of Turkic and Malay sources to such an extrinsic category merely reflects my own limitations and bias. For present purposes, the Turkic and Malay Islamicate traditions will include: (1) selected relevant themes from Central and West Asian stories, (2) examples of heroic stories from Malaysia and Indonesia, and (3) some visual materials produced as illustrations of those themes.

Though the de facto bias of this survey favors literature, it will be our constant endeavor to integrate as much as possible the visual and the literary expressions of heroic themes. Most extant Islamicate visual art is in fact highly literary, in the sense that nearly all the material containing heroic themes either is physically attached to a text (such as in miniature paintings, which provide the bulk of our input), or tells in pictures a story already known to the viewer via written or oral means. By far the most plentiful material is to be found in books, often commissioned and paid for by royalty and executed by artists in the royal atelier. For a variety of reasons— not the least of which is that the work most frequently illustrated, the *Shahnama,* is in Persian—the majority of the relevant creations come from Iran. Mughal India, Ottoman Turkey, and Mamluk Egypt and Syria are the other crucial points of origin, listed here more or less in descending order of productivity.

The Arabicate Tradition

Works in Arabic[1]

Folk and Popular Literature. Within the larger category of Arabic narrative poetry, one can identify several major types: the *ayyam al-arab,* the *hamasa* or *malhama,* and the *sira.*

The *ayyam al-arab.* The earliest archives of Arab history, these "Days of the Arabs" recount the brave deeds of combatants in defense and the spread of tribal honor prior to the beginning of Islam. The chronicle form blends prose with poetry and brims with specific references to places and persons. Often the offender is a blood-relative of the one offended, and a poem traditionally signals the high point of the conflict. Key features of the literature include an emphasis on the chivalric manner of the ancient heroes as embodied in the notion of *futuwwa* or *furusiya* (horsemanship and all its attendant manners).[2]

The *hamasa* or *malhama.* Two meanings of the term *hamasa* ("bravery") deserve attention here. First, the *hamasa* gathers together pre-Islamic, mostly narrative and descriptive, poetry so that the term becomes virtually synonymous with "anthology." Originally the term connoted a vigorous spirit and thus reflected the tone of the poetry judged suitable for inclusion within it. That

237

vigor marks all combatants, but especially the hero at war. Poets
extol vengeance as crucial for tribal honor, and belittle those with
no stomach for it. The hero rises above envy and hatred, pride
and arrogance, and demonstrates magnanimity by modesty. But
never does the hero acquiesce in poverty or injustice. Staunchly
loyal to father and family, the hero also exemplifies patience in
adversity.[3] Secondly, *hamasa* can refer to poetry of a more truly epic
character, with a strong element of the marvelous. These are also
known in modern Arabic as *malahim* (pl. of *malhama*), and much of
the material derives from early Islamic occupation of conquered
lands. Though tribal strength is crucial, individual strength looms
large, along with generosity and bravery: a shorter sword betokens
a braver fighter. "The Story of King Umar an-Nuʿman" from the
Thousand and One Nights exhibits features of both the *malhama* and
sira genres. Umar possesses all the qualities of the Arabic epic hero:
skill in battle, ferocious anger, command of global respect and admiration, justice and magnanimity. Although this hero can extend
his dominion over many peoples, he does so in a purely Bedouin,
rather than imperial, manner. Byzantine, Persian, or Coptic notions of royalty were not originally current in Arab culture.[4]

The *Sira*. Among the earlier sources in terms of literary type
are works of the *sira* genre, often referred to as "saga." These
expandable collections of tales and legends tell sometimes of historical, sometimes of fictitious, characters who overcome various
obstacles to bring honor and justice to their people. Stitched together into cycles, the narratives were probably intended always to
be recited rather than read, even after they were committed to
writing. Poetry and rhymed prose often punctuate the narratives.
In some cases, the final product incorporates stories from varied
cultural origins over a period of several centuries. It has been suggested that the *sira* genre's relative lack of historicity results from
oral transmission and continual recompilation. Historical details
are gradually lost and thus yield to elements of action and romance.
During the eighth and ninth centuries, religious concerns led to
an increase in popular fables and stories. These would eventually
give rise to the historical novel or epic poem. Even so, some find
the antecedent of the *sira* form in the more historically detailed
ayyam al-arab.[5]

Several important representatives of the type are the stories
of Banu Hilal, Antar ibn Shaddad, Dhat al-Himma wa 'l-Battal,

Baybars I, and Sayf ibn Dhi Yazan. Many of the chief themes appear also in the *hamasa* literature: chivalrous courage, adamantine loyalty, vengeance, sanguinary combat (either among Arabs or between Arabs and Christians) that yields much booty and countless prisoners. Commenting on the content of these works, C. Pellat observes that they generally do not exhibit "a feeling of the greatness of the fatherland represented by a hero who possesses all the virtues"; but he explains further that "if epics are linked with the awakening of nationalities, the Arabs hardly needed this element during the most brilliant period of their literature which corresponded with the apogee of their power."[6]

The *sira* of the Banu Hilal (in two versions and three cycles) traces the migrations and wars of the tribe, including struggles for seven thrones and fourteen stout castles. The Hilal tribe fights the enemies of the Fatimid Caliph al-Mu'izz during the eleventh century, and that conflict forms the framework within which the adventures and trials of the hero, Abu Zayd, occur. Along with Abu Zayd, major characters are his heroine Alja, his half-brother Dhiyab ibn Ghanim, and the mysterious *femme fatale* Zaziya (or Jaziya). The stories remain popular in much of the Arab world, all the way across North Africa. Glass paintings in a folk-art style, popular especially in North Africa, depict major characters from the Hilali epic.[7]

Also of nomadic/tribal origin, but more important for us here, is the *sira* of Antar. Perhaps the nearest thing to an Arabic national epic, it includes traditions from at least seven, and possibly as many as twelve, centuries. In over thirty volumes, the work came to embrace pre-Islamic Arabian material along with Islamic stories of Abraham and Muhammad, Persian features (especially in the form of court ceremonial, divinely sanctioned royalty, the hunt/chase, and messages sent by bird), Christian material relating to the Crusades, and folkloric themes such as exceptional longevity and a rock-rending sword. In recent times, playwright Ahmad Shawqi has named one of his works after the hero of this tale.[8] Comic books and glass painting remain popular visual media for telling the story.

The Antar story grows from the adventure of an historical poet into the epic of a slave who rises to rule the world. The main work was composed progressively from the late eleventh to the mid-fourteenth centuries.[9] Much early material was reworked, per-

239

haps around the time of the Mamluk Sultan Barquq (1382–98), so that the whole now reflects a Cairene perspective on Africa. The story shares many key features with those of Sayf ibn Dhi Yazan and Abu Zayd al-Hilali: Sayf also liberates the Yemenis from the Abyssinians, and Antar's battle scenes are structured like those of Abu Zayd and Dhiyab. According to H. T. Norris, Sayf, Abu Zayd, and Antar all stem from a "common pre-Islamic archetype preserved in the oral folklore and ballads of the Arabian nomads and popular histories of Arabia."[10]

Princess Dhat al-Himma and her sometime rescuer al-Battal star in their own *sira*. Rhymed prose interspersed with some poetic verses tells of the Umayyad dynasty hero al-Battal (d. ca. 740) in the context of the Muslim dynasty's conflict with the Byzantine empire, conflated with stories of tribal rivalry between the Banu Kilab and the Banu Sulaym. A later Turkish romance focuses on the exploits of this warrior who relied more on his wits than on his biceps. Al-Battal shares some important characteristics of the picaresque hero in that he often employs outrageous disguises and gets away with it. But the heroine from whom the work takes its name, Dhat al-Himma (or Delhemma), is an equally interesting character, owning the distinction of being one of the earliest "Amazons" in the tradition.[11]

Finally, the earliest written epic of Sayf ibn Dhi Yazan predates that of Antar. The story found its present form around the late fourteenth century, although the hero is of pre-Islamic origin. Historically, the tale relates to the expulsion of the Abyssinians from southern Arabia. This Yemenite prince's slave mother abandoned him at birth to be reared by a gazelle. Sayf appears as a Muslim fighting the heathen Ethiopians, and as in the Antar story, the hero gradually discovers the common ancestry of Arabians and Ethiopians. The strong presence of Egyptian folkloric elements suggests an Egyptian origin. Sayf's tale traveled far to the east and enjoyed greater popularity in Southeast Asia than any of the older Arabic *sira* stories.[12]

The *Maqamat*. Another Arabic genre of importance to us, particularly because of its popularity as a text to be illustrated, is the form called "Assemblies" *(maqamat)*. Badiᶜ az-Zaman al-Hamadhani (969–1008) developed what was formerly a brief narrative, recited from memory at an informal gathering, into a series of some four hundred discrete scenes in which a narrator recounts the wanderings and exploits of a wily, unscrupulous rogue. After gleefully dazzling his audience with his wit and eloquence, he proceeds to relieve them of their money. Hariri of Basra (1054–1122) later wrote the most important of the imitations of Hamadhani, in a rhymed prose style of extraordinary complexity. Some fifty-one vignettes tell of Abu Zayd's adventures in a time of upheaval due to the Crusades—the hero's home town, Saruj, just over the Syrian border in Turkey, was taken by the Crusaders in 1101.

J. T. Munroe explains the *Assemblies* as "countergenre," in that, for example, the last of Hariri's *Maqamat* constitutes a parody of more serious literary forms, such as the *Sirat Antar* and *Shahnama*. The story inverts the major thematic elements of the classical forms—romance, father-son conflict, chivalry, etc. For example, in the Antar story, "the son of an *apparently* ignoble marriage between a free-born Arab and a negro slave (who is *in fact* a princess) must prove his worth time after time and against all odds. . . . In 'Bishr' [the name of Hariri's *maqama*] we have instead the example of a man with no background whatsoever, who through his base actions not only heaps shame upon himself but also bequeaths it to a son as ignoble as himself."[13]

Hariri's *Maqamat* inspired numerous book illustrations, especially in the thirteenth and fourteenth centuries, in Iraq and Mamluk Egypt. These seem to have been paid for either by an urban middle class (in Iraq) or by a ruling elite made up of relative outsiders of non-royal descent (the Mamluks). Among the Hariri manuscripts, one finds a fascinating variety of levels and styles of visual exegesis of the text.[14] Of all the heroic characters of the Arabicate tradition, those of the *maqamat* were by far the most frequently pictured in illustrated manuscripts.[15] The second most significant type of visual imagery that tradition produced were the witty under-glass paintings, mentioned above, and pulp-print images of folk heroes such as Abu Zayd al-Hilali and Antar.

Historiographical Literature: The Universal Histories. Early Arabic universal histories of Mas'udi (d. 897), Ya'qubi (d. 956), and Tabari (d. 923) provide information on both prophets and kings in a global setting that dates back virtually to creation. Although the Arabic works were not popular in the manner of epic and romance, the stories they tell were widely known and exemplify an important aspect of what the public knew of many important religious and royal characters. If any major illustrated versions of these Arabic histories were ever produced, none remain.[16]

Islamic Legendary and Hagiographical Literature. Here one can include two major types, divided according to general kinds of subject matter. First come those that relate to the lives of Muhammad or of pre-Islamic prophets; and second, those that deal with either the heroic deeds of Muhammad and his Companions or the conquests of the earliest Caliphs.

Lives of the Prophets. Three kinds of works fall within this category. Probably the most famous *sira* is that of the Prophet Muhammad. Popular storytellers still derive much material from this source, the most important version of which is that of Ibn Ishaq, later revised by Ibn Hisham. I know of no illustrated version of the work, although numerous episodes prominently developed in this most important biography of Muhammad (such as the Ascension, for example) became the subjects of miniature paintings in other works of literature.[17]

A number of works featuring the events around the birth of Muhammad comprise a second type known as the *mawlid* ("birthday story"). This type emphasizes the signs and wonders that occurred in creation when the greatest of prophets came into the world. Much of the same kind of imagery occurs in accounts of many heroic nativities.

A third type includes a number of works called "Stories of the Prophets." The *Qisas al-Anbiya* especially of al-Kisaʾi (ca. 1200) and ath-Thaʿlabi (d. 1036) deserve mention here because of their importance as sources of stories about explicitly religious personalities. All of the prophets form an unbroken line of heroic figures whose deeds link them together. In addition, items such as Moses's staff, Adam's sarcophagus, Joseph's shirt, and the stones with which David slew the Philistine become heirlooms passed down among prophets as emblems of authority. As chapter ten suggests, prophetic genealogy is of a piece with the larger concept of heroic lineage.[18]

Heroes and the Early Muslim Community. Two major types of literature are here distinguished by subject matter.[19] A series of works called *maghazi* ("Raiding Stories") tell of the exploits of Muhammad and the principal heroes among his companions. Al-Waqidi (d. 823) composed the most famous of these. The latter include especially Abu Bakr, Umar, Uthman, and, most of all, Ali. *Futuh,* or "Conquest Narratives," deal with the wars of expansion under the earliest Muslim caliphs. One example is the *Futuh Ifriqiyya* (*Conquest of North Africa*), which features a still-popular hero named Abdallah ibn Jaᶜfar and his beloved Amina. Glass paintings show the two racing together across the landscape mounted on a fiery steed.[20]

Swahili Literature: The Utenzi Epic

Swahili culture has produced some of the most important sources of heroic material in the Arabicate tradition. According to J. Knappert, even though the Swahili has been predominantly an oral culture, some African bards did commit their works to writing—for their own use only. That surely explains, at least in part, why none of the many extant Swahili heroic works includes any visual illustrations. All such written epics occur among Islamized groups. In addition, of all examples of Swahili literature, the Islamic materials are the most numerous (over half of all Swahili epics), the oldest, and the easiest to analyze as a category.[21] Knappert contends that "the ethos of the Islamic epic was not originally an African one but of Arabic provenance; it follows that the feelings of national appurtenance and personal loyalty for the poet, the bard and the audience is extended from their homeland all the way to Mecca, to the Prophet Muhammad and his family and friends. In this way we have to extend the criterion of nationality which an epic has to satisfy (cp. the Cid, Roland, Prince Marko) to the nation of Islam. And this was indeed the intention of the writers of the Islamic literature: it was propaganda in the shape of poetic beauty."[22]

Many of the longer Swahili epics take their subject matter from Arabic *maghazi* literature. Parallel to the Arabic *mawlid* form are a number of shorter *tenzi* that celebrate Muhammad's birth. According to L. Harries, "There can be no doubt that the Swahili *tendi* (northern variant of *tenzi*) derived from the Maghazi legendary literature."[23] Like the *maghazi,* Swahili epic literature is made up of cycles of independent stories meant to entertain. As a result, even though the *tenzi* bear a direct relationship to the *maghazi,* they exhibit numerous variations in story line.[24] As a literary form, on the other hand, the *utenzi* finds no parallels in Arabic or Persian literature.[25] What remains of the fast-disappearing art of oral recitation suggests that heroic poems still recited are abridgements of older, more complete epics. Unlike the singer of Yugoslav tales, a Swahili singer must remain strictly faithful to an original work as he narrates the story.[26]

For the sake of convenience, I have arranged the material according to subject: works relating to the earlier prophets, then those devoted to Muhammad, then those featuring members of his family and his companions, then poems treating later historical struggles between Muslims and non-Muslims.

As for its subject matter, the Swahili repertoire of religious epics begins with stories of the prophets. *The Epic of Adam and Eve* offers important insights into the Swahili tranformations of the story of God's first "caliph" and prophet.[27] Several other *utenzi* tell the stories of such prophets as Job, Noah, and Joseph, and Jesus.[28]

Epics that deal with the life of Muhammad and his family are most important. Knappert reports on a recent manuscript (dated 1965) of the "Legend of the Miiraji," or Ascension of the Prophet Muhammad, that is full of miracles and monsters. The story features Muhammad's airborne journey on a winged quadruped named Buraq. This Swahili version serves here as an excellent example of a literary genre that has become devoted entirely to one segment of the heroic saga, namely, the journey to another world. Here the Prophet embarks on the ultimate search for enlightenment as he makes his way toward the very Throne of God. Patterned after earlier versions in Arabic, Persian, Turkish, and Malay, this popular Swahili version testifies to the undiminished fascination the tale has held for Muslims everywhere throughout many centuries.[29]

According to tradition, the original version of the nineteenth-century *Epic of the Battle of Uhud (Utenzi wa wita vya Uhud)* came from a now-forgotten Arab of the Buhriy tribe who lived during Muhammad's lifetime. A tragic story not written down until 1951, the 739-stanza epic narrates the reversal of fortunes against the Muslim armies at the battle of Mt. Uhud in the year 625, fought against the Quraysh of Makka.[30]

Aidarusi son of Uthaima's *Hamziya* dates to 1652, and is thus the oldest Swahili work of Islamic poetry. It tells the story of Muhammad's heroic uncle Hamza, with color and detail uniquely Swahili. Written in Kingozi or archaic Swahili, the work is a versified translation of the thirteenth-century Arabic original by the famous Egyptian poet Busiri, more noted perhaps for his encomium of Muhammad known as the *Burda*. Its meter is the *ukawafi,* "easily the most advanced and sophisticated prosodic form in the Swahili repertoire." The utenzi meter (4 × 8 syllables) is probably the oldest metrical form, used for texts of epics set in Muhammad's time.[31]

A certain Sayidi Hamadi Bin Sayidi Hasani al-Mutaliba composed the *Epic of Mwana Fatuma* (in the utenzi meter) about 1750, or slightly later, and may have been familiar with the writings of Bwana Mwengo and his son Abu Bakari. The story features Muhammad's oldest daughter, Fatima, by his wife Khadija. She bears the distinction of being the only woman with a part in all three major eighteenth-century Swahili epics. The story is what J. Knappert calls a "popular narrative," because of its currency in rural towns and villages, and a "typical story for women" in which exemplary feminine behavior and God's gift of the ideal husband play a central part.[32]

The *Epic of Husayn's Death (Utenzi wa Kufa kwa Huseni),* now extant in only 93 stanzas, may be (if not a purely liturgical text) part of a once longer work. Like Hamadi el-Buhriy's *Epic of Our Master Husayn (Utenzi wa Sayidina Husein),* the fragment extols the Shi'i protomartyr's bravery in the face of terrible odds. Not out of love for battle does he go, but in response to a call for help. To his final fight his duty urges him; alone but undeterred he advances to his destined encounter with the forces of the Caliph Yazid at Karbala.[33] The work belongs to the genre known as the *maqtal,* important and popular from Turkey to Malaysia (where it was absorbed into the genre *hikayat*—see below).

Hamadi Abdallah of the al-Buhriy family wrote the longer of two epics about Abd ar-Rahman *(Amdu Rehemani),* son of Muhammad's father-in-law and best friend, Abu Bakr. Though he was Muhammad's brother-in-law through the Prophet's marriage to Abu Bakr's daughter Aisha, Abd ar-Rahman plays a disaffected warrior won over by the villainous Abu Sufyan, who had given Abd ar-Rahman his daughter in marriage. At length Abd ar-Rahman repents of kidnapping a young knight, sets the youth free, and decides to fight his former patron Abu Sufyan. When Abd ar-Rahman falls victim to Abu Sufyan, the converted hero's wife straps on a sword and enters the fray, preferring fidelity to her husband

and his faith over obedience to her father. It is left to Ali, however, ably assisted by his companion Miqdad, to quell the villain and restore the dying Abd ar-Rahman to health.[34]

Called in Swahili the *Chuo cha Utendi* (*Book of Action*—probably a reference to the action of making poetry, *poiesis,* but may refer to the heroic action within the poem) or *Utendi wa Tambuka (Action at Tabuk)* or merely *Herekali,* the *Epic of Heraklios,* was written in or before 1728 by Bwana Mwengo at the beginning of major developments in Swahili epic. The Sultan of Pate invited to his court the perhaps illiterate but certainly devout Muslim Bwana Mwengo. His poetry truly deserves the name Islamic for all its many direct references and allusions to religious beliefs and personages. The epic treats of events that ensued after the Byzantine Emperor Heraclius spurned a letter in which Muhammad proclaimed his intent to declare war should the Emperor refuse to become a Muslim. Heraclius's adamant refusal sets the stage for scenes featuring miraculous deeds of Muhammad and Ali, culminating in the dramatic victory of the Muslims.[35]

Historically, the action takes place during an eight-year war between the Byzantines and the Arabs, beginning at the battle of Mu'ta in Syria in 628 and ending with the decisive Byzantine defeat at Yarmuk in 636. Beyond that general historical foundation, the epic branches off into largely legendary material, conflating the whole Arab adventure into a single encounter. Muhammad had originally set out apparently to chasten some recalcitrant northern Arab tribes, never actually intending to encounter the Byzantines. Contrary to the epic's chronology, both Muhammad and Abu Bakr died well before the Byzantine campaign ended, while such heroes of the story as Amr ibn al-As and Sa'd made their epic conquests seven years afterward.[36] Abu Bakari, son of Bwana Mwengo, wrote both the *Katirifu* (or *wadi sesebani*) and the *Fatuma,* a non-epic life of Muhammad's daughter, not to be confused with the epic version mentioned above. Named after a pagan king, the *Katirifu* blatantly imitates and embroiders upon the miraculous content of the *Heraklios* epic.[37]

Epic format has proven to be a popular medium for commemorating events of modern times as well. Hamadi al-Buhiry's *Utenzi wa Wadoichi Kutamalaki Mrima (The Epic of How the Germans Captured Mrima)* conjures up the tone and imagery of *jihad* to recount the Swahili peoples' heroic, if futile, battles against the invading Germans in the 1880s. The opening invocations of the Divine Names and prayers to Muhammad set the religious tone of the work. Abushiri ibn Salimu al-Harithiya and his side-kick Jahazi (a word referring to a stout ship, thus making for a nickname equivalent to "Man o' War") star in the work. Later, when the hero has no choice but to consult a seer or magician, the author inserts himself in that role.[38]

The Persianate Tradition

Works in Persian[39]

Shahnama. Firdawsi's epic poem, *Shahnama*, is the earliest and by far the most significant. Completed around 1010, *The Book of Kings* lays out a vast panorama of Iranian myth, legend, and history. Beginning with the father-king of the purely mythical Pishdadian dynasty, Gayumart, the epic proceeds through the heroic struggles of Iran against Turan during the legendary Kayanian dynasty. A more solidly historical series begins with the appearance of the Achaemenid dynasty and proceeds with the introduction of Alexander the Great. The Ashkanian/Parthian dynasty eventually loses out to the Sasanians, and they in turn disappear with the Arabs' defeat of the last Sasanian king, Yazdagird.

Firdawsi retells the Persian patrimony in some fifty thousand couplets in *mutaqârib* meter ($\cup -- \cup -- \cup -- \cup -/ \cup -- \cup -- \cup --$ $\cup -- \cup -$, with the ends of the hemistichs rhyming). Perhaps the most frequently illustrated work of Islamicate literature, *The Book of Kings* was also often imitated by later Persian authors.[40] Because of its enormous popularity among patrons of the arts, the *Shahnama* will furnish us with numerous heroic personages and visual images. Firdawsi's masterpiece and the images produced over more than five centuries to illustrate it are examples of elite or princely literature and art.[41] Since this work has been discussed so often throughout this book, the present notice has been left very short.

Imitators of Shahnama. J. Rypka divides the related epics into secondary and historical types.

Secondary Epics. From the eleventh and twelfth centuries come several large works composed with the intention of "completing the work of Firdausi, who claimed to have by no means exhausted the whole of the national tradition and in fact encouraged others to do so."[42] Unlike the epic that inspired them, these works

Appendix

(1) focus not on the history of a great nation but on the incomparable exploits of the story's one peerless hero; (2) style their heroes members of the Sistanian family and, hence, relatives of Rustam (whom they are said in some instances even to outdo); and (3) include a father-son conflict in which identities are unknown, but which does not end tragically. Like the *Shahnama*, the earlier imitators express few if any distinctively Islamic religious values; later works, however, show heroes of decidedly Islamic conviction. One major example of the type is Asadi's *Garshaspnama* (9,000 verses, written 1064–66), celebrating one of Iranian legend's most ancient warrior heroes who had gradually evolved into a remote ancestor of Rustam. Representing the other end of the Sistanian heroic genealogy, the eleventh- and twelfth-century *Jahangirnama* revolves around a second son of Rustam, Jahangir, born after the death of Suhrab. The latter epic exhibits many Islamized traits, as Rustam and son champion the true faith against all forms of idolatry.[43]

Historical Epics. Among the relevant historical or quasi-historical epics are the *Zafarnama*, Hamdullah Mustawfi of Qazwin's 75,000-line extension of Firdawsi's work up to 1335; and a number of other epics that focus on members of the Prophet's family. Safa includes also in this category Nizami's *Iskandarnama* (which I have treated below along with "court romances"), several works entitled either *Shahnama* or *Shahanshahnama* (*Book of the King of Kings*), and several works named after such important characters as Sam (grandfather of Rustam) and Shah Rukh (one of Timur's most famous descendents).[44]

Shiʿi Literature. Last of the secondary epics done in imitation of the *Shahnama*, the fifteenth-century *Khawarannama* (*Book of the East*) recounts wholly fictitious tales about the battles of Muhammad's son-in-law Ali against the kings of the East. As a literary descendent of Rustam, Ali manifests his spiritual/heroic legitimacy in deeds reminiscent of the earlier hero, slaying demons and dragons. With this latest of the old-style epics, the tradition that had formerly been Mazdaean became Shiʿite.[45]

The *Falnama* (*Book of Divination* or *Omens*), attributed traditionally to the sixth Imam, Jaʿfar as-Sadiq (d. 765), includes fascinating material on the prophets and Shiʿi figures. Turkish patronage produced a number of important illustrations of prophets, especially of Adam and Eve. Another distinctive focus of Shiʿi heroic literature is the tragedy of Husayn's martyrdom, given expression in the "passion plays." Visual imagery has taken the form of murals and large poster paintings meant to accompany and enhance the experience of the drama of Karbala.[46]

Mystical and Other Didactic Epics. Several major heroic/epic themes occur in a genre that has been called the "mystical" or "didactic epic." Farid ad-Din Attar's (d. 1190) *Conference of the Birds (Mantiq at-Tayr)* and *Book of Affliction (Musibatnama)*, for example, are structured around the idea of spiritual journey or pilgrimage. One important type of the genre tells of the Prophet Muhammad's journey through various levels of heaven and hell; a number of texts entitled *Miʿrajnama*, ranging from around the tenth to the fifteenth centuries, describe Muhammad's heroic sojourn, tests, and successes in the unseen world. Sanaʾi's *Hadiqat al-Haqiqa (Enclosed Garden of Ultimate Reality)* features the prophets and saints as the chief heroes, as do a number of other Sufi works of the type, such as Jalal ad-Din Rumi's (d. 1273) *Mathnawi (The Spiritual Couplets).* Another major didactic poem with important romantic elements is the *Makhzan al-Asrar,* or *Treasury of Secrets,* by Sanaʾi's successor, Nizami, which fashions each of twenty stories around an important moral teaching. To works of this type we have referred only incidentally, for the heroic imagery they afford is of secondary importance here.[47]

Persian Heroic Romances. The major Persian genre best described as a heroic or epic romance encompasses a wider range of content, develops its characters in greater detail, and shows affinities with a wider range of other literary forms than does the purely epic poem. Persian authors did not invent the form, but they did advance its development enormously. Two major types of romance need to be taken into account here: popular romances and court romances. Of the romance form, which "reflects a growing disaffection with the values embodies in the epic," J. S. Meisami writes further: "Leaving aside . . . the 'historic' heroes of *sirah* and epic, the ironic 'antiheroes' of the *maqamah,* . . . when we reach the romance we find that emphasis on contrast in character becomes a further means of conveying the complex nature of the human condition, and specifically of the variety of possible responses to that universal human experience, love."[48] Another useful way of understanding the difference between epic and romance comes from P. Heath's definitions of their respective "final causes" or purposes: they investigate "the concerns of honor as balanced between death (epic)/love (romance) and social propriety, within the context of Fate."[49]

Popular Romances. W. Hanaway has defined and described a genre of pre-Safavid (i.e., before 1500) works, transmitted orally and written down long after their composition, as Persian popular romances. Often recounted today by storytellers using scrolls depicting the story's characters, these works focus on heroes whose adventures relate directly to their falling in love. Of the five most famous pre-sixteenth-century romances, *Darabnama, Iskandarnama, Firuz Shahnama, Qissa-i Hamza,* and *Samak-i Ayyar,* the first four connect to stories from the Iranian national legend, while the last reflects an Iranian spirit. Though the first four revolve around historical figures, their content is only vaguely historical.

All survive in non-metrical form. Constructed in straightforward, linear fashion, the stories follow similar patterns: "the family background of the yet-unborn hero, an account of the marriage of his mother and father, his birth and youthful experiences until the time comes for him to begin to assume the role of hero, approximately the age of puberty."[50] Then begins the lover's pursuit through exotic lands—often including islands where marvelous creatures dwell—to win the beloved and to find his father, or in quest of adventure, all interspersed with subplot stories tossed in more or less gratuitously to entertain the listener.

What Hanaway observes concerning the formulaic quality of the popular romance's narrative elements, the viewer will see as well in many Islamic (esp. Persian) miniature paintings designed to illustrate similar stories: "narrative elements may be composed of subelements which can be isolated and recombined in a different order, in the end always producing a recognizable battle or the like." In contrast to the more realistic characters of earlier epic works, popular romance heroes tend to be static, abstract, and unintelligent, so that they must be paired with an alter ego (such as an ayyar) who can make up for what the hero lacks.[51]

One romance of Persian origin, *Qissa-i Hamza (The Tale of Hamza),* has enjoyed such extraordinary and widespread popularity that it merits specific attention here. The Persian work celebrates exploits that may have originated historically with a ninth-century Persian Kharijite insurrectionist named Hamza ibn Abd Allah. In any case, adventures that find the hero galavanting everywhere from Anatolia to China came to be attributed to an uncle of Muhammad. (An earlier Arabic work, perhaps by the author of the *sira* of Sayf ibn Dhi Yazan, entitled *Sirat Hamza* actually features some other Hamza, who is also said to be related to the Prophet). Much simpler in structure than the other major popular romances, and including fewer elements of a miraculous nature than later South and Southeast Asian adaptations, the story's object is "to show the superiority of Islamic Persia over pre-Islamic Persia."[52]

Hamza has been popular across the length and breadth of the Islamic world, for his bravery at the battle of Badr and in other campaigns in Iran and Iraq has secured him a place in the ranks of heroes second only to that of Ali. Legends tell of Hamza's exploits against the forces of evil in many a far-off land on his trusty steed Ashqar, until he dies at the hands of a demon of Hind called the Fur or Porus (also a nemesis of Alexander the Great).[53] To works on Hamza produced in South and Southeast Asia we shall return below in the context of Urdu and Malay literatures. Hamza's ever-present companion, the ayyar Umar (Amr) Umayya, likewise presents an excellent example of a character who undergoes fascinating metamorphoses as he traverses the literary world toward Indonesia. Chapter three deals in some detail with the picaresque and the ayyar character types.[54]

Court Romances. Ayyuqi's *Warqa and Gulshah* (star-crossed chaste-till-death lovers) and Gurgani's *Wis and Ramin* (ca. 1050) were the earliest major works of the type in Iran, the latter showing considerably greater psychological development than the former. In Gurgani's story, a queen promises her yet-unborn daughter in marriage to a neighboring king. Years later, when daughter, Wis, is about to be married to her brother, the king reminds her mother of her promise of old. Mother reluctantly agrees to send Wis away to the king, but en route, the king's younger brother Ramin falls in love with Wis. The conflict unfolds from there.

Nizami (d. 1209) fashioned the greatest corpus of romances in his *Quintet (Khamsa)*. After the didactic work mentioned above *(Treasury of Secrets)* come *Khusraw and Shirin,* with some likenesses to *Wis and Ramin,* about the stormy and tragic affair between the king and his beloved that ends in death for both; *Layla and Majnun,* later retold by Jami and Amir Khusraw, recalling the ill-omened love of *Warqa and Gulshah;* and, most complex of all, the *Haft Paykar,*

251

or *Seven Portraits,* about Bahram Gur's marriages to seven princesses as he journeys through the Seven Climes.[55] Of the heroes in these three works, P. Chelkowski observes that, true to the heroic narrative pattern, "the offspring have been long-awaited; their births are followed by rejoicing. Each hero is described as possessing outstanding qualities, but for all three, the hero's life takes a course different from that expected and desired by those around him. After a period in which he lives out his own desires and frustrations, however, the hero emerges as victor over himself."[56] Nizami's elaboration of the life of Bahram Gur stands between Firdawsi's far less romantic treatment of Bahram Gur in the *Shahnama* and Amir Khursaw's subtler fourteenth-century characterization of Bahram Gur and his beloved in the *Eight Paradises.*

Last in Nizami's *Quintet* comes the two-part work on Alexander from 1191, the *Iskandarnama* (divided into the *Sharafnama* and *Iqbalnama*), still romantic but incorporating more of the traditional heroic deeds of the epic. Jami (d. 1492) later imitated the work in his *Khiradnama-i Iskandari (Book of Alexander's Wisdom).* Last of the great classical Persian poets, Jami also wrote a frequently illustrated romance called *Joseph and Zulaykha* featuring a prominent religious hero and prophet, retold the story of *Layla and Majnun,* and made popular the story of *Salman and Absal.* All three of these elements of the fifteenth-century Sufi's larger *Seven Thrones* anthology are generally interpreted as highly allegorical and much influenced by mystical themes.[57]

Universal Histories.   Rashid ad-Din (fl. ca. 1300) produced the first important universal history in Persian, *Jamiᶜ at-Tawarikh,* in the early fourteenth century. One of the best examples of a work written with the original intent of including illustrations as an integral part, Rashid ad-Din's work embraces everyone from Abraham to Zoroaster in its truly catholic scope.[58] Hafiz-i Abru (d. 1430) also composed a major (and much illustrated) universal history during the fifteenth century. The first quarter of his *Majmaᶜ at-Tawarikh* deals especially with the principal prophets and heroes.[59] Mirkhwand's voluminous *Garden of Purity (Rawdat as-Safa)* and *Habib as-Siyar* provide much material on religious heroic figures, especially on saints.[60]

***Tadhkira* Genre.**   Finally, the genre "recollections of famous holy persons" provides important stories about religious heroes. Attar's

Recollections of the Saints (Tadhkirat al-Awliya)[61] and Jami's *Warm Breezes of Intimacy (Nafahat al-Uns)* are prime examples of the form. Another important type of work deals exclusively with the *Stories of the Prophets,* among which Nishapuri's twelfth-century work ranks among the most significant for present purposes. One could perhaps consider the genre as a bridge between didactic works (for its content) and the tadhkira genre (for its form). Fifteenth-century Timurid Sultan Husayn Bayqara usually gets credit for authoring the *Assembly of Lovers (Majalis al-Ushshaq),* a collection of biographies of saints and mystics, at least one manuscript of which contains numerous famous images of its personages. A similar work by Hilali (d. 1529) called *Sifat al-Ashiqin* exists in several illustrated versions and treats the "Qualities of the Lovers."

It is virtually impossible to leaf casually through a book on Islamicate miniature painting without encountering many pictures of heroic characters. In addition to the multiple royal commissions of *Shahnamas* one finds lavishly illustrated versions of the secondary and historical epics mentioned above, and of the poetic works of Nizami and Jami. Less numerous are heroic miniatures associated with the universal histories, although some important early fourteenth-century illustrations were made for Rashid ad-Din's *Universal History (Jamiᶜ at-Tawarikh),* Biruni's *Chronology of Ancient Peoples (Athar al-Baqiya),* and Hafiz-i Abru's *Universal Histories (Majmaᶜ at-Tawarikh).* Nishapuri's Persian *Stories of the Prophets (Qisas al-Anbiya)* attracted considerable artistic attention. Scenes of heroic figures in mystically tinged works such as those of Nizami and Jami have often been illustrated; rather less frequently have been those of Attar, but there are some important images there as well.[62]

Among the visual arts, but in a category by themselves, are the occasional album pages, now disconnected from their original text and gathered in response to a patron's desire for a book of favorite pieces. Such albums were produced in various parts of the Muslim world, but especially within the Persianate and Turkic traditions.

Two other fascinating but relatively rare sources of visual images-without-texts are ceramics and murals. Iranian potters occasionally depicted heroic figures, especially from the *Shahnama,* on their wares. The most extended narrative sequence occurs on a beaker in the Freer gallery, which shows the *Shahnama* story of Bizhan and Manizha in which the hero Rustam saves the day.[63]

Rustam is again the central figure in a seventh-century mural at Panjikent. Although the mural is a singular find, it raises some fascinating issues concerning the early development of heroic themes later continued under Islamicate rule.[64]

The Indian Subcontinent: Focus on Urdu

Islamicate literatures of the Indian Subcontinent (where now over one quarter of the world's Muslims live) include a vast range of works produced in at least seven major languages. More Persian literature derives from that area than from Iran itself; and although authors of Turkish and Arabic works did not produce comparable quantities, Muslims also wrote widely in those languages. Of relevant works written in the major indigenous Islamic languages—Urdu, Sindhi, Pashto, and Panjabi—we must limit our brief consideration to a few written in Urdu.

Three literary forms merit a mention here: the *mathnawi* (couplets), the rhymed-prose *dastan,* and the Shi'i-inspired lament known as *marthiya.*

Mathnawi: Kamal Khan Rustami's (Bijapur, 1649) 24,000-verse imitation of the Persian Shi'i *Khawarannama* features heroes from the *Shahnama* as well as major religious figures such as Ali, and characters from the Hamza cycle. Later works of the type elaborate on the epic accomplishments of contemporary historical figures. Other seventeenth-century poems recount the stories of such love-pairs as Yusuf and Zulaykha, and Layla and Majnun, or the amorous adventurer Bahram Gur, taking as their models Persian romances on those themes.[65]

Dastan: Eighteenth- and nineteenth-century tales from the Amir Hamza cycle form the subject of numerous prose narratives that revolve around Hamza's literary descendents, their ayyar sidekicks, and their magician foes (possibly to be understood as Hindus). Hamza's popularity in the Subcontinent dates back many centuries, and patrons like Akbar enjoyed illustrated Persian prose versions of the stories. From Persian originals, several Urdu writers produced translations and embellishments filling as many as forty volumes. According to A. Ahmad, "The *dastan* has a repetitive pattern of almost identical stock situations in which heroes aided by *ayyars* challenge sorcerers in a magical landscape with a labyrinthine monotony which drags on to enormous lengths."[66]

Marthiya: Inspired by the martyrdom of Husayn at Karbala in

680, the originally briefer form of *marthiya* grew to epic proportions in the nineteenth century, reinterpreting both setting and affective tone in contemporary Indian idiom. Serving a political function similar to that which mourning for Husayn has often played in Iran, the *marthiya* in India strengthened "the inhabitants of a country in which the traditional national and social order was breaking down and helped them to survive under the increasing pressure when the 'Infidels' intruded upon the land of the Muslims."[67]

Two Major Islamicate Traditions: Turkic and Malay
The Turkic Tradition
Central Asia and Anatolia. For the sake of organization, Turkic materials are here categorized as epic, romance, and religious works.

Turkic Epic Literatures. I. Bashgöz calls it the "greatest epic tradition of the world" on the basis of its geographical spread, its breadth of subject matter, and the sheer bulk of its plot repertoire and length of individual works. I have arranged sample works under the headings of literary, folk, and oral epic.[68]

1. Literary or Classical Epics. Although evidence of the tradition dates back to the twelfth and thirteenth centuries, the earliest complete work dates from the fifteenth. *The Book of My Grandfather Korkut* can perhaps serve as an example of a literary epic, although one could argue that point. Reference to episodes in the epic *Kitab-i Dede Korkut* occur in Arabic, Persian, and Turkish sources as early as the thirteenth century. Of the central figure, the bard who sings epic tales, I. Bashgöz says: "He combines in his personality the characteristics of a mythical ancestor (the eponym of the Turks), of a shaman-sorcerer of the pre-Islamic era, of a political counselor of the rulers, and of a Muslim saint. Thus the bard-sorcerer of the *Grandfather Qorqut* epic embodies traces of several layers of the social and cultural background of the Turkic peoples from the pagan era to the Islamic period of the fifteenth century."[69] Most of the prose stories tell of Muslim raids against Christians to rescue family members taken prisoner in battle. The rest include numerous epic themes, such as the conquest of monsters and animals, and romance between Muslim man and Christian woman. Beneath the stories run two streams of historical background: eighth- through tenth-century struggles of the Oghuz Turks in their former home-

land of Central Asia; and struggles in Anatolia, especially from the thirteenth century, with their new neighbors.[70]

2. *Köroghlu* as Example of Folk Epic. Popular for nearly four centuries among Turkic peoples from Anatolia to Central Asia, the *Köroghlu* epic cycle tells in thirty-four stories (*hikayas,* each in turn made up of episodes called *kols*) the brave deeds of Köroghlu the commoner and his 365 henchmen (Anatolia) or the high-born Guroghlu (Central Asia). In a mixture of prose and poetry, an *ashik* (literally, "lover") entertains his audience to string accompaniment. Further west, the story is mostly prose; the mixture shifts toward the east, and turns entirely to poetry among Tajik bards. The poetic portions are the highly developed *koshma,* "three, five or seven stanzas of four lines with end rhymes *abcb, dddb,* and *eeeb.* It uses the typical metric system of Turkic folk poetry, which is based on the usage of an equal number of syllables in each line. The line consists usually of eight or eleven syllables with a caesura $(4+4$ or $6+5$)."[71]

3. Oral Epics of Central Asia. From the vast range of materials from Turkic Central Asia, three works written down rather recently deserve mention here as examples of the durability of the Turkic epic tradition: the *Manas* (restricted to the Khirgiz tribe), the *Alpamysh,* and the *Edigei* cycles (popular among several peoples). Centered on the hero's unification of the Khirgiz tribes and far-flung exploits, the enormous *Manas* has gradually absorbed by osmosis virtually the whole of Khirgiz lore, including some formerly separate epics. *Alpamysh,* enjoying almost as broad a popularity as the Köroghlu stories, resulted from the gradual historicization of earlier tales (as early as the sixth through the eighth centuries), by inclusion of the movements and conquests of various Turkic tribes. The epic's two parts deal with, first, the hero's romantic exploits (contests among suitors, between bride and groom) and, second, the hero's imprisonment, escape, and return home just in time to prevent his wife's marriage to a competing suitor. Available in some thirty variants, the *Edigei* combines fable elements with the historical fourteenth- and fifteenth-century struggles of the Golden Horde, and features the exile and return of a hero unfairly condemned.[72]

Turkish Romance Works *(hikaya).* As Turkic nomadic leaders began to settle into palace living, tastes in heroic types and adventures changed. From the fifteenth century on, amorous and courtly personages from imported Iranian stories became increasingly popular. Mir Ali Shir Nawaʾi in the fifteenth century, and Fuzuli in the sixteenth, pioneered literary romance; and by the end of the sixteenth century, the formerly epic-singing bards were adapting their stories to changing literary fashions and transmitting the *hikaya* form orally.

More prose than poetry, the romance begins when a hero envisions his beloved in a dream where he receives a love elixir from a character often associated with a Sufi order—a kind of spiritual guide called a *pir*. The hero awakes to a lifelong search for the beloved and marries her in the end. In between, he speaks in the first person of his feelings of painful distance and ecstatic meeting, and the listener hears of his trials along the way. The earliest Turkish romance forms were modeled on the Persian form of *mathnawi* (couplets), but Turkish forms gradually took over—though many of the original Persian characters remain popular today. *Hikaya* repertoires among Turkic peoples equal those of the epic in breadth of material and geographical extension.[73]

Religious Heroic Works. 1. Related to Muhammad. Fourteenth-century Anatolian author Darir composed one of the most important Turkish lives of Muhammad, the *Siyar-i Nabi*. While Darir was in Egypt, he spent five years or so at the court of the Mamluk Sultan Barquq, who commissioned Darir to compose a detailed account of the Prophet. The Sultan wanted, in Z. Tanindi's words, a "work which would contain quotations from the Korʾan, and extracts from tales of saints and heroes, tales which would not only teach their readers gratitude, patience and the praise of God, but which would, in themselves, be a form of prayer." Darir decided to use as a primary source the thirteenth-century Arabic biography by Abu ʾl-Hasan al-Bakri, with occasional reference as well to the more difficult ninth-century Arabic work of Ibn Hisham. Replete with Darir's own supply of popular and folk embellishments, the biography appeared in 1388. Ali plays an extraordinarily large role in the work, suggesting broad tolerance at the Sunni Ottoman court that was pleased to expend enormous sums of money to produce a six-volume version with hundreds of lavish illustrations.[74]

2. Other Works Featuring Religious Heroes. A number of other documents include important information on religious heroes. Late sixteenth-century Turkish author Sayyid Luqman wrote

a kind of historical anthology called the *Zubdat at-Tawarikh (Cream of Histories)*. Ranging back to the creation itself, the work includes numerous episodes from the lives of prophets and saints, with special attention allotted to Muhammad.[75] From the same period comes Fuzuli's *Hadiqat as-Su'ada (Garden of the Felicitous)*.[76] Although Muhammad's uncle Hamza does not function specifically as a religious figure, he is inextricably linked to the authority and popularity of Muhammad. The Hamza cycle originating in Persia also achieved great fame in Turkic areas, including some lavishly illustrated versions in Ottoman times.[77]

3. Shi'i Martyrology. A genre called the *maqtal* focuses on the martyrdom of Husayn as well as on the sufferings of the whole family of the Prophet. One in particular, Lamii Celebi's *Maqtal-i Al-i Rasul (Martyrdom of the Family of the Messenger)*, derives from the late sixteenth century.[78]

4. Religiously Motivated and Oriented Epics. Several Turkic works feature heroes not of the House of the Prophet, but with a decidedly religious coloration. These include, for example, Battal and Abu Muslim, who function as leaders of religiously oriented groups in their stories.

The *Battalnama* features the hero Abd Allah al-Battal (Sayyid Battal) who died during the mid-eighth-century Arab-Byzantine war. The Turkish tale dates back to legends of this hero of the Arabic *Dhat al-Himma* current in Turkey since the thirteenth century. The Turkish version turns the hero into a character from Abbasid times, connects him with the descendents of Ali, and gives him the name Ja'far. Battal remains especially popular among Shi'i-oriented groups. Unlike the traditional Turkish epics, the *Battalnama* centers on the hero's use of magic, intelligence, and prowess, and was read rather than recited to a "religiously oriented audience." I. Mélikoff calls the *Epic of Sayyid Battal the Warrior (Kitab-i Sayyid Battal Ghazi)* the prototype of those works from the Syrian-Iraqi frontiers, dealing largely with the subjugation of Anatolia, that re-cast characters from Arabic works in a Turkic mould (we have just referred to the Arabic *Dhat al-Himma,* in which a certain Battal plays a major role). The author of the *Danishmandnama* borrowed heavily from the Battal epic in composing his work. Dealing mainly with Jihad against the Byzantines, this epic blends a simplified and militant Islamic ideology with the "mystical spirit" that informed many military organizations and "guilds." Danishmand the hero remains somewhat less encrusted with religious and magical imagery than Battal. Similarly indebted to the Battal epic is another work that shares this religious orientation. The tale of Abu Muslim of Khurasan tells of an Abbasid revolutionary who helped bring down the Umayyad caliphate. All three exhibit a large number of common themes; the second and third also contain unique borrowings from the first.[79]

The *Sari Saltuqnama* takes the religious theme one step further, for its leading character is a "dervish-warrior" who serves like a fighting chaplain to the troops confronting the Byzantines. Such a hero marches before the army, chanting litanies and functioning as a mediator between the seen and unseen worlds.[80]

Most often illustrated among the Turkish heroic works are: the *Cream of Histories (Zubdat at-Tawarikh)*, the *Life of the Prophet (Siyar-i Nabi)*, the *Book of Omens (Falnama)*, *The Garden of Felicity (Hadiqat as-Suʿada)*, the *Martyrdom of the Family of the Messenger (Maqtal-i Al-i Rasul)*, and the Central Asian *Book of the Ascension (Miʿraj-nama)* with its forty-eight splendid miniatures of Muhammad's travels through the unseen world. Images of prophets seem generally more popular in Ottoman Turkey than anywhere else in the Islamic world.[81]

The Balkans: Muslim Epics of Yugoslavia. During the month of Ramadan, Muslim men of Yugoslavia often gather in coffeehouses (*kafana*) to break the day-long fast and listen to bards recite lengthy epic songs. During Ottoman times, these recitations occurred in the Sultan's and other lesser court settings. Some singers claim to know thirty epics in their entirety, one for each night of the month of fasting. Ramadan is special, but numerous other occasions bring forth epic recitations as well. The bards work from memory in a free-form fashion, composing their text as they proceed, but always including the salient features of the traditional story at hand.[82]

Of the nine principal Serbocroatian heroic song-cycles M. Coote has described, those of the Muslim Slavs are of chief importance here, while some indirectly significant related data come also from several other sources. Many newly Islamized Slavs of Bosnia and Hercegovina composed *Krajina* songs, originally associated with the Krajina region along the Ottoman empire's northwestern frontier.

These "closest living parallels to the Homeric songs" (M.

Parry) tend to be longer than their Christian counterparts, and mark an evolution from song to true epic. Using formulaic devices to express speech, action, time, and place, the singers spin tales reminiscent in form of the Homeric epics, though usually considerably briefer.[83] Thematic contents often focus on the campaigns of a great Ottoman sultan of old, structured around standard elements such as the sending and receiving of letters, group consultations as to how to handle the message, the fashioning of elaborate disguises and ruses, and detailed catalogues and descriptions of warriors and their acoutrements and castles.[84]

Expansive plot-development, extensive interest in what transpires in the enemy camp and in motivation (as ascertained by "intermediary figures, such as messengers, spies, and eavesdroppers"), and elaborate descriptive detail further distinguish the Krajina among Balkan compositions.[85] Krajinas combine epic and romance elements surrounding heroes noted for their unswerving loyalty to the Ottoman sultan. Battles, against Christians to the west and non-Turkic Muslim enemies to the east, often occur as part of plots turning on such romantic requirements as the rescue of a fair damsel from the clutches of the infidel.[86]

From a cycle featuring Marko Kraljevic ("Prince," "King's Son"), one can glean some rather indirect information. From a Muslim perspective, the Christian Marko surely qualifies as a villain, at least in songs that depict him flaunting Islamic practice (drinking wine openly during Ramadan!). On the other hand, some songs depict Marko as a loyal subject of the Ottomans who helps them fight their enemies, the Arabs, then beards the sultan in his own den to extort a larger reward, or defends the sultan's daughter against a black Arab would-be rapist. From a Christian point of view, Marko underscores the villainous aspect of the Turkish overlords.[87] *Beciragic Meho* and *Prince Marko* are two of many still-popular songs that undergo constant revision with each new singing. Both feature national heroes, rather than the supreme ruler, the sultan.[88]

The Malay Tradition: Malaysia and Indonesia

Two major forms provide material for the study of heroic themes: the *sira (serat)* and the *hikaya (hikayat)*. Of the two types, the *hikayat* is more important in this context, partly because of its continuities with Muslim literature to the west, and partly because the works tend to be much earlier than those of the *serat* genre still extant.

The classical *hikayat* was meant to be performed in recitation rather than read and, as such, differs from ordinary literature. Like epic stories from other parts of the world, the *hikayat* was a living tale, but it generally adhered rather closely to a fixed version, with perhaps less improvisation in performance than in epic recitations based more on memorizations facilitated by formulaic devices.[89] Apparently stories in the *hikayat* form recited on the eve of a battle served to bestir warriors into a fighting mood.

A. Bausani's *Notes on the Structure of the Classical Malay Hikayat* uses literary insights of Propp and psychological perspectives from Jung to arrive at three conclusions about the hikayat. First, the basic theme is the hero's migration from one level of existence to another and back, mirroring both the Hindu idea of avatar and the classical theme of euhemerization. Second, a prominent idea is the existence of a pleroma, involving an ideal number of protagonists, subject to cycles of diminution (separation) and completion (union). And finally, Malay literature may be derivative from an Asian point of view, but in emotional and psychological detail, it shows much originality.[90]

The Achehnese term *hikajat* refers to a poetic genre always composed in the *sandja'* meter (with each *ajat* or verse containing four-times-four syllables, like the Swahili *utenzi* form, set out in eight iambic feet, with at least two lines in succession ending in rhyming syllables), whereas the Malay *hikayat* is always in prose. In the Indonesian genre, the writer changes topics simply by announcing he is about to do so, with no structural division into books or the like. All known examples are clearly transcriptions of works originally recited to special tunes.

Principal Malay *Hikayat* Works. Out of the many scores of works one might study for their heroic content, several are particularly significant here, in that they represent the migration of key literary characters across the Islamic world. The following summary has been limited to only the most important stories. Of the many Malay *Hikayats* of Islamic and Indo-Persian origin, three come from the late fifteenth or early sixteenth century: *Hikayat Iskandar Dhu 'l-Qarnayn*, *Hikayat Amir Hamza*, and *Hikayat Muhammad Hanafiya*.[91]

Stories of Alexander the Great came to Malaysia with Islam,

perhaps around 1300. *Hikayat Iskandar Dhu 'l-Qarnayn* portrays the world-conqueror as a kind of Hanif missionary (in the mould of Abraham) who preceded Muhammad. Thus does Alexander symbolically claim the world in the name of Islam. The conqueror travels in the company of the prophet Khadir (Khizr), who serves as his guide, much as in earlier Persian stories and following the cues of the Qur'an's eighteenth Sura. Alexander's storied marriage to an Indian princess became a reason for proclaiming the royal descent of the rulers of the Malay peninsula.[92]

Hikayat Amir Hamza likewise forms an important link in the chain of global Islamic heroes. Hamza's adventures remain rooted in the Middle East of the Sasanian dynasty with its court at Ctesiphon (Mada'in), and Hamza retains his main sidekick/dunce Amr ibn Umayya and a second who later converts and joins him, Amr ibn Ma'di Karib. Hamza's exploits begin in his youth and proceed through a breathtaking catalogue of conquests and hair-breadth escapes. This medieval Indiana Jones looks suspiciously like Rustam in his feats of prowess, except that Rustam does not enjoy the company of a comic character like either of the Amrs.[93]

A religious work that deserves special attention, the *Hikayat Muhammad Hanafiya* is based on a Persian original from between 1300 and 1500, probably from the fourteenth century. The Malay adaptation occurred before 1511.[94] Some historical background will help one to appreciate the work. Shortly after the tragic death (martyrdom) of Husayn at Karbala, Ali's last surviving son, Muhammad al-Hanafiya—named after his mother, who had been a slave captured from the Banu Hanifa tribe—emerged as contender for leadership of the Family of the Prophet. He could not truly claim descent from Muhammad, but for his supporters his descent from Ali accorded him sufficient legitimacy. Muhammad himself remained politically aloof and refused to challenge the Caliph Yazid. In 685, after Yazid's successor Marwan died, Abdallah ibn az-Zubayr, whose father had rebelled against Ali in 656, led a revolt to take the Caliphate. He would have to contend with the Caliph's son, Abd al-Malik, as well as the Shi'i supporters of al-Mukhtar who claimed prophetic status.

Mukhtar based his legitimacy on his support of Muhammad al-Hanafiya as mahdi, even though the Alid disavowed any association with Mukhtar. When Ibn az-Zubayr attacked Makka and took Muhammad and his family prisoner, however, Muhammad reluctantly had recourse to Mukhtar, who effected his release. Muhammad strove for neutrality in his refuge in at-Ta'if, near Makka, and after both Mukhtar and ibn az-Zubayr had dropped from the picture in 692, Muhammad accepted Abd al-Malik as Caliph. He remained politically inactive until his death in 700 in Madina. The other then-living Shi'i contender, Husayn's son Zayn al-Abidin, who had survived the slaughter of Karbala, died in 712.

As insignificant as the life of Muhammad al-Hanafiya proved in the whole story of Shi'i Islam, he nevertheless became the hero of a romance that enjoyed great popularity in Southeast Asia during the early years of Islam's development there. Shi'i Islam began as political protest and grew to be focused on the suffering of its leaders. By 684, pilgrimages had begun to Karbala and became central to Shi'i doctrine. Two possible reasons for the development of the story and its far-flung popularity are, first, that Husayn's death was soon linked with mourning rites for the slain Mesopotamian fertility deity Tammuz. Second, Ashura was already a day of some significance, a once-obligatory fast of atonement for Muslims. The story of Husayn took on cosmic proportions, so that the martyr came to be considered an eternally predestined savior not unlike the like redemptive Saoshyant of Zoroastrianism.

Husayn traditions apparently became part of a book attributed to Abu Mikhnaf, in two parts: *akhbar maqtal al-Husayn,* complete with *isnads* ("chains of transmission"); and Mukhtar's revenge. Part one especially influenced later Shi'i literature. Firdawsi was also a great influence on developments, but in addition a prose literature geared to the uneducated folk grew up and associated the Persian-Arab war with the Husayn-Yazid conflict (based on the idea that Husayn had married a daughter of Yazdagird III).

Muhammad al-Hanafiya became immortalized because Mukhtar had named him Mahdi, and as such he became the focus of sub-sects of the Kaysaniya which considered Muhammad alive and in the mountains biding his time before reappearing.[95]

Another important tale relating to the Prophet from a Shi'i perspective is the *Hikayat Nur Muhammad (The Light of Muhammad),* dating from around the mid-seventeenth century.[96] Part of a group of four such stories (the others on Muhammad's splitting the moon, his shaving, and his death), the work presupposes the same "mystic cosmogony" as *Muhammad Hanafiya* and *Hikayat Shah Mardan.* The story tells of the spiritual descent of the Light of God, in the form

263

of a bird, from creation through all the prophets to Muhammad and his family, as the mystical heirloom whose possession establishes its owner's place in the ultimate genealogy of religious heroes.[97]

Originally a non-Muslim tale, the *Hikayat Shah Mardan* combines more explicitly religious material with older legends. Its account of the wanderings and metamorphoses of Shah Mardan, the son of Darulhastan's king, Bagerdamantajaya, has developed thus into a vehicle for religious instruction based on the mystical image of a journey in search of special knowledge. Shah Mardan's odyssey begins when he leaves home with the sage who had come to his land to instruct him (a common theme). Romantic and magical elements abound. The hero accomplishes part of his journey in the form of a bird (linking the tale with that of *The Light of Muhammad*), and the story ends with the countries of the prince and his mentor united.[98] Drewes reports the existence of images without text that were evidently used for illustrating a recital of the story.[99]

Finally, we look at a crucial work some call the "Malay National Epic," the *Hikayat Hang Tuah*. Focusing on the kingdom of Malaka, the *Hikayat Hang Tuah* centers around kings who function as the very embodiment of Islam on earth. This absolute and integral relation between royalty and Islam solves the problem left by another Malay royal chronicle, the *Hikayat Raja-Raja Pasai*, in which the kings merely convert to Islam. At the same time, the *Hang Tuah* establishes definitively the desired distance between royalty and common folk, widening the gap by claiming heavenly descent.

Like other *hikayats*, the *Hang Tuah* opens with a royal genealogy; unlike others and unlike, for example, the *Shahnama*, it does not talk of the origins of humanity. Beginning in heaven and gradually opening up onto the wider world as history commences with the descent of the kings to earth, the story eventually comes to the hero Hang Tuah, who serves the king of Malaka, grandson of the first heavenly king. The hero is not himself royal, but a mere shopkeeper who enters into the sovereign's service. The king abides at, and virtually constitutes, the center of the "cultured world" (*bahasa*), and Hang Tuah fights to defend it from the agression of the "amoks" from the outer world—i.e., the world beyond true culture. As a result of his defense, the kingdom of Malaka can be founded.[100] S. Errington describes how the work is organized rather in a spatial than a temporal framework and thus shows little interest in psychological realism or development in the characters. The story is not so much about people as about the royal/Islamic power to maintain order at the center while chaos reigns beyond the pale.[101]

An Example of the *Hikajat* Genre in Indonesia. *The Story of Prince Muhammad (Hikajat Potjut Muhamat)* is probably the most important of the five great Indonesian "epic *hikajat*" works. Extant versions vary in length from about 1,800 to 2,700 lines. Prince Muhammad's tale originated with a certain Teungku (religious scholar) from the village of Lam Rukam at a date unknown, but probably around or after the mid-eighteenth century. Like the other works of its kind, the *Potjut Muhamat* centers around war, in this instance begun by the prince, in frustration at his brother's diminishing control, against a rival sultan. Potjut Muhamat was the youngest son of Sultan Ala ad-Din Ahmad Shah of Acheh, who rose to power after his predecessor was deposed as ruler in 1727. That unseated potentate returned after the death of Ahmad Shah to make life difficult for Ahmad Shah's older son, who had succeeded his father.

Observing with increasing displeasure that his older brother is losing his grip on the reins, Muhamat decides to intervene. The story begins with an overture that describes preliminaries to the hostilities, followed by military preparations which take the prince out to gather allies. Twenty-three episodes tell of Muhamat's efforts to win over a certain power-broker without whose help he cannot succeed. Once the main action begins, the prince thus shares center stage with another hero, Bentara Keumangan, formerly one of the deposed sultan's staunchest allies. The drama of the Bentara's defection forms a constant theme of the tale and "lifts it to a higher plane than that of a mere battle-saga."[102] But still at the heart of the story stands the young prince who devotes himself to a sovereign (his elder brother, but weaker in character). Unlike some other tales, the *Potjut Muhamat* deals not with wars against unbelievers but strictly with internal royal political strife.[103]

We have some interesting information on the use of illustrated manuscripts in Malaysia that hints at a much broader pattern. A nineteenth-century Malay named Encik Apla owned texts of the epic of Amir Hamza *(Menak)* and of two Panji romances which he rented by the evening—one *Menak* shows Hamza smoking a Dutch clay pipe. The illustrations in all three extant manuscripts are in

265

"wayang style," but the Hamza work, whose figures lift their legs and bend their necks, exhibits a difference in its non-wayang naturalism.[104]

Although it is, strictly speaking, a performance art, the Javanese *wayang* deserve mention here. These shadow plays bear an important reciprocal relationship to the Malay literary genre of the *hikayat*. Several *hikayats* of Hindu origin and content evidently grew out of *wayang:* stories from the *Mahabharata* and *Panji* cycles clearly developed into *hikayats* that way, and, although no examples remain, so may the tales of Rama and Krishna in the *Hikayat Sri Rama* and *Hikayat Sang Boma*. Meanwhile, the immensely popular *Hikayat Amir Hamza* has made its way into the *wayang* repertoire.

These two-part shadow plays evidently function religiously by portraying a cosmos divided by the opposition of demonic and heroic forces. In part one, the demons pose their threat, and in the second part, the heroes counter-charge with divine aid and, of course, prevail. By identifying with some character on the good side, the viewer can participate in the heroic office of protecting the cosmos against dissolution. From the point of view of function, watching a *wayang* yields the same kind of religious benefits as listening to or reciting a *hikayat*.[105]

Glossary

Ashiq: (Ar., Turk. *ashik* = lit. lover.) Term Turkic tradition uses to refer to the reciter or singer of a heroic tale.

Ayyar: (Pers.; see chapter two for etymologies.) Originally, member of social grouping; came to refer to heroic supporting cast figure usually subordinate to a leading character.

Alp: (Turk.) Hero, knight.

Babad: (Mal.) Literary type of chronicle.

Batir, Bogatyr: (Turk.) Common terms for hero in Turkic traditions.

Batl: (Ar., pl. *abtal;* variant *battal.*) Most common Arabic term for hero knight.

Dastan: (Pers.) Story, narrative; sometimes synonymous with *hikayat,* sometimes used to refer to a much longer work that is a cluster of shorter narratives, e.g., *Story of Hamza.*

Diw: (Pers.) Demon, devil.

Futuh: (Ar., *sing. fath* = lit. conquest, victory.) Early Arabic narrative of spread of Islam.

Futuwwa: (Ar., Pers. *fotuvvat;* Turk. *futuvvet* = lit. young men's organization.) Came to refer to a code of behavior (see *javanmardi*) associated with heroic conduct.

Hamasa: (Ar.; Pers. *hamase.*) Originally, anthology of poems; eventually became more generic term including a variety of heroic narratives.

Hikaya: (Ar., Pers. *hekayat,* Turk. *hekaye,* Mal. *hikajat.*) Originally, "recitation" or narrative story used to make a moral point; eventually came to refer to a wide range of story-types across the Islamicate world.

Javanmardi: (Pers. = lit. youngmanhood.) A code of behavior for members of brotherhood, especially asociated with *ayyar* characters.

Khamsa: (Ar., Pers. *khamse* = lit. five.) Popular form of five-part anthology of long romantic, didactic, or mystical works (see *mathnawi*), made popular by Nizami and later copied by numerous Persian, Urdu, and Turkic poets.

Kol: (Turk.) Story.

Maghazi: (Ar. = lit. campaign) Literary type that recounts conquests of early Muslim community.

Majalla: (Ar.) Anthology.

Malhama: (Ar., pl. *malahim.*) In medieval times, referred to prognosticatory texts related to horticultural and or astrological phenomena, and by

267

association referred to apocalyptic texts describing end-times and cos-mic cataclysm; more recently, refers to a wide range of heroic tales still popular in the Arab world.

Maqtal: (Ar. and Pers., pl. *maqatil;* Turk. *mektel* = lit. death or killing of.) Literary form mostly associated with Shi‘i accounts of martyrs, detail-ing every moment in the suffering of Muhammad's family members.

Marthiya: (Ar., Pers. *marsiye*). Literary form of lamentation or threnody, bemoaning usually the martyrdom of Shi‘i heroes. Especially popular Urdu form.

Mathnawi: (Ar., Pers. *masnavi* = lit. couplets.) A poetic form used for lengthy romantic, didactic, or mystical poems especially in Persian, but also in Urdu and Turkish. First hemistich rhymes with second; $\cup$ ---/- $\cup$ --/- $\cup$ - metric scheme.

Mutaqarib: (Pers. *motaqareb.*) Popular meter for heroic poems, such as *Shah-nama;* $\cup$ -- $\cup$ -- $\cup$ -- $\cup$ -.

Nama: (Pers. *name.*) A suffix indicating "book of . . ." as in *Shahnama,* the *Book of Kings.*

Naqqali: (Pers.) Storytelling.

Naqqash: (Pers.) Painter.

Naqqashkhana: (Pers. and Turk. *nakkashhane.*) Studio or atelier, usually under princely or royal patronage.

Pahlawan: (Pers. *pahlavan,* pl. *pahlavanan;* also used in Malay as *pahlawan.*) Most common term in Persianate literature for the hero and knight.

Panakawan: (Mal.) The Southeast Asian version of the *ayyar.*

Parda dari: (Pers. *parde dari* = lit. painting or picture holder.) Process of narrating with picture.

Parda: (Pers. *parde.*) Painting on cloth depicting scenes related to *ta‘ziye.*

Penglipur lara: (Mal. = lit. dispeller of sorrow.) Type of popular story; also refers to the storyteller.

Qissa: (Ar. pl. *qisas,* Pers. *qesse.*) Another basic form of narrative tale, earliest important usages apparently in the Qur’an's moralistic stories of past prophets.

Rawda khani: (Pers. *rowze khani* = lit. reciting the passion play.) The process of narrating the story of Husayn's martyrdom and related events by a *rowze khan,* storyteller.

Shabih: (Pers. = lit. likeness or impersonator.) Refers to either an actor in *ta‘ziyeh* or a likeness in a painting illustrating the passion story.

Shamayil gardani: (Pers., *shemayel gardani* = lit. picture presenting or keep-ing.) Refers to the action of a narrator who tells story with pictures.

Ta’rikh: (Ar., pl. *tawarikh,* Pers. *tavarikh,* Turk. *tevarih* = lit. history.) For pres-ent purposes, usually used in plural after *jami‘* or *mujma‘* (collection) as genre of "Universal History" which includes numerous episodes about heroes.

Ta'ziya: (Pers. *ta'ziye* = lit. mourning.) Persian passion plays to commemorate the martyrdom of Husayn and suffering of all the prophets and Family of the Prophet.

Tabaqa: (Ar., pl. *tabaqat.*) A literary type somewhat similar to the *tadhkira* form, designed to show associations and interrelationships among famous peoeple who belonged to a social group, such as *sufis.*

Tadhkira: (Ar., Pers. *tazkere,* Tur. *tezkere* = lit. recollections.) A literary type made up of brief quasi biographical or hagiographical notices on famous people, such as saints.

Tendi: (Sw., pl. *utendi/tenzi, utenzi* variant.) Poetic form using four lines of eight syllables each, first three lines ending in same rhyme, fourth line rhyming with all other fourth lines.

Ukawafi: (Sw.) Metric system used for some important narrative poetry.

Wayang kulit: (Mal.) Shadow play using puppet-like figures whose arms are manipulated with sticks.

ABBREVIATIONS

AA	*Arts Asiatiques*
AFS	*Asian Folklore Studies*
AI	*Ars Islamica*
AIEO	*Annales de l'Institut des Études Orientales*
AION	*Annali di l'Istituto Orientale, Napoli*
BKI	*Bijdragen tot de Taal-, Land- en Volkenkunde*
BSOAS	*Bulletin of the Schools of Oriental and African Studies*
CA	*Cahiers Algeriennes*
CAR	*Central Asian Review*
CSP	*Canadian Slavic Papers*
DI	*Der Islam*
EI2	*Encyclopedia of Islam,* New Edition
FO	*Folia Orientalia*
GAL	*Geschichte der Arabischen Literatur,* 2nd Edition
IBLA	*Revue/l'Institut des belles lettres arabes a Tunis*
IL	*Islamic Literature*
IO	*L'Islam et l'Occident*
IrS	*Iranian Studies*
JA	*Journal Asiatique*
JAAR	*Journal of the American Academy of Religion*
JAL	*Journal of Arabic Literature*
JAOS	*Journal of the American Oriental Society*
JARCE	*Journal of the American Research Center Egypt*
JEASC	*Journal of the East African Swahili Committee*
JFI	*Journal of the Folklore Institute*
JKRC	*Journal of the K. R. Cama Oriental Institute*
JMBRAS	*Journal of the Malayan Branch Royal Asiatic Society*
JRAS	*Journal of the Royal Asiatic Society*
JSAI	*Jerusalem Studies in Arabic and Islam*
JSAS	*Journal of Sophia Asian Studies*
KO	*Kunst des Orient*
LMI	*Le Monde Iranien et l'Islam*
MW	*Muslim World*
NC	*La Nouvelle Clio*
OM	*Oriente Moderno*

Abbreviations

RA	*Revue Africaine*
REI	*Revue des Études Islamiques*
RHCM	*Revue d'Histoire et de Civilization du Maghreb*
RHR	*Revue d'Histoire de Religion*
RIMA	*Review of Indonesian and Malaysian Affairs*
RNL	*Review of National Literatures*
RSO	*Rivista di Studi Orientali*
SEI	*Shorter Encyclopedia of Islam*
SI	*Studia Islamica*
STF	*Studies in Turkish Folklore*
ZDMG	*Zeitschrift für Deutsche Morgenlandische Gesellschaft*

NOTES

Introduction

1. Campbell 1949:viii.
2. Campbell 1949:16–20.
3. Hawkes 1977:67ff., 89ff.

Chapter One: Heroic Themes as Invitation to the World of Islam

1. Hodgson 1974:1: 58.
2. Bausani 1970:759–68. See also Biebuyck 1972: 269f. on applying DeVries's criteria for the heroic life-cycle pattern as link to other heroic traditions. See also Kailasapathy 1968: 229ff. on "The World of the Heroes," where the author compares Homeric Greek and Tamil literature to show how both are reflections of a "Heroic Age." One might extend the comparison to include several other heroic traditions, as does Ahmad 1966b: 1–5. See Coyajee 1939 on comparisons between Persian and Arthurian traditions.
3. Khouri and Algar 1975:143–49.
4. Khouri and Algar 1975:175–79, quoting 179; 181–91, quoting 187.
5. Vereno 1974:182ff. Dumezil's three-part structure of sacred, military, and mercantile functions relates myth/epic characters to actual historical settings. Sacred function is related to "sovereignty"—when these split, the problem of a power struggle arises: "The more complete the transfer of sovereignty from the first to the second function in any given culture at any given time, the sharper the distinction between sacred and secular."
6. Brakel 1970:14–15, quoting Winstedt's translation. Brakel further defines the function of the *hikayat* in Malay culture as "power-strengthening, enhancing the *mana* of whoever participates in the act of reciting, be it as reader or as listener . . . [Furthermore] to recite it or to have it recited is a meritorious act which atones for sins" (6–7).
7. See *Soviet Epics* 1956 (no author listed) on the ideological implications of epic changes and the insertion of religious elements (e.g., making Köroghlu a saint who wins by God's power, etc.)

272

8. Marcos 1971:237–69. See Meisami 1987: 134ff. on hero as model. See Norris 1980:69 on Antar and Islam and development beyond pre-Islamic forms and values. See Connelly 1986: chapters 8–10 on related issues in Hilali saga.
9. Norris 1980:14–22.
10. Hurreiz 1977:34.
11. Levy 1967:152ff.
12. Southgate 1978:54, 57.
13. Levy 1967:350–51.
14. Levy 1967:50.
15. Goldziher 1967a and 1967b.
16. Izutsu 1966.
17. Bravmann 1972:2.
18. Ringgren 1952:130.
19. Santoso 1971:9.
20. Santoso 1971:9–10.
21. Santoso 1971:16–18.
22. Winstedt 1921:121 and passim.
23. Santoso 1971:20–24.
24. Bausani 1970:759–68; schematic diagram, 768.
25. Brakel 1979:21–22; he makes a similar argument for the introduction of the Islamicate genres known as *kitab* and *sya'ir,* 22ff.; see also Brakel 1970 on Persian influence.
26. Hanaway 1970:265.
27. Hanaway 1970:263–69.
28. See Ras 1968:133 and passim for parallels with other stories. See also Mazaheri 1979 and Soroudi 1980 on Islamization of Rustam and the Persianization of Ali.
29. Hamid 1982:130ff.
30. Ahmad 1966b.
31. Maaruf 1984:48.
32. Summarized from Maaruf 1984:9–16. Maaruf says that along with feudalism, the second ingredient in the distortion of the heroic image is materialism, the archetype of which is J. Paul Getty. See Mbele 1986: 468–69 for an example of the processes of Islamization and Arabization in Swahili tradition.
33. Marcos 1971:314.
34. See Cahen *EI*2 and Taeschner *EI*2 and *EI*2a for for further details.
35. See Bürgel 1988b on woman as person in Nizami. On women in the Lamtuna Berber epic, see Norris 1972:108–10.
36. Winner 1958:75–78.

Chapter Two: Issues in the Interpretation of Heroic Themes

1. See von Grünebaum 1975 for an example of the negative assessment; see Ettinghausen 1979 for a move in a more positive direction.
2. Moghaddam 1982:34–57 and passim.
3. Idris 1963:149.
4. Meisami 1987:134–35.
5. Meisami 1987:81–82.
6. Meisami 1987:131.
7. Pérès 1958:7–12, quoting 8.
8. Pérès 1958:19–20.
9. Pérès 1958:23ff.
10. Canova 1977.
11. Biebuyck 1972:268–69.
12. Corbin 1983:163–70, 205–18.
13. See Hillenbrand 1978 for survey of recent iconographic studies; see Safani 1982 on battle scene prototypes.
14. See Simpson 1979.
15. Gutmann and Moreen 1987:111.
16. Gutmann and Moreen 1987:118ff.
17. Milstein 1987:137.
18. On epic as mirror of contemporary history, see Grabar and Blair 1980. Molé 1958 on Seljuk *Wis and Ramin* presupposes the presence of images that decidedly nuance the interpretation of the text.
19. On Timurid use of portraits of contemporary figures, inserted into miniatures, see Lentz and Lowry 1989, e.g., cat. no. 140.
20. Levy 1967:50.
21. Levy 1967:44.
22. See Meisami 1987:300 on links between the arts.
23. Connelly 1986:206–07. Day 1983: 154 makes a remark interesting in this context, concerning "the possible effect of Islamic doctrine on the paratactical nature of Malay literary style."
24. Klimburg-Salter 1977:60–68. Color plate: Landscape in Anthology, Lentz and Lowry 1989:57; Gray 1979: XXXVI; Kevorkian and Sicre 1983: 91 (all same miniature).
25. Simpson 1985:141.
26. Simpson 1985 mentions L. Golombek's unpublished thesis on how an image gave rise to a story, which then in turn inspired further images.
27. Belenitsky 1960.
28. Atasoy 1972.
29. Chelkowski 1989.

30. Grabar 1974 and 1984. Color plate: Ettinghausen 1962: 117.
31. See Grabar and Blair 1980 for color plate.
32. Golombek 1972, quoting 29. Color plate: Lentz and Lowry 1989: 294; same in Kevorkian and Sicre 1983:119. See also Lukens-Swietochowski 1974.

Chapter Three: The Folk Hero

1. See Grech 1977:323ff. on three categories of popular narrative: the pure Bedouin type with emphasis on the male hero; the "heroic-philosophic" epic, with its main female character; and the religious epic with its sense of communal empowerment as exemplified by the values of the earliest Islamic heroes. The three functions of the Bedouin epic listed in my text are from 325.
2. See Connelly 1986 for analysis of the work and its context; on folk tale variants in Sudan, see Hurreiz 1977 passim, and Hurriez 1972 for more texts. See Galley 1977 on images of Jaziya.
3. On the history of scholarship on this and other works of "popular sira," see Heath 1985. See Norris 1980 and Hamilton 1981 for partial translation.
4. See Norris 1980 and Blachere *EI*2 for general background on Antar. Color plates: Masmoudi 1972:54–55, 71; Williams 1978:2–5 and back cover. Another historical heroic figure shown in many glass paintings is Abdallah ibn Jaʿfar, usually seen riding with his beloved Yamina. He was involved in the early conquests of North Africa. Color plates: Masmoudi 1972:2–3, 45, 51, 78–79.
5. See J. Allen 1971:268–369 and J. and R. Allen 1961 for translations of *Utenzi wa Abdirrahmani na Sufiyani* and *Utendi wa Mikidadi na Mayasa*.
6. Knappert 1979:212–14. I have found no samples of images of Miqdad.
7. Knappert 1985:422–30.
8. Knappert 1985:417–21.
9. Bashgöz 1987a:316–17.
10. Marcos 1971:222ff.
11. See Grabar 1970, 1974. Color plates available, *Maqama* number in parentheses: Lewis 1990:I; all remaining from Ettinghausen 1962: (4) 112; (7) 118; (8) 150; (10) 114; (26) 151; (27) 152; (29) 146; (30) 113; (31) 82; (32) 117; (37) 107; (38) 106; (39) 108, 121; (43) 111, 116.
12. Burrill 1970 provides texts; Burrill 1974:245–47 gives references to pictures; Constantin 1967 discusses the character's variations among Turks, Balkans, and Rumanians. Color plate: Petsopoulos 1982:212.

13. Hurreiz 1977: 47, 60–61, quoting 60; Hurreiz also notes that in some Near Eastern versions, the part of Jiha is actually filled by Khoja Nasruddin (63, n. 38); see also Hurreiz 1972:157–63 for texts. On Jha, the Tunisian variant of the character, see Dundes and Bradai 1963; see also Dejeux 1978 on the Arabo-Berber variant. On the Malay version of the comic figure, Si Junaha, see Knappert 1980:270ff. Color plate: Williams 1978:5.
14. Canard 1961:167–68.
15. One color plate whose theme is pertinent here shows Zal consulting magi, S. C. Welch 1972:73v.
16. Lewis 1974:151, 141–43, and passim on names.
17. Winstedt 1921:101, 118–19.
18. Errington 1975:92–100; for a summary of various interpretations of the *Hikayat Hang Tuah,* see Hussein 1974:26–28.
19. Mazaheri interprets *ayyar* as an Arabization of the Persian compound *ab-yar,* "irrigation-protector." Because those originally charged with protecting the water supply were associated with Iranian attempts to fight off Muslim invaders, the plural of the word *(ayyarun)* gradually came to have the Arabic meaning of something like "gangs of young men up to no-good," troublemakers, hooligans. From there one moves rather easily to a connotation of rogue or trickster. In Persian, the term continued to carry a more positive connotation, and long after the Arab Muslim conquest, it was associated with a number of historical heroes who had fought to reassert Iranian identity, such as Ya'qub ibn al-Layth as-Saffar (867–79) and Mardawiz (927–35). Mazaheri 1979:20 refers to the two, respectively, as a latter-day Rustam and Isfandiyar. Still later usage associates the word with courtiers in the Persian tradition. See Bausani 1974:458–59 for other attempts at etymology.
20. See, e.g., *EI2* 2:961ff. on "Futuwwa"; see also Taeschner 1931 and 1944 on same. Mélikoff 1962a:32–33 on an *Ayyarnama;* 64 on connections with *futuwwa* organizations; 103, n. 2 indicates an unavailable work by Jean Deny, *Un conte picaresque des 1001 Nuits, Conférence de l'Université de Paris* 1940; see 78 and 83 on Ahmad ad-Danaf and Dalila.
21. See Simpson 1985 on various images without text. Stern 1971:544 interprets a poem on the tenth-century Iranian heroic figure Ya'qub ibn al-Layth the Coppersmith and makes an interesting link between Kawa and Ya'qub: the poem says Ya'qub carries the "banner of Kawi," the Sasanian dynastic panther-skin escutheon captured by the Arabs in 636/37. "Banner of Kawr" originally meant simply "king's (*kawi/ kay* = king) banner," but eventually the "true etymology was forgotten, and the word gave rise to legends about the smith" Kawa and his

apron-banner. Ya'qub gains this dual prestige by showing himself as both heir to royal lineage and as a liberator of the oppressed. Color plates relating to Kawa's revolt and Dahhak's downfall: S. C. Welch 1972:36; Titley 1984:15; A. Welch 1973:14a; Ashrafi 1974:78–79; Falk 1985:231.

22. Hanaway 1970:129–77.

23. Gaillard 1985. Partial trans. in Razavi 1972. Summary in Hanaway 1970.

24. Drewes 1979:1–27, including summary of, and comparison with, the older *Hikajat Malem Dagang,* in which the hero—prince and younger brother—plays a similar supporting role.

25. Bausani 1974:461; 467, n. 26.

26. Norris 1980:51.

27. See Calasso 1979 for extensive details and translation of an Amr story in *Khawarannama.*

28. Color plates: Brand 1985:11; Glück 1925:8, 48; Beach 1981:40.

29. Knappert 1980:100. See also Pigeaud 1950:237–40.

30. Coote 1978:268; Parry and Lord 1974:1:336 and 2:30–32. For another example of the type, Ali Zaybaq ("Quicksilver"), see the *Thousand and One Nights* cycle of the clever Dalila.

31. Hodgson 1974:2:157.

32. On etymology, Rudra-stama, etc., see Mazaheri 1979:13f., n. 29.

33. See Soroudi 1980:372.

34. See Hanaway 1978 for general background. Color plates: Rogers 1986:38; Lillys 1965:29; Lowry 1988:18; S. C. Welch 1972:110v; Goswamy 1988:5.

35. Color plates of Rustam's birth: Ashrafi 1974:82; Grube 1966; Robinson 1976a:XVI right; Lewis 1990:IV; Goedhuis 1976:88i; Karahan 1971:9; Walther 1981:29.

36. Color plates featuring Rakhsh: Gray 1961:98; Karahan 1971:11; Goedhuis 1976:19x.

37. Maguire 1974a. Color plates of some scenes from the seven courses: Rustam—Lowry 1988:26; Lentz and Lowry 1989:59rt; Grube 1972; Lillys 1965:21; Robinson 1976a:X; Goswamy and Fischer 1987:17; Karahan 1971:12; Pinder-Wilson 1958:6; Lowry 1988:25; S. C. Welch 1972:120v; Çağman and Tanindi 1979:9; Ashrafi 1974:99. Isfandiyar—Lewis 1990:XI; Rogers 1986:3, 37, 52, 53; A. Welch 1976:14, 16; Gray 1956:3.

38. See Mazaheri 1979 from beginning for full argument, 16–17 for these conclusions.

39. On longing for the return of a Rustam, see poems of Mihdi Akhawan Salis in Soroudi 1980:371, n. 15. A roughly parallel major figure from Serbocroatian works, Djerzelez Alija, epitomizes loyalty of Bos-

nian Muslims to the Ottoman sultan. Like Rustam, the hero comes to the monarch's aid to extricate him from tight spots, from threats both internal and external. He alone proves a match for the more redoubtable Christian heroes, and only Djerzelez could bring success at last to the two-decade siege of Baghdad. Coote 1978:268; Luka 1983:177–83.

40. See Beach 1981:58ff. Color plates: Falk 1985:119; Goswamy and Fischer 1987:7, 95; Falk 1985:120; Gluck 1925:2, 9, 23, 27, 30, 31, 33, 45; S. C. Welch 1978:1, 2, 3; Grube 1972; Brand 1985:12; Robinson 1976b:29, 30.

41. For an excellent summary of modern Arabic writers, see Idris 1963.

42. Shojai 1975, quoting 230. Three of the four novelists Shojai studies "see heroic action as possible."

43. Moghaddam 1982:9–15, 92–100.

44. Navabpour 1980:89.

45. Markus 1985a. See also Elwell-Sutton 1971 on folk tale influences.

46. Haye 1967.

47. Oshikawa 1986 explores the transformation of the historical character. Includes two plates of novel cover-art.

Chapter Four: The Royal Hero

1. Meisami 1987:182 and n. 6.

2. Color plates: Wilkinson 1931:15; Ashrafi 1974:8, 9; Falk 1985:32, 56; A. Welch 1976:9; Çağman and Tanindi 1979:4; Karahan 1971:26; Kevorkian and Sicre 1983:68; Robinson 1980:XIII. Related scenes: Ashrafi 1974:63–64, Lowry 1988:23, Gray 1961:164; Goedhuis 1976:55iii; same, Kevorkian and Sicre 1983:253.

3. Meisami 1987:147.

4. Related color plates: Kevorkian and Sicre 1983:37; Lentz and Lowry 1989:283.

5. Color plates: Titley 1984:24; Lentz and Lowry 1989:116, 176, 277; Petsopoulos 1982:195.

6. Color plates: Ipširoglu 1980:26; Robinson 1976a:II; Gray 1979:LV; Yusupov 1982:276; Gray 1961:153; A. Welch 1976:25; Rogers 1986:59; Kevorkian and Sicre 1983:159, 247.

7. Color plates: Ashrafi 1974:10, 89; Robinson 1976a:III; Goedhuis 1976:52; Rogers 1986:120; Çağman and Tanindi 1979:17.

8. Color plates: Titley 1984:38; (note astrologer) Gray 1961:134; Rogers 1986:71; Ashrafi 1974:95.

9. Color plates: Lowry 1988:38; Ashrafi 1974:18, 90; Falk 1985:17b, 184, 194; Titley 1984:9, 21; Yusupov 1982:271, 272, 274; Rogers 1986:65, 138; Gray 1961:54; Ipširoglu 1980:27; Robinson 1980:VIII; Lentz and Lowry 1989:297; S. C. Welch 1976:12.

10. Color plates: Ashrafi 1974:19, 42, 57; Robinson 1980:IX; Gray 1979:XXXIII; Goedhuis 1976:14vii; Karahan 1971:37; Kevorkian and Sicre 1983:55, 135.
11. Color plates: A. Welch 1976:10; Rogers 1986:54; S. C. Welch 1976:26–27; Falk 1985:61; Kevorkian and Sicre 1983:161.
12. See Chelkowski 1988 for summary and analysis; see Burrill 1974a on the Farhad and Shirin love as developed in later Persian and Turkish works. Color plates: Robinson 1976a:XII; S. C. Welch 1972:742v; Kevorkian and Sicre 1983:42, 249.
13. Stchoukine 1977:167–68. Color plates dealing with scenes other than those already noted: Titley 1984:22; Falk 1985:38; Lentz and Lowry 1989:108, 163; Rogers 1986:56, 69, 142, 143; Lowry 1988:16; Robinson 1980:II; Gray 1979:LXX.
14. Color plates: Ashrafi 1974:17; Karahan 1971:36; Wilkinson 1931:20; Ashrafi 1974:5, 12; Falk 1985:229; S. C. Welch 1976:13; Rogers 1986:41; Yusupov 1982:280; Çağman and Tanindi 1979:18.
15. Bürgel 1988c:172–74. Color plates: Yusupov 1982:281; Titley 1984:20; Goedhuis 1976:14xiii.
16. Color plates: Yusupov 1982:279; Gray 1961:112; Ipširoglu 1980:21; Kevorkian and Sirce 1983: 26–27, 41; Titley 1984:10; Gray 1979:XXX; Grube 1966 and 1972; Çağman and Tanindi, 1979:13,26–27; Lentz and Lowry 1989:112, 282 and copy 175; Robinson 1976a:II; S. C. Welch 1972:568r; Grabar and Blair 1980:53; Ashrafi 1974:77; Falk 1985:23. See also Mostafa 1942 for further iconographic details.
17. Color plates: Ashrafi 1974:13; Kevorkian and Sicre 1983:93, Gray 1961.
18. Color plates: white—Rogers 1986:121, 131; Yusupov 1982:76; blue—Yusupov 1982:75; green—Titley 1984:23; Rogers 1986:129; Robinson 1980:III; Ipširoglu 1980:28; Gray 1979:LXVII; Kevorkian 1983:251; red—Rogers 1986:30; Robinson 1980:X; yellow—Rogers 1986:72; Yusupov 1982:74; Ashrafi 1974:88; Kevorkian and Sicre 1983:113; black—Rogers 1986:60; Yusupov 1982:73; Gray 1979:LXXIII.
19. See Krotkoff 1984 for further interpretation of the symbolism; quoting 102.
20. Meisami 1987:234, n. 65.
21. The prophet Idris/Enoch plays a similar role among the prophets, albeit with the more limited function of teaching humankind how to make clothing. As a culture-hero, Idris remained the patron of tailors. See Falk and Archer 1981:3 for color plate of Idris in this role.
22. Levy 1967:5.
23. Color plates of Gayumart's court: Pinder-Wilson 1958:5; S. C. Welch

1972:20v; Gray 1961:59; Lowry 1988:24; Atil 1987:32; Robinson 1976b:6; Karahan 1971:3. See chapter five for references to Solomon's court.

24. Color plates: Karahan 1971:4; S. C. Welch 1972:22v, 23v; A. Welch 1976:4–5, 10.

25. Color plates: Ashrafi 1974:14; Gray 1979:XX; Beach 1981:73; Holter 1981:5r.

26. Color plates: Falk 1985:43; S. C. Welch 1972:30v. Rahman 1971:51 sees a connection between this and use of the cow-headed mace as royal emblem thereafter, and Kawa's hoisting a "cow's skin" leather apron as the banner of revolt—an interesting idea, but stretched a bit too thin.

27. See Molé 1958a. Color plates: Falk 1985:46; Ashrafi 1974:15; Gray 1979:LIII; Kevorkian and Sicre 1983:143.

28. See Rubin 1979.

29. Color plates: S. C. Welch 1972:42v; same, Kevorkian and Sicre 1983:155; Rogers 1986:32; Grabar and Blair 1980; Ashrafi 1974:2, 16; A. Welch 1976:15. Lowry, 1988:7, 8; Karahan 1971:5, 6; Ipširoglu 1980:20.

30. See Navabpour 1980:86–89, on a connection with a modern Iranian novel.

31. Color plates: Robinson 1976a:XI; Ashrafi 1974:98; Gray 1961:77.

32. Color plates: Titley 1984:7; Lentz and Lowry 1989:178rt; Falk 1985:94, 51; Ashrafi 1974:3, 29; Karahan 1971:14, 15, 16; Kevorkian and Sicre 1983:189; Goswamy 1988:3, 8–11; Gray 1956:4. Another favorite theme for miniaturists is the prince's royal activities with Afrasiyab: Kevorkian and Sicre 1983:187.

33. Color plates: Robinson 1980:XII; Rogers 1986:33, 39; Gray 1979:XL; Lillys 1965:33, 35; Grabar and Blair 1980:21; Karahan 1971:27, 28, 29, 30, 32.

34. See Yarshater 1979, Chelkowski 1989, and Peterson 1979.

35. An interesting exception is Banu Gushasp, one of Rustam's daughters, who has her own epic; see Safa 1954:300–302.

36. Hanaway 1970:28–29. He explains that "The warlike woman as a motif in Islamic Persian literature is an unexpected one and its presence here may be ascribed partly to the survival of a pre-Islamic tradition and partly to the widespread distribution of this theme in world folklore."

37. Motlagh 1971:52–54. Plate: Lentz and Lowry 1989:177.

38. Hanaway 1970:26–29.

39. See Lewis 1974 for stories of Bamsi Bayrek and other women as warriors. Also Canard, Christides, and Grégoire on Dhat al-Himma and the Amazons in the story of Umar an-Nu'man.

40. Hanaway, 1970:32.

41. Hanaway 1970:39–54 analyzes the relationship between Purandukht and the goddess Anahita, via their threefold connections with water and springs, conferral of legitimacy on a king, and bestowal of victory in battle.
42. Chelkowski 1988:187. See also Bürgel 1988b.
43. Other important women in Firdawsi include: Pishdadian (to 100 B.C.): Shahrinaz and Arnawaz (Jamshid's daughters); Faranak (wife of Abtin and mother of Faridun); Arzu, Mah Azadekhuy, and Sahi (daughters of Sarv of Yemen, chosen by Faridun to wed his three sons); Mahafarid and her daughter (Iraj's concubine and his daughter by her, born after Iraj's death). Kayanian (100–330 B.C.): Tahmina (Rustam's beloved in Turan, mother of Suhrab); Gurdafarid (fighter who challenges Suhrab); Sudaba (wife of Kay Kawus who lusts after Siyawush); Farangis (oldest daughter of Afrasiyab and widow of Siyawush); Jarira (daughter of Piran and first wife of Siyawush); Katayun (oldest daughter of Byzantine emperor, wife of Gushtasp and mother of Isfandiyar); Humay and Bihafarid (daughters of Gushtasp); Queen Humay Shahrzad (daughter and wife of Bahman, sister of Sasan); Nahid (Alexander's mother); Rawshanak (Dara's wife, later wife of Alexander). Ashkanian (330 B.C.–225 A.D.): none important. Sasanian (226–651): Gulnar (Ardashir's lover); Gurdya (sister and wife of Bahram Chubin, later wife of Khusraw Parwiz); Purandukht and Azarmdukht (daughters of Khusraw Parwiz—the first by Maryam—and short-reigning queens). Earlier figures are less personalized, the later more individualized. See Motlagh 1971:22–98.
44. Color plates: S. C. Welch 1972:67v; Ashrafi 1974:81; Falk 1985:49; Rogers 1986:51; Gray 1979:XXII; Robinson 1976b:31; Walther 1981:36; Lowry 1988:9.
45. Levy 1967:152–72; Motlagh 1971:61–66. Color plates: Kevorkian and Sicre 1983:147; Ashrafi 1974:84; Atil 1973a:44; Rogers 1986:42, 144; Goswamy and Fischer 1987:16; Karahan 1971:19; Goswamy 1988:14. See also Simpson 1981 for an analysis of the beaker depicted in Atil 1973a. Another famous trysting couple from the *Shahnama* whose rendezvous is a favorite of miniaturists are King Ardashir and the slave girl Gulnar; color plates: Gray 1956:8; S. C. Welch 1972:516v; Falk 1985:22, 57.
46. Color plates: Lentz and Lowry 1989:294; same in Kevorkian and Sicre 1983:119, 181; Walther 1981:100; Gray 1961:144; Titley 1984:33; S. C. Welch 1976:41.
47. For detailed analysis of how Iskandar's story developed through various sources, see Hanaway 1970:66–128, "Alexander: The Persianization of a Foreign Hero."
48. See Southgate 1978:196–201.

281

49. On which, see Polignac 1982; Hanaway 1970:109–15 on the historians' judgments of Alexander.
50. Color plates: S. C. Welch 1976:14; Titley 1984:8, 32, 43; Gray 1961:128, 74; Yusupov 1982:283, 285; Falk 1985:62.
51. Color plates of same in Grabar and Blair 1980:30; Gray 1961:29. Iskandar's dealings with India: Goedhuis 1976:46xii; Lowry 1988:11.
52. Color plates: Robinson 1976a:VIII; S. C. Welch 1976:24; Ashrafi 1974:102; Rogers 1986:66.
53. See Hanaway 1970:84–98 on analysis of *Shahnama* content; Southgate 1978:169–73; Levy 1967:232–50; see Molé 1953:388ff. on *Kushnama* as source on Alexander. Color plates: Gray 1961:28, 131; Çağman and Tanindi 1979:19; Petsopoulos 1982:194; Grabar and Blair 1980:28; Pinder-Wilson 1958:10; Rogers 1986:67, 73, 122; Ashrafi 1974:67; Goswamy and Fischer 1987:49.
54. Hanaway 1970:102–07, here quoting 106–7; for comparison with contents of Firdawsi, see summary of *Darabnama*, Hanaway 1970:297–305; Southgate 1978:181–84.
55. Hanaway 1970:118.
56. Hanaway 1970:125–27.
57. Southgate 1978:173–81.
58. Ras 1968:130–31.
59. Ras 1968:131–33.
60. Color plates: S. C. Welch 1976:48; Gray 1961:32; Grabar and Blair 1980:39. See also Stchoukine 1977 on the frequency of death and mourning scenes in Nizami.

Chapter Five: The Religious Hero

1. Norris 1980:8.
2. Renda 1976: figure 26. Color plates: Petsopoulos 1982:197–98, 208.
3. Several manuscripts of the *Falnama* depict a variety of scenes in and around the Garden. Color plates: Lowry 1988:33; Lillys 1965:79; Grube 1966.
4. See Rubin 1979:46–47.
5. See Knappert 1967a:64–138 and 1970:13–34 on the Adam and Eve epics; Knappert 1964c on *Utenzi wa Maisha ya Nabii Adamu na Hawaa;* Knappert 1967a: 83–91 on the role of Satan as link to an *Epic of Job;* Allen 1971:370–425 and Werner 1923 for translations of *Utenzi wa Ayubu*. On Adam and Eve in other traditions, see Thackston 1978 and Knappert 1980. See Hamid 1982:147ff. and Knappert 1980:27–44 on Malay stories on various minor prophets.
6. Knappert 1967a:64 says he cannot trace the work, but has been as-

sured there is an *Utenzi wa Nuhu.* Color plates: Falk 1985:18, 45r; Beach 1981:60; S. C. Welch 1978:9.

7. See chapter three on Hamza, and Hanaway 1970 on the Hamza romance.

8. Color plates: Atil 1973b:10; Titley 1984:25; Gray 1961:25, 79; S. C. Welch 1985:89. On images of Nimrod's other follies, especially his attempt to fly heavenward to fight God, see Milstein 1987:124–26.

9. See Knappert 1967a:223–24 on Abraham in seventh heaven. See Shapiro 1943 on sacrifice.

10. See Rahman 1971:60–61.

11. On miniatures of Yusuf among the Ishmaelites, see Milstein 1987:126–32. Color plates: Kevorkian and Sicre 1983:175, 185; S. C. Welch 1976:40; Meredith-Owens 1969:VIII; Robinson 1976b:43; Petsopoulos 1982:201; Çağman and Tanindi 1979:35; Robinson 1980:I; Lowry 1988:29; Grube 1972; Falk 1985:187.

12. Text in Knappert 1964a:9–58. Partial translation of Jami's work in Pendlebury 1980.

13. See chapter four on Zulaykha as lover.

14. See Knappert 1970:41–55; Damman 1938 on Swahili epic. On related images, see Hanaway 1985. Color plates: Holter 1981:7v; Petsopoulos 1982:209; Ashrafi 1974:45; Goswamy and Fischer 1987:99; Rogers 1986:118; Gray 1961:162.

15. See Gutmann and Moreen 1987.

16. Rubin 1979:47.

17. On related miniatures, see Milstein 1987:133–37.

18. Knappert 1964a:122–24.

19. See Knappert 1967a:234 on the chain mail theme in Swahili literature. See also Knappert 1969b:81ff. Color plate: Holter 1981:8r.

20. Color plates: Lowry 1988:60; Titley 1984:14; Yusupov 1982:186–87; Falk 1985:131; Goswamy and Fischer 1987:25; Aslanapa 1971:XXVII.

21. See Soroudi 1980:376ff. on connections among Solomon, Rustam, and Ali.

22. See, e.g., article on *Zubdat at-Tawarikh,* Renda 1976. On Swahili stories, Knappert 1964a:136–38, 131. Color plates: Holter 1981; Gray 1961; Lillys 1965:83; Gray 1979; XLIV.

23. On Khadir in courtly poetry, see Meisami 1987 passim. On miniature paintings, see Coomaraswamy 1934:176ff.

24. See Masmoudi 1972.

25. See Drewes 1963:334ff.

26. Drewes 1977:16–18.

27. See Mélikoff 1960 and 1962a on *Saltuqnama.*

28. See Knappert 1971:1:67–69 on Swahili stories of Mary.

29. Norris 1972:100ff.
30. See Rubin 1979 on these two main metaphors used to explain the prophetic heritage.
31. Knappert 1983:77.
32. See Knappert 1971:1:30ff. and Knappert 1961 for Swahili material on Muhammad.
33. Knappert 1979:111; 1967a:42–43, quoting 143. Color plates: Tanindi 1984; Séguy 1977. Related studies: see Ettinghausen 1957 on images from the fourteenth century; on the life of the Prophet, see Soucek 1988 and Grube 1965.
34. Knappert 1979:104–6.
35. Knappert 1979:121–22.
36. Knappert 1985:198–203.
37. See Schimmel 1975b:137 on a 1649 illustrated Dakhni Urdu version of the *Khawarannama*. Color plates: Tanindi 1984:IX, 56, 68, 71, 84; Gray 1961:105–7; Titley 1984:203; Lentz and Lowry 1989:132; Meredith-Owens 1969:VII.
38. See Calasso 1974 and 1979 for full treatment and analysis.
39. On Ali and Rustam, see Soroudi 1980. See also Winstedt 1940b:279ff.
40. Knappert 1979:112, 114. On Ali against the villain Ra's al-Ghul, see text and translation in Harries 1962:27–49.
41. Knappert 1979:212, 214; Knappert 1985:413.
42. Knappert 1983:113–15; see text of *Utenzi wa Seyidina Ali* in Knappert 1964a:106–59. Knappert also reports on the epic *Utenzi wa Shehe Ali*.
43. Knappert 1985:258–59.
44. Knappert 1985:431–34.
45. Knappert 1985:259–61.
46. Knappert 1985:126–27.
47. Knappert 1985:434–37.
48. Knappert 1985:282.
49. Knappert 1979:122–27.
50. Knappert 1985:272–77.
51. Knappert 1967a:147–49.
52. Soroudi 1980:373. Color plate: Falk 1985:163.
53. Knappert 1985:268ff.
54. Knappert 1985:283–84.
55. Knappert 1983:59–73, prayer quoted from 68; Knappert 1985:283–97. On Persian versions of the tragedy, see Virolleaud 1950 and Pelly 1879. For a treatment of various aspects of the Shi'i *ta'ziya*, see Chelkowski 1979.

56. See Brakel 1975 and 1977 for text, translation, and analysis; see also Knappert 1985:306–11.
57. On specific miracles, see Knappert 1967a:159–63; Knappert 1971:1:38–40. Further see Knappert 1967a:151ff., Tanindi 1984:2:13ff. Color plates: Tanindi 1984:15, 36, VII.

Chapter Six: Villains and the Forces of Evil

1. Knappert 1967a:83–90. Color plates: Gray 1979:XLIII; Lowry 1988:32.
2. Knappert 1967a:94–113.
3. Knappert 1967a:91; for more on Satan, see Knappert 1971:1:71–72.
4. Paret 1930:131 lists various Arabic editions.
5. Knappert 1967a:4; for excerpted text and translation of Swahili epic, see Harries 1962:29–47.
6. Color plates: Masmoudi 1972:36, 38.
7. Warner 1925: 2:103–5; Levy 1967:59ff. Color plates: Falk 1985:29; Karahan 1971:13.
8. Levy 1967:57–58. Color plates: Gray 1956:6; Lowry 1988:15; Titley 1984:17; Lentz and Lowry 1989:166; Grube 1972.
9. Color plates: Lowry 1988:26; Lentz and Lowry 1989:59rt; Grube 1972; Lillys 1965:21; Robinson 1976a:X; Robinson 1976b:16; Goswamy and Fischer 1987:17; Goswamy 1988:2; Karahan 1971:12.
10. Color plates: Welch and Welch 1982:22B; Falk 1985:54; S. C. Welch 1972:294r; Kevorkian and Sicre 1983:151; Lentz and Lowry 1989:127; Gray 1979:XXXVII; Gray 1961:90; S. C. Welch 1985:73; Karahan 1971:10.
11. Levy 1967:146–51, quoting 151.
12. See Warner 1925:3:281 on full text of the allegorizing comment. Color plates: Robinson 1976a:IX; Ashrafi 1974:6, 97; S. C. Welch 1985:75.
13. Norris 1980:101–2.
14. See chapter three for notes on color plates of *Hamzanama*.
15. Related to Polyphemus of the *Odyssey;* see Lewis 1974:15 for bibliography.
16. Lewis 1974:140–50; Hickman 1988:173ff. for further psychological interpretation. Other significant giant stories include Moses's battle with Og, mentioned in chapter five, and Miqdad's victory over Zoro, mentioned in chapter three.
17. Examples from *sira* of the literally hundreds of enemy knights: Lawn az-zalam ("Color of Darkness") is the "sword of Ghawwar ibn Dinar";

Wajh al-Ghul is killed by Antar; Antar story catalogues Antar's competitors, but the list does not include Amr ibn Maʿdi Karib, since he was known "historically" to have defeated Antar—Norris 1980:108ff., 121ff., 62ff., noting especially the case of Abd Hayyaf.

18. See Dumezil 1970:153, 14–15.

19. One might be reminded of the Bible's deliberate inclusion of several unsavory types in the genealogy of Jesus. Color plates: S. C. Welch 1972:28v, 29v, 37v; Goedhuis 1976:19iv; Kevorkian and Sicre 1983:149; Falk 1985:42.

20. See Warner 1925:v1–3 for the complete story of Afrasiyab. Color plates: Grube 1972; Ashrafi 1974:85, 96; S. C. Welch 1972:105r; A. Welch 1976:4; Goswamy 1988:13, 15, 16. Concerning Garshasp, the Iranian king at the end of whose reign Afrasiyab made his move, see Falk 1985:20. Concerning relations of Kay Khusraw with Afrasiyab's survivors, see Lowry 1988:21; Karahan 1971:24. See chapter ten for more on Afrasiyab's daughters Farangis and Manizha.

21. Errington 1975:113–16, quoting 114.

22. Errington 1975:89.

23. For a cross-cultural study of the phenomenon, see Spores 1988.

24. Knappert 1967a:155–56 and passim.

25. For further analysis of the enemy in the Turkic epic *Danishmand-nama*, see Mélikoff 1960:131–38.

26. See J. W. T. and R. Allen 1961 for text and translation. On infidels (Jews and Frankish Crusaders) in *sira*, see Norris 1980:64. See also Knappert 1967a:74ff and 140.

27. Levy 1967:246–47.

28. Color plates: Lentz and Lowry 1989:178; Lowry 1988:12. Other color plates on the theme of outsiders as black peoples: Lewis 1990:XII, XIII, XIV, XV.

29. Coyajee 1939:161–64. Color plate: Lowry 1988:17.

30. See Awn 1983 and Calasso 1971 on Iblis's moral ambiguity. On Muslim as villain, see: Coote 1978:265 on Serbo-Croatian songs of the liberation of Yugoslavia from Ottoman invaders; Skendi 1954:46ff. on Iskanderbeg; Daniel 1984; Grégoire 1931, 1942 and 1975; Nasralla 1980; Senac 1983; Sivan 1968; Tonguc 1958.

Chapter Seven: Heroic Identity and Legitimacy

1. See Campbell 1949 passim. See also DeVries 1959:194–208 for his analysis of the life cycle of the hero.

2. Errington 1975:80; Winstedt 1921:111.

3. Qurʾan Sura 19; Levy 1967:47–48; Lewis 1974:27–28, 59–60, and passim; see Naimi 1938 on Rustam's birth.

4. Norris 1980:25–29, 34–35.
5. Levy 1967:35.
6. Winner 1958:72–73.
7. Levy 1967:33.
8. The same ruse is used in the story of Egrek, on which see chapter nine.
9. Lewis 1974:171–81.
10. Color Plates: Rogers 1986:50; A Welch 1976:8, 11; Falk 1985:48; S.C. Welch 1972:63v; Lentz and Lowry 1989:179; Grube 1972; Karahan 1971:7, 8; Kevorkian and Sicre 1983:18, 145; Goswamy 1988:1.
11. Norris 1980:16.
12. Hanaway 1970:207–08.
13. See Krotkoff 1984 for further details.
14. Levy 1967:181–97.
15. Levy 1967:99ff.; Warner 1925:2:325ff.
16. See Zhirmusnky 1963:248–49 on the Turkic Edigei epic.
17. Connelly 1986:139–40.
18. Peter Heath, "Plot Formation in *Sirat Antar,*" unpublished paper, to be incorporated in a larger work on Antar now in progress.
19. Southgate 1974:154.
20. Color plates: Çağman and Tanindi 1979:5; Lentz and Lowry 1989:133; Lillys 1965:25; Ashrafi 1974:76; Karahan 1971:17, 18; Goswamy 1988:6, 7; Gray 1956:5.
21. Knappert 1967b:183–84; Knappert 1983:142; Harries 1962:48ff. provides text and translation; see Mbele 1986 on discussion over the hero's identity.
22. See Azarpay 1981:109ff on visual aspects of the theme.
23. Levy 1967:25ff. Color plates: Ashrafi 1974:80; Goedhuis 1976:19vi.
24. Levy 1967:38.
25. Knappert 1979:213.
26. Norris 1980:106.
27. Lewis 1974:60, 62.
28. Lewis 1974:161.
29. Southgate 1978:176.
30. Nizami 1972:1028ff. after the section on Iskandar's visit to the hermit, a scene mentioned briefly in chapter two and further discussed in chapter nine.
31. Levy 1967:20.
32. Color plate: Holter 1981:9r.
33. Mélikoff 1960:1:163, 300.
34. Color plate: Goswamy 1988:12.
35. Marcos 1971:219–21.
36. Lewis 1974:168.

37. Walker and Unsal 1966:194ff.
38. Norris 1980:174–75; 196, n. 61 describes a parallel theme in *Dhat al-Himma.*
39. Knappert 1983:116–17.
40. Norris 1980:133ff.; Lewis 1974:177.
41. Norris 1980:162ff.
42. Coote 1978:268.
43. Christides 1962:595.
44. Christides 1962:570.
45. Meisami 1987:147.
46. Meisami 1987:149–57. See Bürgel 1988a on Khusraw and Shirin as an example of recognition/love on sight of painting.
47. Norris 1980:35.

Chapter Eight: Journey as Context of Quest and Test

1. See Maguire 1974a.
2. Norris 1980:100–101.
3. Drewes 1975:8ff.
4. Hamori 1971:10–12.
5. Color plates: Lentz and Lowry 1989:250; Gray 1979:XLV; Gray 1961:140; Kevorkian and Sicre 1983:74 (unfinished image of similar scene); Pinder-Wilson 1958:1.
6. Color plate: Gray 1979:LXII.
7. Color plate: Gray 1961:134.
8. Levy 1967:362–64.
9. Knappert 1983:78–80.
10. Knappert 1967a:191ff.
11. Harries 1962:26–27.
12. Knappert 1971:3:227ff.
13. See Ettinghausen 1957; Séguy 1977.
14. Levy 1967:45–46.
15. Southgate 1978:54–58.
16. According to Knappert 1980:69–79, another Malay source concerns itself with Khadir's relationship to Iskandar as part of a larger interest in establishing the royal legitimacy of the Malay sultans. In *Sejara Melayu* Khadir acts rather as Iskandar's vizier or press secretary and as counsel to other sultans as well. Khadir's association with Iskandar even makes the guide function as a progenitor of kings as Iskandar himself functioned. One story makes Khadir the crucial link in a chain of divine descent: Khadir's wife bears a pumpkin, which, when discarded, breaks open to reveal a baby, who then speaks and demands that the prince build her a palace. Meisami 1987:228–29

notes that in the context of Bahram Gur's spiritual journey, Khadir appears as the only true guide in the story of Mahan as he wanders in the garden of fifth tale in the *Haft Paykar*. In the midst of false guidance aplenty to be had in a world of sense, only Khadir can lead to where renunciation of the senses frees the traveller from the snares of illusion.

17. Drewes 1975:8ff.
18. Corbin 1976:307ff.
19. On the role of the Simurgh in initiation and guidance into the realm of spirit, see Corbin 1976:195ff.
20. Knappert 1980:67; Levy 1967:248.
21. Chelkowski 1988:182.
22. Hanaway 1970:258–61, quoting 261; and 1971:151ff.
23. Norris 1980:97–98. See also Marcos 1971:285ff.
24. Color plate: Lentz and Lowry 1989:134.
25. Maguire 1974a. See also Hamori 1971:19, n. 38 on Isfandiyar's Seven Feats and the Brazen Hold; also 18, n. 32 on spiritual/actual journey.
26. Norris 1972:1.
27. Norris 1980:53–54, fort mentioned once as in Uman, once as in Yemen.
28. Knappert 1971:3:231–32, 251–55.
29. Coyajee 1939:168–71 draws some parallels with Arthurian temptresses Guinevere and Morgan La Fee.
30. Christides 1962:569ff.
31. For further related examples, see Hanaway 1970 passim; Knappert 1985:192ff. on Khadija's marriage to Muhammad; Knappert 1979:104 on Khadija's meeting with Muhammad, and 122ff. on Ali and Fatima; Knappert 1985:417ff. on Miqdad and Mayasa.

Chapter Nine: The Geography of Quest and Conquest

1. See, e.g., Hanaway 1970:217–25 on sparing use of descriptions of nature—sunrise and sunsets.
2. This threefold division does not correspond exactly to the traditional Iranian cosmos that Corbin describes as "an intelligible universe, a sensory universe, and between the two a universe for which it is difficult in our language to find a satisfactory term." He calls the middle realm the "imaginative." Of the Iranian eighth clime, Corbin says: "The ancient sages were alluding to this world when they declared that besides the sensory world there is another world with shape and dimensions also extending in space, but the shape, dimensions, and extent of his other world are not identical with those we perceive in the world of physical bodies, although what exists in the

sensory world has its analogue there; it is not a question of sensory dimensions, but of exemplary imaginative dimensions." Corbin 1979:78.

3. See, e.g., Ahmad *EI2* 4:119.
4. Rubiera 1981:27–33.
5. Rubiera 1981:55ff. on Iram.
6. Norris 1980:9.
7. Nizami 1972:1021ff.; see 1025–26 for the text the artist has included within the frame of the miniature described below.
8. Color plate: Lentz and Lowry 1989:250, catalog no. 140.
9. The Malay version in Knappert 1980:63–64, quoting 64. Nizami's description of the visit to Iram is in the Persian text, 1281ff.
10. See Meisami 1987:230–31, 287–88, 290–93.
11. Levy 1967:248–49.
12. Rubiera 1981:39–41 translates a text of Qazwini on the construction of the palace.
13. Southgate 1978:53.
14. Color plate: Goedhuis 1976:33.
15. Markus 1984:75, n. 25.
16. Norris 1980:147ff. Norris 1972:71 also mentions a dome built by Idris at the point where a river deriving from the Nile divided into branches after emerging from high mountains.
17. Norris 1980:60; he notes further that each sub-segment in turn is "influenced by the tripartite division of the pre-Islamic ode, the erotic prelude *(nasib)*, the march *(rahil)*, and an ending of praise *(madih)* and heroic triumph."
18. Norris 1980:126–27.
19. Norris 1980:116.
20. Norris 1980:133ff.; on the historical background of the actual geography, see 73ff.
21. Norris, 1980:61.
22. Knappert 1971:1:97.
23. Knappert 1983:91.
24. Hamori 1971:17–18, n. 32.
25. Norris 1972:50–51, 76.
26. Errington 1975: 176–78; on spatial organization and outsiders/amoks, see 60–68.
27. Brakel, 1975:67–71.
28. See Ahmad *EI2a* 4:376 on *Dastan-i Amir Hamza.*
29. Knappert 1980:93ff.
30. See chapter three on Hamza for references to color plates.
31. Rubiera 1981:63ff. According to Hamori 1971:10–12, a Black Castle with inscriptions about former monarchs and their attempts to fend

off death prefigures the City of Brass and leads to the less realistic stage of the city; sculptures lead and point the way to the city as reminders of Solomon's (1) "mortal magnificence" and (2) "fall from grace and power"; and in the City of Brass are many "life-like corpses and other deceptive exteriors" (perhaps like the dead bodies Iskandar sees on thrones?). See also Norris 1972:1ff. on the sea tale and the City of Brass; 6–7 on mountains and Sea of Darkness; 11 on Alexander and the dragon of the western sea; 14ff. on Khadir as guide; 52–53 on the city's location in the Sahara; 99ff. on a Berber hero's "City of Equality." Norris indicates that the City of Brass was located in either the remote East or West. One version, perhaps, is the City of Sosso in African legend with 188 fortresses. The gateless Arabian city, guarded by jinns, was made for Solomon as a ruse, with a lake next to it full of jinn, and with a magical forest nearby (inside or near the lake). The whole complex sets up a pattern of symbols consisting of palace/city, water source and tree and grove. A modification of the palace is a copper tower, a flood-age castle in the clouds or tree tops. Solomon's brass palaces in Spain (Tadmur) and Africa had magnetic properties. Palace and well combine and contrast as do the progenitor Semitic king/hero and the heroine, who is a Semitic or Cushitic queen or princess. Alexander builds a raised palace of *baht* stones with magnetic properties, irresistibly attractive, with a well of magnetic ebb and flow nearby. Norris also tells of a Palace of Alexander with a "cupola of locks," and of cities of copper and lost groves in Africa. Norris 1980:10–13, 31, 85–86. On apocalyptic connections, see Destrée 1971.

32. See Destrée 1971 for further discussion of the question of whether the city is purely mythical or based on some quasi-historical foundation.

33. Calasso 1974 and 1979 provide detailed analysis of the work. The latter includes an Italian translation of the text of Ali's journey to the City of Gold, 513–39. See Basset 1893 on another version (in Arabic) of the story. Farther east, the hero Shah Mardan also finds a magical city on his travels, but the narrative is much less extensive and detailed; See Drewes 1975:11.

34. Rubiera 1981:33–34.

35. In Arabic legend, Sinimmar was also the sculptor of the images of Khusraw Parwiz, his wife Shirin, and the world's fastest horse, Shabdiz, carved at Taq-i Bustan on Mt. Bisutun. Arabic sources also depict Khawarnaq as an occasion for that contemplation of beauty that uniquely raises the mind to thoughts of God and of this world's impermanence. The palace and its trappings, inevitably and so soon reduced to ruin, often serve as a reminder not so much of human

might as of the passing nature of all that is not God. See Rubiera 1981:35–37 for translations of selected Arabic sources.

36. Krotkoff 1984.

37. Bahram Gur sends his princesses off to fire temples after he marries Justice; Meisami 1987:300, n. 1. Further connections are in Zulaykha's seven-room palace in Jami's *Yusuf and Zulaykha,* in which she hopes to seduce the prophet; Zulaykha also has a small model of the same building made of food created for her banquet. And in the *Haft Paykar* there is also the palace of Mundhir with a special room associated with the seven climes. Color plates: Lentz and Lowry 1989:120, 288; Gray 1961:75, 116; Kevorkian and Sicre 1983:123.

38. Rubiera 1981:41–43.

39. Corbin 1979:75. See also Southgate 1978:56ff., 91–92; even Solomon did not make it there.

40. Corbin 1979:30. He uses as an example of the "landscape of Xvarnah" (the divine-royal aura of legitimacy surrounding such heroes as Faridun and his descendents) a manuscript full of intriguing landscape paintings. For a color plate, see Kevorkian and Sicre 1983:91. See also Milstein 1986 on connections between light and landscape.

41. Knappert 1967a:148–49.

42. Knappert 1967a:207.

43. Knappert 1967a:205ff.; 1971:1:87ff.

44. See Attar's *Musibatnama,* in which the thought-wanderer journeys through another world, visiting forty sources of knowledge.

45. Waugh 1975:236.

46. Waugh 1975:240ff.

47. Waugh 1975:243.

48. Meisami 1987:227.

49. Meisami 1987:227–32.

50. Corbin 1983:163ff., quoting 180; on the Twelver Shi'i metaphysical elaboration of this type of interpretation, see Corbin 1983:181–205.

51. Suhrawardi might have taken a similar approach to Bahram Gur's disappearance in Nizami's rendition.

52. The following description is largely a summary of Corbin 1983:205–19.

53. Corbin, 1983:207.

54. On several fascinating parallels with the Arthurian legend, see Corbin 1983:163ff. and passim, and Coyajee 1939:37–194. Color plates: Ipširoglu 1980:13; Karahan 1971:22, 25; Wilkinson 1931:13; Rogers 1986:40; Lillys 1965:31; Ashrafi 1974:93; Kevorkian and Sicre 1983:16; Grube 1972.

55. Klimburg-Salter 1977:esp. 60–69. See also Nasr 1972 and Sakisian 1938.

Chapter Ten: Relational Motifs: The Hero and the Human Family

1. See also Knappert 1967b:183 and Harries 1962:48–71 on the case of Liongo Fumo, who virtually set it up so that his son could kill him.
2. Markus 1984:61–64 also describes the three levels of the prince's affront to his father.
3. Drewes 1963:346–47.
4. Drewes 1963:351.
5. See Clinton 1990.
6. Color plates: Ashrafi 1974:7; A. Welch 1976:1; Karahan 1971:20, 21.
7. Lewis 1974:90.
8. Lewis 1974:93.
9. Lewis 1974:88–107; the eleventh story has Uruz rescue father, and the first story has a son rescue father; in the second, Kazan frees his whole family from captivity to the infidels. See also Shojai 1975:221ff. on the theme in modern Iranian literature. See Shariati 1982 for a psychoanalytic approach to these and other "oedipal" themes in the *Shahnama*. On grandfather/grandson relationship, see Dumezil 1983:77–78; Rustam at birth is likened to grandfather Sam, etc., Levy 1967:48.
10. Knappert 1985:428.
11. Levy 1967:92ff.
12. Levy 1967:210ff.
13. Winstedt 1921:116–17.
14. See Shariati 1982 for full analysis from the Freudian perspective.
15. Markus 1984:61–64.
16. Motlagh 1971:26–28.
17. Other mothers noteworthy for the intensity of their grief over the loss of their hero sons are Katayun and Jarira, the mothers of Isfandiyar and Farud. Color plates: Kevorkian and Sicre 1983:64, 221; Ashrafi 1974:30; Pinder-Wilson 1958:4. Among religious women of deep sorrow are Fatima, mother of Hasan and Husayn, the major Shiʿi martyrs; and Shahrbanu, wife of Husayn, on whom see Knappert 1985:302–6.
18. Color plates: Lentz and Lowry 1989:130; Çağman and Tanindi 1979:7; Lillys 1965:23; Wilkinson 1931:5; Ashrafi 1974:83. Goedhuis 1976:19xi.
19. Canard 1961:163–67 and *EI*2:2:233ff. Also from the Arabic *sira* tradition comes Ghamra, consort of Antar, mother of his sons Maysara

and Ghasub. Both sons of this warrior mother show prowess as leaders of the troops. Norris 1980:102–3.

20. Lewis 1974:117–32.
21. Wilson 1924:144ff.
22. Lewis 1974:133–39.
23. Lewis 1974:151–60.
24. Levy 1967:20–22. See also Dumezil 1970:14–15.
25. Levy 1967:29–30. Color plates: A. Welch 1976:5, 9. Falk 1985:47; Kevorkian and Sicre 1983:15.
26. Christides 1962:565.
27. Potjut Muhamat as youngest son and brother provides an interesting Southeast Asian parallel to the theme. See Drewes 1979.
28. Lewis 1974:161–70.
29. Thanks to Peter Heath for these observations.
30. Zhirmunsky 1963:250.
31. Lewis 1974:140–50.
32. Color plates: Titley 1984:16; Karahan 1971:31.
33. Color plate: Ashrafi 1974:31.
34. Motlagh 1971:24–26.
35. Stern 1971:543–44.
36. Holter 1981.
37. Color plate: Aslanapa 1971:XXVII.
38. Norris 1980:62.
39. Levy 1967:33.
40. Norris 1980:171–76; 196, n. 61.
41. Meisami 1987:233ff.
42. See Corbin 1978 and Chittick 1979.

Chapter Eleven: The Two Struggles and the Enemy's Many Faces

1. Knappert 1983:68; see 64–73 on the Swahili version of the story.
2. Markus 1987:98.
3. Norris 1980:38; for more detail on background of weaponry, see all of n. 26, 37–38. See also Bellamy 1987.
4. Norris 1980:31–32, 18–19. Other related materials: Suʿada gives Zayd a magical sword, according to Knappert 1985:439. See also Lord 1960:86–89; Marcos 1971:225ff. and Dumezil 1970:148ff.
5. Levy 1967:50.
6. Coyajee 1939:244–45.
7. Winner 1958:84.
8. Knappert 1979:112–14; 1983:87–90.
9. Knappert 1983:103–6; Knappert 1985:261.

10. Knappert 1980:92.
11. See Roux 1982:59–82 on bow and arrow within Turkic cultures.
12. The phrase frequently appears as an inscription on medieval Islamic swords. According to Ibn Hisham, someone else made the statement, and according to Ibn Taymiyya, Gabriel gave the sword to Muhammad at Badr.
13. Marcos 1971:228–30; on 210, Marcos refers to another hero with a two-pointed sword.
14. Further information in Mittwoch *EI*2a, Zawadowski 1943, Zaky 1954 and 1959. Color plates: Meredith-Owens 1969:VII; Falk 1985:163; Gray 1961:105; Tanindi 1984:63, 71.
15. Errington 1975, quoting 89, n. 6; see also 98–100.
16. Josselin 1965:143; Winstedt 1921:20–21. See Frey 1988 for an art-historical and cultural study of the kris.
17. Knappert 1985:423ff. See also Marcos 1971:231–36 on horses and their names.
18. Roux 1982:35; Roux also mentions that the winged horse featured in the *Saltuqnama* is called Semender.
19. Bashgöz 1978:316 lists names of major Turkic horses.
20. Winner 1958:83–84.
21. Levy 1967:50ff. Color plates: Gray 1961:98; Karahan 1971:11; Goedhuis 1976:19x.
22. Knappert 1967a:204–5; for bibliography, see Knappert 1966a.
23. Color plates: Tanindi 1984:IV; Lentz and Lowry 1989:276; S. C. Welch 1976:33; Gray 1979:XXVI; showing lion/Ali in sky also, Lowry 1988:31; Kevorkian and Sicre 1983:49; Gray 1961:105.
24. Knappert 1979:114.
25. Knappert 1967a:all of chapter three, esp. 177, 186ff. Also Knappert 1979:111ff., 114ff. on Abu Bakari's Katirifu (third oldest Swahili text); Knappert 1983:80–82 on infidel tyrant. See also Knappert 1985:203–9, 223; Dajani-Shakeel 1976. A color plate related to this theme: Titley 1984:44.
26. Color plates: Rogers 1986:36; Gray 1956:7; Kevorkian and Sicre 1983:21, 107, 219; Ipširoglu 1980:19; S. C. Welch 1972:241r; Goedhuis 1976:15, 19 xvii; Lowry 1988:20; Tanindi 1984:55; Grube 1966 and 1972; Karahan 1971:23; Robinson 1980:VII.
27. Hanaway 1971:153–54. For Southeast Asian parallels, see Drewes 1979 passim.
28. Norris 1980:183; a similar tale is told about the enemy Ghawwar: see 158–59.
29. Errington 1975:92; Winstedt 1921 passim.
30. Norris 1980:105–6, 114–15.
31. Norris 1980:16–17.

32. Lambert 1962:49–55, quoting 53–55. For more on single combat scenes in Swahili sources, see Knappert 1983:92–103, 106–9, 119–22.
33. Color Plates: Tanindi 1984:77; Ashrafi 1974:4, 92; Lowry 1988:19; Titley 1984:11; Lillys 1965:27; Falk 1985:33, 53, 55; Goswamy 1988:4; Rogers 1986:34, 141; Goedhuis 1976:19xx; Gray 1961:89, 98; S. C. Welch 1972:102v, 341v.
34. Color plates: Falk 1985:56, 110; Ashrafi 1974:9; A. Welch 1976:8–9; Çağman and Tanindi 1979;4; Karahan 1971:26; Kevorkian and Sicre 1983:68; Goswamy 1988:17; Robinson 1980:XIII; Titley 1984:203; Rogers 1986:55; Tanindi 1984:5, 18; Pinder-Wilson 1958: 6.
35. Coyajee 1939:127–94. Color plates: Falk 1985:50, dupe in Goswamy and Fischer 1987:94; Goedhuis 1976:19 xviii; 34ii; S. C. Welch 1972:225v.
36. For one listing, see J. and R. Allen 1961:81.
37. Norris 1980:106. See also wife of Abd ar-Rahman, daughter of Abu Sufyan in Knappert 1979:211ff.
38. Connelly 1986:199–203.
39. Connelly, 1986:207; see 203–8 on visual imagery. Further on warrior women, see Christides 1962:580ff.; Zhirmunsky 1963:247; on Dhat al-Himma, Canard *EI*2 234ff.; Hanaway 1970:25–54; Norris 1980:161.
40. Connelly 1986:218. Another famous fighting couple are Humay and Humayun in in Khwaju Kirmani's poem. Color plate: Gray 1961:47; Kevorkian and Sicre 1983:29.
41. Sumer 1972:44–46; for more on the importance of the hunt, see Hanaway 1976 and Shepherd 1974.
42. Shariati 1982:51–52.

Chapter Twelve: Rediscovery of Authentic Humanity: The Heroic Mind and Heart

1. Campbell 1949:17–18.
2. See for example von Grünebaum 1975 for one not very persuasive argument that the characters are too flat to have acted as human or ethical models.
3. A contemporary American analogy might be the "professional wrestler," with either goodness or badness emphasized to the point of caricature.
4. Hanna 1968:302–3.
5. See Josselin 1965:140–43.
6. Saʿdi 1969:14.

7. Color plate: Beach 1981:164, plate 73.
8. Southgate 1974:158; Warner 1925:2:168.
9. On Hafiz's treatment of the imagery, see Meisami 1987:287–93.
10. Norris 1980:97–98.
11. Lewis 1974:58; see also 40, 106, 132, 181, 188 for almost identical wording, after which the bard wishes the royal listener long life.
12. Lewis 1974:12–13.
13. Mélikoff 1960:1:456–60.
14. Southgate 1978:180–81; Norris 1972:49–51.
15. Southgate 1978:93.
16. Shariati 1982:esp. 41ff.
17. Connelly 1986:208ff.
18. Knappert 1983:58.
19. Norris 1980:207–27; see 59 for text and further analysis.
20. Josselin 1965:144; Winstedt 1921:121–22.
21. Lewis 1974:108–116.
22. See Corbin 1983:163–235; also Coyajee 1939:185ff.
23. Levy 1967:134.
24. Krotkoff 1984:102.
25. Levy 1967:250.
26. Meisami 1987:195; see also 156–57, n. 23.
27. Meisami 1987:196; also see 198, n. 26 on the piety of kings in their old age.
28. Hamori 1971:14.
29. Color plates: Titley 1984:3; Lillys 1965:37, 91.
30. Connelly 1986:140.
31. Lewis 1974:27–41.
32. Levy 1967:217.

Appendix: Sources of Heroic Images: The Major Literary and Artistic Traditions

1. General background on related Arabic works on Brockelmann 1949; Sezgin 1967; Nicholson 1969; Gibb 1962.
2. See Mittwoch *EI2*.
3. Marcos 1971 discusses the *hamasa* of Abu Tammam, an Abbasid-period collection of mostly pre-Islamic and early Muslim poets, with its newly Islamized derogation of vengeance and blood feud. See Gabrieli 1970 on epic elements in pre-Islamic poetry. See Bravmann 1960, Canova 1977 and 1983 for further background on Arabic literary and popular heroic themes.
4. Marcos 1971:78; Pellat *EI2* 4:110–12 as well as adjacent series of

articles on *hamasa* across the Muslim world; on *malhama*, see also al-Mahasini 1960, who discusses *malhama* in the sense of "stories our mothers and grandmothers told us on winter nights," rather than in the sense of apocalyptic or prognosticatory text as described in Fahd 1966:224ff.

5. See Marcos 1971:58–92 for more thorough discussion of these three types of literature. See also *EI*2 articles on Kissa (narrative, story). On the "romance" in Arabic literature, see Pérès 1957 and 1958.

6. Pellat *EI*2 4:111; see *EI*2 articles on Antara (Sirat) Antar, Baybars I (Sirat) Baybars, Dhu 'l-Himma, al-Battal (Banu) Hilal.

7. Schleifer *EI*2 4:387; see Connelly 1973 and 1986 for excellent background on this work and the genre as a whole. On glass painting, see Galley 1977; Masmoudi 1968, 1969, and 1972.

8. See Abel 1970 for analysis of the *sira's* overall makeup.

9. Norris 1980:42.

10. Norris 1980:1–6, quoting 6. A related but, for present purposes, less important work is the *sira* of Baybars, a collection of *urban* tales, combined with elements of other traditional stories (e.g., *Thousand and One Nights*). Although ostensibly a life of the early Mamluk sultan Baybars I (1260–77), the story is replete with fictitious details. See Paret *EI*2 1:1126–27.

11. See Canard 1932, 1935, 1937, 1961, and his articles on Dhu 'l-Himma, *EI*2 2:233–39 and al-Battal, *EI*2 1:1102–03; for the most recent and complete single study, see Steinbach 1972.

12. Norris 1980:20ff.; Winstedt 1940b:98–99, 273ff.

13. Munroe 1983:31ff., quoting 35–36. See also Kilito 1976 for further analysis of the literary type; texts of Hamadhani translated in Prendergast 1915/1973; see Irving 1954 on influence on a later genre.

14. See Grabar 1970 and 1974.

15. Grabar 1984 provides a thorough analysis of all extant illustrated manuscripts, including a complete set of images on microfiche.

16. See, for example, on Mas'udi, Khalidi 1975.

17. See Guillaume 1955 for complete translation.

18. See Thackston 1978 for a translation of Kisa'i.

19. See especially Paret 1930 and 1970.

20. Masmoudi 1968 and 1969.

21. Knappert 1983:76.

22. Knappert 1983:7.

23. Harries 1962:25.

24. Harries 1962:24–28.

25. Knappert 1983:170, n.28.

26. Knappert 1983:2ff.

27. Knappert 1967a:69–138; Knappert 1964c.
28. On Job, for example, see J. Allen, 1971:370–425 (complete text), and Werner 1923. On Jesus, see Damman 1980.
29. Knappert 1967:201ff.
30. Lambert 1962, introduction; offers dual language text. Knappert 1985:203–9 summarizes the story.
31. Knappert 1979:102–4, quoting 104. See also Knappert 1969 on same work.
32. Knappert 1979:120ff.
33. Knappert 1983:59–63.
34. Knappert 1979:210–17; Knappert 1985:407ff.
35. Knappert 1979:109–12.
36. Knappert 1967a:139ff. analyzes and gives excerpts of the text in dual language.
37. Knappert 1979: 114; story summarized, 115–20.
38. Knappert 1979:217–21. Good examples of other African Muslim material from areas neighboring the Sahil region come from a Sudanese people called the Jaʿaliyyin. Hurreiz (1977:30) delineates four categories of subject matter found in the genre known as *qissa* or *hikaya* (terms used synonymously): (1) historical legends of the tribe, (2) legends of saints and popular Islamic religious narratives, (3) stories of adventure and love in quasi-fictitious setting, (4) comical tales featuring picaresque/trickster characters.
39. For general information on Persian literature, see Rypka 1968:162ff.; Morrison 1981; Ethé 1901; Browne 1930; Yarshater 1988.
40. See Safa 1954:120–70 on Firdawsi's predecessors, and 171–283 on Firdawsi. English translations of the *Shahnama:* Warner 1925 (complete); Levy 1967 (selections). Major studies also in Nöldeke 1925 and Coyajee 1939.
41. Works dedicated to the visual art of the *Shahnama:* Wilkinson 1931; S. C. Welch 1972; Robinson 1950, 1972, and 1983; Atasoy 1972; Belenitsky 1960; Grabar and Blair 1980; Grabar 1969; Gharavi 1357/1979; Simpson 1979 and 1982; Brian 1939; Karahan 1971; Corning Museum of Glass 1973; Lillys 1965; Norgren and Davis 1969.
42. Rypka 1968:163.
43. Molé 1953:381ff.; Massé, Hamasa/Persian, *EI*2 4:112–14. Safa 1954:283–341 discusses these and over a dozen other major "national" epics. See Barthold 1944 on the history of the Persian epic. See also Hanaway 1978.
44. Safa 1954:343–76. See also Davar 1927 on the *Shahnama* as an historical epic.

45. Molé 1953: 391–92; Calasso 1974 and 1979; Safa 1954:377–92 labels this category "religious epics," including in it a dozen other works, several of which focus on the exploits of Ali.
46. See Peterson 1979 on related visual arts.
47. Darbandi and Davis 1984 gives complete translation of *Conference of the Birds*. Excellent background on important Sufi-influenced literature in Schimmel 1975a. On related visual imagery, see Baer 1977; Klimburg-Salter 1977; Lukens-Swietochowski 1967 and 1972.
48. Meisami 1987, first quote 80, second 136.
49. Heath 1987:13–14, here conflating his two separate statements.
50. Hanaway 1970:13.
51. Hanaway 1971:139–61, quoting 148. Southgate 1978, in addition to a complete translation, includes in appendices excellent background on Alexander literature. Razavi 1972 offers a partial translation of *Samak-i Ayyar.*
52. Hanaway 1970:238.
53. Knappert 1985:401–4.
54. Meredith-Owens *EI2* 4:153; Hanaway 1970:337–49 provides a summary of the romance.
55. Translation in Wilson 1924.
56. Chelkowski 1988:180.
57. Bürgel 1988c:161–78. Pendlebury 1985 translates excerpts of *Yusuf and Zulaykha*. See Meisami 1987, ch. 4 on *Wis and Ramin, Warqa and Gulshah, Khusraw and Shirin, Majnun and Layla;* ch. 5 on *Haft Paykar.* On the latter, see Krotkoff 1984. On related visual arts, see Stchoukine 1977; Ashrafi 1974; Chelkowski 1975; Binyon 1928.
58. On illustrated versions, see Gray 1978; Robinson 1977; Rice and Gray 1976.
59. Ettinghausen 1955.
60. Rehastek 1892 has translated the former work.
61. English translation in Arberry 1966.
62. See, for example, Lukens-Swietochowski 1972. Of related interest: Baer 1977 and Klimburg-Salter 1977.
63. Atil 1973a; Simpson 1981.
64. See Azarpay 1981.
65. On Alexander in Urdu *mathnawis,* see Gaeffke 1989.
66. Ahmad *EI2* 4:376.
67. See Schimmel 1973 and 1974 passim for the broader picture; 1975b:137ff. on mathnawi; 203ff. on dastan; 199ff. on marthiya; quoting 202. Ahmad *EI2* 4:119 on Hamasa/Urdu, and 375–76 on Hikaya/Urdu.
68. Bashgöz 1978a.
69. Bashgöz 1978a:313.

70. Translations of *Dede Korkut:* G. Lewis 1974; Sumer 1972.
71. Boratav, Hikaya/Turkish, *EI2* 4:373–75; Bashgöz 1978a:317.
72. Hatto, Hamasa/Central Asia, *EI2* 4:115–19; Zhirmunsky 1963, 245ff.
73. Bashgöz 1978a:324–28; Bashgöz 1976.
74. Tanindi 1984 (English text) 10–13, quoting 10. On illustrations to same, see Grube 1965.
75. On illustrated work, see Renda 1976.
76. Tanindi 1984:6–8 (English text).
77. Meredith-Owens, Hamza, *EI2* 4:153–54.
78. Tanindi 1984:6–8 (English text).
79. Mélikoff 1960:I:43ff.; see 161–70 for summary of themes. See Mélikoff 1962a on Abu Muslim. Bashgöz 1978a:324; Mélikoff, Al-Battal, *EI2*a 1:1103–4; same, Hamasa/Turkish, *EI2* 4:114–15.
80. Mélikoff 1960:I:50–51.
81. See Soucek 1988 on life of Muhammad; see also Séguy 1977 for color plates.
82. Lord 1960:14ff.
83. Lord 1960:33ff., quoting Parry.
84. Lord 1960:67ff.
85. Coote 1978:273–74.
86. Coote 1978:267–69.
87. Coote 1978:264–66.
88. Lord 1960:223ff. See also Skendi 1954:60–71, 117–33 on relationships between Muslim and Christian traditions of epic poetry; Luka 1983 passim.
89. Errington 1975:1ff.
90. Bausani 1979:10; intro. by Lode Brakel. Bausani gives a translation (18–41) of *Hikayat Maharaja Ali,* with paragraph-by-paragraph commentary (43–67), conclusion, and notes.
91. Hamid 1982:115–69 provides background and summaries of the major works.
92. Winstedt 1940:85–87, 92–95.
93. Winstedt 1940:94–97; summary, 258–65.
94. Brakel 1975:54ff.
95. Brakel 1975:1–6; Winstedt 1940:105–7.
96. Winstedt 1940:88, 100ff.
97. Winstedt 1940:101–4.
98. For a summary of one version, see Winstedt 1940:79–80; on similarities to the Indonesian *Hikayat Anlin Darma,* see Drewes 1975:8–15.
99. Drewes 1975:32–34.
100. Errington 1975:44–56, 68.
101. Errington 1975:4ff., 60–68; see 45 concerning the differences between the *Hikayat Raja-raja Pasai* and *Hang Tuah.*

102. Drewes 1979:18.
103. Drewes 1979:3ff.; see 9–16 for summary and background of the related *Hikayat Malem Dagang;* 17ff. for summary and background of *HPM.*
104. Day 1983:150–51; Pigeaud 1950.
105. Brakel 1970:7–8.

BIBLIOGRAPHY

Abd al-Badi, Lutfi. 1964. *La épica Arabe y su influencia en la épica Castellana.* Santiago de Chile: Instituto Chileno-Arabe de Cultura, 1964.

Abel, Armand. 1970. "Formation et constitution du Roman d'Antar." *La Poesia Epica e la sua Formazione.* Rome: Accademia Nazionale dei Lincei, 1970. 717–30.

Abu-Haidar, Jareer. 1974. "Maqamat Literature and the Picaresque Novel." *JAL* 5 (1974) 1–10.

Afshar, Iraj. 1936. "The Landscape Miniatures of an Anthology Manuscript of the Year 1398 A.D." *AI* 3 (1936) 77–98.

Ahmad, Aziz. *EI2.* Hamasa/Urdu Literature. *EI2* 4:119.

———. *EI2*a. Hikaya/Urdu. *EI2* 4:375–76.

Ahmad, Kassim, ed. 1966a. *Hikayat Hang Tuah.* Kuala Lumpur: Dewan Bahasa dan Pustaka, 1966.

———. 1966b. *Characterization in Hikayat Hang Tuah.* Kuala Lumpur: Dewan Bahasa dan Pustaka, 1966.

Al-Mahasini, Zaki. 1960. *Adab al-malahim waʾl-malhamat al-ʿarabiyya (Epic Literature and Arabic Epic).* Cairo: Al-Azhar, 1960.

Allen, J. W. T. 1971. *Tendi.* New York: Africana, 1971.

———. trans. 1965. *Utenzi wa Seyidina Huseni Bin Ali* by Hamadi Abdallah al-Buhriy. Dar es-Salaam: East African Literature Bureau, 1965.

———, and Allen, Roland, trans. 1961. *Utenzi wa Abdirrahman na Sufiyani* by Hamadi Abdallah al-Buhriy. Dar es Salaam: East African Literature Bureau, 1961.

Allen, Roland, trans. 1950. *Utenzi wa Kiyama* by Hamadi Abdallah al-Buhriy. Dar es Salaam: Supplement Tang. Notes and Records, 1950.

———. trans. 1956. *Utenzi wa Kutawafu kwa Nabii* by Hamadi Abdallah al-Buhriy. Kampala, 1956.

Arberry, A. J., trans. 1966. *Muslim Saints and Mystics.* London: Routledge and Kegan Paul, 1966.

Arendonck, C. van, and Fares, Bishr. 1974. "Futuwwa." *SEI.* Leiden: Brill, 1974. 109–10.

Arnakis, Georges G. 1953. "Futuwwa Traditions in the Ottoman Empire: Akhis, Bektashi Dervishes and Craftsmen." *JNES* 12 (1953) 232–47.

Ashrafi, M. 1974. *Persian-Tajik Poetry in XIV-XVII Centuries Miniatures.* Dushanbe: Irfan Printing House, 1974.

Bibliography

Aslanapa, Oktay. 1971. *Turkish Art and Architecture.* New York: Praeger, 1971.

Atasoy, Nurhan. 1972. "Illustrations Prepared for Display during Shah-Name Recitation." *Memorial Volume, Fifth International Congress of Iranian Art and Archaeology.* Tehran (1968) 2:262–72. Tehran, 1972.

Atil, Esin. 1973a. *Ceramics from the World of Islam.* Washington: Smithsonian, 1973.

———. 1973b. *Turkish Art of the Ottoman Period.* Washington: Smithsonian, 1973.

———. 1987. *The Age of Sulayman the Magnificent.* Washington: National Gallery of Art, 1987.

Awn, Peter. 1983. *Satan's Tragedy and Redemption: Iblis in Sufi Psychology.* Leiden: Brill, 1983.

Azarpay, Guitty. 1981. *Sogdian Painting: The Pictorial Epic in Oriental Art.* Berkeley: University of California Press, 1981.

Baer, Eva. 1965. *Sphinxes and Harpies in Medieval Islamic Art: An Iconographical Study.* Jerusalem: Hebrew University, 1965.

———. 1977. "Aspects of Sufi Influence on Iranian Art." *Acta Iranica* 12/ Varia 1976, 3d ser: *Textes et Memoires* 5 (1977) 1–12.

Balashova, G. N. 1972. "A Twelfth-Thirteenth Century Pottery Jug Decorated with Epic Subjects." *Sredniaia Aziia i Iran.* Leningrad, 1972. 91–106; English summary 181–82.

Banani, Amin. 1971. "Firdawsi and the Art of Tragic Epic." In *Islam and Its Cultural Divergences: Studies in Honor of G. E. von Grunebaum,* edited by G. L. Tikka. Urbana: University of Illinois Press, 1971. 3–9.

Barthold, W. 1944. "Zur Geschichte des persischen Epos." *ZDMG* 98 (1944) 121–57. German by H. H. Schaeder.

Bashgöz, Ilhan. 1976. "The Structure of Turkish Romances." In *Folklore Today: A Festschrift for Richard M. Dorson,* edited by Linda Degh, H. Glassie, F. J. Oinas. Bloomington: Research Center for Language and Semiotic Studies, 1976. 11–23.

———. 1978a. "The Epic Tradition Among Turkic Peoples." Oinas 1978:310–35.

———. 1978b. "Epithet in a Prose Epic: The Book of My Grandfather Korkut." In *Studies in Turkish Folklore: In Honor of Pertev N. Boratav,* edited by Ilhan Bashgoz and Mark Glazer. Bloomington, IN: MacCallum, 1978. 25–45.

Basset, René. 1893. "L'expédition du château d'or et le combat de ʿAli contre le dragon." *Giornale della Societa Asiatica Italiana* 7 (1893) 3–81.

Bausani, Allessandro. *EI2.* Hikaya/Persian Literature. *EI2* 4:372–73.

———. 1970. "Elementi Epici Nelle Letterature Islamiche." *La Poesia Epica e la sua Formazione.* Rome: Accademia Nazionale dei Lincei, 1970. 759–68.

————. 1974. "An Islamic Echo of the 'Trickster'? The ʿayyars of Indo-Persian and Malay Romances." *Gururajamanjarika: Studi in onore di G. Tucci.* Naples: Istituto Universitario Orientale, 1974. 457–67.

————. 1979. *Notes on the Structure of the Classical Malay Hikayat.* Clayton, Vic: Monash University, Centre of Southeast Asian Studies, 1979.

Beach, Milo C. 1981. *The Imperial Image: Paintings for the Mughal Court.* Washington: Smithsonian, 1981.

Belenitsky, A. M. 1960. "Ancient Pictorial and Plastic Arts and the Shah-Nama." *Proceedings of the 25th International Congress of Orientalists* 3 (1962) 96–101.

Bellamy, James A. 1987. "Arabic Names in the *Chanson de Roland:* Saracen Gods, Frankish Swords, Roland's Horse, and the Olifant." *JAOS* 107:2 (April–June 1987) 267–77.

Bennigsen, A. A. 1975. "The Crisis of the Turkish National Epics, 1951–1952: Local Nationalism or Internationalism." *Canadian Slavic Papers* 17 (1975) 463–74.

Bertels, Y. E., et al., eds. 1971. *Shahnama.* 9 vols. Moscow: AN SSSR, 1960–71.

Biebuyck, Daniel. 1972. "The Epic as a Genre in Congo Oral Literature." In Dorson 1972:257–74.

Binney, III, Edwin. 1962. *Persian and Indian Miniatures.* Portland: E. Binney, 1962.

————. 1973. *Turkish Miniature Paintings and Manuscripts.* New York: Metropolitan Museum of Art, 1973.

Binyon, Lawrence. 1928. *The Poems of Nizami.* London: The Studio Limited, 1928.

————. et al. 1971. *Persian Miniature Painting.* New York: Dover, 1971.

Blachere, Regis. *EI*2. ʿAntara. *EI*2 1:521–22.

Bombaci, Alessio. 1969. *La Letteratura Turca: Con un Profilo della Letteratura Mongola.* Firenze: Sansoni and Milano: Accademia, 1969.

Boratav, Pertev Naili. 1965b. "L'Épopée et la Hikaye." *Philologiae Turcicae Fundamenta* II. Wiesbaden, 1965. 11–44.

————. 1969. "Le conte et la Narration épico-Romanesque." *Turcica* 1 (1969) 95–122.

————. *EI*2. Köroghlu. *EI*2 5:270.

————. *EI*2a. Hikaya/Narrative Genres of Turkish Literature and Folklore. *EI*2 4:373–75.

————, and Bazin, L., trans. 1965a. *Er-Töshtük, épopée kirghiz du cycle de Manas.* Paris: Maisonneuve, 1965.

Boullata, Isa, ed. 1989. *Oral Tradition* (Arabic) 4:1–2 (1989) ALL.

Bowra, C. M. 1952. *Heroic Poetry.* London: Macmillan, 1952.

Brakel, Lode F. 1970. "Persian Influence on Malay Literature." *Abr Nahrain* 9 (1969–70) 1–16.

Bibliography

――――. 1975. *The Hikayat Muhammad Hanafiyyah*. Hague: Nijhoff, 1975.
――――. 1979. "On the Origin of the Malay Hikayat." *RIMA* 13:2 (1979) 1–33.
――――, trans. 1977. *The Story of Muhammad Hanafiyyah*. Hague: Nijhoff, 1977.
Brand, Michael, and Lowry, Glenn. 1985. *Akbar's India: Art from the Mughal City of Victory.* New York: Asia Society, 1985.
Bravmann, M. M. 1960. "Heroic Motives in Early Arabic Literature." *Islam* 33 (1958) 256–79; 35 (1960) 1–25; 36 (1960) 4–36.
――――. 1968. "The Return of the Hero: An Early Arab Motif." *Studia Orientalia in Memoriam C. Brockelmann.* Halle: Univ. Halle-Wittenberg, 1968. 9–28.
――――. 1972. *The Spiritual Background of Early Islam.* Leiden: Brill, 1972.
Brian, Doris. 1939. "A Reconstruction of the Miniature Cycle in the De-motte Shah Namah." *AI* 6 (1939) 97–112.
Brockelmann, Carl. 1949. *Geschichte der Arabischen Literatur.* 2nd ed. Leiden: Brill, 1943–49.
Browne, E. G. 1930. *A Literary History of Persia.* London: Routledge and Kegan Paul, 1902–30.
Bürgel, J. Christoph. 1988a. "Love on Sight of Pictures." In his *The Feather of Simurgh: Licit Magic in the Arts of Medieval Islam.* New York: New York University Press, 1988. 119–37.
――――. 1988b. "Die Frau als Person in der Epik Nizamis." *Asiatische Studien* 42:2 (1988) 137–55.
――――. 1988c. "The Romance." Yarshater 1988:161–78.
Burrill, Kathleen R. F. 1970. "The Nasreddin Hoja Stories, I. An Early Ottoman Manuscript: Groningen a g 8." *Archivum Ottomanicum* 2 (1970) 7–114.
――――. 1974a. "The Farhad and Shirin Story and Its Further Develop-ment from Persian into Turkish Literature." Chelkowski 1974:53–78.
――――. 1974b. "From *Gazi* State to Republic: A Changing Scene for Turk-ish Artists and Men of Letters." Chelkowski 1974:239–89.
Çağman, Filiz, and Tanindi, Zeren. 1979. *Islamic Miniature Painting.* Istan-bul: Ali Riza Baskan, 1979.
Cahen, Claude. *EI2.* Futuwwa/Pre- and Early Islamic. *EI2* 3:961–65.
Calasso, Giovanna. 1971. "Intervento di Iblis nella creazione dell'uomo: l'ambivalente figura del 'Nemico' nelle tradizioni islamiche." *RSO* 45 (1971) 71–90.
――――. 1974. "Il *Xavar-name* di Ibn Hosam: note introduttive." *RSO* 48 (1973–74) 153–73.
――――. 1979. "Un 'epopea musulmana' di epoca timuride: il *Xavar-name*

di Ebn Hosam." *Memorie della Classe di scienze morali, storichi e filologichi, Accademia dei Lincei,* 8th ser., vol. 23, fasc. 5 (1979) 383–541.

Campbell, Joseph. 1949. *The Hero With a Thousand Faces.* Princeton: Bollingen, 1949.

Canard, Marius. 1926. "Les expéditions des Arabes contre Constantinople dans l'histoire et dans la légende." *JA* 208 (1926) 61–121.

———. 1932. "Un Personnage de roman arabo-byzantin." *RA (Extraits des Actes du IIe Congrés National des Sciences Historiques).* Algiers: Typographie Adolphe Jourdan, 1932.

———. 1935. "Delhemma, épopée arabe des guerres arabo-byzantines." *Byzantion* 10 (1935) 283–300.

———. 1936. "La guerre sainte dans le monde Islamique et dans le monde Chrétien." *RA* 79 (1936) 17–27.

———. 1937. "Delhemma, Sayyid Battal et ʿOmar-an-Noʿman." *Byzantion* 12 (1937) 183–88.

———. 1961. "Les principaux personnages du roman de chevalerie arabe Dat al-Himma wa-l-Battal." *Arabic* 8 (1961) 158–73.

———. *EI*2a. (al-)Battal, ʿAbd Allah. *EI*2 1:1102–03.

———. *EI*2. Dhu ʾl-Himma. *EI*2 2:233–39.

Canova, Giovanni. 1977. "Gli Studi sull'epica popolare araba." *OM* 57 (1977) 211–26.

———. 1983. "Il poeta epico nella tradizione araba: note e testimonianze." *Quaderni di Studi Arabi* 1 (1983) 87–104.

Carbonetto, Arturo, comp. 1970. *Epica e ideali Umani.* Palermo: Palumbo, 1970.

Caussin de Perceval, A. P. 1833. "La mort d'Antar." *JA,* 2e. ser., 12 (1833) 97–123.

Cejpek, J. 1968. "Iranian Folk-literature." Rypka 1968.

Chadwick, Nora K., and Zhirmunsky, Victor. 1969. *Oral Epics of Central Asia.* Cambridge: Cambridge University Press, 1969.

Chelhod, J. 1967. "La geste du roi Sayf." *RHR* 171 (1967) 181–205.

Chelkowski, Peter. 1975. *Mirror of the Invisible World: Tales from the Khamseh of Nizami.* New York: Metropolitan Museum of Art, 1975.

———. 1988. "Nizami: Master Dramatist." Yarshater 1988:179–89.

———. 1989. "Narrative Painting and Painting Recitation in Qajar Iran." *Muqarnas* 6 (1989) 98–111.

———, ed. 1974. *Studies in the Art and Literature of the Near East in Honor of Richard Ettinghausen.* Salt Lake City: University of Utah Press, 1974.

———, ed. 1979. *Taʿziyeh: Ritual and Drama in Iran.* New York: New York University Press, 1979.

Chittick, W. C. 1979. "The Perfect Man as the Prototype of the Self in the Sufism of Jami." *SI* 49 (1979) 135–57.

Bibliography

Christensen, A. 1925. "The Smith Kaveh and the Ancient Persian Imperial Banner." *JKRC* 5 (1925) 22–39.

Christides, V. 1962. "An Arabo-Byzantine Novel 'Umar b. al-Nu'man' Compared with Digenes Akritas." *Byzantion* 32 (1962) 549–604.

Clarke, H. Wilberforce, trans. 1881. *The Sikander Nama, E Bara; or, Book of Alexander the Great.* London: W.H. Allen, 1881.

Clinton, Jerome W. 1984. "The Tragedy of Suhrab." In *Logos Islamikos: Studia Islamica in honorem G. M. Wickens,* edited by Roger Savory and D. A. Agius. Toronto: Pontif. Inst. Med. Studies, 1984. 63–77.

———. 1987. *The Tragedy of Sohrab and Rostam.* Seattle: University of Washington Press, 1987.

———. 1990. "The Story of Sam and Zal." *Acta Iranica.* 3d ser., 16 (1990) 38–47.

Connelly, Bridget. 1973. "The Structure of Four Bani Hilal Tales: Prolegomena to the Study of Sira Literature." *JAL* 4 (1973) 18–47.

———. 1986. *Arab Folk Epic and Identity.* Berkeley: University of California Press, 1986.

———. 1988. "Three Egyptian Rebab-Poets: Individual Craft and Poetic Design in *Sîrat Bani Hilal.*" *Edebiyat* 2:1–2 (1988) 117–48.

Constantin, Gh. I. 1967. "Nasr ed-Din Khodja' chez les Turcs, les peuples Balkaniques et les Roumains." *DI* 43:1–2 (March 1967) 90–133.

Coomaraswamy, A. K. 1934. "Khwaja Khadir and the Fountain of Life in the Tradition of Persian and Mughal Art." *AI* 1 (1934) 173–82.

Coote, Mary P. 1988. "Serbocroatian Heroic Songs." Oinas 1978:257–85.

Corbin, Henri. 1966. "The Visionary Dream in Islamic Spirituality." In *The Dream and Human Societies,* edited by G. E. Von Grünebaum and Roger Caillois. Los Angeles: UCLA Press, 1966.

———. 1976. *L'Archange empourpré.* Paris: Fayard, 1976.

———. 1978. *The Man of Light in Iranian Sufism.* Boulder: Shambhala, 1978.

———. 1979. *Spiritual Body and Celestial Earth.* Princeton: Princeton University Press, 1979.

———. 1983. *Face de Dieu, Face de l'Homme: Herméneutique et Soufisme.* Paris: Flammarion, 1983.

Corning Museum of Glass. 1973. *Tales From a King's Book of Kings: The Houghton Shah-nameh Miniatures.* Ithaca: Corning Museum, 1973.

Corriente Cordoba, F. 1967. "Dos elementos folkloricos comunes en la version etiopica de la leyenda de Alejandro y la literatura arabe." *al-Andalus* 32, fasc. 1 (1967) 221–30.

Coyajee, J. C. 1939. "Studies in the Shahnameh." *JKRC* 33 (1939) 13–307. Also in book form, Bombay: Taraporevala, 1938.

Czegledy, K. 1958. "Bahram Chobin and the Persian Apocalyptic Literature." *Acta Orientalia Hungaria* 8 (1958) 20–40.

Dajani-Shakeel, Hadia. 1976. "Jihad in Twelfth-century Arabic Poetry: A Moral and Religious Force to Counter the Crusades." *MW* 66 (1976) 96–113.

Dammann, Ernst. 1938. "Eine Suaheli Dichtung uber Moses den Habicht unde die Taube." *Zeitschrift fur Eingeborenensprachen* 28 (1937–38) 1–13.

———. 1980. *Eine Suahelidichtung des Sheikhs Muhammed bin Abubekr bin Omar Kidjumwa Masihii uber Jesus.* Munich/Marburg: W. Finck Verlag, 1980.

Daniel, Norman. 1984. *Heroes and Saracens: An Interpretation of the Chansons de Geste.* Edinburgh: Edinburgh University Press, 1984.

Darbandi, A., and Davis, D., trans. 1984. *The Conference of the Birds.* New York: Penguin, 1984.

Davar, Firoze C. 1927. "The Historical Epic, with Particular Reference to the *Shahnameh*." *JKRC* 10 (1927) 4–23.

Davidson, H. R., ed. 1975. *The Journey to the Other World.* Cambridge: Cambridge University Press, 1975.

Day, A. 1983. "Islam and Literature in South-East Asia." In *Islam in South-East Asia,* edited by M. B. Hooker. Leiden: Brill, 1983. 130–59.

De Francovich, Geza. 1984. *Persia, Siria e Bisanzio nel Medioevo artistico Europeo.* Napoli: Liguori, 1984.

Dejeux, Jean. 1978. *Djoh'a, héros de la tradition orale arabo-berbere, hier et aujourd'hui.* Paris: Naaman, 1978.

Deny, Jean. 1920. "Fütüwwetnâme et Romans de Chevalerie Turque." *JA* (1920) 182–83.

Destrée, Annette. 1971. "Quelques reflexions sur les héros des recits apocalyptiques persans et sur le mythe de la ville de cuivre." *Atti del Convegno Internazionale sul tema: La Persia nel Medioevo.* Rome: Accademia dei Lincei, 1971. 639–52.

DeVries, Jan. 1959. *Heldenlied en Heldensage.* Utrecht: Het Spectrum, 1959.

Dhar, Somnath. 1978. *Folktales of Turkey.* New Delhi: Sterling, 1978.

Dorson, Richard M. 1972. *African Folklore.* Bloomington: Indiana University Press, 1972.

Drewes, Gerardus Willebrordus Joannes. 1963. "The Struggle between Javanism and Islam as Illustrated by the Serat Dermagandul." *BKI* 122:3 (1963) 309–65.

———. 1970. "Hikajat Muhammad Mukabil." *BKI* 126 (1970) 309–31.

———. 1975. *The Romance of King Anlin Darma in Javanese Literature.* The Hague: M. Nijhoff, 1975.

———. 1977. *Directions for Travellers on the Mystic Path.* The Hague: M. Nijhoff, 1977.

———. ed. and trans. 1979. *Hikayat Potjut Muhamat: An Achehnese Epic.* The Hague: M. Nijhoff, 1979.

Bibliography

Dumas, C. 1917. *Le héros des Maqamat de Hariri: Abou-Seid de Saroudj.* Alger: Typographie Adolphe Jourdan, 1917.

Dumezil, Georges, 1970. *The Destiny of the Warrior.* Chicago: University of Chicago Press, 1970.

———. 1983. *The Stakes of the Warrior.* Berkeley: University of California Press, 1983.

Dumoulin, Heinrich. 1984. "The Person in Buddhism: Religious and Artistic Aspects." *Japanese Journal of Religious Studies* 11:2–3 (1984) 143–67.

Dundes, Alan, and Bradai, Toufik. 1963. "Tales of a Tunisian Trickster." *Southern Folklore Quarterly* 27:4 (Dec. 1963) 300–15.

Egger, Gerhart. 1969. *Der Hamza Roman.* Vienna: Oesterreichisches Museum fur angewandte Kunst, 1969.

Elwell-Sutton, L. P. 1969. "The Unfortunate Heroine in Persian Folk-literature." *Yadname-ye Irani-ye Minorsky* (Tehran: 1348/1969) 37–50.

———. 1971a. "The Influence of Folk-tale and Legend on Modern Persian Literature." *Iran and Islam, in Honor of the Late Vladimir Minorsky,* edited by E. C. Bosworth. Edinburgh: Edinburgh University Press, 1971. 247–54.

———. 1971b. "Magic and Supernatural in Persian Folk-Literature." *Actes du Ve Congres Inter. d'Aribisants et Islamisants.* Louvain, 1971. 189–96.

———. 1980. "A Narrator of Tales from Tehran." *ARV: Scandinavian Yearbook of Folklore* 26 (1980) 201–8.

———. *EI2.* Kissa/Persian Literature. *EI2* 5:197–201.

Errington, Shelly. 1975. *A Study of Genre: Meaning and Form in the Malay "Hikayat Hang Tuah."* Ph.D. diss., Cornell University, 1975.

Esin, Emel. 1970. "Le dévelopment heterodoxe de la peinture figurative religieuse Turque-islamique." In *Congresso di Studi Arabi e Islamici: Atti 5,* edited by Armand Abel. Brussels: Centre pour l'Étude des Problémes du Monde Musulman Contemporain, 1970.

Ethé, Hermann. 1872. *Die Fahrten des Sajjid Battal.* Leipzig: Brodhaus, 1872.

———. 1901. *Neupersische Literatur.* In *Grundriss der Iranischen Philologie,* edited by W. Geiger and E. Kuhn. Vol. 2. Strasburg, 1901.

Ettinghausen, Richard. 1955. "An Illuminated Manuscript of Hafiz-i-Abru in Istanbul." *KO* 2 (1955) 30–44.

———. 1957. "Persian Ascension Miniatures of the Fourteenth Century." *Accademia Nazionale dei Lincei, Convengo Volta, Atti* 12 (1957) 360–83.

———. 1962. *Arab Painting.* London: Skira, 1962.

———. 1972. *From Byzantium to Sasanian Iran and the Islamic World: Three Modes of Artistic Influence.* Leiden: Brill, 1972.

———. 1979. "World Awareness and Human Relationships in Iranian

Painting." *Highlights of Persian Art,* ed. R. Ettinghausen and Ehsan Yarshater. New York: Wittenborn Art Books, 1981. 243–71.

Fahd, Toufic. 1966. *La Divination Arabe.* Leiden: Brill, 1966.

Falk, Toby. 1985. *Treasures of Islam.* London: Philip Wilson, 1985.

——, and Archer, Mildred. 1981. *Indian Miniatures in the India Office Library.* London: Sotheby, Parke, Bernet, 1981.

Fares, Bishr. 1931. *L'Honneur chez les arabes avant l'Islam: Étude de Sociologie.* Paris: Maisonneuve, 1932.

Flemming, B. *EI2.* Kissa/Older Turkish Literature. *EI2* 5:193–94.

Forough, Mehdi. 1967. "Abraham's Sacrifice in Persian Passion Plays and in Western Mystery Plays." *A Survey of Persian Art,* edited by A. U. Pope. New York: Asia House, 1967. 3120ff.

Frey, Edward. 1988. *The Kris: Mystic Weapon of the Malay World.* Singapore: Oxford University Press, 1988.

Frohock, W. M. 1987. "The Idea of the Picaresque." *Yearbook of Comparative and General Literature* 16 (1987) 43–52.

Gabrieli, Francesco. 1970. "Elementi epici nell'antica poesia araba." *La Poesia Epica e la sua Formazione.* Rome: Accademia Nazionale dei Lincei, 1970. 751–57.

——. 1971. "L'Epopea Firdusiana e la Letteratura Araba." *La Persia nel Medioevo.* Rome: Accademia Nazionale dei Lincei, 1971. 209–14.

Gaeffke, Peter. 1987. "The Garden of Light and the Forest of Darkness in Dakkini Sufi Literature and Painting." *Artibus Asiae* 38 (1987) 224–34.

——. 1989. "Alexander in Avadhi and Dakkini *Mathnawis.*" *JAOS* 109:4 (Oct./Dec. 1989) 527–32.

Gaillard, Marina. 1985. "Samak-e ʿAyyar et Xorshid Shah: Héros reel et Héros Apparent." *Studia Iranica* 14:2 (1985) 199–221.

Galley, Micheline, and Ayoub, Abderrahman. 1977. *Images de Djazya: à propos d'une peinture sous verre de Tunisie.* Paris: Éditions du Centre National de Rechérche Scientifique, 1977.

Galmes de Fuentes, Alvaro. 1978. *Epica Arabe y epica Castellana.* Barcelona: Ariel, 1978.

Gerhardt, Mia. 1963. *The Art of Story Telling.* Leiden: Brill, 1963.

Gharavi, M. 1357–1979. "The White Simorgh: A Survey of Shahnameh Paintings." *Honar va Mardom* 181 (1357) 65–69; 188 (1357) 46–53; 189 (1357) 11–20; 191/192 (1357) 81–89.

Gibb, H. A. R. 1962. *Arabic Literature.* Oxford: Oxford University Press, 1962.

Glück, Heinrich. 1925. *Die Indischen Miniaturen des Hamzae-Romanes im österreichischen Museum für Kunst und Industrie in Wien und in anderen Sammlungen.* Leipzig: Amalther Verlag, 1925.

311

Bibliography

Goedhuis, Michael, et al. 1976. *Persian and Mughal Art.* London: Colnaghi, 1976.

Goldziher, Ignaz. 1967a. "What Is Meant by 'al-Jahiliyya?'" *Muslim Studies.* London: Allen and Unwin, 1967. 1:11–44.

———. 1967b. "Muruwwah and Din." *Muslim Studies.* London: Allen and Unwin, 1967. 1:203–8.

Golombek, Lisa. 1972. "Towards a Classification of Islamic Painting." In *Islamic Art in the Metropolitan Museum of Art,* edited by Richard Ettinghausen. New York: Metropolitan Museum of Art, 1972. 23–34.

Goswamy, B. N. 1988. *Jainesque Sultanate Shahnama.* Zurich: Museum Rietberg, 1988.

———, and Fischer, Eberhard. 1987. *Wonders of a Golden Age.* Zurich: Museum Rietberg, 1987.

Grabar, Oleg. 1969. "Notes on the Iconography of the 'Demotte' Shah-Nama." Pinder-Wilson 1969:32–47.

———. 1970. "The Illustrated Maqamat of the Thirteenth Century: The Bourgeoisie and the Arts." In *The Islamic City,* edited by A. H. Hourani and S. M. Stern. Oxford: Oxford University Press, 1970. 207–22.

———. 1972. "History of Art and History of Literature: Some Random Thoughts." *New Literary History* 3 (1972) 559–68.

———. 1974. "Pictures or Commentaries: The Illustrations of the Maqamat of Hariri." Chelkowski 1974:85–104.

———. 1984. *The Illustrations of the Maqamat.* Chicago: University of Chicago Press, 1984.

———, and Blair, Sheila. 1980. *Epic Images and Contemporary History: The Illustrations of the Great Mongol Shahnama.* Chicago: University of Chicago Press, 1980.

Gray, Basil. 1956. *Iran: Persian Miniatures—Imperial Library.* Paris: UNESCO/New York Graphic Society, 1956.

———. 1961. *Persian Painting.* London: Skira, 1961.

———. 1978. *The World History of Rashid al-Din: A Study of the Royal Asiatic Society.* London, 1978.

———, ed. 1979. *The Arts of the Book in Central Asia.* Boulder: Shambhala, 1979.

Grech, R. 1977. "Le recit héroïque de source arabe dans la littérature populaire algérienne." *Libyca* 25 (1977) 319–28.

Greenbaum, Steven E. 1974. "Vrtrahan—Verethragna: India and Iran." In *Myth in Indo-European Antiquity,* edited by Gerald James Larson. Berkeley: University of California Press, 1974. 93–97.

Grégoire, Henri. 1931. "L'Épopée byzantine et ses rapports avec l'épopée turque et l'épopée romane." *Bulletin Classe Lettres, Acad. Royale Belgique* 17 (Brussels 1931) 463–93.

———. 1936. "Comment Sayyid Battal, martyr musulman du VIIIe siècle, est-il devenu, dans la légende, le contemporain d'Amer (d. 863)." *Byzantion* 11 (1936) 571–75.

———. 1975. *Autour de l'épopée byzantine.* London: Variorum Reprints, 1975.

Grillon, Pierre. 1967. "Le Mythe d'Alexandre à travers le roman grec et la Tradition Islamique." *RHCM* 3 (1967) 7–28.

Grube, Ernest J. 1964. "The Spencer Siyer-i Nabi and the Gulestan Shah-Nama." *Pantheon* 22 (1964) 9–28.

———. 1965. "The Siyar-i Nabi of the Spencer Collection in the New York Public Library." *Atti del Secondo Congresso Internazionale di Arte Turca, Venice 1963.* Naples: Ist. Universitario Orientale Seminario di Turcologia, 1965. 149–76.

———. 1966. *The World of Islam.* New York: Macmillan, 1966.

———. 1972. *Islamic Paintings from the Eleventh to the Eighteenth Centuries from the Collection of Hans P. Kraus.* New York: Hans P. Kraus, 1972.

Guillaume, A., trans. 1955. *The Life of Muhammad.* Oxford: Oxford University Press, 1955.

Gutmann, Joseph, and Moreen, Vera B. 1987. "The Combat Between Moses and Og in Muslim Miniatures." *Bulletin of the Asia Institute,* n.s., 1 (1987) 111–22.

Hamid, Ismail. 1982. *Arabic and Islamic Literary Tradition.* Kuala Lumpur: Utusan, 1982.

Hamilton, Terrick, trans. 1981. *Antar: A Bedoueen Romance.* Delmar, NY: Scholars' Facsimiles & Reprints, 1981.

Hamori, Andras. 1971. "An Allegory from the Arabian Nights: The City of Brass." *BSOAS* 24, pt. 1 (1971) 9–19.

———. 1974. *On the Art of Medieval Arabic Literature.* Princeton: Princeton University Press, 1974.

Hanaway, William L. 1970. "Persian Popular Romances Before the Safavid Period." Ph.D. diss., Columbia University, 1970.

———. 1971. "Formal Elements in the Persian Popular Romance." *RNL* 21 (1971) 139–61.

———. 1976. "The Concept of the Hunt in Persian Literature." *Boston Museum Bulletin* 68 (1976) 21–34.

———. 1978. "The Iranian Epics." Oinas 1978:76–98.

———. 1985. "The Symbolism of Persian Revolutionary Posters." In *Iran Since the Revolution,* edited by Barry M. Rosen. Boulder: Social Science Monographs, 1985. 31–50.

Hanna, Sami A. 1968. "'Antarah: A Model of Arabic Folk Biography." *Southern Folklore Quarterly* 32:4 (Dec. 1968) 295–303.

Harries, Lyndon. 1962. *Swahili Poetry.* Oxford: Clarendon Press, 1962.

Hasan, Hamid. 1970. *Hikayat Hang Tuah: Ulasan dan kajian.* Kuala Lumpur: Pustaka Melayu Baru, 1970.

Bibliography

Hatto, Arthur Thomas. *EI2*. Hamasa/Central Asia. *EI2* 4:115–19.

———. 1970. *Shamanism and Epic Poetry in Northern Asia*. London: SOAS, University of London Press, 1970.

———, ed. and trans. 1977. *Kökötödün asi. The Memorial Feast for Kökötöy Khan. A Kirghiz Epic Poem*. Oxford: Oxford University Press, 1977.

———. 1980. "Kara Kiircit—An Inquiry into Brother-Sister Relations in Yakut Epic Poetry." *Zentralasiat. Studien* 14 (1980) 109–34.

Hawkes, Terrence. 1977. *Structuralism and Semiotics*. Berkeley: University of California Press, 1977.

Haye, Kh. A. 1967. *Heroes and Heroines of Islam*. Lahore: Ferozsons 1967.

Haywood, J. A. *EI2*. Kissa/Urdu Literature. *EI2* 5:201–4.

Heath, Peter. 1985. "A Critical Review of Modern Scholarship on *Sirat ʿAntar ibn Shaddad* and the Popular *Sira*." *JAL* 15 (1985) 19–44.

———. 1987. "Romance as Genre in *The Thousand and One Nights*, Part I." *JAL* 18 (1987) 1–21.

———. 1988a. "Romance as Genre in *The Thousand and One Nights*, Part II." *JAL* 19 (1988) 1–26.

———. 1988b. "Lord and Parry, *Sirat ʿAntar*, Lions." *Edebiyat* 2:1–2 (1988) 149–66.

Heller, B. *EI2*. Sirat ʿAntar. *EI2* 1:518–21.

Hickman, William. 1988. "ʿBasat and Tepegöz': A Reappraisal." *Edebiyat* 2:1–2 (1988) 167–89.

Hikmet, Nazim. 1977. *The Epic of Sheik Bedreddin and Other Poems*. Translated by R. Blasing and M. Konuk. New York: Persea Books, 1977.

Hill, A. H., trans. 1960. "Hikayat Raja-Raja Pasai." *JMBRAS* 33, pt. 2 (1960).

Hillenbrand, Robert. 1978. "Recent Work on Islamic Iconography." *Oriental Art* 26 (1978) 201–13.

Hinds, M. *EI2*. Maghazi. *EI2* 5:1161–64.

Hodgson, Marshall. 1974. *The Venture of Islam*. 3 vols. Chicago: University of Chicago Press, 1974.

Holter, Kurt. 1981. *Rosenkranz der Weltgeschichte*. Graz, Austria: Akademische Ausdruck u. Verlagsanstalt, 1981.

Huart, Clement. *EI2*. Bahram. *EI2* 1:644–45.

Hurreiz, Sayyid H. 1972a. "Afro-Arab Relations in the Sudanese Folktale." Dorson 1972:157–63.

———. 1972b. "Manasir and Jaʿaliyyin Tales." Dorson 1972:369–85.

———. 1977 *Jaʿiliyyin folktales: An Interplay of African, Arabian and Islamic Elements*. Bloomington: Indiana University Press, 1977.

Hussain, Khalid, comp. 1966. *Taj Us-Salatin*. Kuala Lumpur: Dewan Bahasa dan Pustaka, 1966.

Hussein, Ismail. 1974. *The Study of Traditional Malay Literature*. Kuala Lumpur: Dewan Bahasa dan Pustaka, 1974.

Idris, Suhayl. 1963. "L'héroisme dans la littérature arabe, le roman arabe moderne." (Extraits traduits et notes: M. Borrmans.) *IBLA* 26:101 (1963) 145–61.

Ipširoglu, M. S. 1980. *Masterpieces from the Topkapi Museum: Paintings and Miniatures*. London: Thames and Hudson, 1980.

Irving, Thomas B. 1954. "Arab Antecedents of the Picaresque Novel." *IL* 6 (December 1954) 683–88.

Iskandar, Teuku. 1970. "Some Sources Used by the Author of Hikayat Hang Tuah." *JMBRAS* 43:1 (1970) 35–47.

Iz, Fahir. *EI2*. Kissa/More Recent Turkish Literature. *EI2* 5:194–97.

Izutsu, Toshihiko. 1966. *Ethico-Religious Concepts in the Qur'an*. Montreal: McGill University Press, 1966.

Johns, A. H. *EI2*. Kissa/Malaysia and Indonesia. *EI2* 5:205.

Jones, A. M. 1976. "Swahili Epic Poetry." *African Music Society Journal* 5:4 (Johannesburg, 1976) 105–29.

Josselin de Jong, P. E. 1965. "The Rise and Decline of a National Hero." *JMBRAS* 38:2 (1965) 140–55.

Kailasapathy, K. 1968. *Tamil Heroic Poetry*. Oxford: Clarendon Press, 1968.

Karahan, A.; Yazici, T.; and Milani, A. 1971. *Shahnamelerden Seçme Minyatürler (Miniatures from the Shahnameh Manuscripts in the Topkapi Saray Museum)*. Istanbul: Birinci Baski, 1971.

Kevorkian, A. M., and Sicre, J. P. 1983. *Les Jardins de Desir*. Paris: Phebus, 1983.

Khalidi, Tarif. 1975. *Islamic Historiography: the Histories of Mas'udi*. Albany: SUNY Press, 1975.

Khanlari, P. N. 1343/1964. *Scenes from the Shahnameh*. Tehran: Iranian Cultural Foundation, 1343/1964.

Khouri, Mounah, and Algar, Hamid. 1975. *An Anthology of Modern Arabic Poetry*. Berkeley: University of California Press, 1975.

Khwandamir, Ghiyas al-Din. 1353/1974. *Tarikh-e Habib al-Siyar*. Edited by M. Dabirsiyaqi. Tehran, 1353/1974.

Kilito, Abd al-Fattah. 1976. "Le genre 'séance': une introduction." *SI* 43 (1976) 23–51.

Klimburg-Salter, Deborah E. 1977. "A Sufi Theme in Persian Painting: The Divan of Sultan Ahmad Galair in the Freer Gallery of Art." *KO* 11 (1976–77) 43–84.

Knappert, Jan. *EI2*. Kissa/Swahili Literature. *EI2* 5:205–6.

———. 1961. "The Figure of the Prophet Mohammed according to the Popular Literature of the Islamic Peoples." *JEASC* 31 (1961) 24–31.

———. 1964a. *Four Swahili Epics*. Leiden: Drukkerij "Luctor et Emerigo," 1964.

———. 1964b. "Utenzi wa Miiraji." *Afrika und Ubersee* 48 (1964) 241–74.

315

Bibliography

————. 1964c. *"Utenzi wa Maisha ya Nabii Adamu na Hawaa." JEASC* 34:1 (1964) c. p. 130.

————. 1966a. "Miiraji, the Swahili Legend of Mohammed's Ascension." *Swahili* 36:2 (1966) 105–56.

————. 1966b. "Ukawafi wa Miiraji." *Swahili* 36:2 (1966) 141–50.

————. 1967a. *Traditional Swahili Poetry.* Leiden: Brill, 1967.

————. 1967b. "The Epic in Africa." *JFI* 4:2/3 (1967) 171–90.

————. 1969. "The Hamziya Deciphered." *African Language Studies* 9 (1968) 52–81.

————. 1969b. "Utenzi wa Katirifu." *Afrika und Ubersee* (1969) 81ff.

————. 1970/1978. *Myths and Legends of the Swahili.* London: Heinemann Educational Books, 1970/1978.

————. 1971 *Swahili Islamic Poetry.* 3 vols. Leiden: Brill, 1971.

————. 1976. "Al-Husain Ibn Ali in the Epic Tradition of the Swahili." *Al-Seraat* 2:1 (1976) 20–27.

————. 1977. *Myths and Legends of Indonesia.* Singapore: Heinemann Educational Books, Asia, 1977.

————. 1979. *Four Centuries of Swahili Verse.* London: Heinemann Educational Books, 1979.

————. 1980. *Malay Myths and Legends.* Kuala Lumpur: Heinemann Educational Books, Asia, 1980.

————. 1983. *Epic Poetry in Swahili and Other African Languages.* Leiden: Brill, 1983.

————. 1985. *Islamic Legends: Histories of the Heroes, Saints and Prophets of Islam.* 2 vols. Leiden: Brill, 1985.

Knudson, Ch. A. 1968. "Le thème de la Princesse Sarrasine dans *La Prise d'Orange." Romania* 22 (1968).

Kowalski, T. 1940. "Les Turcs dans le Sah-Name." *Rocznik Orientalistyczny* 15 (1939–40) 84–99.

Krasnowolska, A. 1978. "Rostam Farrokhzad's Prophecy in Shan-name and the Zoroastrian Apocalyptic Texts." *FO* 19 (1978) 173–84.

Krotkoff, Georg. 1984. "Colour and Number in the *Haft Paykar." Logos Islamikos,* edited by R. Savory and D. Agius. Toronto: Pontifical Institute of Medieval Studies, 1984.

Kyriakidès, Stilpon P. 1936. "Eléments historiques byzantins dans le roman épique turc de Sayyid Battal." *Byzantion* 11 (1936) 563–70.

Lambert, H. E., trans. 1962. *Utenzi wa vita vya Uhud (The Epic of the Battle of Uhud).* Collected and compiled by Haji Chum. Dar es Salaam: E. African Literature Bureau, 1962.

Lazard, G. 1956. "Un texte persan sur la legende de Gayomart." *JA* 244 (1956) 201–16.

Lentz, Thomas W., and Lowry, Glenn D. 1989. *Timur and the Princely Vision.* Los Angeles: County Museum of Art, co-published with Smithsonian, 1989.

Levy, Reubens. 1967. *The Epic of the Kings* (selections). London: Routledge and Kegan Paul, 1967.

Lewis, Bernard. 1990. *Race and Slavery in the Middle East.* Oxford: Oxford University Press, 1990.

Lewis, Geoffrey, trans. 1974. *The Book of Dede Korkut.* Harmondsworth, Middlesex, England: Penguin, 1974.

Lichtenstaedter, Ilse. 1935. *Women in the Aiyam al-Arab.* London: Royal Asiatic Society, 1935.

Lillys, William; Rieff, Robert; and Esin, Emel. 1965. *Oriental Miniatures: Persian, Indian, Turkish.* Rutland, VT: Charles E. Tuttle, 1965.

Littmann, Enno. 1950. *Mohammed in Volksepos, Ein Neuarabisches Heiligenlied.* Copenhagen: E. Munksgaard, 1950.

Lord, A. B. 1960. *Singer of Tales.* Cambridge, MA: Harvard University Press, 1960.

Losty, J. P. 1982a. *The Art of the Book in India.* London: British Library, 1982.

———. 1982b. *Masterpieces of Indian Paintings in the British Library.* New Delhi: British Library, 1982.

Lowry, Glenn, with Nemazee, Suzanne. 1988. *A Jeweler's Eye: Islamic Arts of the Book from the Vever Collection.* Washington: Sackler Gallery, 1988.

Luka, Kole, trans. 1983. *Chansonnier épique albanais.* Tirana: Academie de sciences de la RPS d'Albanie, Ins. de Culture populaire, 1983.

Lukens-Swietochowski, Marie G. 1967. "The Language of the Birds: The Fifteenth Century Miniatures." *Bulletin of the Metropolitan Museum of Art,* n.s., 25:9 (May 1967) 317–38.

———. 1972. "The Historical Background and Illustrative Character of the Metropolitan Museum's Mantiq al-Tayr of 1483." *Islamic Art in the Metropolitan Museum of Art,* edited by R. Ettinghausen. New York: Metropolitan Museum of Art, 1972. 39–72.

———. 1974. "Some Aspects of the Persian Miniature Painter in Relation to His Text." Chelkowski 1974:111–32.

Maalouf, Amin. 1985. *The Crusades Through Arab Eyes.* Translated by Jon Rothschild. New York: Schocken, 1985.

Maaruf, Shaharuddin B. 1984. *Concept of a Hero in Malay Society.* Singapore: Eastern Universities Press Sdn Bhd, 1984.

Maguire, Marcia E. 1974a. "The Haft Khvan of Rustam and Isfandiyar." Chelkowski 1974:137–47.

———. 1974b. "The *Shahnamah* and the Persian Miniaturist." Chelkowski 1974:133–36.

Mahmoud, Mohammed. 1984. "The Unchanging Hero in a Changing World: Najib Mahfuz's Al-liss wa ʾl-kilab." *JAL* 15 (1984) 58–75.

Marcos Marin, Franscisco. 1971. *Poesia Narrativa Arabe y épica hispánica: Elementos Arabes en los origenes de la épica hispánica.* Madrid: Gredos, 1971.

Bibliography

————. 1979. "Epica Arabe y épica hispánica" (Contribución a una crítica de la historia en España, capitulo medieval). *Boletín de la Asociación Española de Orientalistas* 15 (1979) 169–75.

Markus, Kinga. 1984. "Prince Noshzad;a, Royal Martyr? Christianity, Rum, and the Sasanians in the *Shah-nama.*" *JSAS* 2 (1984) 58–79.

————. 1985a. "Experiments with the Künstlerroman in the Modern Persian Fiction—*The Patient Stone* of Sadeq Chubak and *The Night's Journey* of Bahman Sholevar." *JSAS* 3 (1985) 225–39.

————. 1985b. "The Wars Between the Sasanian Iran and the Imperial Rome and Their Legendary Interpretation in Firdausi's *Shahname.*" *Transactions of the International Conference of Orientalists in Japan*, no. 30. Tokyo: The Toho Gakkai, 1985. 38–53.

Masmoudi, Mohamed. 1968. "Une Peinture sous verre à thème héroique." *Cahiers des arts et traditions populaires*, no. 2. Tunis: Institut National d'Archéologie et d' Art, 1968. 5–14.

————. 1969. "Deux autres peintures sous verre à thème héroique." *Cahiers des arts et traditions populaires*, no. 3. Tunis: Institut National d'Archéologie et d'Art, 1969. 85–98.

————. 1972. *La Peinture sous-verre en Tunisie.* Tunis: Ceres Productions, 1972.

Massé, Henri. *EI2.* Hamasa/Persian Literature. *EI2* 4:112–14.

————. *EI2a.* Fal-Nama. *EI2* 3:760–61.

————. 1935. "Les épopées persanes—Firdowsi." Perrin: Librairie académique, 1935.

————. 1956. "La survie des héros iraniens." *Mélange de G. Jamati.* Paris: CNRS, 1956.

Mazaheri, Aly. 1979. "L'Iran de Ferdovsi et le héros culturel Rustam." *Zaman* 1 (1979) 4–20.

Mbele, Joseph L. 1986. "The Identity of the Hero in the Liongo Epic." *Research in African Literatures* 17:4 (Winter 1986) 464–71.

Meeker, Michael. 1988. "Heroic Poems and Anti-Heroic Stories in North Arabic; Literary Genres and the Relationship of Center and Periphery in Arabia." *Edebiyat* 2:1–2 (1988) 1–40.

Meisami, Julie Scott. 1987. *Medieval Persian Court Poetry.* Princeton: Princeton University Press, 1987.

Mélikoff, Irène. *EI2.* Hamasa/Turkish Literature. *EI2* 4:114–15.

————. *EI2a.* (al-)Battal (Sayyid Battal Ghazi). *EI2* 1:1103–4.

————. 1960. *La Geste de Malik Danishmend.* 2 vols. Paris: Maisonneuve, 1960.

————. 1961. "Les Georgiens et les Armeniens dans la littérature épique des Turcs d'Anatolie." *Bedi Karthlisa, Revue de Karthveologie* 11–12 (1961) 27–35.

————. 1962a. *Abu Muslim, de "Porte Hache" du Khorassan dans la tradition épique turco-iranienne.* Paris: Adrien Maisonneuve, 1962.

318

————. 1962b. "Nombres Symboliques dans la littérature épico-religieuse des Tucs d'Anatolie." *JA* 250 (1962) 435–45.

————. 1966. "Le drame de Kerbela dans la littérature épique turque." *REI* 34 (1966) 133–48.

Meredith-Owens, G. M. 1969. *Turkish Miniatures.* London: British Library, 1969.

————. 1969. "A Copy of the Rawzat as-Safa with Turkish Miniatures." Pinder-Wilson 1969:110–23.

————. *EI*2. Hamza b. ʿAbd al-Muttalib. *EI*2 4:152–54.

Meskub, Shahrokh. 1969. *Muqaddama-i bar Rustam va Isfandiyar.* Tehran: Pocket Books, 1969.

Milstein, Rachel. 1977. "Sufi Elements in the Late Fifteenth-Century Painting of Herat." In *Studies in Memory of G. Wiet,* edited by M. Rosen-Ayalon. Jerusalem, 1977. 354–69.

————. 1986. "Light, Fire, and the Sun in Islamic Painting." In *Studies in Islamic History and Civilization in Honor of Professor David Avalon,* edited by M. Sharon. Jerusalem: Cana, 1986. 533–52, plates 1–9.

————. 1987. "Nimrod, Joseph and Jonah: Miniatures from Ottoman Baghdad." *Bulletin of the Asia Institute,* n.s., 1 (1987) 123–38.

————. 1989. *Miniature Painting in Ottoman Baghdad.* Costa Mesa, CA: Mazda, 1989.

Mittwoch, E. *EI*2. Ayyam al-ʿArab. *EI*2 1:793–94.

————. *EI*2a. Dhu ʾl-Fakar. *EI*2 2:233.

Moghaddam, Mahmood Karimpour. 1982. *The Evolution of the Hero Concept in Iranian Epic and Dramatic Literature.* Ph.D. diss., Florida State University, 1982.

Molé, Marijan. 1953. "L'épopée iranienne apres Firdosi." *NC* 5 (July–December 1953) 377–93.

————. 1958. "La Partage du Monde dans la tradition iranienne." *JA* 240 (1952) 455–63.

Moosa, Matti I. 1969. "The Revival of the Maqamah in the Modern Arabic Literature." *The Islamic Review,* pt. 1 57 (July–August 1969) 12–19, 40; pt. 2 (October 1969) 30–37, 40; pt. 3 (November–December 1969) 25–36.

Morrison, G., ed. 1981. *History of Persian Literature from the Beginning of the Islamic Period to the Present Day.* Leiden: Brill, 1981.

Mostafa, M. 1942. "Bahram Gur's Representation in Islamic Painting." *Al-Risalah* 10 (1942) 211–16.

Motlagh, Djalal Khaleghi. 1971. *Die Frauen im Schahname: ihre Geschichte und Stellung unter gleichzeitiger Brucksichtigung vor- und nachislamischer Quellen.* Freiburg im Breisgau: K. Schwarz, 1971.

————, ed. 1988. *The Shahnameh.* (Persian text) Vol. 1. New York: Bibliotheca Persia, 1988.

319

Bibliography

Munroe, J. T. 1983. *The Art of Hamadhani.* Beirut: American University Press, 1983.

Na'imi, N. A. 1938. "La naissance de Rustem. Miniatures persanes du 15 siecle." *Afghanistan* (1938) 168.

Nagel, Tilman. 1978. *Alexander der Grosse in der fruhislamischen Volksliteratur.* Waldorf-Hessen: Verlag fur Orientkunde H. Vorndran, 1978.

Nasr, S. H. 1972. "The World of Imagination and the Concept of Space in Persian Miniatures." *Islamic Quarterly* 13 (1969) 129–34.

Nasralla, Abderrahim Ali. 1980. *The Enemy Perceived: Christian and Muslim Views of Each Other During the Crusades.* Ph.D. diss., New York University, 1980.

Navabpour, R. 1980. "Static Heroes and Revolutionary Characters in Some of the Modern Fiction of Iran." *Bulletin of British Association of Orientalists* 11 (1979–80) 85–93.

Neklyudov, S. 1973. "The Common and the Specific in the Central Asian Epic." *Social Sciences* [Moscow] 4:2 (73) 94–104.

Nicholson, R. A. 1969. *A Literary History of the Arabs.* Cambridge: Cambridge University Press, 1969.

Nizami of Ganja. 1351/1972. *Kulliyat-i Khamsa.* N.Ed. Tehran: Chapkhana Sipihr, 1351/1972.

Nodushan, Muh. Ali Eslami. 1349/1970. *Zendegi va marg-e pahlavanan dar Shahnama (Life and Death of the Heroes in the Shahnama).* Tehran, 1349/1970.

Nöldeke, Theodor. 1925. "The Iranian National Epic." Translated by L. Bogdanov. *JKRC* 6 (1925) 1–161. [Also rpt., Philadelphia: Porcupine Press, 1979.]

Norgren, J., and Davis, E. 1969. *Preliminary Index of Shah-Nameh Illustrations.* Ann Arbor: University of Michigan Press, 1969.

Norris, Harry T. 1972. *Saharan Myth and Saga.* Oxford: Clarendon Press, 1972.

———. 1980. *The Adventures of Antar.* Warminster: Aris and Phillips, 1980.

Oinas, F. J. 1978. *Heroic Epic and Saga.* Bloomington: Indiana University Press, 1978.

Olrik, Axel. 1965. "Epic Laws of Folk Narrative." In *The Study of Folklore,* edited by Alan Dundes. Englewood Cliffs: Prentice-Hall, 1965. 129–41.

Oshikawa, Noriaki. 1986. "Patjar Merah Indonesia and Tan Malaka: A Popular Novel and a Revolutionary Legend." *JSAS* 4 (1986) 121–55.

Pagliaro, A. 1940. "Lo zoroastrismo e la formazione dell'epopea iranica." *AION,* n.s., 1 (1940) 241–51.

Paksoy, H. B. 1989. *Alpamysh: Central Asian Identity Under Russian Rule.* Hartford: Association for the Advancement of Central Asian Research, 1989.

Paret, Rudi. *EI2*. Sirat Baybars. *EI2* 1:1126–27.

———. 1930. *Die legendäre Maghazi-Literatur.* Tubingen, 1930.

———. 1970. "Die Legendäre Futuh-Literatur, ein arabisches Volksepos?" *La Poesia Epica e la sur Formazione.* Rome: Accademia dei Lincei, 1970. 735–47.

Parry, Milman, and Lord, A. B. 1974. *Serbocroatian Heroic Songs.* 4 vols. Cambridge, MA: Harvard University Press, 1953–74.

Parsay, Javid and Rouhani, M. 1354/1975. *The Illustrated Shahnameh Manuscripts.* Tehran: Ministry of Art and Culture, 1354/1975.

Pellat, Charles. 1965. "L'idée de Dieu chez les 'Sarrasins' de chansons de geste." *SI* 22 (1965).

———. *EI2.* Hamasa/Arabic Literature. *EI2* 4:110–12.

———. *EI2a.* Hikaya/Arabic Literature. *EI2* 4:367–72.

———. *EI2b.* Kissa/Semantic Range. *EI2* 5:185–87.

Pelly, L. 1879. *The Miracle Play of Hasan and Husain.* Revised with explanatory notes by A. N. Wolleston. 2 vols. rpt. of 1879 ed. London: Variorum Reprints, 1970.

Pendlebury, David, trans. 1980. *Jami: Yusuf and Zulaykha.* London: Octagon, 1980.

Pérès, H. 1957. "Le Roman historique dans la littérature arabe." *AIEO* 15 (1957) 5–39.

———. 1958. "Le Roman dans la littérature arabe des origines a la fin du Moyen-Age." *AIEO* 16 (1958) 5–40.

Peterson, Samuel. 1979. "The Ta'ziyeh and Related Arts." Chelkowski 1979:64–87.

Petsopoulos, Yanni, ed. 1982. *Tulips, Arabesques, and Turbans.* New York: Abbeville Press, 1982.

Piemontese, A. M. 1976. "Magia e mito nel romanzo persiano di Hamza." *Magia. Studi di storia delle religioni in memoria di R. Garosi.* Rome: Bulzione Editore, 1976. 151–76.

Pigeaud, Th. G. 1950. "The Romance of Amir Hamza in Java." *Bingkisan Budi: een Bundel opstellen voor P. S. van Ronkel.* Leiden: A. W. Sijthoff's Uitgeversmaatschappij N. V., 1950. 235–40.

Pinder-Wilson, Ralph. 1958. *Persian Painting of the Fifteenth Century.* London: Faber and Faber, 1958.

———. 1969. *Paintings from Islamic Lands.* Oxford: Oxford University Press, 1969.

———. 1976. *Paintings from the Muslim Courts of India.* London, 1976.

Polignac, F de. 1982. "L'image d'Alexandre dans la littérature arabe: l'Orient face à l'Hellénisme?" *Arabica* 29 (1982) 296–306.

Poppe, Nikolaus N. 1976. *Mongolische Epen.* Wiesbaden: Harrassowitz, 1975.

———. 1979. *The Heroic Epic of the Khalkha Mongols.* Translated by J.

Krueger, et al. 2d ed. Bloomington: University of Indiana Press, 1979.

Prendergast, W. J., trans. 1915/1973. *The Maqamat of Badiᶜ al-Zaman al-Hamadhani.* London: Variorum Reprints, 1915/1973.

Qandil, Barbara. 1970. "A Comparative Study of a Near Eastern Trickster Cycle." *Southern Folklore Quarterly* 34 (1970) 18–33.

Rahman, M. 1971. "Influence of Legendary Kings and Heroes on Persian Literature." *Indo-Iranica* 24:1–2 (1971) 50–63.

Rank, Otto. 1959. *The Myth of the Birth of the Hero.* New York: Vintage, 1959.

Ras, J. J. 1968. *Hikayat Bandjar: A Study in Malay Historiography.* The Hague: Nijhoff, Bibliotheca Indonesica 1, 1968.

Rast, N. A. 1955. "Russians in the Medieval Iranian Epos." *Amer. Slav. E. Eur. Rev.* 14 (1955) 260–64.

Razavi, Frederique, trans. 1972. *Samak-e Ayyâr.* Persian Heritage Series. Vol. 1, intro. by Henri Massè. Paris: J. P. Maisonneuve et LaRose, 1972.

Rehastek, R. 1892. *Rawdatu 's-Safa.* 2 vols. London: 1891–92.

Renda, Günsel. 1976. "New Light on the Painters of the 'Zubdet al-Tawarikh' in the Museum of Turkish and Islamic Arts in Istanbul." *IVeme Congres International d'art Turc.* Provence: Editions de l'Université de Provence, 1976. 183–99.

Rice, David T., and Gray, Basil. 1976. *The Illustrations to the World History of Rashid al-Din.* Edinburgh: Edinburgh University Press, 1976.

Ringgren, Helmer. 1952. *Fatalism in Persian Epics.* Uppsala: A. B. Lundequistska, 1952.

———. 1954. "The Problem of Fatalism in Pre-Islamic and Early Islamic Literature." *IL* (June 1954) 5–17.

Robinson, B. W. 1950. "The National Hero in Persian Painting." *Journal Iran Society* 1 (1950) 80–85.

———. 1976a. *Persian Paintings in the India Office Library.* London: Sotheby Parke Bernet, 1976.

———, et al. 1976b. *Islamic Painting and the Arts of the Book.* London: Faber and Faber, 1976.

———. 1977. "Rashid al-Din's World History: The Significance of the Miniatures." *JRAS* (1980) 212–22.

———. 1980. *Persian Paintings in the John Rylands Library.* London: Sotheby, Parke, Bernet, 1980.

———. 1983. *Persian Painting and the National Epic.* Oxford: Oxford University Press, 1983.

———, and Gray, B. 1972. *The Persian Art of the Book.* Oxford: Oxford University Press, 1972.

Rogers, J. M., ed. 1986. *The Topkapi Saray Museum: The Albums and Illustrated Manuscripts.* Boston: Little, Brown, 1986.

Rohani, Nasrin. 1982. *A Bibliography of Persian Miniature Painting.* Cambridge, MA: Agha Khan Program for Islamic Architecture, 1982.

Ronkel, Ph. S. Van. 1895. *De Roman van Amir Hamzah.* Leiden: Brill, 1895.

Roth, G. 1959. "The City of Iron in Ancient Indian Literature and in the Arabian Nights." *Journal Bihar Research Society* 45 (1959) 53–76.

Roux, Jean-Paul. 1977. "Symboles et archetypes dans les arts islamiques." *Archeologia* 106 (1977) 18–37.

———. 1981. "Le combat d'animaux dans l'art et la mythologie iranoturcs." *AA* 36 (1981) 5–11.

———. 1982. *Études d'Iconographie Islamique.* Leeuven: Editions Peeters, 1982.

Rubiera Mata, Maria Jesus. 1981. *La arquitectura en la literatura arabe.* Madrid: Editora Nacional, 1981.

Rubin, Uri. 1979. "Prophets and Progenitors in the Early Shi'a Tradition." *Jerusalem Studies in Arabic and Islam* 2 (1979) 41–65.

Rypka, Jan. 1951. "Les sept princesses de Nizhami." *L'âme de l'Iran.* Paris: Albin Michel, 1951. 101–25.

———. 1968. *History of Iranian Literature.* Dordrecht: D. Reidel, 1968.

Sa'di, 1348/1969. *Gulistan-i Sa'di,* ed. Nurallah Iran Parast. Tehran: Danish-i Sa'di, 1348/1969.

Safa, Zabihollah. 1333/1954. *Hamasa Saray dar Iran. (Epic Poetry in Iran: From the Earliest Period of Iranian History to the 14th/20th Century.)* Tehran: Priouz Press, 1333/1954.

Safani, Alan. 1982. "The Battle Scenes of Varqa va Golshah and Their Prototypes." *Marsyas: Studies in the History of Art* 22 (1981–82) 1–6.

Sakisian. A. 1938. "Le Paysage dans la Miniature Persane." *Syria* 19 (1938).

Santoso, Soewito. 1971. "The Islamization of Indonesian/Malay Literature in Its Earlier Period." *Journal of the Oriental Society of Australia* 8:1–2 (1971) 9–27.

Schimmel, Annemarie. 1973. *Islamic Literatures of India.* Wiesbaden: Harrassowitz, 1973.

———. 1974. *Sindhi Literature.* Wiesbaden: Harrassowitz, 1974.

———. 1975a. *Mystical Dimensions of Islam.* Chapel Hill: University of North Carolina Press, 1975.

———. 1975b. *Classical Urdu Literature from the Beginning to Iqbal.* Wiesbaden: Harrassowitz, 1975.

Schleifer, J. *EI2.* Hilal/Saga of Banu Hilal. *EI2* 4:387.

Séguy, Marie Rose. 1977. *The Miraculous Journey of Mahomet: The Miraj Nameh in the Bibliotheque Nationale.* Translated by R. Pevear. New York: Braziller, 1977.

Senac, Philippe. 1983. *L'image de l'autre: l'Occident medieval face a l'islam.* Paris: Flammarion, 1983.

Bibliography

Sezgin, Fuat. 1967. *Geschichte des arabischen Schrifttums.* Leiden: Brill, 1967.

Shapiro, M. 1943. "The Angel with Ram in Abraham's Sacrifice: A Parallel in Western and Islamic Art." *AI* 10 (1943) 134–47.

Shariati, Ali. 1982. "Psychanalyse d'un cas de révolte juvenile a travers la littérature épique persane." *Ethnopsychologie* 37:3–4 (1982) 33–58.

Shepherd, Dorothy. 1974. "Banquet and Hunt in Medieval Islamic Iconography." *Gathering in Honor of Dorothy E. Miner.* Baltimore: Walters Art Gallery, 1974. 79–92.

Shojai, D. A. 1975. "The Fatal Rage: Heroic Anger in Modern Iranian Fiction." *IrS* 8 (1975) 216–33.

Simpson, Marianna Shreve. 1979. *The Illustration of an Epic: The Earliest Shahnama Manuscripts.* New York: Garland, 1979.

———. 1981. "The Narrative Structure of a Medieval Iranian Beaker." *AO* 12 (1981) 15–24.

———. 1982. "The Pattern of Early *Shahnama* Illustration." *Studia Artium Orientalis et Occidentalis.* Vol. 1, *Problems in the Relation between Text and Illustration* (1982). 43–53, with 10 full-page ills.

———. 1985. "Narrative Allusion and Metaphor in the Decoration of Medieval Islamic Objects." In *Pictorial Narrative in Antiquity and the Middle Ages,* edited with Herbert L. Kessler. Washington: National Gallery of Art, 1985. Vol. 16: *Studies in the History of Art.* 131–49.

Sivan, Emmanuel. 1968. *L'Islam et la croisade: ideologie et propagande dans les reactions Musulmanes aux croisades.* Paris: Maisonneuve, 1968.

Skendi, Stavro. 1954. *Albanian & South Slavic Oral Epic Poetry.* Philadelphia: American Folklore Society, 1954.

Slyomovics, Susan. 1988. *The Merchant of Art: An Egyptian Hilali Oral Epic Poet in Performance.* Berkeley: University of California Press, 1988.

Soroudi, Sorush. 1980. "Islamization of the Iranian National Hero Rustam as Reflected in Persian Folktales." *Jerusalem Studies in Arabic and Islam* 2 (1980) 365–83.

Soucek, Priscilla. 1974. "Farhad and Taq-i Bustan: The Growth of a Legend." Chelkowski 1974:27–52.

———. 1975. "An Illustrated Manuscript of al-Biruni's *Chronology of Ancient Nations.*" *The Scholar and the Saint,* edited by Peter Chelkowski. New York: New York University Press, 1975. 103–68.

———. 1988. "The Life of the Prophet: Illustrated Versions." In *Content and Context of Visual Arts in the Islamic World,* edited by Priscilla Soucek. University Park, PA: Pennsylvania State University Press, 1988. 193–217, with 9 ills.

Southgate, Minoo. 1974. "Fate in Firdawsi's 'Rustam va Suhrab.'" Chelkowski 1974:149–59.

————. 1977. "Portrait of Alexander in Persian Alexander-Romances of the Islamic Era." *JAOS* 97 (1977) 278–84.

————. 1985. "Conflict Between Islamic Mores and Courtly Romance of Vis and Ramin." *MW* 75:1 (January 1985) 17–28.

————, trans. 1978. *Iskandarnamah: A Persian Medieval Alexander-Romance.* New York: Columbia University Press, 1978.

Soviet Epics. 1956. "The Re-examination of the Soviet Asian Epics." *CAR* 4:1 (1956) 66–71.

Spores, John C. 1988. *Running Amok: An Historical Inquiry.* Monograph in International Studies, Southeast Asian Series, No. 82: Athens, OH: Center for International Studies, Ohio University, 1988.

Stchoukine, Ivan. 1977. *Les peintures des manuscrits de la Khamseh de Nizami au Topkapi Sarayi Muzesi d'Istanbul.* Paris: Paul Geunther, 1977.

Steck, M. *EI2.* Kaf. *EI2* 4:400–02.

Steinbach, U. 1972. *Dat al-Himma: Kulturgeschichtliche Untersuchungen zu einem arabischen Volksroman.* Wiesbaden: Freiburger Islamstudien 4, 1972.

Stern, S. M. 1971. "Yaʿqub the Coppersmith and Persian National Sentiment." In *Iran and Islam: In Memory of the Late Vladimir Minorsky,* edited by C. E. Bosworth. Edinburgh: Edinburgh University Press, 1971. 535–55.

Sumer, Faruk; Uysal, Ahmet; and Walker, Warren, trans. and eds. 1972. *The Book of Dede Korkut.* Austin: University of Texas Press, 1972.

Taeschner, Franz. 1931. "Futuwwa-Studien, die Futuwwabünde in der Türkei und ihre Litteratur." *Islamica* 5 (1931) 285–333.

————. 1944. "Das Futuwwa-Rittertum des islamischen Mittelalters." *Beiträge zur Arabistik, Semitistik und Islamwissenschaft.* Leipzig, 1944. 340–85.

————. *EI2.* Futuwwa/Post-Mongol Period. *EI2* 3:966–69.

————. *EI2a.* Ayyar. *EI2* 1:794.

Tanindi, Zeren. 1984. *Siyer-i Nebi.* 2 vols. Istanbul: Hurriyet Foundation, 1984.

Tauer, F. *EI2.* Hafiz-i Abru. *EI2* 4:57–58.

Taylor, Jean Gelman. 1989. "Kartini in Her Historical Context." *BKI* 145:2–3 (1989) 295–307.

Thackston, Wheeler M., trans. 1978. *The Tales of the Prophets of al-Kisaʾi.* Boston: Twayne, 1978.

Titley, Norah M. 1977a. *Catalogue and Subject Index of Paintings from Persia, India, Turkey in the British Museum.* London: British Museum, 1977.

————. 1977b. *Miniatures from Persian Manuscripts: A Catalogue and Subject Index of Painting from Persia, India, and Turkey in the British Library and the British Museum.* London: British Museum, 1977.

Bibliography

―――. 1981a. *Miniatures from Turkish Manuscripts.* London: British Museum, 1981.

―――. 1981b. *Dragons in Persian, Mughal, and Turkish Art.* London: British Museum, 1981.

―――. 1984. *Persian Miniature Painting.* Austin: University of Texas Press, 1984.

Tonguc, Sencer. 1958. "The Saracens in the Middle English Charlemagne Romances." *Litera* 5 (1958) 17–24.

UNESCO. 1961. *Turkey: Ancient Miniatures.* Pref. by R. Ettinghausen, intro. by M.S. Ipširoglu and S. Eyuboglu. Greenwich, CT: New York Graphic Society, 1961.

Vaglieri, L. Veccia. *EI2.* (Al-)Husayn b. ʿAli b. Abi Talib/The Legend of Husayn. *EI2* 4:612–15.

Van Leeuwen, P.J. 1937. *De Maleische Alexanderroman.* Ph.D. diss., University of Utrecht, 1937.

Vereno, Matthias, 1974. "On the Relations of Dumezilian Comparative Indo-European Mythology to History of Religions in General." In *Myth in Indo-European Antiquity,* edited by Gerald J. Larson. Berkeley: University of California Press, 1974. 181–90.

Vial. C. *EI2.* Kissa/Modern Arabic Literature. *EI2* 5:187–93.

Virolleaud, C. 1950. *Le théatre persan ou le drame de Kerbela.* Paris: Maisonneuve, 1950.

―――. 1959. "Le roman de l'Emir Hamza, oncle de Mahomet." *Ethnographie,* n.s., 53 (1958–59) 3–10.

Von Grünebaum, G.E. 1953a. "The Spirit of Islam As Shown in Its Literature." *SI* 1:1 (1953) 101–9.

―――. 1953b. "Firdausi's Concept of History." *Melanges Köprülü* (1953) 177–93.

―――. 1975. "The Hero in Medieval Arabic Prose." In *Concepts of the Hero in the Middle Ages and the Renaissance,* edited by N. Burns and C. Reagan. Albany: SUNY Press, 1975. 83–100.

―――, and Caillois, Roger, eds. 1966. *The Dream and Human Societies.* Los Angeles: University of California Press, 1966.

Walker, Barbara G. 1985. *The Crone: Woman of Age, Wisdom, and Power.* San Francisco: Harper and Row, 1985.

Walker, Warren, and Unsal, Ahmet. 1966. *Tales Alive in Turkey.* Cambridge, MA: Harvard University Press, 1966.

Walther, Wiebke. 1981. *Woman in Islam.* London: G. Prior, 1981.

Warner, A. G., and Warner, E. 1925. *The Shanama of Firdausi.* 9 vols. London: Kegan Paul, Trench, Trubner, 1905–25.

Waugh, Earle H. 1975. "Religious Aspects of the Miʿraj Legend," in *Journey to the Other World,* edited by H. R. Davidson. Ipswick: Folklore Society, 1975.

Welch, Anthony. 1973. *Shah Abbas and the Arts of Isfahan*. New York: Asia Society, 1973.

———. 1976. *Artists for the Shah*. New Haven: Yale University Press, 1976.

———. 1979. *Calligraphy in the Arts of the Muslim World*. New York: Asia Society, 1979.

———, and Welch, S. C. 1982. *Arts of the Islamic Book: The Collection of Prince Sadruddin Aga Khan*. Ithaca: Cornell University Press, 1982.

Welch, Stuart Cary. 1972. *A King's Book of Kings*. New York: Metropolitan Museum of Art, 1972.

———. 1976. *Persian Painting*. New York: Braziller, 1976.

———. 1978. *Imperial Mughal Painting*. New York: Braziller, 1978.

———. 1985. *India: Art and Culture 1300–1900*. New York: Metropolitan Museum of Art, 1985 [1988 rpt.].

Wensinck, A. J. *EI2*. (al-)Khadir. *EI2* 4:902–5.

Werner, Alice, trans. 1923. *Utenzi wa Ayubu*. BSOAS 2 (1921–23) 85–115; 297–319; 347–418.

Wilkinson, James Stewart. 1931. *The Shah-namah of Firdausi: The Book of the Persian Kings*. London: Oxford University Press, 1931.

Williams, Penny. 1978. "Through a Glass Brightly." *Aramco World Magazine* 29:4 (July-August 1978) 2–5.

Wilson, C. E., trans. 1924. *The Haft Paikar (The Seven Beauties), Containing the Life and Adventures of King Bahrum Gur, and the Seven Stories Told by His Seven Queens*. 2 vols. London: Probsthain, 1924.

Winner, Thomas. 1958. *The Oral Art and Literature of the Kazakhs of Russian Central Asia*. Durham: Duke University Press, 1958.

Winstedt, R. O. *EI2*. Hikaya/Malaya. *EI2* 4:377.

———. 1921. "Hikayat Hang Tuah." *JSBRAS* 83 (1921) 1101–22.

———. 1940. "A History of Classical Malay Literature." *JMBRAS* 17 (1940). Oxford/Kuala Lumpur: Oxford in Asia Historical Reprints, 1969.

Yarshater, Ehsan. 1962. "Some Common Characteristics of Persian Poetry and Art." *SI* 16 (1962) 61–72.

———. 1979. "Taʿziyeh and Pre-Islamic Mourning Rites in Iran." Chelkowski 1979:88–94.

———. ed. 1988. *Persian Literature*. Albany: SUNY Press, 1988.

Yusupov, E. Y., ed. 1982. *Miniatures: Illustrations of Alisher Navoi's Works of the XV–XIXth Centuries*. Tashkent: Fan Publishing House, 1982.

Zafrani, H. *EI2* Kissa/Judaeo-Arabic and Judaeo-Berber. *EI2* 5:206–7.

Zaky, A. 1954. "Islamic Swords in the Middle Ages." *Extrait du Bulletin de l'Institut d'Egypt* 35 (1953–54) 365–79.

———. 1959. "The Sword in Islamic Art." *Bull. Coll. Arts Baghdad Univ.* 1 (1959) 93–100.

Bibliography

Zawadowski, G. 1943. "Note sur l'origine magique de Dhu 'l-Faqar." *En Terre d'Islam* 1 (1943) 36–40.

Zhirmunsky, V. M. 1963. "On the Comparative Study of the Heroic Epic of the Peoples of Central Asia." *Proceedings of the XXV International Congress of Orientalists, Moscow 1960,* no. 3. Moscow: Izd. vostocnoj literatury, 1963. 241–52.

Index

Index

166–69. *See also* Castles; Cities; Cosmology; Palaces

Aristotle, 86, 90, 91, 151

Arnawaz, 199–200

Art historical issues, 31–33. *See also* Interpretation

Arts, visual. *See* Art historical issues; Ceramics; Painting

Ayyam al-Arab, 237, 238

Ayyar (folk subtype), 19, 55–59; etymology of term, 276n.19; and heroic virtue, 22; and Islamization, 58; in Urdu literature, 254; in Southeast Asia, 57–59. *See also* Amr ibn Ma'di Karib; Amr ibn Umayya; Kawa; Potjut Muhamat; Samak-i Ayyar

Azada. *See* Bahram Gur

Bahram Chubin, 69–70, 152, 174

Bahram Gur: battles beast, 216 (Figure 16); compared to Rustam, 70; death or disappearance of, 74; hunting with harpist, as developed by Firdawsi, Nizami, Amir Khusraw, 71–72; life story of, 222; likened to imam and mahdi, 74 (*see also* Hang Tuah); and the seven pavilions, 72–74, 73 (Figure 3); stories of, 39 (Table 2); spiritual transformation of, 179–80

Bamsi Bayrek, 141, 218

Banu Chichek, 218

Banu Hilal: stories of, 13; under glass paintings of, 34; *sira* of, 44. *See also* Abu Zayd al-Hilali; *Sira*

Barbad, 69

Basat, 124–25

Bashgoz, Ilhan, 255

Battal, al-, 53, 258

Battle scenes, 210

Bausani, Alessandro, 16

Baybars I: *sira* of, 45

Beast: as metaphor of evil, 213–15. *See also* Evil, Weapons

Biebuyck, Daniel, 30

Bihafarid, 199

Birth, of hero: portents attending, 125–26, 131

Birthmark, 142, 143, 144, 201. *See also* Amulet; Talisman

Bizhan, 83–85, 130, 186 (Table 4)

Boghach Khan, 231–32

Brakel, Lode, 17

Bravmann, M., 14

Cain, 96, 115

Calasso, Giovanna, 174

Campbell, Joseph, 2, 93, 220

Canova, Giovanni, 29

Castle (fortress): Black, 150, 290n.31; Brazen Hold, 158, 199; of the Clouds, 169; of the Eagles, 170; of Kay Khusraw on Alburz, 169; Seven Fortresses, 109, 174; of Talisman of Dal, 174; White, 81. *See also* Cities; Cosmology; Kang Dizh; Settings; Siyawushgird

Ceramics: Bizhan and Manizha, story of, in, 253; Kawa, Dahhak, Faridun pictured in, 56

Champion (folk hero subtype). *See* Hamza, Rustam

Chanson de geste, 28

Characterization, 24, 221–23

Chelkowski, Peter, 82, 252

Christides, V., 162

Chubak, Sadiq, 27, 63

Cities, symbolic: Babylon, 168; of Brass, 150, 174, 230, 290–91n.31; of Copper, 173–74; Ctesiphon, 169; of Gold, 174; Qayrawan, 171. *See also* Castle, Cosmology, Geography, Iram, Palaces, Settings

Combat, single: champion-cham-

330

pion, 210–13; father-son, 138; male-female, 49, 194, 218. *See also* Battle scenes, Jihad

Confraternities, knightly, 55, 59, 215–17. *See also* Ayyar; Futuwwa; Hang Tuah; Jawanmardi; Kay Khusraw; Muhammad

Connelly, Bridget, 34, 138, 217–18, 226, 231

Corbin, Henri, 30, 176, 180–81, 202

Cosmology: Arabo-centric, in Swahili literature, 171; and *axis mundi* 171, 172, 181; eighth clime, 30, 180, 289n.2; and epic structure, 30–31; and Land of Darkness (*see* Iskandar); and Land of Flags and Ensigns, 170; and quadripartite structure, 169–70, 172; seven climes, suggested in painting, 37, in Bahram Gur's seven pavilions, 72, 175; and spiritual or mysterious power, 118–19; of three levels, 165–66. *See also* Castle; Cities; Geography; Palaces; Settings

Crusades, 44–45, 51, 104, 239

Dahhak: as evil force, 26, 70; succumbs to Ahriman, 122–23; abducts Jamshid's sisters, 199–200; chained to Mt. Damavand, 126

Darabnama, 81, 88–89, 137

Dastan genre, 17 (Table 1), 254

David, 100, 95 (Table 3)

Dawud. *See* David

Death: of Antar, 226; and Bahram Gur, 228; and Dede Korkut, 224; and Hang Tuah, 226–27; as heroic risk, 204–5; and, of Iskandar, 225, 228–30; and Kay Khusraw, 228; of Khusraw Parwiz, 230; and Wild Dumrul, 227

Dede Korkut: as bestower of names, 54, 141; book of: stories from,

11, 124–25, 189–90, 195–96, 218, 227, 231–32; as epic character and bard, 143, 255; as wisdom figure, 53–54

Demon. *See* Diw, Evil

Demythologization, 16–17

Developmental issues: character identity, 140–47; sense of purpose, 139–40; survival of trials, 161–62

Dhat al-Himma, 53, 193, 258

Dhu 'l-Faqar, 96, 105, 142, 206–7

Dhu 'l-Qarnayn. *See* Iskandar

Disguise, 85, 145–47, 199, 218

Dilaram. *See* Bahram Gur

Diw, 77, 89, 119, 123

Djerzelez Alija, 145, 277–78n.39

Dragon, 77–78, 98, 111, 231–15

Dreams and visions: of imminent death, 111, 224; revealing foe's location, 199; function of in popular romance, 156–57; of future of future hero's birth, 67, 77, 125, 126, 135–36, 137; interpretation of, 89, 156; in which Muhammad or other prophets appear, 116, 117, 173; in Turkic *hikaya*, of beloved, 257. *See also* Omens

Drink, drunkenness, 49, 128, 192, 199, 211

Drugs, 83, 162, 193

Egrek, 196–97

Eighth clime. *See* Cosmology

Elijah, 89, 102, 154 (Figure 11)

Emotion: expression of, 232–33

Emren, 195

Epic: Arabic popular, 29, 275n.1; didactic, 249; heroic, 28, 30, 180; Kazakh, 23; mystical, 30, 35, 180–81, 249; Persian: historical, 248, secondary, 247–48; romantic, 28; Slavic *Krajina* songs

Index

(Bosnia-Hercegovina), 259–60; Swahili, 243–47; Turkic: classical, 224–25, 255; Turkic: folk, oral, 256; Turkic: religious, 258–59

Errington, Shelly, 30, 127–28, 172, 207

Eʿtimazadeh, Mahmud, 64

Eve: image of, 121 (Figure 10); in religious lineage, 95 (Table 3); in Swahili literature, 96, 121–22. See also Adam

Evil: inward and outward forms, 26–27; interpretations of, 122, 123–24, 130–31; trials as metaphors for, 158. See also Beast; Jihad; Weapons

Faramarz, 189

Faranak, 192

Farangis, 198

Farhad, 69, 146

Faridun: against evil, 26, 56; grieves over Iraj, 78; and mortality, 223; names sons, 139; partitions world among sons, 77; as progenitor, 75–77; tests sons in form of dragon, 77–78; as younger son, 196

Farr, 140. See also Khwarna

Fate, 14, 118, 131. 230

Fatima, 95 (Table 3), 112–13

Faylaqus (Philip of Macedon), 87, 88, 90, 186 (Table 4)

Firdawsi: and composition of Shahnama 60; and fear of the feminine, 218–19; and function of heroic tale, 13; on mortality, 223, 225–26; and story of Bizhan and Minizha, 83

Fitna. See Bahram Gur

Formulaic composition: in descriptions of battle, 210; in painting, 34, 210; in reminders of mortality, 224; in romances, 240

Fortress. See Castle; Palaces

Furusiya, 237

Futuh genre, 243

Futuwwa, 12, 21, 56, 237. See also Virtues, heroic

Gabriel: escorts Adam from Garden, 96; represents Ali in heaven, 113; with Hasan and Husayn, 114; in well with Joseph, 98, 99 (Figure 7); disguised as merchant, 111; as guide to Muhammad, 152; as messenger to Muhammad, 47; preventing Muhammad from fighting, 212; in Swahili literature, 106, 152

Gayumart, 74–75, 76 (Figure 4), 186 (Table 4)

Garshasp, 126, 186 (Table 4)

Garsiwaz, 130, 186 (Table 4), 198

Gender-related issues, 21–23, 145–47, 217–19. See also Relationships; Women

Genres, literary: and cultural values 28–29; and Islamization, 16–19. See also Epic; Futuh; Hamasa; Hagiography; Hikaya; Historiography; Maghazi; Malhama; Maqama; Maqtal; Marthiya; Mathnawi; Mawlid; Penglipur lara; Romance; Sira;, Utenzi

Geography: and heroic itineraries, 163–64; psychological, 176. See also Castles; Cities; Cosmology; Settings

Ghamra, 45, 124, 211, 217, 218

Ghasub, 212

Ghawwar ibn Dinar, 124, 211

Giw, 85, 198, 186 (Table 4)

God: name(s) of, 19, 158, 247; power of, 222; will of, 19

Gog and Magog, 129–30. See also Iskandar

Goldziher, Ignaz, 14

Index

Jihad, 203–4; greater, 104, 209–10; lesser, 209, 246
Jinn, 48, 102 (Figure 8), 115, 119, 150, 167
Job (Ayyub), 122
John the Baptist, 102
Jonah, 32, 100
Joseph: image of, 32, 36; in religious lineage, 95 (Table 3);as tragic prince parallel, 97–98; in well: image of, 99 (Figure 7); well likened to Bizhan's pit, 97, and to Jonah's whale, 100; Zulaykha's attempted seduction of, 85–86
Journey: motives for, 148–49, 179; through seven valleys, 181. *See also* Cosmology; Geography; Micraj
Jung, C. G., 220

Kacba, 91, 96, 105, 177
Kang Dizh, 31, 180–81. *See also* Architecture; Castles; Cities; Cosmology; Palaces
Kan Turali, 193–94
Katayun (alias Kitabun, Nahid), 186 (Table 4), 198–99
Kawa: as ayyar, 56; confronting evil, 26; in images, 56; in modern Persian literature, 64
Kay Kawus, 78, 122–23, 174, 198
Kayanian dynasty, Persian, 60, 88
Kay Khusraw: sends Bizhan to Armani forest, 83; life story of, 222; likeness to father, Siyawush, 143; portents at birth of, 135, 137; prevented from knowing father, 137–38; "Round Table" knights of, 205, 215–17; sends Rustam to rescue Bizhan, 85; in Suhrawardi's interpretation, 30, 180–81;
Kay Qubad, 126, 186 (Table 4)
Khadija, 95 (Table 3), 106

Khadir (Khizr): and analogy to lone knight, picaresque, wisdom figure subtypes, 102; guide to Moses, 58, 102–3; as healer, 232; as spiritual initiator, 230; image of, 154 (Figure 11); and Islamization, 16; and Iskandar 86, 88, 91, 102, 153–55; as lunar/aquatic figure, 91; as progenitor, 288n.16
Khalid ibn al-Walid, 106
Khamsa (Quintet) of Nizami, 166. *See also* Romance, courtly
Kharijites, 45, 240
Khawarnaq, palace of, 72, 174–75. *See also* Architecture; Bahram Gur; Cosmology
Khawarannama: and Ali's exploits, 109, 174, 213; ayyars in, 59; imitator of *Shahnama,* 248; Urdu imitation of, 254
Khoja Nasruddin, 51–52
Khumayni, Ruhullah, 11, 98
Khurshid Shah, 57
Khusraw Parwiz: against Bahram Chubin, 174; and heroic stories, 13; in relationship to Shirin, 146–47; as romantic adventurer, 67–70; spies Shirin bathing, 67, 68 (Figure 2), 146
Khwarna, 114, 140, 292n.40. *See also Farr; Fate*
Kinana, 47, 141
Klimburg-Salter, Deborah, 34–35, 181–82
Knappert, Jan, 204, 243
Köroghlu: epic of, structure, 256; as folk hero, 50; as Guroghlu (Central Asian), 50; stories of, 39 (Table 2)
Kris, 54, 207–8. *See also* Weapons
Krotkoff, Georg, 74, 175, 228

Land of Darkness. *See* Cosmology; Iskandar; Khadir

336

Languages: gift of. *See* Amr ibn
Umayya; (al-)Battal; Hang Tuah;
Solomon (Sulayman); Tahmurat
Lawn az-Zalam, 211–12
Lineage, heroic: Buwayhid dynasty
(to Bahram Gur), 200; Iskandar
(to Faridun), 87; Malay kings (to
Iskandar), 74, 201; of religious
heroes, 95 (Table 3); Saffarid dy-
nasty (to Jamshid), 200; Samanid
and Ziyarid dynasties (to Bahram
Chubin), 200; Sasanian Persia (to
Isfandiyar), 74; in *Shahnama*, 186
(Table 4); Tahirid dynasty (to
Rustam), 200; various, 201. *See
also* Amulets; Birthmarks; Heir-
looms
Lone Knight subtype. *See* Cham-
pion subtype
Luhrasp, 198–99
Luqman, 89, 155. *See also* Guides,
spiritual

Maaruf, Shaharuddin b., 20–21,
27–28
Maghazi genre, 122, 242–43
Maguire, Marcia, 61, 158–59
Mahafarid, 191
Mahdi, 74, 173
Malaka, Tan, 65
Malhama genre, 238, 297n.4
Mammad, Shir, 64
Manizha, and Bizhan: story of, 13,
83–85, 130
Manuchihr, 77, 83, 136, 201
Maqama genre, 29, 36–37, 51, 240–
41
Maqtal genre, 17 (Table 1), 107,
258. *See also* Muhammad Ha-
nafiya; and Genres, literary
Markus, Kinga, 64, 187
Marmadi. *See* Amr ibn Maʿdi Karib
Marmaya. *See* Amr ibn Umayya
Marriage, 44, 162–63, 193–95. *See*

also Gender-related issues; Rela-
tionships, human
Marthiya genre, 254–55. *See also
Maqtal*
Martyr(dom), 114–17, 209. *See also*
Hasan; Husayn, Jaʿfar
Mary, 95 (Table 3), 104
Maryam, 69, 186 (Table 4)
Mathnawi, Urdu, 254. *See also* Epic,
didactic
Mawlid genre, 242–43
Mayasa, 45, 49
Mazaheri, Aly, 61
Meisami, Julie S.: on character de-
velopment, 66, 74; on *Haft Pay-
kar*, 175, 179, 202; on *Khusraw
and Shirin*, 67, 146; on Persian
court romance, 28; on romance
as genre and its values, 249
Menak, 59
Metaphor: visual, levels of, 37
Meter, poetic: *koshma*, 256; *muta-
qarib*, 247; *sandja'*, 261; *ukawafi*,
245; *utenzi*, 245
Mihrab, 82–83
Miqdad: compared to Bahram Gur,
48; compared to Rustam, 47; and
Islamization, 45–47; and missing
father, 136; stories of, 45–49
Miraculous element, 18, 52, 106,
109, 118–19
Miʿraj, Muhammad's Ascension: image of, 178 (Figure 13); interpretations of, 179; in modern Iranian fiction, 64; *Miʿrajnama* (*Book
of the Ascension*), 104, 249; story
of mystical journey, 11, 105, 152–
53; in Swahili, 177. *See also* Muhammad
Mortality: intimations of, 223–26.
See also Death
Moghaddam, M. K., 26–27
Moses: Khumayni as new, 11, 98;
against giant Og, 32, 98–99;

rasul (pl. *rusul*; messenger), 93
Recitation: of Malay *hikayat* form, 261–62, 272n.6; as moral exhortation, 11–13; visual illustration to accompany, 36; in Yugoslavia during Ramadan, 259
Relationships, human: with adopted sons and half-brothers, 197; of daughters, 198–99; father-son, 136–39, 185–90; general interpersonal, 145–47; mentor-disciple (or foster-parent-foster-child), 190–91; and reconciliation, 231–32; romantic, 162–63; among siblings, 195–96; of heroines as sisters, 199–200; of worthy son to parents, 195–96; between spouses, 193–95. *See also* Disguise; Gender-related issues
Ringgren, Helmer, 14
Rizal, Jose, 21
Romance: Arabic popular, 28–29
Romance: Persian courtly, 28–29, 80, 251–52; of Amir Khusraw, 71; of Jami, 86, 252; of Khwaju Kirmani, 80; of Nizami, 80, 146, 251–52
Romance: Persian popular, 250–51; ayyars in, 56–57; and Hamza, 250–51; and Islamization, 18–19
Romantic adventurer subtype: royal. *See* Bahram Gur; Gushtasp; Khusraw Parwiz
Rubiera, M. J., 167
Rudaba, 61, 82–83, 84 (Figure 6), 186 (Table 4)
Rumi, Jalal ad-Din, 62
Rustam: and Ali, 109; describes his armor, 205; birth of, 60–61; as champion, 60–62; in single combat, 213, 214 (Figure 15); battles diws, 123; disguised as merchant, 85; against moral evil, 26; fighting Isfandiyar, 37, 78–80;

iconography of, 61, 143; Islamized, 109; itinerary of, 164; and heroic stories, 13; kills son Suhrab, 138, 144, Figure 14; life story of, 221–22; in heroic lineage, Table 4; as mentor to Bahman, 80, 191; as mentor to Siyawush, 78, 190–91; as model for modern literary characters, 63–64; on mortality, 223–24; and need of guide, 149; rescues Bizhan, 85; in secondary epics, 248; seven courses (or feats) of, 61, compared to those of Isfandiyar, 158–59; Rakhsh, horse of, 61; and Solomon, 102; stories of, 39 (Table 2); and Tahmina, 192–93. *See also* Lineages

Sa'di of Shiraz, 223
Saga. *See Sira*
Sajn, 135, 206
Salih, 102, 111
Salm, 77, 186 (Table 4)
Salur Kazan, 136, 145, 189–90
Sam, 62–83, 186 (Table 4)
Samak-i Ayyar, 18, 56–57, 81
Santoso, Soewito, 15
Sari Saltuq, 104
Sasanian Persia, 48–49, 74, 174
Satire, visual, 37
Sayf ibn dhi Yazan, 13
Scouts, 149–50
Segrek, 196–97
Sejara Melayu (Malay Chronicles): and function of tales, 11; Hang Tuah in, 222–23; Iskandar in, 19–20, 91; and Islamization 15–16
Settings, geographical: of stories, 39 (Table 2); Abyssinia, 13, 87; Acheh (Sumatra), 57; Arabia, 13, 47, 49, 106; Armenia, 67–69; Byzantium, 67–69; Malaka, 11, 54; Sarandib (Sri Lanka), 173. *See*

Index